The Catholic Tradition

The Catholic Tradition

Before and After Vatican II
1878–1993

Timothy G. McCarthy

A Campion Book

Loyola University Press
Chicago

∞

Loyola University Press
3441 North Ashland Avenue
Chicago, Illinois 60657

Cover and book design by Tammi Longsjo.
Cover artwork by Dick Mlodock.

Library of Congress Cataloging-in-Publication Data
McCarthy, Timothy, 1929–
    The Catholic Tradition : before and after Vatican II, 1878–1993 /
    Timothy G. McCarthy.
        p.   cm.
    Includes bibliographical references and index.
    ISBN 0-8294-0776-6
    1. Catholic Church—History—20th century.   2. Vatican Council
    (2nd: 1962–1965)   3. Modernism—Catholic Church.
    4. Catholic Church—Doctrines.   I. Title.
BX1389.M38   1994
282' . 09'04—dc20   93-44446
                                                   CIP

Contents

Abbreviations

Throughout this book, letters enclosed in parentheses identify the sixteen documents of Vatican II by their abbreviated Latin title and paragraph number.

AA Apostolicam actuositatem: Decree on the Apostolate of the Laity

AG Ad gentes: Decree on the Church's Missionary Activity

CD Christus Dominus: Decree on the Bishops' Pastoral Office in the Church

DH Dignitatis humanae: Declaration on Religious Freedom

DV Dei Verbum: Dogmatic Constitution on Divine Revelation

GE Gravissimum educationis: Declaration on Christian Education

GS Gaudium et spes: Pastoral Constitution on the Church in the Modern World

IM Inter mirifica: Decree on the Instruments of Social Communication

LG Lumen gentium: Dogmatic Constitution on the Church

NA Nostra aetate: Declaration on the Relationship of the Church to the Non-Christian Religions

OE Orientalium ecclesiarum: Decree on Eastern Catholic Churches

OT Optatam totius: Decree on Priestly Formation

PC Perfectae caritatis: Decree on the Appropriate Renewal of Religious Life

PO Presbyterorum ordinis: Decree on the Ministry and Life of Priests

SC Sacrosanctum concilium: Constitution on the Sacred Liturgy

UR Unitatis redintegratio: Decree on Ecumenism

Preface

Several years ago the religious studies faculty at St. Mary's College of California reorganized its course offerings. We instituted a four-course sequence in order to provide our students with a coherent, chronological, and ecumenical understanding of "the one and only Church of Christ" (UR 24) from Jesus to the present. I took on the fourth course, The Twentieth-Century Church and the Challenge of Modernity.

There were no books that covered this history in a way in which the students could appreciate it and as I understood it. After using chapters of books and magazine articles for several semesters, I decided to write my own text. The present book was used in manuscript form by 180 students during the spring semesters of 1991, 1992, and 1993. I am grateful to the students for their patience and interest; their challenging questions helped me to rewrite each edition.

This book could be used in a classroom setting. Nonetheless, I hope it will reach a wider audience of adult Christians. The book does not have a textbook format. Since it has an ecumenical perspective, I believe it can be helpful to all Christians, especially those interested in the institutional, intellectual, and devotional developments within the Catholic community.

Vatican II is the pivotal point of the history of the Catholic Church in the twentieth century. I cite the conciliar documents extensively, using a text edited in 1966 by Walter M. Abbott, a Jesuit scholar. This text does not use inclusive language. Nevertheless, I retain this edition because it captures the style and ethos of the conciliar period. Readers who prefer inclusive language should make their own adjustments as they read along.

In addition to my students' responses, I received help and encouragement from many colleagues and friends, much too many to name. However, I would be remiss if I did not acknowledge the special insights and encouragement of Margaret Duffner, Odile Dwyer, and Honey O'Leary. John C. Dwyer, theologian, author, former colleague, and true and generous friend, provided invaluable theological and technical assistance with the organization and production of the manuscript.

I am most grateful to the staff of Loyola University Press for their gracious assistance: to Joseph F. Downey, S.J., editorial director, for taking on this project; to Jeremy Langford, editor, who, with his associates, gave the manuscript a meticulous review and proposed many positive changes.

The most help came from my wife, Virginia. This book could not have been written without her support, patience, and love. With deep affection and gratitude, I dedicate this book to Virginia.

Introduction

The twentieth-century Catholic Church has undergone startling shifts and developments in theology, spirituality, and demography. Concerning the latter, for example, approximately 77 percent of Catholics lived in Europe and North America in 1900, and 23 percent in what is now known as the third world. In 1990, 70 percent of Catholics lived in the third world and 30 percent in Europe and North America. This book is a thematic history of the major events, issues, and concerns that have shaped and often defined the church and the Catholic tradition before and after Vatican II.

There are several ways to write institutional, intellectual, and devotional history. This book focuses on significant events, such as the rise of modernity and the loss of Papal States, and important personalities, particularly the popes, bishops, and theologians. The popes and bishops, called the hierarchical magisterium, are the official teachers in the church; the theologians, called the scholarly magisterium, seek to understand, interpret, and teach the faith. The popes and bishops lead the theologians; sometimes the popes and bishops learn from the theologians as they aid in explaining, correcting, and refining their teachings. Often both sets of teachers are in tension, even serious disagreement and distrust. Nonetheless, both work toward a common goal: to foster, under the inspiration of the Holy Spirit, the faith, hope, and love of the disciples of Christ in the concrete conditions of their daily lives. This is called spirituality.

This study begins with the pontificate of Leo XIII (1878–1903) and ends with the visit of John Paul II to the

Baltic States in September 1993. Vatican II (1962–65), the decisive ecclesial event of the century, is the pivotal point of the story. There were theologies and spiritualities before and during the Council—and since. I report on these, but occasionally I go beyond reporting and personally evaluate and challenge some of them.

In the first three chapters, I introduce the popes, explain the concept of modernity, and report on Vatican II. These chapters form the background for the remaining eight chapters, which investigate the issues that received the greatest attention at Vatican II: the identity and mission of the church, authority, ecumenism, interreligious dialogue, liturgy, social justice, sexual morality, and Mary. There are no chapters about such important topics as christology, feminist theology, religious orders, the nature of the priesthood, or religious education because these issues did not receive significant refinement and development during the Council. Nevertheless, throughout this book I frequently refer to these important topics, especially feminist issues.

1

The Popes of the Twentieth Century

Baron Friedrich von Hügel (1852–1925), the son of an Austrian father and a Scottish mother, was a prominent English theologian who made his home in London. Due to poor health, he never received a formal university training. He studied with tutors, especially in philosophy, Hebrew, biblical criticism, and mysticism. His studies led him to propose that a religion is as strong as the individual strengths and interrelationships of its three principal elements: the institutional, the intellectual, and the mystical (1932). He believed the history of a religion is the story of the shifting relationships and tensions among all three elements.[1]

In the Roman Catholic Church the institutional comprises such factors as the papacy, bishops, parishes, canon law, and the Roman curia; the intellectual includes theologians, church historians, Scripture scholars, philosophers, and other thinkers; the mystical includes the sacramental, scriptural, and prayer life of the church, as well as the involvement of Christians in social justice and works of mercy. In order for Catholicism to flourish, the three elements, embodiments of the Spirit, should be in balance. Finding this balance, however, is not an easy task. Although all three elements are indispensable and complementary, they are often in tension, and more often than not, in conflict. Like three spirited horses in a troika, they clash because each is totalitarian in tendency. Consequently, these three elements must work together in order to offset one another's weaknesses and provide a healthy equilibrium.

This book uses Von Hügel's triad (or troika) and begins by highlighting the popes and their roles in shaping the church. After all, the papacy is distinctive of the Catholic tradition and, as Raymond Brown, Sulpician priest and biblical scholar, has suggested, it has been "a strong cohesive force (perhaps the single most powerful force holding us Catholics together)" (1975a, 80). Peter Hebblethwaite, theologian and Vatican affairs writer, has also described the importance of the papacy:

> The papacy is not a static institution, frozen once for all in its present form. And popes are not just a mass-produced series of figures in white who appear on distant balconies and mouth interchangeable platitudes. It matters very much who is pope. Each pope makes his own distinctive contribution (1978a, 195; 1980d).

Today there is a movement in historical writing to avoid such a conventional, top-down approach that features great public events and great figures. Instead, historians now often begin from the bottom. They write "people history," in which "all human behavior, the actions and thoughts of peoples from all cultures and all segments of all societies within these cultures come within its purview" (Greene 1975).

Jay P. Dolan and other church historians have written histories from the perspective of the people (1975, 1978a, 1985). However, sometimes the "new social historians" are too dismissive of general histories of the church. For example, Dolan, in his negative review of Thomas Bokenkotter's *A Concise History of the Catholic Church* (1977), maintains that a history of the church limited to the actions of popes and bishops will not truly tell the history because the church is primarily the people of God. Dolan acknowledges that the biblical image people have of God does not exclude the role of the hierarchy, "but neither does it permit the history of the church to be reduced to a narrative of hierarchical and administrative activities." He then adds, "Popes die and councils come to a close, but the pilgrimage of the people of God never ends" (1978b).

It seems to me that to make his point, Dolan dismisses too easily the far-reaching and long-lasting effects of the papal and episcopal actions and teachings on the very pilgrimage of the people of God he wants to underscore. Is not the pilgrim church still crossing rocky terrain in some places because of the papal condemnations of modernity in the early part of this century? Has Vatican II "come to a close," or are we not hoping against hope that the pilgrim church will catch up to the Council's vision of the Catholic tradition at least by the early part of the twenty-first century? The thesis of this book is that the pilgrimage moves along in great measure due to the interplay among the faithful, the theologians, and the hierarchy.

The Twentieth Century: Its Beginning

For over one thousand years the popes exercised sovereignty over a vast area of Italy called the Papal States. It has been suggested that "the twentieth century began for the papacy in 1870, when Rome was occupied by the new Italian State, and papal fortunes fell to their lowest ebb since the Reformation" (Rhodes 1983, 9).

The Papal States comprised some sixteen thousand square miles through north-central Italy. According to tradition and some more-than-dubious documentation dating back to Constantine (288–337), Pepin, king of the Franks, bestowed the land on the pope in 754. In 1870, when Italy was going through a process of unification as a nation, the Italian armies occupied Rome and confiscated the Papal States. The pope, Pius IX (1846–78), declared himself a "prisoner of the Vatican" and the occupation a "profanation." "Barrels of holy water," he declared, "would be needed to wash away the profanation of the Quirinal," which was once the summer residence of the popes where the king had installed himself. The conflict between the Vatican and Italy that began in 1870 became known as the "Roman question."

The loss of the Papal States meant a major loss of political and financial power for the church. It was difficult for Pius IX and many Catholics to imagine that the papacy could carry on both its apostolic mission and its international role without the trappings of regal power and while confined to Vatican City, a mere 108 acres (Schoof 1970, 31). It took Rome a long time to realize that the loss of the Papal States not only provided the popes with the opportunity of enhancing their religious and moral authority, but it also freed the church for its real mission in Italy and around the world. Nonetheless, the unresolved Roman question hobbled the activities of the popes until 1929, almost sixty years.

The following sections briefly review the life of each of the nine popes of the twentieth century, from his birth to his election. Included is also a brief review of some significant events that affected either each pope personally or the society in which he lived during his pontificate.

Leo XIII (1878-1903)

Gioacchino Pecci was born on March 2, 1810, in Carpineto, a town just south of Rome. He was a brilliant, hard-working student who eventually studied for the papal diplomatic service at the Academy of Noble Ecclesiastics (1832–37). Ordained a priest in 1837, he joined the papal service and was made governor in the Papal States, first of Benevento (1838–41) and then of Perugia (1841–43). He gained a reputation as a firm and capable administrator. At the age of thirty-three, only six years after his priestly ordination, he was made by Gregory XVI (1830–46) an archbishop and nuncio to Belgium (1843–46). He was next appointed bishop of Perugia, where he stayed for thirty-two years, the entire pontificate of Pius IX. As bishop he modernized the curriculum of his seminary, promoted a revival of Thomism, and wrote pastoral letters calling for a reconciliation between Catholicism and contemporary culture. He was made a cardinal in 1853 and attended Vatican Council I (1869–70).

Upon the death of Pius IX, he was elected the 256th pope on February 20, 1878. Because Cardinal Pecci had a frail physique and was in fragile health, it seemed his election may have been no more than a stopgap measure after the thirty-two-year reign of Pius IX. When pressed by the cardinals to take the papal throne, the sixty-seven-year-old Pecci warned, "My pontificate will be short. The conclave will soon have to be held again. My pontificate will be like that of Marcellus II" (Rhodes 1983, 70). Marcellus was pope for twenty-one days in April 1555. Leo's pontificate, however, lasted twenty-five years. Toward the end of Leo's long life, one wit is supposed to have remarked, "We elected a holy Father, not an eternal Father."

Cardinal Pecci took the name Leo because he admired Leo XII (1823–29), who was pope when Pecci was a teenager. Leo XII had been a papal nuncio in a number of countries and had acquired wide and intimate knowledge of Europe and all of its changes, which led him to realize that the church must adapt itself to a newly emerging society. Leo XIII intended to follow the course of his namesake and not the ultramontane policies (those that encourage excessive loyalty to the pope) of both Gregory XVI and Pius IX. Leo realized that under both his predecessors the papacy had been extremely powerful, but only for Catholics. Leo's aim, therefore, was to restore the power and prestige of the papacy throughout the world.

The recovery of the Papal States dominated Leo's foreign policy. Nevertheless, according to J. N. D. Kelly, Anglican priest and Oxford scholar, his "main achievement was his attempt, within the framework of traditional teaching, to bring the church to terms with the modern world" (1986, 311; see also John 1964; Walsh 1980; Cheetham 1983). Agreeing with the traditional teaching, he considered most of the liberalism of his day as essentially godless, as exemplified by the principle of the separation of church and state. The real aim of his dialogue with society was to rechristianize it and to make the church what she had always been: the spiritual mentor of society (Aubert 1978, 41). In some of his encyclicals (major papal statements of theology and policy), Leo tried to show that the ideals of democracy were best served by Christian principles. He believed the lawful aspirations of freedom could only be fulfilled through Christianity.

Leo's pontificate was a period of wrenching social change. Nevertheless, the judgment of historians is that he did restore the prestige of the papacy throughout the world, mainly because he championed social reform, especially for the poor, and because he was more conciliatory toward governments than his predecessor. When he died at the age of ninety-three on July 20, 1903, flags flew at half-mast in major cities around the world. This sign of respect is in sharp contrast to the scorn heaped upon Pius IX at his funeral procession. On that occasion, a cursing, stone-throwing mob followed the funeral cortege to the body's final resting place at San Lorenzo-Outside-the-Walls and threatened to throw the pope's corpse into the Tiber River.

Pius X (1903-14)

Giuseppe Sarto was born at Riese on June 2, 1835. At the age of fifteen he enrolled in the seminary at Padua and was ordained on September 18, 1858. He spent the next seventeen years as a country priest. From 1875 to 1884, he was chancellor of the diocese of Treviso and spiritual director of the seminary. In 1884 he became bishop of Mantua and in June 1893, Leo XIII appointed him patriarch of Venice and a cardinal.

Cardinal Sarto was elected pope on August 4, 1903, at the age of sixty-eight. He chose the name Pius "out of regard for recent popes of that name who had bravely resisted persecution" (J. Kelly 1986, 313). Pius was of medium height and had a somewhat florid complexion. This simple, straightforward, and extremely pious man was capable of severity and was greatly concerned with church order.

Pius X was not distinguished for learning and had no experience with politics or the wider problems of the church and world. As one who had been a pastor during his entire priestly career, he made it clear from the start that he intended to give his pontificate a pastoral orientation rather than a political one. He adopted as his motto "to sum up all things in Christ" (Eph. 1:10). Since his chief concerns were the internal problems of the church and the spiritual life of the people, he set three goals for his pastoral ministry: to renew religious instruction, to foster liturgical piety, and to develop devotion to the Eucharist (Falconi 1967, 20). His strategy for the church was that of defensive centralization. For example, he had a fundamental hostility toward liberalism, especially the separation of church and state. He was convinced that religion, politics, and society formed a continuous whole and their separation was a sacrilege. Any separation would divorce a nation from Christianity. He did not perceive the distinction between spheres of competence whereby the state can do certain things and the church others. Someday the year 1904 may be known as "the year of the theologians" because born that year were the three theologians who, I believe, have made the greatest contributions to theology, the church, and Vatican II; namely, Yves Congar in France, Bernard Lonergan in Canada, and Karl Rahner in Germany.

Pius X's reign of eleven years came to an end on August 20, 1914, when, it was said, he died heartbroken by the outbreak of World War I. The preliminary process of the canonization of this humble and prayerful man was initiated by Pius XII in 1943 and completed in 1953 when two miracles attributed to him were declared genuine. He was canonized on May 29, 1954, and August 21 was designated his feast day. He was the first pope to be canonized since Pius V (1566–72) was so honored in 1712.

Benedict XV (1914-22)

Giacomo Della Chiesa was born in Genoa on November 21, 1854. He earned a doctorate in civil law from the Genoa University in 1875. He then studied for the priesthood in Rome, being ordained on December 21, 1878.

After training for the papal diplomatic service (1878–82), he was assigned as secretary to the papal nuncio, Mariano Rampolla, in Spain (1883–87). When Rampolla became Leo XIII's secretary of state and a cardinal in 1887, Della Chiesa returned to Rome with him, eventually being promoted to undersecretary of state (1901–7). Pius X appointed him archbishop of Bologna in 1907 and a cardinal in May 1914. Some three months later (on September 3) he was elected pope. He took the name Benedict in honor of his last great predecessor from Bologna, Benedict XIV (1740–58).

As mentioned, Pius X's death coincided with the outbreak of World War I. The choice of Cardinal Della Chiesa was probably due to the need for an experienced diplomat during this time of crisis. In fact, the conclave was so hurriedly called—only eleven days after Pius' death, in order to have a pope who could persuade the warring powers to stop fighting—that the cardinals from the United States did not arrive in time for the election.

Benedict was small of stature, had poor eyesight, and was matter-of-fact and precise, without much outward geniality and charm. On his very first day in office, he set forth his major concerns. First, he focused on the issue of peace among nations. As a symbol of his compassion for the sorrow caused by the war, he stipulated that his installation would not take place in Saint Peter's but at a simple ceremony in the Sistine Chapel. His second concern was reconciliation within the church. He personally wrote an invitation to the president of France to attend his installation mass, despite the separation

between state and church in that country during the previous
ten years. Third, he inquired about Vatican finances and
immediately set aside a generous sum for charitable donations
to be made without delay (Falconi 1967, 114).

Benedict's pontificate of seven years and four months was
overshadowed by the war and its aftermath. Because the Roman
question remained unresolved, the papacy was subject to diplomatic isolation and unable to play any significant role in major
world affairs. Benedict protested inhumane methods of warfare
and published several peace plans, which went unheeded.

During the war he maintained strict impartiality, never condemning any of the belligerents, with the result that each side
accused him of favoring the other. For example, on August 1,
1917, he sent a peace message to all the belligerents, urging
them to "accept a just and lasting peace," not to strive for "victory," and to end their "useless struggle." His message antago-
nized just about everybody. His talk of "useless struggle"
undermined Italian morale; the Allies thought he was pro-
German; while the Germans thought he was pro-French
(Hebblethwaite 1983).

After the armistice, Benedict was not allowed any part in
the peace settlement of 1919. In fact, "the Allies [had] secretly
(treaty of London: April 1915) agreed with Italy that the
Vatican should be excluded" (J. Kelly 1986, 315). Woodrow
Wilson, the first United States president to be received by a
pope, visited Benedict in December 1918. The two leaders
had previously exchanged correspondence on Wilson's
"Fourteen Points," the president's proposals for the peace that
would follow the war (Hanson 1987, 42).

Benedict died unexpectedly at the age of sixty-seven on
January 22, 1922, from influenza that had developed into
pneumonia. Some of his initiatives were to be carried forward
by two of the men he selected for diplomatic posts: in 1917
he sent Pacelli (the future Pius XII) as nuncio to Munich; in
1918 he sent Ratti (the future Pius XI) as nuncio to Poland.

Pius XI (1922–39)

Achille Ratti was born on May 12, 1857, at Desio, near Milan
and within sight of the Alps. Vigorous in body and mind, he
excelled in his youth as a mountain climber. He was educated
at several seminaries, including Milan, the Lombard College,

the Academy of St. Thomas in Rome, and the Gregorian University. His ordination to the priesthood took place in December 1879 at the Lateran. After a stint as professor at the seminary at Padua (1882–88), he worked at both the Ambrosian Library in Milan (1888–1911) and the Vatican Library (1911–18), becoming the prefect in 1914.

Benedict XV, recognizing Ratti's flair for languages, sent him as his emissary to Poland in April 1918. In 1919 Ratti was promoted to nuncio and made an archbishop. In 1921 he came back to Italy as the cardinal archbishop of Milan. On February 6, 1922, being almost sixty-five, he was elected pope. Pius was stocky in build, had a broad, high forehead, and maintained an expression at once benevolent and extremely firm.

Early in his pontificate, Pius set forth his three goals for the church: there would be a holy year (1925); he would inaugurate a new feast of universal importance (Christ the King in 1925); and he would reassemble Vatican I. This Council had quickly adjourned with the outbreak of the Franco-Prussian war on July 19, 1870, having completed only two of its fifty-one proposed documents. After protracted consultations with bishops around the world, Pius decided that the reconvening of the Council would be impracticable until the Roman question had been settled. Then it might not even be necessary.[2]

Pius's motto was "Christ's peace in Christ's kingdom," expressing his belief that the church should not isolate itself from society but actively participate in it. For example, he installed a radio station in the Vatican in 1931, becoming the first pope to use the radio to teach the gospel.

During his seventeen years in office, Pius had to handle many volatile issues: communism in Russia, nazism in Germany, persecution in Mexico, civil war in Spain, and fascism in Italy. His "most significant diplomatic achievement was the Lateran Treaty (February 11, 1929) which he negotiated with Benito Mussolini, Italian prime minister since 1922, and which established the Vatican City as an independent, neutral state" (J. Kelly 1986, 317).

The Lateran Treaty meant that for the first time since 1870 the Vatican recognized Italy as a sovereign country with Rome as its capital. Mussolini granted the Vatican many privileges, hoping in return to obtain its support for his fascist regime. By agreement, Catholicism was accepted as the official religion of Italy and the Vatican received ninety million dollars in compensation. The Roman question had been resolved.

The treaty was revised on February 18, 1984, after fifteen years of negotiations. Some of the major changes include the following: Catholicism would cease to be the state religion of Italy and Vatican City would no longer be called a "sacred city," a designation that permitted the church to take such steps as banning books, plays, and films (Lavin 1984; Hebblethwaite 1984a).

Pius XI's last years were especially troubled. In the 1930s there were worldwide economic disorders brought on by the great depression; the Sino-Japanese war was fought in 1931; Mussolini conquered Ethiopia in 1936; and the French and British appeased Hitler by signing the Munich Pact in 1938, which surrendered part of Czechoslovakia to Germany. When Pius died on February 10, 1939, World War II was a mere seven months away.

Pius XII (1939-58)

Eugenio Pacelli was born in Rome on March 2, 1876. After his seminary studies at the Gregorian and Lateran universities in Rome, he was ordained in 1899. He entered the papal service in 1901. In 1902 he earned a doctorate in church law (canon law) and from 1904 to 1916 he assisted Cardinal Pietro Gasparri in codifying the canon law, a project begun in 1905 by Pius X and completed under Benedict XV in 1918.

In April 1917, Pacelli was appointed nuncio to Munich and made an archbishop. As nuncio, he was deeply involved in the negotiations sponsored by Benedict XV on behalf of peace. Pacelli remained in Germany, briefly in Munich but mainly in Berlin, until 1929. In December of that year he became a cardinal. On February 7, 1930, he succeeded Cardinal Gasparri, his friend and mentor, as secretary of state. This office enabled him to travel extensively, even permitting him to make an unprecedented visit to many parts of the United States in 1936.

Pacelli, a talented linguist, statesman, diplomat, and scholar, was elected the 260th pope on March 2, 1939, his sixty-third birthday. This tall, slender man with an aristocratic yet pale and ascetic appearance kept a tight grip on the global church, ruling with authority. Animated in conversation, often with a most winning and boyish smile, Pius made a profound impression on the thousands who attended his numerous public audiences in Rome. He gave a speech virtually every day. He ranged widely over ecclesial and world problems, giving frequent attention to medical ethics and social teachings. However, just as World War I and its aftermath dominated Benedict XV's contact with the nations of the world, so World War II and the troubles wrought by communism, fascism, and nazism preoccupied the pontificate of Pius XII. He envisioned himself as the pope of peace.

One event—one of the most shameful in world history—haunts the history of Pius's tenure: the Holocaust. The Nazis, who came to power under Hitler in January 1933, ruthlessly and systematically executed six million Jews in concentration camps such as Dachau and Buchenwald in Germany and Treblinka and Auschwitz in Poland from 1938 to 1945. This genocide shocked the world and its horrors continue to reverberate through world politics and theology. For example, when Germany's united Parliament held its first meeting in Berlin on October 4, 1990, the session opened with a minute of silence in tribute to the victims of nazism, including those of the Holocaust.

Within the church there have been several references to the significance of the Holocaust for society and the church itself. In his address in 1979 to the United Nations, John Paul II declared that the contemporary world's recognition of human rights was generated as a response to the Holocaust. Johann Baptist Metz, a priest-theologian who served in the German army as a teenager, wrote in 1989 that the Holocaust takes on "paradigmatic character through its very incomparability" (Metz 1989; see also Baum 1974b). The Holocaust, he said, points us away from any idealistic system of thought that does not take into account people. Auschwitz, more than any other event, turns theology to the people who are victims of oppression, exploitation, and other forms of human degradation. Metz's view was seconded by Nicholas Lash, professor of divinity at the University of Cambridge, just before the first Congress of the European Society for Catholic Theology, held in Stuttgart, Germany, in April 1992. Commenting on the theme of the congress, "The Christian Faith and the Future of

Europe," Lash wrote: "All talk of 'Christian' Europe finds its final silencing in those bleak fields that now lie in Europe's heart and center: Treblinka, Dachau, Auschwitz. In the demands that these memories lay upon our actions and imagination is to be found, I think, the key to much else that should shape European theology now and in the future" (Lash 1992a, 268; see also Lash 1992b).

The theses of Metz, Lash, and John Paul are debatable since there were other horrible genocides in the twentieth century, for example, the seven million killed in the Ukrainian Holocaust in the Russian-made famine of 1932–33. The point, nonetheless, is that the Holocaust continues to resonate throughout world history, politics, and religion. The question is: What did Pius XII do about it? And the answer is that he never publicly spoke out against the Nazi atrocities. Some angrily maintain that the pope was shamelessly silent; others argue that he did everything humanly possible to save lives. What is the truth?

One of those who said the pope was shamelessly silent was Rolf Hochhuth. In 1963 this thirty-two-year-old German Protestant wrote a play about Pius XII titled *The Deputy.* In this play, which was translated into more than twenty languages, Pius was depicted as one who knew in fine detail about the systematic annihilation of the Jews but was silent because of his own Germanophile tendencies, his concern for church property, and his obsessive fear of communism.

On the other hand, some recent scholarship indicates that not only did Pius do everything humanly possible to save lives—including keeping silent—but that he knowingly risked his own personal reputation rather than jeopardizing the day-to-day practical work of the rescue of Jews sponsored by the Vatican and others. It is estimated that the Catholic Church was successful in helping save from 700,000 to 860,000 Jews from certain death, some 30,000 in Rome itself. Not only were Jews sheltered in monasteries, convents, schools, and churches, but Pius also took the advice of Roman rabbis in softening condemnation of the Holocaust atrocities. When Pius died in 1958, Golda Meir, foreign minister (1956–66) and prime minister (1969–74) of Israel, declared: "When fearful martyrdom came to our people in the decade of Nazi terror, the voice of the pope was raised for the victims" (Lapomarda 1986).

J. Derek Holmes, church historian at Ushaw College, England, published a book in 1981 defending Pius XII. His arguments are based on new materials released from the Vatican archives and other sources over the previous fifteen years. For example, after the war the World Jewish Congress sent twenty million lire to Vatican charities in gratitude for the involvement of Pius XII in their cause.

Owen Chadwick, professor of history at Cambridge, wrote a book about Pius and the Holocaust (1987), based in large measure on the wartime diaries and diplomatic reports of d'Arcy Godolphin Osborne, the British Minister to the Vatican from 1936 to 1947. Chadwick quotes a letter in which Osborne criticized Hochhuth's appraisal of the pope: "So far from being a cool (which, I suppose, implies cold-blooded and inhumane) diplomatist, Pius XII was the most warmly humane, kind, generous, sympathetic and (incidentally saintly) character that it has been my privilege to know in the course of a long life." Osborne was not a Catholic.

Finally, Sister Pascalina Lehnert (1894–1984), a German nun who was officially Pius's housekeeper from 1918 to 1958 (but, in fact, was his secretary, confidant, and adviser) said in 1983 in the first interview she had granted since the pope's death that Pius condemned the Nazi massacres in the Netherlands in a scathing letter but decided at the last minute against its publication. She reported that Pius was "profoundly shaken" when the Nazis reacted to a critical pastoral letter of the Dutch bishops by deporting another forty thousand people to concentration camps. Pius said: "I wanted this protest to be published this very afternoon. But then I thought that if 40,000 people ended up in the death camps because of the Dutch bishops' words, Hitler would intern at least 200,000 for those of the pope."[3]

John XXIII (1958-63)

Angelo Roncalli, the third of thirteen children, was born on November 25, 1881, in Sotto il Monte, a town near Bergamo. After his seminary training in Bergamo, he studied at the Saint Apollinare Institute and graduated with a doctorate in theology in 1904, the year of his ordination.

From 1905 to 1914 he was secretary to Bishop Giacomo Radini-Tedeschi of Bergamo and also a lecturer on church history at the seminary. During World War I he served four years in the medical corps and then as chaplain. In 1921 Benedict XV took him out of Bergamo and placed him in charge of fund-raising for the missions throughout Italy. In his spare time he engaged in research in church history. His studies in the Ambrosian Library in Milan brought him in contact with Achille Ratti, the future Pius XI. It was Pius XI who appointed him an archbishop in 1925 and launched him on his diplomatic career, first in Bulgaria (1925–34) and then in Turkey and Greece (1934–44).

Pius XII appointed him nuncio to France in 1944, a very sensitive assignment because, among other things, Roncalli would have to deal tactfully yet firmly with the problem of the many bishops accused of collaborating with the Vichy regime. In 1953 he was made a cardinal and three days later, patriarch of Venice, at the age of seventy-one. After twenty-eight years of service outside of Italy, he was back in his native land. It looked as if Cardinal Roncalli would end his earthly days in the pastoral work for which he had always kept a strong love. However, at the conclave on October 28, 1958, he was elected pope, a month before his seventy-seventh birthday. An editorial in a New York paper stated: "In the secular affairs of men he would be old and ready to retire. Yet in the affairs of God, he is beginning a new and tremendously arduous task."[4]

Roncalli was elected on the twelfth ballot by the fifty cardinals present. Apparently, the cardinals were uncertain about who should succeed the powerful Pius XII. Roncalli seems to have been a neutral and compromise candidate who would provide time for the cardinals to determine the next pope. At his age, Roncalli could be nothing but a transitional pope in the temporal sense of having a brief pontificate. What no one expected was that he would be a transitional pope in the metaphysical sense: confronting the church with a totally new approach to its own identity and mission. By calling Vatican Council II, he forced the church to redefine its meaning for the world (Murphy 1981, 20).

Cardinal Roncalli took the name John because it was his father's name; it was the name of the church where he was baptized; and because John the Baptist, the one who prepared the way of the Lord, was one of his models. In choosing the name John, he also made a historical statement. From 1410 to

1415 there was a John XXIII (Baldassare Cossa), whose very complicated story as antipope includes his election by the Council of Pisa and his subsequent resignation and deposition at the ecumenical Council of Constance (1414–18), where he was accused of such crimes as simony and perjury. However, until 1958, historians debated his authenticity. Roncalli, a church historian, settled the matter without blinking an eye: "There have been twenty-two authentic popes called John. I will be the twenty-third" (ibid., 77).

John was a short, stout, smiling old man who radiated goodness, warmth, and gentle wit. The Vatican always prepares three sets of robes for the new pope: a small, a medium, and a large. It was a struggle to fit John into the large white robes waiting for him. He quipped: "Everyone wants me to be pope except the tailors."

When John died after a brief pontificate of less than five years, the philosopher-journalist Walter Lippmann said the pope "had reached across all the barriers of class, caste, color and creed to touch the hearts of all kinds of people" (Donohue 1981). What was it about this man that evoked such admiration and praise? At his installation mass on November 4, 1958, John described himself in his homily. The new pope, he said, "through the events of life, is like the son of Jacob, who meeting with his brothers showed them the tenderness of his heart and, bursting into tears said, 'I am Joseph, your brother.'"

Peter Hebblethwaite believes these words tell us about the greatness of John: "This text of Genesis 45 is the key to understanding Roncalli. It is the passage in which Joseph, now powerful in the land of Egypt, reveals himself to his discomfited brothers. Roncalli used it on countless occasions: when addressing socialists in Venice, the prisoners in the Regina Coeli prison in Rome, the Jews who came to visit him in the Vatican. The message was the same each time. . . . To paraphrase Blaise Pascal, people expected to meet a pontiff, and they met a brother human being" (Hebblethwaite 1981b).

Paul VI (1963-78)

Giovanni Battista Montini was born on September 26, 1897, at Concesio, near Brescia. After his ordination in 1920, he pursued graduate studies in Rome. In May 1923 he went to

Poland as an attaché in the apostolic nunciature (home of the papal representative) until ill health forced his return to Rome. In October 1924, he entered the service of the secretary of state of Pius XI, being appointed undersecretary of state (one who can represent the secretary of state) in December of 1937. In 1952, Pius XII promoted him to pro-secretary (the assistant to the secretary of state) and then, in 1954, appointed him archbishop of Milan. Why Milan after twenty-five years of close collaboration? No one really knows. Various reasons have been proposed. For example, it has been suggested that Montini proposed that the Vatican open a dialogue with the communist governments as a way to gain limited freedom for the church. This approach was in sharp contrast to Pius XII's open resistance to Soviet attempts to repress and eradicate religion in the Soviet Union and Eastern Europe.

Pius XII had offered Montini the cardinal's hat in 1952. This honor Montini declined, but later accepted when offered by John XXIII in December 1958. He actively participated in the first session of Vatican II in October 1962.

The June 1963 conclave (a closed meeting of the College of Cardinals, ordinarily held at the Vatican to elect a new pope) was attended by eighty cardinals, the largest in the church's history. Montini was elected on the fifth ballot. The new pope had a high forehead, chiseled features, a strong mouth with compressed lips, and sensitive and keen blue eyes beneath somewhat bushy brows. He carried himself with grace and dignity. His choice of the name Paul was due in part to his keen interest in the Pauline epistles and spirituality. The name also suggested an outward-looking approach like the missionary Paul. And one of his first acts was to announce that the Council would continue, thereby making John XXIII's reform irreversible.

Wilton Wynn, Vatican correspondent for *Time* magazine from 1962 to 1987, surmised that if Montini had been a cardinal in 1958, Roncalli would not even have been considered for the papacy. Montini had more extensive diplomatic experience in Rome and, at that time he was sixty-one, the right age. In 1958 the average age of the fifty-one cardinals at the conclave was seventy-four. Some irreverent observer remarked, "There is one requirement for the pope to be elected by this conclave—he must be able to walk" (Wynn 1988, 20–21).

John XXIII called for an ecumenical council in 1959. If Montini had been elected in 1958, would he have called a council? No one can answer this question, but it seems clear today that Paul VI was the ideal choice to steer John's council to its conclusion by putting John's spirit into church life and law.

No pope has an easy road to travel. For example, Paul had defended and reaffirmed priestly celibacy in his 1967 encyclical *Sacerdotalis celibatus* by describing it as a "heavy and sweet burden" and a "total gift" of the priest to God and the church. Nevertheless, toward the end of his life he admitted that his "heaviest cross" was signing the laicization papers of thousands of priests leaving the priesthood. During his fifteen years, 32,357 priests asked for laicization and he granted all but 1,033 (ibid., 248).

Paul was called "the pilgrim pope" because between 1964 and 1970, he made nine trips overseas. Perhaps his finest hour occurred on October 4, 1965, when he addressed the United Nations in New York City. His presence was historic: the first time a pope had set foot in the western hemisphere. Paul's emotional speech drew a standing ovation from the general assembly. The most evocative passage was the following:

> And now, we come to the most important point of our message, which is, at first, a negative point. You are expecting us to utter this sentence, and we are well aware of its gravity and solemnity: *not some peoples against others,* never again, never more! It was principally for this purpose that the organization of the United Nations arose: against war, in favor of peace! Listen to the lucid words of a great man, the late John Kennedy, who proclaimed four years ago: "Mankind must put an end to war, or war will put an end to mankind." Many words are not needed to proclaim this loftiest aim of your institution. It suffices to remember the blood of millions of men, that numberless and unheard-of sufferings, useless slaughter and frightful ruin, are the sanction of the past which unites you with an oath which must change the future history of the world: No more war, war never again! Peace, it is peace which must guide the destinies of peoples and of all mankind.

Paul died quietly at Castelgandolfo, outside of Rome, on August 6, 1978. "History will be generous to Paul because it possibly will say he was the first to bear the full burden of the modern papacy. John XXIII opened Catholicism's Pandora's box and left Paul with the consequences."[5]

John Paul I (August 26 to September 28, 1978)

Albino Luciani was born of poor, working-class parents on October 17, 1912, in northern Italy in the village of Canale d'Agordo in the Belluno diocese. Ordained a priest in 1935, he later earned a doctorate in theology from the Gregorian University. A man of wide literary culture and of deep but simple piety, he was appointed professor of dogmatic theology for his diocese. He was consecrated bishop of Vittorio Veneto in 1958 by John XXIII. Paul VI appointed him patriarch of Venice in 1969 and a cardinal in 1973. He participated in the international synods of 1971, 1974, and 1977.

Cardinal Luciani, a man with an infectious smile and kindly manner, was elected the 263rd pope on August 26, 1978, a few months short of his sixty-sixth birthday. The vote was decisive: on the third ballot he received more than two-thirds of the 111 ballots. The decisive election took the church by complete surprise because Luciani had seldom left northern Italy and had neither curial nor international experience. At any rate, the world was captivated by this pastoral man of practical common sense and welcomed his warm and beaming smile. The first pope ever to choose a double name, John Paul did so to symbolize his esteem for his two predecessors, his desire to combine their best qualities, and his plan to continue their reform policies.

Both John XXIII and Paul VI had a great impact on Luciani's ecclesial career and vision. Both, he said, "had provided me with an example and a program" (Hebblethwaite 1978b). Unfortunately, neither the church nor the world had a chance to learn what policies he would have pursued because he died most unexpectedly on September 28, 1978, having served a mere thirty-three days as the vicar of Peter. His term was the shortest since 1605, when Leo XI served for just twenty-seven days.

Almost immediately after John Paul I's death, rumors of foul play began to circulate in Rome because of odd discrepancies concerning his sudden death. Precise answers to obvious questions were in short supply: Who found the body and when? What caused the death and when? Was there a secret autopsy or none at all? The Vatican officials had not performed an autopsy—the papal constitution forbids them—but did announce that John Paul died of a heart attack.

In 1984, David Yallop, a British journalist and author, published a controversial book that purported to be an exhaustive and thoroughly objective investigation into the death of the pope. His conclusion: the pope was the victim of an assassination plot devised by six high-ranking prelates. Allegedly, the pope was poisoned by members of a secret Masonic lodge. Yallop, invoking journalistic privilege, provided no verifiable evidence for his sensational allegations and refused to identify his alleged sources.

Yallop's irresponsible thesis that the pope was murdered provoked the Vatican—including John Paul II and Paul Marcinkus, a United States archbishop who had been labelled a prime suspect[6]—to invite John Cornwell, a former Catholic, a former editor of the *Observer* in London, and an award-winning crime writer and novelist, to make an official investigation into the mysterious death of the pope. Cornwell used his talents to produce a fascinating account of the people and events surrounding the death (Cornwell 1989).

Having ready access to reliable Vatican officials, secretaries, funeral attendants, reporters, and relatives, Cornwell convincingly demonstrated that Yallop's fanciful murder plot was full of gaping holes. His own conclusion was that the pope died of a blood clot in the lung, possibly from not taking his anticoagulant drugs. However, although Cornwell never accused anyone of murder, he did find the papal staff culpable for the pope's death. Cornwell claimed to have uncovered evidence leading to a conclusion that he found "more shameful and more tragic than any of the conspiracy theories." John Paul died, said Cornwell, "scorned and neglected by the institution that existed to sustain him." In other words, those charged to watch over the pope never summoned medical assistance when the pope complained of feeling slightly ill on the night that he died. But this seems more like culpable incompetence than scornful neglect (Hebblethwaite 1991a).

Most people conclude that Cornwell's theory, while believable, is unsupported by concrete evidence, and thus ultimately settles nothing. Unless someone comes forward to support Cornwell's thesis, the circumstances surrounding John Paul's sudden death will remain a mystery.

The answer could simply be that the pope, who did not have robust health, was unprepared for the pressures of the office. After all, the papacy is demanding, being probably the most sensitive and public position in the world. The day before his death, John Paul jokingly asked an aide "to buy a machine that could do his reading for him" (Watson 1978). Cornwell devoted two lengthy chapters to his interviews with Archbishop Marcinkus. At one point the archbishop said: "They called him the 'smiling pope.' But let me tell you something . . . that was a very nervous smile." Another curial official said John Paul's death "could have had something to do with passing from responsibility for a relatively small diocese of 600,000 Catholics in Venice to responsibility for the entire Catholic world."[7]

John Paul II (1978-)

Karol Wojtyla was born on May 18, 1920, in the town of Wadowice in southern Poland. When he was nine years old, his mother died while giving birth to a stillborn daughter; his father died in 1942. In his youth Wojtyla was an outstanding student who became extremely keen about poetry, acting, and sports, especially swimming, canoeing, hiking, and skiing.

His university studies at the Jagiellonian in Krakow were interrupted by the German occupation of Poland in September 1939, but resumed after the Russians conquered the country in January 1945. He was graduated with distinction in theology in August 1946, receiving ordination that November 1. Sent to Rome, he obtained a doctorate in theology at the Angelicum in 1948, writing his dissertation on the concept of faith in John of the Cross (1542–91). From 1948 to 1951 Wojtyla served as a parish priest back in his native land. In 1952 he returned to the Jagiellonian to study philosophy, defending his doctoral dissertation on Max Scheler (1874–1928) in 1959. Scheler and other German phenomenologists reacted against nineteenth-century subjectivism and historicism (the identification of recorded history with history as actually lived by people), seeking a return to objectivity and the principle of human solidarity (Baum 1970a, 10–11). From 1952 to 1958, Wojtyla lectured on social ethics at the Krakow seminary and became professor of ethics at the Catholic University of Lublin.

Pius XII made him an auxiliary bishop to the diocese of Krakow in 1958; Paul VI named him archbishop of Krakow on December 30, 1963, and a cardinal on June 26, 1967.

Wojtyla was an active participant at Vatican II and at four of the five international synods called by Paul VI. During the 1960s and 1970s he had a chance to travel extensively, sometimes on curial business, to the Middle East, Africa, Australia, south and east Asia, and the United States, where he attended the eucharistic congress in Philadelphia in 1976. Cardinal Wojtyla was thus well-known and widely respected when the 109 cardinals assembled to elect a successor to John Paul I.

With twenty-seven members, the Italians were still the largest single group of cardinals, yet they could not reach a consensus in appointing an Italian candidate. Also, the frailty and sudden death of John Paul I "may have been a symbol of the weakness of the remaining group of Italian cardinals, a signal that the time had come to break the pattern of electing Italian popes" (Wynn 1988, 262). On October 16, 1978, Wojtyla was elected the 264th pope by an overwhelming majority (103 of 109 votes) at the age of fifty-eight. He was the youngest pope since Pius IX, who was elected at the age of fifty-four. It is said that he first thought of taking the name Stanislaus, after a Polish church leader murdered by the king in 1078. Stanislaus, the Polish equivalent of the English archbishop Thomas Becket (1118–70), is, for John Paul, "the patron of church-state relations." Dissuaded by the cardinals, Wojtyla chose the name John Paul "as less nationalistic and to make the point that he would continue the work of his predecessors" (Hebblethwaite 1992b).

John Paul II is an extraordinary man: intelligent, serious yet witty, charismatic, energetic, a talented manipulator of the media, an inspiring liturgist, an eloquent homilist, and a linguist. On his inauguration day he "addressed the world's Catholics in 11 languages, including Ukrainian and Lithuanian, which significantly are languages of restless minorities in the [then] Soviet Union."[8]

John Paul's election was marked by a series of firsts: the first Slavic pope, the first non-Italian in 455 years, and the first pope to live his life as student, priest, professor, bishop, and cardinal in a communist society.

John Paul has been extremely active. His eight-day trip in August 1993 to Jamaica, Mexico, and the United States (in Denver for World Youth Day) was his sixtieth overseas pilgrimage. Unfortunately, John Paul's active pontificate was almost cut short when he was shot and nearly killed in Saint Peter's Square on May 13, 1981, by an alleged Turkish terrorist.[9] The gunman was caught and given a life sentence for the attack, but the investigation into who had masterminded the shooting was inconclusive. John Paul recovered quickly and continued to make his presence felt in the contemporary world, thanks in part to the extensive coverage his words and deeds receive in the media.

Leo XIII was elected in 1878 at the age of sixty-seven and helped bring in the twentieth century. John Paul was elected in 1978 at the age of fifty-eight and could well bring in the twenty-first.

Conclusion

This chapter began with Von Hügel's thesis that a religion (read: Catholic Christianity) is as strong as the individual strengths and interrelationships of its institutional, intellectual, and devotional elements. Since the papacy is distinctive of the Catholic Church, vignettes of those who became popes were presented to show how their lives were inextricably intertwined with the institutional, intellectual, and devotional life of the church. Most had advanced degrees from prestigious academic institutions in Rome and were teachers. Each was an expert in some area of church life: church law, church music, philosophy, church history, or theology. All were known for their piety and commitment to Christ and his church.

Once elected to the church's highest office, each pope manifested in his own special way his devotion to the integrity of the institutional church, especially through his writings, addresses, and decrees about theological, liturgical, ethical, devotional, and social matters. As this thematic history of the Catholic tradition during the twentieth century unfolds, it will become clear that these men did not "mouth interchangeable platitudes." Each made his own distinctive contribution to the tradition, at times positive and helpful, and at other times negative and counterproductive. For example, the preconciliar popes wrote 184 encyclicals: Leo XIII wrote eighty-six and Pius XII wrote forty. Most of these documents had a tangible effect on the church. Avery Dulles, a Jesuit expert on ecclesiology, indicates that in the twentieth-century preconciliar church, "Catholic theology . . . depended heavily on the encyclicals of the popes" (1992, 107). However, to understand more clearly the distinctive contributions of these men to the church's institutional, intellectual, and devotional life, it is necessary to turn to the historical and cultural context of the twentieth-century church, namely, the rise of modernity.

2

The Church and Modernity

In a 1984 book on church history, Stephen Happel and David
Tracy wrote that "the most significant cultural force in our
world is the spirit of modernity: the rational science born in
the early modern period and the Enlightenment critique of
reason, history, politics and religion" (p.163). In 1987, three
years after his original statement, Tracy, a priest-theologian at
the University of Chicago's Divinity School, declared that "we
have left modernity behind" (1987b, 73). Whether modernity
is still with us or behind us, the twentieth-century Catholic
Church and Vatican II cannot be understood unless they are
placed within the context of the challenge of modernity.

Modernity is not a fully precise term or notion. In each
period of history thoughtful persons attempt to be in touch with
modernity. For example, the attempt in the thirteenth century of
Thomas Aquinas to correlate with new Aristotelianism was the
modernity of that period. In this book *modernity* denotes the
mentality or mindset that developed in the seventeenth century
as a result of the scientific revolution. This mindset is associated
with the Enlightenment of the eighteenth century and it has continued into the nineteenth and twentieth centuries. Modernity
unleashed major critiques of the past understanding of the physical sciences, politics, philosophy, economics, and religion, and
was concerned with the progressive enhancement of human life
by controlling the natural world; by creating a perfect society;
by focusing on human reason, dignity, and autonomy; and by
rejecting religion, faith, and revelation.

In addition to modernity, two other terms pervade this chapter: *modernists* and *Modernism*. Those Christians who tried to reconcile modernity with historical Christianity were called modernists. A modernist movement within the Roman Catholic Church that was condemned in 1907 as heretical was called Modernism.

The way to modernity was opened in the fifteenth century by the Renaissance and in the sixteenth century by the Protestant Reformation—two massive cultural events opposed to the medieval world. The Renaissance rejected medievalism and called for a return to the classical humanism of Greco-Roman culture. The ideal of the Renaissance was for humans to control the natural world and create a perfect society—two goals carried forward by the Enlightenment. The Protestant reformers wanted to escape the medieval church by returning to the early church, especially its emphasis on the Bible. They protested the church's authoritarianism, doctrinal confusion, fiscal abuses, widespread ignorance, and corrupt clergy. The Reformation's insistence on the primacy of the individual conscience opened the gates for the Enlightenment's stress on human autonomy; its stress on "faith alone" helped the Enlightenment divorce faith from reason and reject faith in revelation altogether.

Can the rise of modernity be assigned a specific date? Several European and North American scholars fix on the year 1680 (Butterfield 1966; Congar 1968; Lonergan 1974, 55), because this date marks the rise of modern science, in which modernity has its roots. The scientific revolution of the seventeenth century—probably the greatest intellectual accomplishment in the history of the human race—was so significant that Sir Herbert Butterfield (1901–79), professor of modern history at Cambridge, did not hesitate to categorically declare that the scientific revolution "outshines everything since the rise of Christianity and reduces the Renaissance and the Reformation to the rank of mere episodes, mere internal displacements, within the system of medieval Christendom" (1966, 7).

The Scientific Revolution

Modernity began when modern science asked this radical question: Could nature "be understood as in itself a perfect system, governed by laws discoverable through repeated observation and controlled experimentation" (Clebsch 1979, 188)? Scientists believed that once the laws of nature were understood, nature could be brought into the service of humankind. Furthermore, nature would no longer need grace to perfect it.

To understand how the scientific question was answered, we turn first to Nicolaus Copernicus (1473–1543), a Polish priest and astronomer, who published in 1543 his immortal work *On the Revolutions of the Heavenly Bodies*. In what has become the foundation for modern astronomy, Copernicus advanced a heliocentric theory of planetary motion and in the process directly challenged the existing Ptolemaic geocentric system. According to Copernicus, the sun is motionless at the center of the universe with the planets, including the earth, revolving around it. Copernicus's findings caused considerable consternation, in part because it contradicts how human senses perceive earth's place in space. More important, it contradicts the world view expressed in the Bible. For example, Joshua 10:12–14 depicts Joshua, in his battle with the Amorites, asking God to halt the sun in the middle of the sky for a whole day.

Galileo Galilei (1564–1642), the Italian astronomer and physicist, ushered in the age of science. He examined the acceleration and deceleration of moving bodies and wrote in defense of Copernicus's hypothesis in his 1632 masterwork *Dialogue on the Two Great World Systems*. Galileo's teachings got him in trouble with the church because sixteen years earlier the Vatican had proclaimed the Copernican heliocentric view "formally heretical, inasmuch as it expressly contradicts the doctrines of holy scripture in many places, both according to their literal meaning" and the common interpretation of the early Church Fathers. Galileo was formally brought to trial in Rome on April 30, 1633, condemned as "vehemently suspected of heresy," made to adjure the Copernican theory, silenced, and forced to live under house arrest.

The facts surrounding the condemnation of Galileo in 1633 are controversial. Whatever the real motives for the silencing, what is most significant is that modern science, with its rigorous method of verifying experiments, undermined the medieval view that there were only two sources of the truth, namely, authority and philosophy. The church's authoritative teaching was rooted in God's word in Scripture and tradition. The Scriptures present a geocentric view of the universe with humans on earth the central point of the universe. The heliocentric thesis called this scriptural view into question.

The other source of truth was philosophy, especially the deductive, metaphysical methods of Aristotle and medieval scholasticism. Galileo's scientific method relativized philosophy. Science became a third route to the truth and a threat to the established order.

The findings of other major scientists also conflicted with church teachings. For example, Sir Isaac Newton (1642–1727), the English mathematician and physicist from Cambridge, was convinced the world was rational because it came from an intelligent Creator. But when he discovered the laws of gravity, his findings evoked a serious religious question: if the laws of gravity control all things and if scientists can manipulate these laws, what is God's function? Sir Charles Lyell (1797–1875), an English geologist, published a three-volume work, *Principles of Geology* (1830–33), in which he demonstrated that the earth had evolved over millions of years and not six days.

Charles Darwin (1809–83), an English naturalist, published two books, *Origin of Species* (1859) and *Descent of Man* (1871), in which he claimed that the development of both plants and animals was the result of "natural selection," a process in which random mutations in the offspring of a species enabled some to adapt themselves to their environments more readily than others, thereby surviving in greater numbers and passing on to their offspring these invaluable assests. Such a doctrine dealt a lethal blow to the view of biological theists who regarded the plant and animal worlds as one large, happy family crafted by God during the six days of creation. In contrast to this vision of nature as a peaceable kingdom of flawless specimens, Darwin's evolutionary view pitted the species against each other, each competing furiously for the limited resources available, either becoming extinct when they failed to adapt or overpopulating when they adapted too well.

When this theory was extended to humankind, it not only challenged the Genesis story that humans were created a perfect species who later fell from grace, but it also asserted that humans had a close kinship with other primates and had perhaps evolved from some other forms of life.

The condemnation of Galileo in 1633 illustrates that right from its very beginnings modern science was on a collision course with the church, and that the church retreated from science. Today most agree that religion and science need not be in conflict. Galileo himself knew this when he wrote: "All that has been discovered and observed recently was due to the telescope that I invented, after being inspired by divine grace." Albert Einstein (1879–1955) addressed this tension: "Science without religion is lame; religion without science is blind." During an address commemorating Einstein's centennial on November 10, 1979, John Paul II said that Galileo had suffered at the hands of the church and that more study is needed "to dispel the mistrust that still opposes, in many minds, a fruitful concord between science and faith" (Hebblethwaite 1979c). That study, at least as it concerned Galileo, came to closure on October 31, 1992, when John Paul II read a formal statement before the Pontifical Academy of Sciences. In his address he asked this question: "Has not this case long been shelved and have not the errors committed been recognized?" In his answer, John Paul explained that, since the seventeenth-century theologians did not recognize the formal distinction between the Bible as theology and as cultural and historical interpretations of the faith, "This led them unduly to transpose into the realm of the doctrine of the faith, a question which in fact pertained to scientific investigation" (Cowell 1992).[1]

The Effects of the Scientific Revolution

Galileo and Newton introduced a radical shift in the methodology of science by rejecting the Aristotelian method, which, in its attempt to determine the universal, the necessary, and the essential, simply examined nature, recorded its doings, and profited from this information. Aristotelian science viewed nature as a finished clay vessel. It could be studied, but both its fixed nature and the intent of the potter had to be respected (Milhaven 1970, 119).

Modern science, by contrast, since it searches for the complete explanation of all the data in terms of their intelligible relationships, deals with the changing, the probable, and a pluralism of perspectives from the best scientific opinions. Consequently, nature is not a completed clay vessel, but clay to be broken and remolded responsibly and creatively for human and social needs.

Modern science has had three major effects on human interaction with the world and nature (Johann 1968, 70–78, 154–70). First, it has allowed people to discover and explore their control over the world. Through scientific means it is people themselves who can plant crops, plan economies, dredge rivers, make rain, fly above the clouds, and eliminate illnesses. Is there any wonder, considering these accomplishments, that some would ignore or deny the presence of God? The papal nuncio to Munich reported to the Vatican in 1871 a public speech by a defrocked priest who had declared: "If 12 ignorant heads could regenerate the world, what shall we not be able to do—we who have the power of science on our side?" (Rhodes 1983, 13).

Second, it has given people a different appreciation for the scope of time that encompasses human life. Formerly, human history was viewed as short and static, with the past holding a place of honor. Modern science has helped people understand that human history is quite long and dynamic, and it gives the future and its potential for greater achievements the place of honor.

Since human history is not a short span, it is clear that it took long ages to shape the present order of the world. Consequently, moderns do not view things as having been the way they are now from the beginning of time or even as having been divinely established. Rather, they hold that this present world has evolved out of many cultures and traditions, and is the result of an endless series of both accidental and controlled forces. People became aware that the patterns of nature and society are open to their continued influence. Moderns see the world as a system shaped by their own technological achievements. Furthermore, since people themselves shape their institutions, art, laws, and so on, these things are conditioned by their time and place. And so, flowing from the historicity of things, moderns believe that instead of evolving from a supposed golden past, they are, possibly, progressing toward a golden future.

Third, humans have developed a different understanding of distance. Science expands and intensifies the scope of communications and people's approach to truth. Formerly, people knew few traditions and conceived them as permanent and universally accepted. Communication was slow and limited. Since people lived within a limited horizon of ideas and culture, what they knew became the tradition. Traditions developed and solidified. People grew up within a tradition. They made it their own and passed it on to their children.

Modernity challenged tradition, not out of disregard or disrespect, but in order to free people "from the mystifications and ideologies inevitably present in all traditions" (Tracy 1989a, 38–39). Modern science invented a whole series of instruments that made it possible to discover among nations a rich pluralism of thought and cultures, all of which are relative to changing history. In our day the communications explosion offers people varied world views so that no single tradition can hold undisputed primacy over communities and individuals. As people try to make important choices and decisions, especially those that orient the whole direction of their lives, they do so knowing there are other points of view and that the evidence that justifies their decisions may not be conclusive.

Classical and Historical Consciousness

The result of the rise of modern science in the seventeenth century was a new view of the world, space, and time. Beginning around 1680, people began to develop a wholly new psychological outlook or ideal, such as had happened only once before in human history (Voegelin 1956–87).

Until the time of the Greek pre-Socratics (the sixth century B.C.), people interpreted the interrelationships among the four constants—the created world, self, others, and the deity—in terms of myth: symbolic stories that explained the origins and inner meaning of the universe and of life, especially human life. People sought harmony among the constants, and focused on nature as the sacred manifestation of the divine. The Greeks, especially Plato and Aristotle, differentiated the four constants in philosophical terms. Their goal was to find harmony among science, politics, anthropology, and theology by focusing on the divine being who grounds all reality and lures humans to himself. The rise of philosophy slowly sub-sumed peoples' mythic consciousness into what is called a classical consciousness.

Classical consciousness comprised a universal and abstract way of knowing that was fundamentally applicable in all times and circumstances. It highlighted traditional ways, unchanging institutions, hierarchical rule, and authority figures. The real was a fixed order that was objective, unchanging, universal, and abstract. The ideal person was the wise person or sage.

Modern science gave rise to historical consciousness. Tradition and authority were subsumed under freedom, equal-ity, dialogue, community, and democracy. Instead of underscor-ing the objective, unchanging, universal, and abstract, people concentrated on the subjective, changeable, particular, and practical. The ideal person was the free or autonomous person.

Classical consciousness stressed philosophy; historical con-sciousness stresses history. To live authentically and freely, our radical historicity has to be given full play. History encom-passes the past, present, and future. To appreciate some past person or event, it is essential that the cultural and temporal context be studied. History made things the way they are. To understand ourselves today, a study must be made of our social, economic, educational, and religious context. History makes us. To understand the future, we have to recognize that we can determine it, to some extent. We make history.

The Economic Revolution

The attempt of modern science to enhance human life by con-trolling the natural world resulted in the Industrial Revolution. This revolution started in England around 1750 and took root in France in 1830, in Germany in 1850, and in the United States in 1860. In these countries there was an impressive improvement in living standards: better food, clothing, homes, transportation, communications, and medicine. The Industrial Revolution transformed the economy and the social structures of society. Due to the impact of science, a factory system of large-scale machine production was introduced. Although there were improvements in agriculture and breeding live-stock, many people moved from the farms to the factories in urban centers. Landowners lost much of their economic impor-tance to bankers, merchants, and industrialists.

In order to meet the problems created by the new social structures, various theories were proposed. The most famous came from Karl Marx (1818–83), the German philosopher and revolutionary who founded communism, a radical form of socialism. In collaboration with Friedrich Engels (1820–95), he published the *Communist Manifesto* in 1848. Some of his main teachings are the following: Progress in history does not come from Christian charity but economic greed. Economic events shape history and are the result of the class struggle between the proletariat and capitalists. The proletarian revolution will bring about communism and the end of the class struggle.

The Intellectual Revolution

The Enlightenment was first and foremost an assertion of emancipation from past views of philosophy, authority, and tradition. Human reason became the primary focus and was viewed as an instrument for spiritual liberation from ignorance, superstition, and passivity. The Enlightenment encouraged a search for a universal morality (including social justice for all) and an emphasis on respect for individuals.

The intellectual revolution was given form and substance by such famous philosophers as Locke, Hume, Kant, Hegel, Comte, and Feuerbach. In order to appreciate their thought, especially in relation to religion and the Catholic Church, it is necessary to return to the seventeenth century and the father of modern philosophy, René Descartes (1596–1650).

The seventeenth century was an age of philosophical skepticism. The skeptics said that certain and valid knowledge of universal truth is unattainable. According to them, people only know appearances (phenomena) and not the real thing; for example, people see colors and even patterns of color but not the being that supports or has the color. Furthermore, the skeptics maintained that evil in the world is incompatible not only with a solid, ordered universe but also with the existence of God.

Descartes, a master mathematician and a devout Catholic, tried to answer the "mental suicide" of the skeptics. In his search for an undeniable truth, Descartes refused to appeal to religion, the philosophy of Aristotle, science, or even the senses. The latter are fallible, as is clear, for example, from our original geocentric view of the universe. Furthermore, he realized, the skeptics would simply dredge up other authorities and probable arguments. So, Descartes began with universal and systematic doubt: to doubt is to think, to think is to be. He is known for his famous assertion, "I think, therefore I am."

Concerning God, Descartes maintained that the idea of a substance that is infinite, eternal, immutable, independent, and all powerful—in other words, perfect—is innate and not derived from sense experience. Since the notion of perfection present in this idea could not come from the ideas of other beings or have been manufactured from ideas of himself, it must have been placed there by God himself. And, since we humans are finite, God is the ultimate guarantor of our search for truth.

Descartes's principle of universal doubt threatened the authority of both revelation and the church, and his demand for clear and irrefutable evidence opposed the notion of revelation and religious mysteries. His "turn to the subject" (i.e., the theory that a person should never accept anything as true until it is presented to the mind "so clearly and distinctively" that he has no occasion to doubt it) became an important Enlightenment theme. All philosophers after Descartes had to deal with his theories about God, innate ideas, and the relationship between spirit and matter.

John Locke (1632–1704) founded British empiricism. The term *empiricism* is derived from a Greek word meaning "experience." Opposing the theory of innate ideas favored by Descartes, Locke argued instead that all knowledge is derived from experience, whether of the mind or the senses.

David Hume (1711–76), a Scottish philosopher and historian, picking up on Locke's empiricism, carried it to the extreme of skepticism. Since the only knowledge that is valid is that acquired through experience, then there is no valid knowledge of such matters as cause and effect or the idea of substance. All we can do is speak of the attributes of a thing and not of the substance behind them. For example, we see the attributes of an apple and assume there is the substance apple. But we have not experienced the substance itself. Pure reason does not allow us to affirm that there are such things as substance in which the various attributes that we perceive reside (Gonzalez 1984, 192).

Hume's ideas left little room for religion. He rejected natural theology—the attempt to acknowledge the existence of God through reason rather than revelation. Claims about the order of the world and a divine cause were considered improbable at best. The order of the world, he said, does not necessarily speak of a God beyond the world since there is evil as well as order, suffering as well as joy. He also denied the validity of miracles. Since matter-of-fact experience is our sole source of knowledge, what we know is that nature is uniform and regular. Since miracles violate the laws of nature, it can never be reasonable to accept them. It would be more sensible to seek other explanations that have their psychological origin in experience. For Hume, then, "Any philosophical, scientific, or religious language that required metaphysical statements, positions that once met the world of experience but transcended it, was suspect" (Happel and Tracy 1984, 115–16).

Immanuel Kant (1724–1804), a German philosopher of logic and metaphysics considered the foremost Enlightenment thinker, has influenced modern thought right up to the present. He had been a rationalist (one who holds that reason is to be granted the primary role in explanation) until, as he later acknowledged, it was Hume who awakened him from his "dogmatic slumber." By this he meant he now also acknowledged the inability of speculative reason to establish in purely rational and objective terms the truth of theology, especially its explanation of God, freedom, and immortality. All these truths belong not to "pure reason" but to "practical reason."

Kant granted primacy to our practical reason, which knows the existence of God as the judge of our actions; of our soul and its freedom by which we choose moral actions; and of life after death when good will be rewarded and evil punished. His distinction between pure and practical reason opened the way out of skepticism and renewed the possibility of religion and morality. However, religion for Kant was primarily an ethical matter. He reasoned that morality requires a belief in God, freedom, and immortality, for without these our sense of duty and our ability to act would vanish. Furthermore, this moral life should flow from a life of trust in oneself rather than authoritarian decrees. Kant espoused the autonomy of reason vis-a-vis any opposition from the outside. He argued that the freedom and dignity of the human person required that the individual obey only those laws given by himself or herself. To have laws imposed from the outside, even when the outside lawgiver is God, is to lose one's autonomy.

G. W. F. Hegel (1770–1831) was the most influential thinker of the nineteenth century. In reaction to Kant's teachings that reason was seriously limited, he identified the findings of the human mind with the divine Spirit. In effect, Hegel divinized human consciousness. He argued that universal reason (Spirit) is not only what distinguishes humans from the animals, but also represents the full content of our humanity. But universal reason can only be understood concretely as it objectifies itself in human institutions, laws, customs, art, science, and philosophy. Hegel thus immersed humankind within history with a completeness beyond any previous thinker. Twentieth-century existentialists would eventually capitalize on his thought, declaring, "We have no nature, only a history."

Auguste Comte (1789–1857), a French philosopher considered the founder of positivism, was also a sociologist who actually originated the term *sociology*. In his major work, *The Course of Positive Philosophy* (1842), he called for the reform of society so that both individuals and nations could live in harmony and comfort. His thesis was that history had passed from a long childhood to a recent era of change and now to a third stage of development. First there was the religious stage, with its belief in the supernatural; second was the philosophical stage, with its belief in ideas as reality; now we had reached the positive (or science of humanity) stage, in which phenomena are explained by observation, hypotheses, and experimentation. Sociology would provide a scientific basis for leading human history into a golden age. In this stage the structures of society could be changed to make life better. History, which is neither planned nor directed by a God, has its own inherent principles that can be directed toward inevitable progress.

Ludwig Feuerbach (1804–72), a German philosopher, also denied the existence of God. In his famous work *The Essence of Christianity* (1841), he declared that God is simply a projection of our best qualities. The notion of a real, personal being called God was helpful at one stage of human development because it enabled us to realize ourselves in self-transcendence. However, to remain at that stage only alienates people from themselves and one another. Feuerbach posited, then, that we are God. Feuerbach was not opposed to religion. In fact, he wanted to keep it as long as it was understood as he defined it, namely, as the glorification of the human. In other words, religion is humankind. Feuerbach's theory that alienation results when we view God as other was to influence both Freud and Marx.

The Political Revolution

The freedoms brought on by the scientific, economic, and intellectual revolutions naturally led people to seek the perfect society and liberation from various forms of oppressive inequalities. The ideas for such a political revolution were sparked by the writings of philosophers like Locke and Rousseau.

One of Locke's most important works, *Two Treatises on Civil Government* (1690), quickly established him as a leading philosopher of freedom. Contradicting his predecessor Thomas Hobbes (1588–1679), Locke maintained that the original state of nature was not nasty, brutish, and short but was, rather, happy and characterized by reason and tolerance. Furthermore, he stated that all human beings were equal in dignity and free to pursue "life, health, liberty, and possessions." Locke advanced the idea that governments were formed when the people made a social contract to establish them and that they should guarantee people's inalienable rights. Locke epitomized the Enlightenment's faith in the middle class and human goodness.

Jean-Jacques Rousseau (1712–78), a Swiss-French philosopher and political theorist, was one of the great figures of the French Enlightenment. He popularized the liberal ideas for the common people. He taught that religious sentiment and intuition were more important than the rationalism of the philosophers. By this he meant that our knowledge of God rests upon a religious impulse or feeling. The inner consciousness of God and morality is first a feeling which is later aided by reason; it is not a product of cognition. It is feeling that is primary and instinctive. All thought and intellectual arguments follow from feeling. It was actually Rousseau who had set Kant in the direction of practical reason.

Rousseau also taught that the poor were the victims of the rich. His most celebrated theory was that of the natural man ("the noble savage"). His epochal work of political theory, *The Social Contract* (1762), begins with the thunderous assertion, "Man is born free, and everywhere he is in chains."

Rousseau argued that humans in their natural state of innocence were naturally good and had equal rights and freedom, but were corrupted by the introduction of such things as religious dogmas and institutions, ownership of property, science, and commerce. People entered into a social contract among themselves, thereby establishing social, economic, and political structures, in order to correct the inequalities brought about by the rise of civilization. He advocated a return to our natural state with its natural religion, consisting of belief in God, the immortality of the soul, and freedom.

The political revolutions of the eighteenth century were historical consciousness in action. The American Revolution (July 4, 1776) called for government of, by, and for the people, and enumerated many inalienable rights. The revolution took place because, in our terms, the people wanted to control their own social and economic history. They wanted freedom of the press, speech, and religion, and freedom to vote, work, and travel. The tradition of monarchical rule had ended as far as the citizens were concerned and the people took on the responsibility of personally determining their own history.

The French Revolution (July 14, 1789) proclaimed an end to the authority of God, the church, and the monarchy. It exalted the rights of the individual. Its slogans were, "No one stands above man" and "Liberty, fraternity, and equality."

Pius VI (1775–99) opposed the civil liberties of the French Revolution and condemned its 1789 "Declaration of the Right of Man" because it challenged the old order, encouraged indifferentism, and impugned Christianity.

An Evaluation of Modernity

Modernity began with the promise of science and technology to assure the progressive enhancement of human life by controlling the natural world. Science has been eminently successful. We now have better homes, food, medicine, means of communication, and travel than before 1680. On the other hand, we witness the negative results of the modern scientific promise of freedom and progress: ecological damage, more destructive warfare, genocide, and the threat of nuclear annihilation. As a result of the many ideas and ills brought on by modernity, many people have rejected a relationship with God, religion, and the traditional Christian view of life. For many there is no ultimate meaning to daily life and work, which may be why the suicide rate is higher now than in the past.

Modernity began with the promise of unlimited growth through the creation of a perfect economic and political society. As a result, humankind has benefitted greatly. Never before in the history of the world have so many people enjoyed a standard of living that even medieval kings and lords would have envied. Workers have received many rights and privileges. On the other hand, we witness materialism, consumerism, the erosion of the human community, neocolonialism, labor-management conflicts, monopolies, the marginalization of the poor, and the physical impossibility of extending modern Western standards of living throughout the globe.

Modernity began with the promise of political freedoms within independent sovereign states. It insisted that people should be judged by their abilities and achievements and not by social origin or some other arbitrary measure of status. It produced major advancements in human rights, dignity, freedom, and pluralism. The principles of democracy as realized in the United States have caught the imaginations of many people around the globe—as witnessed, for example, by the collapse of the Berlin Wall on November 9, 1989. On the other hand, there has been no end to colonialism, totalitarianism, and religious oppression. Pluralism often becomes relativism, historical consciousness becomes historicism,[2] and autonomy is reduced into self-centered individualism. Robert Bellah and his coauthors showed, in *Habits of the Heart*, a 1985 study of American individualism, that most middle-class Americans do not even have "a moral language that transcends radical individualism." The result is that there is little sense of mutual obligation, personal or political, which leads to a crisis of community.

Postmodern Movement

The deaths of 38.8 million people during World War II have given moderns a sobering view of our prospects for making this a world of peace, autonomy, and freedom. We have gone beyond such Enlightenment assumptions as "Progress is inevitable" and "Reason by itself can provide a basis for morality and society." Denise Lardner Carmody and John Tully Carmody assert that "it is precisely the spread of this sobriety that justifies calling World War II the death-knell of modernity" (1983, 157).

We are moving into what is being called a postmodern culture. The internationally-acclaimed Jesuit theologian Bernard Lonergan (1904–84), writing in the early 1980s, declared that the Enlightenment "still enjoys a dominant position. But, as it were, from within it there has developed an antithesis, no less massive though, as yet, it has not crystalized. To it I refer when I speak of a second enlightenment" (1985, 63–65). A few years later, David Tracy, a student of Lonergan, described *postmodern* as "an ever-elusive word in search of a definition." Actually, the word is "more an acknowledgment that we now live in an age that cannot name itself than that we should simply reject modernity" (1990, 902).

This postmodern movement—this second enlightenment— did not begin in the 1980s. It was anticipated by perceptive thinkers like Kierkegaard, Nietzsche, Marx, and Freud who called into question some of the rationalist claims of the Enlightenment. "These 'masters of suspicion' forever cast doubt on the belief that the solitary autonomous rational thinker could achieve, much less had achieved, 'enlightenment'" (Tracy 1975, 8).

What binds these four masters of suspicion together is their conviction that one's primary task as a human is not to become a finely tuned rational person but to attempt something more difficult: to become a true self, that is, one who struggles to be an authentic person despite one's own radical limitations. To become an authentic, decentered self entails a willingness to enter real dialogue with others; to take sides; to start a constructive argument; to expose ideologies, frauds, and illusions; and to shape the world. Since World War II, authenticity also entails acknowledging and dealing honestly with "the radical plurality of our different languages and the ambiguity of all our histories" (Tracy 1987a, 82).

Søren Kierkegaard (1813–55), a Danish existentialist philosopher and religious writer, believed that over the course of life people normally become increasingly aware of God. But this awareness, he said, often leads to despair once they realize the antithesis between their temporal existence and eternal truth.

According to Kierkegaard, the ethical person who subordinates himself to Kant's view of morality cannot bridge the "infinitely qualitative difference" that separates humans from God. Also, reason is no help in realizing the final religious state of union with God. Therefore, Kierkegaard proposed the idea that a leap of faith is required. As his model, Kierkegaard cited Abraham, the father of the Jews who obeyed the call of faith without seeking to be justified before anything less than the presence of God. Kierkegaard taught that each person must always be ready to stand alone before God without benefit of some social, even ecclesiastical, shield.

Friedrich Nietzsche (1844–1900), a German philosopher, anticipated the end of modernity by questioning the major role given to reason by the Enlightenment. What really drove "the genteel and urbane value-system of the Enlightenment thinker," said Nietzsche, was the powerful will-to-power. Another sign that the Enlightenment was not working was the disintegration of Western culture. Things were so bad that Nietzsche felt called to announce the death of God, arguing that the divine no longer had any effective power because it was submerged in the evils of the times. To counteract these massive evils that pervade society, he said people must reject externally imposed values and, in freedom, create their own in order to survive. Nietzsche concluded that since people are on their own to survive, each person had better become a "superman," a person with a dominative power beyond good and evil.

Karl Marx maintained that the task of philosophy is not simply to interpret the world but to change it. In order to change it, the ideologies operative in the political and economic structures of each society must be uncovered. "In the Marxian terminology, ideology is always something false, a distortion of the truth for the sake of social interest, a symbolic framework of the mind that legitimates the power and privileges of the dominant group and sanctions the social evils inflicted on the people without access to power" (Baum 1975, 34). In his day, Marx attacked the bourgeois intellectuals who refused to note or to struggle against the ideologies within the economic systems that allowed them to maintain their privileges. These privileges existed mainly because the working conditions of the proletariat were so inhumane. In other words, Marx showed that there were economic conditions intertwined with hidden motives that allowed, even enforced, the illusion of the autonomy of the rational bourgeois thinkers.

Sigmund Freud (1856–1939), an Austrian psychiatrist and founder of psychoanalysis, explained that people do not live by a pure and autonomous conscious rationality. Rather, he said, people are also driven and motivated by subrational forces of the unconscious that run contrary to reason and civilization. As an example, Freud argued that the natural urge for sexual gratification underlies people's entire mental life and drives them to seek as much pleasure as possible. This impulse for pleasure remains a permanent aspect of the human psychic makeup and is even the foundation of the drive toward religion. Religion, he concluded, is not a rational commitment but the result of wishing for comfort and security. While religious people disagreed with Freud's conclusions, they did agree that religion is rooted in the preconscious imagination.

Modernity and Christianity

The Enlightenment was an all-out attack on Christianity (Lonergan 1974, 57).[3] On the one hand, specific facts justified the attacks: over many years European Christians had engaged in religious persecutions and wars; the condemnation of Galileo in 1633 alienated many scientists; as an institution the church often came across as bureaucratic, rigidly authoritarian, and uncompromising. On the other hand, this wholesale attack was not fully justified. History makes clear that the church had made many major educational, cultural, and political contributions to the development of Europe.

The belief popular in the Enlightenment that religion was giving way to critical reason undermined the church's roles as guardian of revelation, source of truth, and moral guide.

As guardian of revelation, the church teaches about God and his son, Jesus. During the eighteenth and nineteenth centuries, reason and science were set against Christian revelation. The Christian God was replaced by the God of the philosophers, and, eventually, with deism, agnosticism, or atheism. The teachings of the scientists, philosophers, and other scholars during these centuries rendered some Christian teachings (e.g., those concerning the creation of the world and the human race) "at worst false and at best quaint" (Clebsch 1979, 243).

It should be pointed out that not all scientists, philosophers, and historians set out to attack Christianity. For example, while it is true that Darwin's works "made fables of the notion of human uniqueness and the story of the animals in Noah's ark" (ibid., 245), Darwin himself was a devout Christian who was deemed worthy of burial with Chaucer, Newton, and other noted English heroes in Westminster Cathedral, a national shrine.

The church, since it is founded on Christ, the light of the world, professes to be a source of truth. However, with the Enlightenment, the secular state and the secular university replaced the church as the source of truth. And the church's role of moral guide was undermined by the Enlightenment's assertion of freedom and autonomy, which declared the individual's moral conscience free of clerical direction and control.

Because the institutional church failed to see the positive values set forth by the modernists and because it refused to face the justifiable criticism of its own absolutism, fundamentalism, and failure to respect fundamental human rights, the church found itself on the fringes of the political, cultural, and intellectual life of society. By choice the church became an isolated fortress surrounded by an alien world made up not only of other Christian churches and other religions but also of atheists, secular scientists, and governments that had overthrown such traditional values as monarchical rule and the union of church and state in the name of liberalism and democracy. The church developed what Maisie Ward aptly called "a state of siege mentality."

The Popes and Modernity

This section opens with Gregory XVI (1831–46) and Pius IX (1846–78), as these are the two popes who governed the church for most of the nineteenth century and who set the stage for the twentieth century. Both were hard-working, morally upright, and strong of character. They rejected many of the social, economic, and political movements of their time and were unfriendly to those Catholic intellectuals and clergy who were open to new scientific and historical developments.

There were three reasons why the popes rejected liberalism and denied civil rights (Baum 1979b). First, traditional Catholic teaching highlighted the integration of the individual and society. The private good of the individual, the church taught, should be subordinated to the common good. The task of government was to enhance the common good. Liberal political philosophy, on the other hand, elevated the individual to such great heights, the popes complained, that the common good was being undermined and the traditional order of society destroyed. Furthermore, classical liberalism maintained that government should govern as little as possible and should allow maximum liberty in all spheres of activity: freedom of production and trade, religion, thought, speech, press, assembly, and so on. Second, the Catholic Church regarded itself as the divinely appointed embodiment of true religion. It called for the acknowledgment of Catholicism as the religion of the state wherever possible. The popes maintained that implicit in the demand for freedom of religion was indifferentism—the belief that one religion is as good as any other. Third, the Catholic Church had always expressed concern for the poor. The popes related political liberalism to economic liberalism, and so argued that in an unbridled free market system the rich could suppress the poor.

Gregory XVI
Bartolomeo Cappellari became a Camaldolese monk at the age of eighteen in 1783, and, although he eventually left his monastery in 1826 to become involved in the Vatican's international missionary ventures as prefect of the Propagation of the Faith, he had "little comprehension of the contemporary world" (J. Kelly 1986, 308). As Pope Gregory XVI he ruled the Papal States with a heavy hand, fighting off attempts to introduce liberal reforms for the three reasons outlined above.

Many nineteenth-century Catholics, on the other hand, had come to grips with modernity's concern for freedom and strove to Christianize the culture, some by reforming it and others by transforming it (Clebsch 1979, 281). Since modernity recognized the intimate link between freedom and moral and intellectual creativity, the theme of many Catholic liberals was, "There is nothing more liberal than religion and nothing more religious than liberalism" (ibid., 256). Their goal was to take the boundless opportunities offered by modernity to deliver the Christian message afresh.

Three French champions of Catholic liberalism were Father Felicité de Lamennais (1782–1854), Count Charles Montalembert (1810–70), and Henri-Dominique Lacordaire (1802–61), who became a Dominican in 1839. This group published the newspaper *L'Avenir*, in which they explicitly championed the role of the pope in the church but also, at the same time, advocated social and civil liberties: freedom of conscience and of the press, and separation of church and state. Gregory, who shared the attitudes of the restored monarchs of Europe, condemned all these liberal ideas in his encyclical *Mirari vos* on August 15, 1832.

Pius IX

During this pope's pontificate, Catholics made more attempts to reform the church by introducing some of the principles of liberalism. In August 1863, Charles Montalembert, the leader of the French liberal Catholics, gathered an impressive assembly of Catholics—cardinals, bishop, priests, laity—at Malines, Belgium, to urge the church to embrace modernity and get in step with the rest of the world. He proposed that Belgium, a country both Catholic and liberal, proved that the church could flourish in the climate of liberty.

One month later, in September 1863, Ignaz von Döllinger (1799–1890), a priest, church historian, and leader of the German liberal Catholics, organized a congress at Munich to discuss whether or not modern culture was hopelessly secular, rationalist, and inimical to the church. In his presidential address he made a personal plea as a scholar for his right to work untrammeled by authority. He argued that intervention into the work of scholars was needed only in those rare cases where their conclusions were in obvious contradiction with the dogmas of the church. The only effective weapons against error, he further declared, "were the weapons of science, not ecclesiastical censure" (G. Daly 1985, 774). Finally, he proclaimed that post-Reformation scholasticism was dead and should now be replaced by greater attention to biblical criticism and scientific history. By post-Reformation scholasticism he meant those schools of theologians and philosophers that emerged in the fourteenth century and developed after Trent that emphasized the interpretation of texts, especially those of other theologians and philosophers, rather than the Scriptures and Church Fathers (major writers of the first seven hundred years of Christianity). This theology, written particularly for seminarians, neither stimulated original inquiry nor engaged new philosophical or historical developments. The result is that Thomism stagnated.

Criticism from various quarters of society that the papacy was out of step with the enlightened views of the times as well as the meetings at Malines and Munich seem to have convinced Pius IX that he should compile a summary of the condemnations of modernity he had issued over the previous seventeen years. On December 8, 1864, he published the famous *Syllabus of Errors*, accompanied by the encyclical *Quanta cura*. The *Syllabus* listed eighty errors, including absolute rationalism, naturalism, pantheism, socialism (one that would subject the family and school systems totally to the state), liberal capitalism (one that had no other end than material gain), and freedom of religion. Error number 80 summarized the document: it is an error to think that "the Roman pontiff can and ought to reconcile and harmonize himself with progress, with liberalism, and with modern civilization." This document shocked many Catholics and angered many who were not Catholic. Were such liberties as freedom of the press, freedom of conscience, and civil rights now considered evil?

Five years later, Vatican Council I was assembled. In 1870 the bishops declared the doctrine of papal infallibility. This teaching was controversial then and remains so to this day. For example, Döllinger spurned the dogma and was excommunicated in 1871. According to Gabriel Daly, the first Vatican council "was summoned to copper-fasten the Catholic church's radical opposition to modern thought" (ibid., 775). The doctrine of papal infallibility dramatically reminded the world of the church's claim to have a divine guarantee for its role as teacher of the truth.

Leo XIII

The negative response of Leo's immediate predecessors to the intellectual, economic, and political life of their times effectively pushed the church to the margins of public life. "Leo's main achievement was his attempt, within the framework of traditional teaching, to bring the church to terms with the modern world" (J. Kelly 1986, 311). A review of Leo's sponsorship of neo-Thomism and his censure of Americanism should confirm this judgment.

Döllinger had declared post-Reformation scholasticism dead in 1863. A neoscholastic or neo-Thomist revival was launched by Leo in 1879, a year and a half after his election, when he issued his encyclical *Aeterni Patris*. This document, drafted with the assistance of the influential Jesuit Thomist Joseph Kleutgen (1811–83), officially "imposed the philosophico-theological system of St. Thomas Aquinas on the whole church. This was an unprecedented act, and its significance is often underrated" (G. Daly 1985, 775). In his encyclical, Leo called Aquinas "a singular safeguard and glory of the Catholic Church" because "with his own hand he vanquished all errors of ancient times; and still he supplies an armory of weapons which brings us certain victory in the conflict with falsehoods ever springing up in the course of years."

The goal of neo-Thomism was to offer a coherent, unified systematic philosophy and theology as an alternative to the philosophy of Kant and other modern philosophers. While some theologians were attempting to use some of the insights of Kant, the neo-Thomists judged modern philosophy intrinsically unsatisfactory for the development of Catholic theology. Neo-Thomism became the theology of all the popes from Leo XIII to Pius XII (Gallagher 1990, 49).

Leo's decree slowed the development of historical consciousness within the church in two ways: it continued the trend begun with Vatican Council I whereby history (ancient tradition) was replaced by an appeal to the "living tradition" of papal pronouncements and authority; and it advocated the "timeless" philosophy and theology of the neoscholastics that left no room for history (Hennesey 1989, 675).

From the moment of this country's birth, United States Catholics have had to struggle to reconcile Catholicism and democratic institutions. By 1890 the Catholic bishops had polarized into two parties. Some bishops, led by Archbishop Michael Corrigan of New York City, were satisfied with upholding the compatibility of Catholicism and democracy and opted for traditional Roman Catholic ways. Others, led by Cardinal James Gibbons of Baltimore and Archbishop John Ireland of St. Paul, wanted more than the compatibility approach. They believed "Catholicism should Americanize" because the church could learn from the American experience (Portier 1983, 323–28).

The Americanists claimed that, since there were obvious differences between American and European Catholics, the church in the United States should incorporate the American ideals into itself. This meant that there should be separation of church and state, that religious pluralism should be tolerated, and that the church should be remodeled along democratic lines. The latter meant that in the church there should be freedoms analogous to those enjoyed in America's liberal democracy (e.g., active participation, personal initiative, and open communication); and that the church should protect individual consciences in preference to ideas such as loyalty, obedience, and uniformity. Gibbons and Ireland advocated these positions because they desired to enhance the identity and mission of the church in a pluralistic society. Americans would never respect—much less join—a church that did not respect and foster the American ideals of liberty and justice.

Leo did not denounce the liberal movements with the same vigor as did Pius IX. In fact, he called on Catholics to search for practical, positive solutions to their country's social, economic, and political problems. Neverthess, Leo XIII had little regard for the United States' principle of separation of church and state. He interpreted the American willingness to work within the framework of religious pluralism as a weakness toward indifferentism. In his 1895 encylical, *Longinqua oceani,* he stated he was pleased that religious freedom had brought the church in the United States prosperity and other blessings. Nevertheless, he claimed the church would develop even more if, in addition to liberty, "she enjoyed the favor of the laws and the patronage of the public authority."

On January 22, 1899, Leo sent a personal letter, *Testem benevolentiae,* to Cardinal Gibbons about the church in the United States. In it he set forth two principles. In doctrinal matters, there can be no modification of Roman Catholic beliefs. It is wrong to foster an apologetics that would whittle down church teaching to suit modernity in order to attract those not of the faith. According to Leo, Catholicism did not "admit modifications, according to the diversity of time and place." In disciplinary matters, the church, he said, must adapt its laws to the conditions of local areas as long as they are drawn up by the responsible hierarchy.

Leo censured the church in the United States for holding views he called "Americanism," a term created by French theologians. The French distrusted American democracy, the easy rapprochement between the church and the United States government, the pro-labor tendencies of many of the bishops, and the willingness of many of the bishops to make decisions without necessarily looking to Rome (A. Jones 1992, 8). Leo condemned the following views: the desire of the church in the United States to be different from the rest of the Roman Catholic world; the conviction that the church should show more indulgence to modern theories and methods; and the belief that individuals can act confidently and independently based on their natural capacities in such a way that the Catholic Church's powers would be limited.

With this letter Leo simply cut short any conversation about the religious significance of the American system of government.

Pius X

The reform of the inner life of the institutional church was the major concern of Pius X. He promoted frequent communion, reformed the code of canon law, restored Gregorian chant, and improved the formation of priests. He also checked the smallest moves toward disobedience or doctrinal error.

During his pontificate some scholars sought to adopt the modern methodologies and findings of historians, scientists, and other thinkers to the church's interpretation of its doctrines, discipline, and Scriptures. In doing so, they rejected that unconditonal obedience that Roman authorities had come to expect, and some of their adaptations of the implications of biblical or historical criticism were deemed heretical. The scholars who believed that the church should adapt to the new situation were called modernists and their teachings were labeled *Modernism* (G. Daly 1980; Haight 1990). Modernism was not a single movement or a complete system of thought. As George Tyrrell wrote in 1910: "By a modernist, I mean a churchman of any sort, who believes in the possibility of a synthesis between the essential truth of religion and the essential truth of modernity" (1910, 5).

The underlying problem in this controversy was that traditional theology overemphazised the objective, the intellectual, and the unchangeable, whereas modernists, such as Loisy, Tyrrell, and Von Hügel, were attempting to introduce the subjective, psychological, and changeable into the church's interpretation of Christianity.

Alfred Loisy (1857–1940), a French priest and Scripture scholar, published his famous book *The Gospel and the Church* in 1902. This book touched off the conflict between Rome and the scholars. In his day the church did not conceive of itself as the product of historical development. Loisy proposed a radically historical view of the church, explaining that the church was a historical organism that grew out of the gospel of Jesus, adapting its doctrines and itself as an institution to different circumstances in history.

Loisy published his research to refute *What is Christianity?*, the best seller by the German scholar, Adolf von Harnack (1851–1930). Harnack's thesis was that Jesus' basic teachings—"God as the Father, and the human soul so ennobled that it can and does unite with him"—were covered over by the church's dogmas and structures. In other words, Harnack viewed the church's dogmas and structures as distortions of Christianity. He believed the essence of Christianity was the interior and individual realization of the kingdom of God in the heart of each individual. Loisy agreed that there were historical developments of the church's structures and teachings, but these were not distortions. "To reproach Catholicism for all its developments," wrote Loisy, "is to reproach it for remaining alive."

George Tyrrell (1861–1909), an English Jesuit and philosopher of religion, wrote essays and reviews in the area of popular spirituality. He wrote for those he sensed were under a strain trying to live a spirituality that came out of the prevailing neo-Thomist theology. "He was an eclectic rather than a systematic thinker. The recurring theme in his work is experience and how both historical and inward experience must be integrated into theology" (Haight 1990). He believed that the distinguishing note of the Catholic Church was that it was the "divinely conceived fulfillment of all man's natural religious instincts." The church had amazing adaptive power whereby it could relate to any culture in which it found itself.

Baron von Hügel is often listed among the modernists because in his frequent travels he became a go-between, putting various modernist writers in touch with one another. Neither he nor his writings were ever condemned by the church, whereas both Loisy and Tyrrell were excommunicated.

Modernism was condemned by Pius X in three separate documents. The decree *Lamentabili* (July 3, 1907) branded Modernism a "synthesis of all heresies." The decree was a syllabus of errors, consisting of sixty-five proscribed theses taken from publications in philosophy, theology, social theory, and, above all, biblical criticism. The encyclical *Pascendi* (September 8, 1907) condemned Modernism as a full-fledged philosophical and theological system. Pius X ordered the bishops throughout the world to see to the orthodoxy of biblical studies and scholastic philosophy in the seminaries and to extinguish the modernist movement by ridding seminaries and parishes of those sympathetic to it. The oath against Modernism was promulgated in a decree *(Sacrorum antistitum)* on September 1, 1910. It was imposed on all clergy and was to be renewed on an annual basis.

Some of the most adamant opponents of the new learning—called traditionalists by most writers—were Cardinal Francis Richard of Paris; Cardinal Rafael Merry del Val, Pius's secretary of state; and Monsignor Umberto Benigni, a Vatican functionary. The latter organized a spy system that made its way into many dioceses around the world. "This secret organization urged the reporting to the Holy See of the writings, sermons, speeches, and even the conversations of churchmen, from cardinals to seminarians, in which the slightest hint of divergence from true doctrines, or of nonconformity to papal policies, might be found" (Murphy 1981, 34).[4] There occurred a veritable reign of terror.

The foundations of Modernism as depicted by Pius X in *Pascendi* were the broad philosophical and theological tendencies towards agnosticism, immanentism, evolutionism, and democratism (Kerlin 1973; see also McBrien 1981, 218–19, 644–46).

The first of these, agnosticism, is the belief that it is not rationally possible to determine whether God exists and what our relationship to him might be. Our only means of knowing about God is by an internal personal religious experience. This experience is the real core of faith. All conceptual explicitations are radically changeable, like clothes covering a body.

The real mystery of God is grasped nonconceptually. This is the central experience of faith.

Agnosticism is compatible with Catholic belief in that Catholicism affirms that inner religious experience is an essential element in the act of faith. In fact, "religion in both its origins and its initial expressions is an activity of the preconceptual intellect (preconscious, creative imagination, poetic imagination, agent intellect)" (Greeley 1980). Yet inner religious experience is not the only way we come to a knowledge of God. God's revelation never occurs in a purely internal experience. It is always mediated through symbols—a person, a historical event, nature, words, or liturgical signs (Dulles 1980).

Immanentism asserts that religious beliefs are the culturally relative response to felt human needs and to the unknowable domains beyond phenomena. All people have within them a religious consciousness according to this view—they have an ever-evolving personal knowledge of God that spurs them toward the divine and salvation. Thus, the modernists downplayed the supernatural origin and process of revelation. For some of them, Jesus was a human person and God did not save us through him.

It is true that we always live in the presence of God and that God reveals himself first and foremost for our salvation, rather than for the satisfaction of our intellectual curiosity. Yet Catholicism teaches that our understanding of God's revelation is not a completely natural process. It is a gift from a trancendent God whose continued guidance we need lest we distort the meaning of the gospel and the way of salvation.

Some modernists taught the theory of doctrinal evolution—that people's religious consciousness was given imperfect expression in statements called "dogmas." These statements were effective if they harmonized with the general cultural situation of religious people. They can and should be changed according to the needs and culture of the people and the church because they are only statements about human perceptions of reality. There is no objective reality behind such dogmas as the Trinity, the Incarnation, and the Resurrection. These terms merely point to the mysterious intuitions of God held by those persons who first coined the terms.

It is this point that aroused the greatest opposition from the traditionalists. On the one hand, it is true that the mystery of God cannot be completely captured in dogmatic statements. Also, all the sources of Christian tradition, especially the Scriptures, must be studied according to the most scientifically critical methods at hand. Yet, dogmatic statements and the Scriptures, despite their cultural conditioning, do point to the definitive and unconditional character of God's revelation in Christ, Catholicism holds.

Institutional democratism was the fourth of Pius's concerns. Some modernists taught that the church came into existence when religious people tried to communicate their faith to others and to maintain it. The church did not have its source in Jesus Christ; the church's authority derived from the experience and sensitivity of its members. Faith is shaped and maintained by the conscience of the whole church community.

Catholics agree that God's revelation was only gradually unfolded in the life of the church. Yet the Scriptures and dogmatic statements are more than historical documents. They are also expressions and products of the church's response to the Spirit, and need to be read and interpreted as such.

Benedict XV
Benedict XV became pope in September 1914. On November 1, 1914, he issued his first encyclical, *Ad beatissimi*, calling a halt to the bitter animosity between die-hard traditionalists and modernists. However, clergy were still required to take the 1910 oath against Modernism until Paul VI cancelled it in 1967.

Pius XI
When Pius X decreed in 1911 that bishops had complete authority over all Catholic organizations, he became the forerunner of *Catholic Action*. This term denotes the collaboration of the laity in the apostolic work of the church's hierarchy. The task of the laity was to animate society with a Christian spirit, especially the Catholic understanding of faith and morals. But it was Pius XI who inaugurated Catholic Action in his first encyclical, *Ubi arcano*, on December 23, 1922. He was eager to carry forward the theme of his predecessor

because of the severe shortage of priests in Italy and around the world. Pius wrote: "In our own time especially, when the integrity of the faith and morals is more seriously threatened each day, and the lack of priests, to our great sorrow, renders the clergy absolutely unable to meet the needs of souls . . . [Catholic Action] will help the priests and make up for their small numbers by multiplying their helpers among the laity."

As mentioned earlier, Pius had chosen as his motto "Christ's peace in Christ's kingdom," which reflected his desire that the church not be isolated from society. As a scholar-pope, Pius XI quietly eased the tensions arising from the modernist debate. He also enlarged the Vatican Library and founded both the Pontifical Institute of Christian Archeology (1925) and the Pontifical Academy of Sciences (1936).

Pius XII

We can get a sense of this pope's reaction to modernity from the way he dealt with Scripture scholarship, the "new theology," and papal authority. His approach to the first concern contrasted with Leo XIII's encyclical *Providentissimus Deus* (1893), which turned a cautious eye on the historical-critical method of Scripture interpretation, especially with regard to apparent contradictions between the physical sciences and the Scriptures. The historical-critical method uses all the tools of criticism—archeology, history, the ancient languages themselves—to uncover fully the meaning intended by the inspired author. This method frees the reader from biblical fundamentalism, a reading that fails to consider the context of a scriptural passage, that is, its literary mode, purpose, relationship to other passages, or to the whole work in which it appears. Nevertheless, quoting Thomas Aquinas, Leo said that the inspired writers "went by what sensibly appeared." The Pontifical Biblical Commission he inaugurated in 1902 continued to be wary of the historical-critical method. Although the commission never condemned the method, the negative character of its responses to such questions as the Mosaic authorship of the Pentateuch and the historical character of the four Gospels hardly inspired biblical scholars in the early part of the century.

In 1920 Benedict XV issued *Spiritus Paraclitus* to commemorate the death in 420 of the greatest Latin biblical scholar,

Jerome. Benedict took a negative view of the advances in biblical studies in his encyclical, strongly insisting on the complete historicity of the Bible.

On the fiftieth anniversary of *Providentissimus Deus*, Pius XII issued *Divino afflante Spiritu* (1943), often considered the Magna Charta for biblical scholarship. Pius was influenced by the Jesuit scholar Augustin Bea (1881–1968), rector of the Pontifical Biblical Institute from 1930 to 1949. Unlike Leo and Benedict, Pius encouraged and freed scholars to pursue their research and to use the historical-critical method without threat of condemnation by the Vatican. The encyclical acknowledged an essential finding of the biblical scholars, namely, that the Bible contains many different forms of literature (myths, parables, epistles, miracle stories, infancy narratives, and so forth) which must be recognized in order to understand the meaning of the texts. This means the Bible should not be read as if it were modern history.

Pius XII also addressed the challenge of the "new theology." Even before the 1943 encyclical, some theologians were turning from the prevailing neo-Thomist theology to the patristic, liturgical, and sacramental sources of the Catholic tradition. They did so in order to hear again what was said then, to reasssess the present in light of the past, and to help the church enter a dynamic conversation with the world of modernity. They found that neoscholasticism was oriented toward subtle and abstract discussions that were rather remote from the day-to-day life of people. These theologians tried to show that the ahistorical methodology of the neo-Thomists was not in accord either with Thomas Aquinas and other medieval scholastics such as Bonaventure and Vincent of Lerens or with the Church Fathers. Unlike the neo-Thomists, Thomas never dismissed the challenges of his contemporaries on the grounds that he already possessed the truth. These theologians also opposed the dualisms that characterized the neoscholastic theology and spirituality: body and soul, profane and sacred, church and world, temporal and eternal, nature and grace. For example, in their theology of grace, the neo-Thomists underscored grace as a created gift of God rather than God's personal presence; as a divine healing of the effects of sin rather than as the perfection of a human nature, which is itself God's good creation; and as a gift offered only intermittently and in certain privileged times and circumstances rather than offered constantly and being universally present in the world.

The theology of these scholars was sarcastically dubbed *nouvelle théologie* ("the new theology") by Reginald Garrigou-Lagrange (1877–1964), a Dominican theologian who taught at the Pontifical University of St. Thomas in Rome from 1909 to 1960. There never was an identifiable position that could be described by the term "new theology." It was simply a convenient term of derogatory rejection applied to the "new" positions thought to be a threat to the established neo-Thomist theology. The "new" theologians included such famous scholars as Yves Congar (1904–); Henri de Lubac (1896–1991) and his Swiss pupil, Hans Urs von Balthasar (1905–88); Jean Danielou (1905–74); Marie-Dominique Chenu (1895–1990); and Pierre Teilhard de Chardin (1881–1955).

Most of these theologians were censured by Rome. For example, Teilhard, a Jesuit priest and noted paleontologist, had his first brush with the Vatican in 1924, when he sent to Rome an essay on original sin that was not intended for publication. From then on he was not allowed to publish articles in philosophy or theology without prior Roman approval. When he sought approval for the publication of *The Divine Milieu* in 1927, permission was never granted. After Teilhard's death in 1955, his scientific and spiritual writings, especially his classic of the spiritual life, *The Divine Milieu*, were translated into sixteen languages and read with great enthusiasm in the 1960s. He became something of a folk hero.

Teilhard emphasized that we encounter God primarily through the created world and not through mystical union, the emphasis of the neo-Thomists. He took this position partly as a result of his attempt to integrate Christian theology with the scientific views of evolution and the origin of the universe. God, wrote Teilhard, shines through the universe and through Christ, the Alpha and Omega of evolution and the activating energy of the entire cosmos.

In place of a spirituality that divided spirit and matter, science and religion, and God and humankind, Teilhard's evolutionary humanism envisaged the whole universe as coextensive with the body of the risen Christ. He insisted that theologians give serious consideration to the physical relation between Christ and the material world. He wrote: "The whole of the Church's dogmatic and sacramental economy teaches us to respect matter and to value it. Christ had to assume and wanted to assume real flesh. He sanctifies human flesh by special contact and he prepares its physical resurrection. . . . Because it has been assimilated into the Body of Christ, something from matter is destined to pass into the foundations and walls of the heavenly Jerusalem."[5]

Chenu, a Dominican historian of medieval theology, was silenced a few years after the publication of *A School of Theology: Le Saulchoir* in 1937. In this important book, Chenu argued against a "timeless Thomism," insisting that a text could be understood only in its historical, cultural, social, and political context. He also taught that the source of theology was the involvement of the church with the changing world. This book was placed on the Index in 1942 probably because of its "apparently modernistic recognition of historicity and human experience with theology" (Schoof 1970, 104). Rome feared that any emphasis on the historical context of theology would divorce it from its foundation in revelation and would turn theology into cultural anthopology. Chenu was deprived of his title of Master of Theology, was removed from his post at Le Saulchoir (a Dominican house of study in Belgium), and was ordered to live in Paris (Komonchak 1990a).

One of the great ironies of church history is that although almost all the new theologians were silenced by Pius XII, they were not only all eventually rehabilitated, but many were to become the true architects of the Vatican II documents. They served as experts to the bishops in the composition of the conciliar texts. Yves Congar, for example, worked on three of the constitutions and on the decrees on missionary activity, ecumenism, and the priesthood (Nichols 1990, 252–53). Joseph Komonchak suggests that "there is no theologian who did more to prepare for Vatican II and who had a larger role in the orientation and even in the composition of its documents" than Congar (1983).[6] Although Teilhard de Chardin was dead, his spirit and writings influenced the Council (King 1985). Several bishops cited him during the public discussions. The document on the church in the modern world uses some of his phrases when it speaks of the impact of science and technology on human development (GS 5), of Christ as "the goal of human history" (GS 10), and when it notes that "the human race has passed from a rather static concept of reality to a more dynamic, evolutionary one" (GS 5).

Finally, Pius XII reasserted the strength of papal authority. In his encyclical *Humani generis* (1950), Pius, influenced in great part by Reginald Garrigou-Lagrange, rejected the new theology. He linked it to Modernism because he believed its emphasis on the universality of grace in history undercut both the gratuity of grace and the teaching authority of the hierarchical church. This far-ranging encyclical also pronounced that the Body of Christ and the Roman Catholic Church are "one and the same;" that Catholics owe "religious allegiance of the will and intellect" even to teachings of the pope not declared infallible; that Christian scholars should return to Thomistic orthodoxy in both philosophy and theology; and that the task of theologians is to justify the declarations of the official magisterium by showing how this teaching is found in Scripture and tradition, whether explicitly or implicitly. Pius went so far as to say that once the pope expresses his judgment on a point previously controversial, "there can no longer be any question of free discussion among theologians." Finally, Pius XII asserted that the church's dogmatic formulas were unchangeable, were perfect expressions of the truths contained in the Bible, and were definitive and hence valid always. Pius declared that anyone who dared to suggest otherwise was on dangerous ground.

Modernism in Perspective

During the first half of the twentieth century two popes, Pius X and Pius XII, condemned any theology that carried the ideals of Modernism, and two other popes, Benedict XV and Pius XI, tried to ease the tension arising from the debate over Modernism. Nonetheless, the condemnation of Modernism cast a pall over the intellectual and devotional life of the institutional church during these four pontificates.

In the light of Vatican II, several theologians have evaluated why modernity took hold and what it means for the church today. David Tracy, for example, wrote that because of the way honest scholars were dishonored, academic institutions investigated, and intellectual inquiry silenced, "The modernist and Americanist crises should be acknowledged as Catholicism's Vietnam experience" (1987b, 271). Roger Haight, a Jesuit theologian, judged that, from our vantage point today, the encyclical *Pascendi* was "a document that was politically brilliant, deadly effective, intellectually dishonest, and totally comprehensible in the historical situation" (1990). The historical situation was one of fear. Both Pius X and Pius XII feared the modernists would bring the hostile elements of modernity inside the church. "What was feared, then, were internal forces that would change the very structure of the church" (ibid.).

Conclusion: John XXIII and Vatican II

During the preconciliar period—1878 to 1962—the church solidified its identity and mission, often by challenging the intellectual, economic, and political views of society. The church was positioned against the world, its values, and goals. The church maintained that the world needed to be rechristianized. During this period, the church also strengthened its institutional, intellectual, and devotional life by officially stabilizing these dimensions in such a way that the church as institution, especially as manifested by the papal office, was the dominant image of the church as a whole. The intellectual and devotional dimensions of the Catholic tradition were locked into the timeless philosophy and theology of neo-Thomism. Modernists within the church were marginalized, even excommunicated. However, the intellectual and devotional dimensions of the church have never been monolithic. During this period, for example, Pius XI opened the church to the physical sciences and Pius XII encouraged Scripture scholars to employ the modern methods of textual analysis. The new theologians argued against a timeless Thomism, highlighted the church as Christ's community, and underscored grace as God's personal and universal presence. The new theologians, those Catholic masters of suspicion, would have their say (and way) at Vatican II.

Even the future John XXIII had an encounter with the Vatican over modernity. It seems that when he was a young priest and serving as secretary to Bishop Radini-Tedeschi, he was accused of favoring some modernist positions. In his biography of the bishop, John XXIII admitted that his accusers were more anxious to get at the bishop than at him. Nevertheless, when John became pope and examined his file in the Vatican, the letter he had sent in 1914 protesting his loyalty to the gospel and the church was missing. But he had his notes among his own papers and was able to reconstruct the original letter. This unfortunate incident explains in part John's insistence that Vatican II would issue no condemnations.

With Vatican II, the institutional church's negative response to modernity came to an end. At that historic meeting, the church officially and decisively entered the age of historical consciousness (GS 4), frankly admitted that "the church herself knows how richly she has profited by the history and development of humanity" (GS 44), and placed herself firmly within the modern world. The bishops began their landmark document on the church in the modern world with these eloquent words: "The joys and the hopes, the griefs and the anxieties of the men of this age, especially those who are poor or in any way afflicted, these too are the joys and hopes, the griefs and anxieties of the followers of Christ. Indeed, nothing genuinely human fails to raise an echo in their hearts. . . . That is why this community realizes that it is truly and intimately linked with mankind and its history" (GS 1).

3

Vatican Council II

The church had twenty ecumenical councils before Vatican II, the first at Nicea in 325 and the twentieth, Vatican I, from 1869 to 1870.

On January 20, 1959, John XXIII had the inspiration—what he called "a flash of heavenly light"—to call a council. According to his own journal, John was in his private apartment, talking with his secretary of state, Cardinal Domenico Tardini, when, suddenly and unexpectedly, he exclaimed that there would be a council. Tardini was enthusiastic.

It has become a tradition that each January 18 to 25, the Christian churches pray for Christian unity. On January 25, 1959, at the Basilica of Saint Paul-Outside-the-Walls, Pope John, accompanied by seventeen cardinals, presided over the prayers for unity. After the ceremony, "in a short speech he made an announcement that came as a thunderbolt: his decision to summon an ecumenical council to promote the unity of all the Christian communities" (Falconi 1967, 324). The cardinals were so struck by the announcement that they sat like statues. There were no comments and, surprisingly, not even polite applause.

John returned to the Vatican and soon realized he had to deal with Vatican officials who were on the defensive. Apparently, some feared a universal council would detract from their privileges. Others wondered if a council was even necessary since the institutional church seemed vigorous and powerful. After all, the theologians were firmly under the control of the hierarchy, there was a uniform liturgical life in the world-wide church, and there was no obvious crisis demanding the attention of all the bishops. Nevertheless, some Vatican officials gave the pope the cold shoulder or what Cardinal Giacomo Lercaro called a "great institutional solitude" (ibid., 330). Even Tardini later expressed serious doubts—even scorn—for the proposed council, pointing to the fact that former councils were usually followed by times of serious trouble and confusion (Murphy 1992).

Its Purpose

The Constitution on the Liturgy, the first document approved by the Council in December 1963, listed four goals of the Council: to revitalize Catholics in their spirituality; to adapt church observances to the requirements of the age; to unite all Christians; and to strengthen the church's mission to all peoples (SC 1).

The day Pope John announced the Council, January 25, 1959, he was somewhat vague about his reasons for calling it. In addition to ecumenism, he vaguely mentioned "affirming doctrine" and "ordering discipline." Over the next few months and with the advice of his associates, however, John made the goals of the Council much clearer. The immediate goal was to modernize the church and to involve it in the concerns of the world, especially those efforts at strengthening unity and peace. The ultimate goal was the unification of all Christians.

John also wanted the Council to be a "new Pentecost" for the church. He himself composed a prayer to the Spirit, asking blessings on the Council. He prayed that the Spirit would renew its wonders "in this our day, as by a new Pentecost" (Abbott 1966, 793). John was convinced that the church had to respond to God's presence in the world as manifested through the "signs of the times." When John formally convoked the Council with the apostolic constitution *Humanae salutis* on December 25, 1961, he used the biblical phrase "signs of the times" in an optimistic sense; that is, there were special signs of the presence of God in history that required the attention of Christians. This meaning is quite different from the scriptural usage, which highlighted the apocalyptic events that are to precede the end of history (as in Matt. 16:1–4).

John used the term again in his encyclical *Pacem in terris* (1963) when he indicated that there were developments taking place in history that Christians ought not to fear or resist because some of them "augur well for the fate of the church and humanity." Three signs John singled out were the struggle of colonial people to determine their own future, the effort of workers to obtain their socio-economic rights, and the quest of women for equality in domestic and public life. At the Council the bishops picked up on John's usage, in great part because "Paul VI missed no opportunity to speak of the significance of the signs of the times" (Häring 1992, 49). The bishops declared that "the Church has always had the duty of scrutinizing the signs of the times and of interpreting them in the light of the gospel. . . . We must therefore recognize and understand the world in which we live, its expectations, its longings, and its often dramatic characteristics" (GS 4).

John's word for modernizing the church in light of the signs of the times was the Italian word *aggiornamento,* meaning an updating. Aggiornamento became the guiding principle of the Council. For the longest time the church had followed the principle set forth by Giles of Viterbo (1469–1532) at the Fifth Lateran Council (1512–17) that "men must be changed by religion, not religion by men." What John's aggiornamento called for was precisely the opposite (O'Malley 1989, 47). Aggiornamento meant the church had to change to meet the needs of the times, that is, the changes taking place outside itself. Aggiornamento looked to the needs and legitimate demands of people. It was not a simpleminded rejection of all that was old and a breezy acceptance of everything new, but rather a disengagement from the limitations of the past and from a culture no longer viable. Aggiornamento denoted critical involvement in the new culture without denying its evils and its need for transformation (Lonergan 1974, 113).

The ultimate goal—church unity—was a Promethean and revolutionary project. While it is true that on the eve of Vatican I in 1869, Pius IX wrote a letter inviting all who were not Catholic to enter the church and to let the Council be the occasion to respond to the needs of their hearts and "to extricate themselves from that state in which they cannot be certain of their salvation," nevertheless, once the Council got underway, it "operated at an almost total removal from the concerns, or even the very existence, of other Christians" (Hennesey 1971). In June 1960, John XXIII created the

Secretariat for Christian Unity and gave it the task of inviting leaders of the other Christian churches to attend the Council as observers. By calling Vatican II, John thrust the Catholic Church into the midst of those Christians who were in the vanguard of the ecumenical movement.

Its Preparation

Between the announcement of the Council on January 25, 1959, and its opening on October 11, 1962, there were three years and eight months. A great deal of preparation was needed.

The Roman curia, under the leadership of Cardinal Alfredo Ottaviani (1890–1979), Prefect of the Holy Office, were given the task of organizing the Council. Twelve preparatory commissions were set up to deal with different aspects of the church, such as the sacraments, the clergy, the bishops, and the religious orders. The commissions eventually produced seventy decrees and dogmatic constitutions. The opinion of Joseph Komonchak is that "the preparatory documents were consistent in their analysis and in their response: against the threats of subjectivism and historicism, the council was to provide a massive reaffirmation of authority, the authority of God in revelation, of Christ as his chief legate, of the church as Christ's juridically empowered agent in the world, of the tradition of objective verbal statements which articulate the Christian mysteries" (Komonchak 1985).

Pope John was aware that the preparatory drafts were of a neoscholastic, juridical, and moralistic bent—not his emphasis—but he was not discouraged. After all, the work was getting done at the rate envisaged and the Council would begin on time. Furthermore, the curia's "great institutional solitude" was broken by the interest and support for the Council that came from individual bishops in Europe, the United States, and from the African and Asian countries.

"The most impressive and decisive help" (Falconi 1967, 333) came, however, from some of the other Christian churches—the Orthodox and Protestant churches. For example, there was exuberant praise for the Council from Athenagoras, the Orthodox Patriarch of Constantinople. Similarly, many church leaders visited John at the Vatican, including Dr. Geoffrey Fisher, Archbishop of Canterbury, on December 2, 1960. This was a historic meeting: the first by the leader of the Anglican churches to Rome.

Its Opening

Vatican Council II—the decisive ecclesial event of this century—opened with a solemn liturgy on October 11, 1962. Present were twenty-seven hundred bishops, "the greatest gathering of bishops in the history of the Roman Catholic Church" (Cortesi 1962). In 1869 at Vatican I there were forty-eight United States bishops; in 1962 there were 217. Also present were ninety superiors of religious communities, and fifteen women from as many countries, including Mary Luke Tobin of the Sisters of Loretto, who at that time was president of the Conference of Major Superiors of Women. Also on hand were some four hundred *periti* (experts), thirty-nine representatives from other Christian communities, and some eighty-five ambassadors from different countries (Hebblethwaite 1982).

In his official opening address of October 11, 1962, John gave "the most important speech of [his] life and the most important speech in church history in the twentieth century" (ibid.). John made three points. First, the Council was to be a celebration of Christian faith, of its unity in diversity and catholicity.

Second, John expressed his optimism about the presence of the Holy Spirit in the world. He complained that there were present in the church certain "prophets of doom who continually announce baleful events as if the end of the world were impending." He added that these prophets see an evil world where there is "only prevarication and decay" and that they fail to see that the church, herself a daughter of time, needs to be changed or modernized. John's hopeful message became, "At the present moment in history, Providence is leading us towards a new order in human relations." John admitted that there were many errors in the contemporary world, but he believed these "often vanish as swiftly as they arise, like mist before the sun." To meet the needs of the modern age, John knew the church should show "the validity of her teachings rather than by [issuing] condemnations."

Third, the Council must be pastoral. Instead of simply repeating the church's doctrine, stated John, the Council must reclothe it to meet the needs "which our era demands." He said, "It is one thing to have the substance of the ancient doctrine of the *depositum fidei* [The Christian gospel originating in Christ and handed on over the ages] but quite another to formulate and reclothe it: and it is this that must—if need be with patience—be held of great importance, measuring every-thing according to the forms and proportions of a teaching of preeminently pastoral character." With this latter distinction, John effectively paved the way for accepting legitimate, though differing cultural expressions of the Christian gospel. It is just possible that the spirits of those modernists excommu-nicated by Pius X encircled the throne of John XXIII with smiles on their faces.

Most ecumenical councils have been polemical and juridi-cal. For example, the Council of Trent met for two reasons: to root out heresies and to reform morals. Vatican I set out to condemn rationalism and define papal infallibility. Vatican II, however, was pastoral, that is, it intended to bring out the enduring relevance of the gospel by proclaiming Jesus' word and Jesus himself, in order to meet the needs, hopes, joys, and fears of all people.

Its History
No one knew how long the Council would last. On October 10, 1962, John said he hoped it "will finish before Christmas," but that there might be another session "if we are not able to say all that we would like to in this period" (Cortesi 1962). By November 12, there was talk of a recess on December 8, with a resumption on May 12, 1963 (Dugan 1962b). When it was clear that more time was needed to permit the various work-ing commissions to complete the greater part of their tasks, John ordered a switch in dates. The second session would begin on September 8, 1963 (Dugan 1962c). Eventually, four sessions were held: the first from October 11 to December 8, 1962; the second from September 29 to December 4, 1963; the third from September 14 to November 21, 1964; and the fourth from September 14 to December 8, 1965.

Most of the opening and closing dates were chosen for symbolic reasons. Several of the dates are Marian feast days. For example, in the Orthodox churches, October 11 is the feast of the Motherhood of Mary, an infallible declaration made at the ecumenical Council of Ephesus in 431. Since Mary receives special honor in all the Eastern churches, Catholic and Orthodox, the date served as a point of unity between the West and the East.

Its Mind

There were two events at the beginning of the Council that indicated that there were serious divisions among the bishops. First, within twenty minutes of the first working session on October 13, 1962, when the curia presented their nominations for the working commissions, "frail looking Cardinal Achille Lienart of Lille arose to propose that, on so crucial a point, the council should be given enough time to nominate and elect the members of these commissions on its own" (Outler 1982). He was promptly seconded by Cardinal Joseph Frings of Cologne—to the applause of the junior bishops at the far end of the assembly. In just twenty minutes the Council passed from the tight grip of the Roman curia to the hands of the bishops, becoming an autonomous parliament with a mind of its own. It has been reported that John XXIII was pleased and even excited by this turn of affairs (Häring 1992, 49).

Second, the debate on the first document, the Constitution on the Liturgy, revealed two main trends among the bishops. To state it generally, the conservative, traditional point of view—one based on a classical consciousness—believed the troubles in the church stemmed primarily from a growing secularization in the world, a decrease in faith, and a lessening of respect for authority. The Council's task, they maintained, was to repeat and clarify the traditional teaching. Its first priority was the internal organization of the church. The progressive point of view—based on historical consciousness—maintained that the institutional church needed restructuring and reform because it was too hierarchical, too impersonal, and too detached from modernity. Service to all humankind should be the church's first priority. Therefore, the Council had several tasks: to reclothe the church's teachings and disciplines to meet the modern world and its needs; to reform the liturgy; and, as a result of the example and urgings of John XXIII, to reunite the Christian churches (Komonchak 1990b).

These traditional and progressive mindsets clashed during the Council over issues that are discussed in later chapters—problems such as collegiality, religious freedom, marriage and family, ecumenism, mariology, and so forth. Because of the presence of these two mindsets, it is not surprising that the bishops produced documents marked by different emphases, some inconsistencies, and some compromises. For example, the bishops maintained some of the dualisms that character-ized the neoscholastic spirituality of the times: body and soul, profane and sacred, church and world, and temporal and eternal. Similarly, the bishops declared that the church has a mission in the world and the faithful were urged to engage in social action (GS 9), and yet the bishops said Christ "gave his church no proper mission in the political, economic, or social order" (GS 42). In the postconciliar church both conservatives and progressives have been able to cite the documents selec-tively, pressing either for change or for the status quo.

Its Results
The Council produced sixteen documents (approximately 103,000 words), in the order and on the dates listed here:

December 4, 1963
    Constitution on the Liturgy
    Decree on Communications
November 21, 1964
    Constitution on the Church
    Decree on Ecumenism
    Decree on the Eastern Catholic Churches
October 28, 1965
    Decree on the Bishops
    Decree on Priestly Formation
    Decree on Religious Life
    Declaration on Christian Education
November 18, 1965
    Constitution on Revelation
    Decree on the Laity
November 28, 1965
    Declaration on Non-Christian Religions
    Constitution on the Church in the Modern World
December 7, 1965
    Decree on Priests
    Decree on the Church's Missionary Activity
    Declaration on Religious Freedom

There was another significant result of the Council, but it took a few years for it to be recognized. The church, which had always been global, was perceived as being what was called a "world church."

The church is essentially global: its mission has always been to all people and nations. While it is true that Jesus himself went "only to the lost sheep of the house of Israel," nevertheless, the inner dynamism of his message of the kingdom of God made it inevitable that Christianity would be a faith with world-encompassing claims. The thrust to all corners of the globe is clear in the New Testament, especially in Matt. 28:18–29, Luke 9:1–6, and Acts 1–2.

In 1974, in Germany, Walbert Buhlmann, a Capuchin missionary and theologian, published *The Coming of the Third Church*, a phenomenological study of the notion that Vatican II marked the emergence of the global church as a world church. Karl Rahner (1904–84), a prolific and eminent Jesuit theologian, called the book "the best Catholic book of the year." However, it was Rahner himself who produced a brief essay in 1979 that has become the locus classicus for the discussion of this question and its far-reaching consequences.

Rahner divided church history into three periods. The first was that short period of Jewish Christianity (A.D. 30–49) when Christianity was proclaimed within one culture only: Israel. The second was that very long period (A.D. 49–1962) when the gospel was proclaimed not in Jewish culture but in the Roman-Hellenistic culture in European and, eventually, North American culture and civilization. The third period began with Vatican II, when, due to the Spirit, the church appeared for the first time as a world church in a fully official way. Rahner pointed out a number of signs of this change: the Council brought together indigenous representatives of all the world's countries and cultures; it pushed for the vernacular in the liturgy; it expressed an openness to the world and historical consciousness; it made the first truly positive statements about the other religions; and it produced a document on religious liberty.

These factors indicated that the church was ready to recognize and accept the essential differences among cultures and should find ways to formulate and incarnate the gospel within the traditions and customs of each culture. This acceptance of other cultures relies on a transformational model and not simply a synthesis model, whereby the church merely adapts itself to other cultures, their beliefs and practices. Rahner ended his essay by warning that if the church did not become de-Europeanized and de-Romanized, it would remain a Western church and, in the final analysis, betray the meaning of Vatican II.

Its Decisions

"From the viewpoint of church history, it can be asserted that never before in the history of Catholicism have so many and such sudden changes been legislated and implemented which immediately touched the lives of the faithful, and never before had such a radical adjustment of viewpoint been required of them," commented Jesuit historian John O'Malley (1989, 17). A list of the principles endorsed by the Council is too lengthy to produce here. These ten are some of the most important ones.

1. Aggiornamento. Instead of being hostile and suspicious of the modern world, the church should update itself, that is, live in close union with its contemporaries, since the risen Christ is with us, calling his church to witness his gospel in today's world.
2. Reformation. Instead of regarding itself as spotless and all holy, the church must acknowledge its errors, failings, and sins and continually reform itself.
3. The Scriptures. Catholics should not limit their spirituality to sacraments, ritual, and law. Rather, the faithful must also immerse themselves in the Scriptures because here the Spirit speaks in a special way.
4. Collegiality. Instead of viewing the church primarily as a pyramid (bishops subordinate to the pope, priests subordinate to bishops, and people subordinate to priests), all Catholics should work together according to their proper roles for the common good of the church and its mission.
5. Religious freedom. The church, instead of seeking a privileged status and insisting that all people belong to it, should foster religious freedom: it should respect the right and duty of each person to choose his or her religion.
6. Laity. Instead of reinforcing the principle behind Pius XI's Catholic Action (namely, that the faithful were

called to the apostolate by a mandate from the hierarchy), the Council said the faithful should exercise
their ministry both in the church and in society based
on their baptismal faith and commitment to Christ
(LG 33). This put an end—in theory at least—to episcopal control over all forms of apostolic activities.

7. Regional and local diversity. Instead of emphasizing
    itself as a monolithic society, the church should stress
    the local churches being in communion with the uni-
    versal church.

8. Ecumenism. Instead of viewing the other Christian
    churches with hostility, Catholics should respect
    other churches' heritage, note their salvific impor-
    tance, and admit they possess true elements of the
    one and only Church of Christ.

9. Interreligious dialogue. Instead of viewing other reli-
    gions as false and harmful, Catholics should acknowl-
    edge the truths and goodness they manifest, even as
    Catholics continue to proclaim that Jesus Christ is the
    universal Lord and savior of all humankind.

10. Social mission. Instead of overemphasizing that indi-
    vidual salvation is to be achieved in the next world,
    the church must carry out on earth the mission of
    Christ, especially among the poor. Earthly affairs
    should not be divorced from religious life. The bish-
    ops said: "This split between the faith which many
    profess and their daily lives deserves to be counted
    among the most serious errors of our age" (GS 43).

Its Nature

What did the Council do for the universal and local church?
How was the church different after the Council from what it
had been before 1962? What process did the Council set in
motion—was it a renewal, a reform, a reformation, or a
retrieval and reinterpretation of the Catholic tradition?

We have seen that John XXIII had several specifics in mind:
a new Pentecost; aggiornamento and Christian unity; the presence of leaders of other Christian communities as observers; a
statement on Catholic-Jewish relations; and a policy prohibiting condemnations. Otherwise, declared O'Malley, "there is
not the slightest shred of evidence that he foresaw or

intended the direction it took" (1989, 116). There are several indications that John XXIII leaned toward the progressive outlook while holding onto some traditional views. For example, he issued an apostolic constitution on the importance of the use of Latin in the education of seminarians; on June 30, 1962, he issued a general warning against "numerous ambiguities and serious errors" in the writings of Teilhard de Chardin.

Was the Council a renewal? Renewal takes place when "the church looks to its origins and revitalizes itself by contact with its spiritual sources" (Hebblethwaite 1975, 19). The Council did that, particularly in its decisions about the laity, ecumenism, and religious liberty.

Was the Council a reform? Reform entails a process to correct what is wrong, to remove defects, correct errors, and improve by alteration. The council documents hardly use the word *reform*. The church never admitted that its teachings on religious liberty were a reversal or that it was guilty of persecuting Jews over many centuries. Yet, the council was aware of changes in society and, therefore, progress and development became major conciliar themes. The Decree on Ecumenism acknowledged that, "as she goes her pilgrim way," the church must certainly reform "deficiencies in the formulation of doctrine" that were due "to the influence of events or of the times" (UR 6). Similarly, the Council called for a number of reforms—for example, instead of having one liturgy for the whole church, the liturgy must be adapted to the genius and traditions of people (SC 37–40); and members of religious orders were instructed that instead of holding on to antiquated rules and constitutions, they should adapt "to the needs of our time" (PC 18).

On the other hand, while a reform involves changes and corrections, the changes take place within a given frame of reference and do not change the church's self-understanding. Reform steadies the church on its course. Did the self-understanding of the church actually change at Vatican II? Not drastically. The Council failed to do away with its "absolutistic claims and its antiquated class structure" (Dulles 1988a, 19). In other words, the church never made a decisive break with juridicism, clericalism, and triumphalism. The latter term indicates that the church highlighted its successes in such a way that it assumed privileged status and superiority over the rest of the world's institutions and religious bodies. We have seen that the sixteen documents reflect the huge committees in which they were hammered out. They are marked by qualifications and ambiguities. The result, said O'Malley, was that many of the bishops "went home to resume life pretty much as usual once the work was done" (1989, 116). The reform, then, is ambivalent. There were some important changes, but others were not made—for example, the Council did not restructure the Roman curia so that all authority would not be centralized in Rome.

Was the Council a reformation? This is O'Malley's thesis (1989). By reformation he means "reform by transformation or by revolution." Such a reformation entails "a partial rejection of the past in the hope of creating something new" (ibid., 73). Reformation is "a self-consciously induced change in ecclesial life or consciousness that is based on principles that tend to dislodge old ones" (ibid., 88). In other words, a reformation is an event or period in which the church's self-understanding has changed radically.

To defend his thesis, O'Malley refers to two previous reformations in the church: the reformation of Gregory VII (1073–85), over the issue of investiture, which resulted in the freedom of the church from the state and in the emergence of a strong and centralized papacy that protected local churches from the state; and the reformation of Martin Luther (1517), from which there emerged a new church that separated the Scriptures from the papacy, grace from merits, and faith from works. O'Malley admits that these two reformations "are in no way prescriptive or normative" for other reformations (ibid., 121). Vatican II, he maintains, is a special reformation. The council fathers knew that they were experiencing a new Pentecost and that the Council had radical implications. Also, Vatican II stands in marked discontinuity with the councils that preceded it because of the principle of aggiornamento: the church is in a new era, and religion is to be changed by and for people "in order to accommodate these new historical and cultural differences" (ibid., 121). The main example O'Malley gives to defend his thesis is that "the laity is doing things once reserved exclusively to priests" (ibid., 119).

Is this shift from priest to people a reformation? Evidence indicates otherwise. For example, in his monumental book on the various forms of ministry in the history of the church, Bernard Cooke demonstrated that the charisms of ministry have been plural (1977). In the first centuries these charisms did not exist uniquely in any one ministry, whether bishop or priest. What eventually happened in the history of the church, added John Coleman, is that there developed "what has been called a 'ministerial moloch,' whereby the priesthood gobbled up all ministries in itself" (1981).

Vatican II acknowledged that all the faithful participate in the one priesthood of Christ (LG 10). What is happening in the church, maintained Cooke, is that people are looking past the post-Tridentine, hierarchical, and sacerdotal patterns based on ordination and a celibate lifestyle to the tradition of ministry based on the priority of baptism and ministerial competence rooted in charisms (Cooke 1985). In other words, all ministries in the church—liturgical, educational, social, ecumenical, and special ministries to the sick and dying—are ultimately the reponsibility of the entire Christian community. The ecclesiastical categories of clergy and laity inherited from the classical tradition of Christianity are increasingly irrelevant in the church as she renews herself by retrieving a modified hierarchical view from the past.

To call the Council a reformation seems an exaggeration. What seems more accurate is Robert Imbelli's thesis that the "major theological achievement of Vatican II" was "the recovery of tradition" (1982; see also Van Beeck 1985, 1–21). A thorough review of the sixteen documents makes clear that the church did recover its ancient tradition, reclothing it for our era as requested by John XXIII. "To reclothe" does not mean to reformulate or merely to translate "traditional dogmas into a new idiom" (Baum 1970b). To reclothe is to recover the tradition by reinterpretation for the present age. At Vatican II the church was doing theology: it was seeking an understanding of its faith in the Christ-event for modernity. Good theology has two constants: it is always an interpretation of the Christ-event and an interpretation of the contemporary situation (Tracy 1981, 79, 340). At Vatican II the church turned from neoscholastic theology to its venerable patrimony, attempting to articulate a clearer sense of its own identity and mission in view of such factors as the new humanism, historical consciousness, social justice, ecumenism, and religious and cultural pluralism. As explained in chapter 2, the dominant theologians at the Council were the so-called new theologians (Congar, for example), who returned to the sources of Christianity not only to rehear what was said then but also to reinterpret the present in light of the past.

In addition to the ten decisions outlined earlier, there are many other instances of this recovery of the tradition. Consider the following three examples. First, the church recovered the view that the whole church is both a teaching and a learning church. This perspective had been lost, especially under Pius XII. In *Humani generis* (1950), he wrote that Catholics owe "religious allegiance of the will and intellect" even to non-infallible teachings of the pope. The conciliar bishops wrote: "With the help of the Holy Spirit, it is the task of the entire People of God, especially pastors and theologians, to hear, distinguish, and interpret the many voices of our age, and to judge them in the light of the divine Word. In this way, revealed truth can always be more deeply penetrated, better understood, and set forth to greater advantage" (GS 44). Second, the Declaration on Religious Freedom reversed the teachings of the *Syllabus of Errors* (1864) by returning to biblical insights about human dignity. In this document, the Council declared "that the right to religious freedom has its foundation in the very dignity of the human person, as this dignity is known through the revealed Word of God and by reason itself" (DH 2). Third, the members of religious orders were told that "the appropriate renewal of religious life involves two simultaneous processes: (1) a continuous return to the sources of all Christian life and to the original inspiration behind a given community and (2) an adjustment of the community to the changed conditions of the times" (PC 2).

In my judgment, Imbelli is correct: at the Council the true Catholic tradition was recovered or retrieved. I would add that once the true tradition was recovered, the bishops built on it their renewal and reform of the church.

Its Successes

Vatican II was a stunning success. In Von Hügel's terms, the theolgians (the intellectual) assisted the pope and bishops (institutional) to update the devotional life of the church (mystical). This pastoral Council made many dogmatic and disciplinary decisions: it renewed and reformed the church; it emphasized the community and power-sharing aspects of the church (collegiality); it formalized cooperation with the other Christian churches; it legitimated the transformation of the rites of the various sacraments, especially the Eucharist; it repudiated anti-Semitism; it acknowledged the rights of people to choose their own religion; and it directed Catholics to dialogue with the modern world. If it were not for the Council, said one bishop, "the church would have been like the Loch Ness monster: rumored to exist, of venerable antiquity, actually seen by some, but not of much relevance in the contemporary world" (Hebblethwaite 1975, 13).

A few cautions are necessary. During the Council, considerable tension and even fierce resistance permeated the formal and informal discussions as the progressive and traditional mindsets attempted to hammer out the sixteen documents. The documents, as we have seen, are compromise statements. Also, the full success of the Council will take time, as history teaches. Walter Kaspar was probably correct when he wrote in 1989: "I myself have no doubt that the council's hour is still to come, and that its seed will spring up and bear rich fruit in the field of history" (p. 176).

Its Failures

Some of the Council's failures—scores of articles and books have explained many of them—relate to the pastoral purposes of the Council and its affirmation of the modern world. Andrew Greeley, a priest, sociologist, and novelist, has written extensively on the failure of the Council to be pastoral, that is, "a council concerned about the reformulation [sic] of the gospel message" (1970). Greeley maintains that no attempt was made at the Council to develop catechetical styles for presenting the Christian gospel for people today. To present the gospel today the religious needs of people must be monitored. The council fathers turned instead to administrators and scholars for their agenda. As a result, wrote Greeley, "The council was concerned with institutional structures and doctrinal propositions (the role of bishops, the nature of revelation, collegiality, etc.), and not with religion. . . . Despite its claim to be pastoral, Vatican II was perceived to be (and in fact was) concerned mostly with the distribution of power in the church and (though by silence) with sexual morality. The postconciliar controversies have been almost totally preoccupied with these issues" (1982a).

Greeley was most annoyed that the Council "did not produce a positive statement on sexuality and did not debate the question of human reproduction" (1982b). Greeley's accusations are disturbing because they make such an ugly contrast with the Council's enunciations about ministry as service and the church as a participatory community. On the other hand, it could be that Greeley expected the Council to undertake a theological and hermeneutical task beyond its competence. How could two-thousand bishops from a world church have organized one language that would meet the deep religious needs of the faithful? Even the 204 bishops and delegates assembled for the Synod of 1977 on catechetics did not tackle this project. Similarly, when the two thousand bishops addressed the pastoral issues of liturgy and moral theology, the most they could do was to set forth principles for a liturgical reform and to declare that "special attention needs to be given to the development of moral theology" (OT 16).

It must be noted to Greeley's credit that he has successfully attempted—and not without arousing considerable controversy—to reclothe the gospel message in the articles cited here, in several books on religion, and in dozens of novels.[1]

As to the Council's failure to affirm the modern world, Gregory Baum, a theologian and sociologist, argued that the bishops, by buying into the liberal confidence that the economic, social, and political problems of the world could be gradually solved by human ingenuity, "paid insufficient attention to the limits and ambiguities of the liberal tradition. While the new emphases on personal conscience and personal development represented an undeniable progress, Catholics had not sufficiently thought through the problematic link of these ideas to individualism, the breakdown of social solidarity, the replacement of human values by the exchange value, the utilitarianism of public policies, and the cultural impact of capitalism" (1985).

Baum delineated four weaknesses in Vatican II's optimistic acceptance of liberalism (1984a, 75–104). They are as follows. First, Vatican II affirmed modern industrial, technical, and developmental society as the instrument of justice and said all peoples should share in the positive benefits of modernity. However, it was the bishops and theologians from western Europe, the United States, and Canada who most influenced this vision. They were naturally influenced by the extraordinary economic progress made in the West after World War II. In other words, the bishops of the West viewed the world through the eyes of capitalists and not through those of the poor, the underdeveloped, and the oppressed in the South and the East.

Second, Vatican II encouraged Christians to engage in social action and criticized a purely individual ethic. However, the Council did not go far enough. It said people must change so society would change. While this is true, what is often the case is that societal structures must be changed before people can even have a chance to change and to live more authentically.

Third, Baum pointed out, Vatican II acknowledged the presence of personal sin in society, especially the neglect of the poor. However, Vatican II said not a word about social sin, that is, about our past, personal sinful choices that gave rise to systematic institutions of socioeconomic and political oppression and deprivation. In other words, it is people who create ghettos, homelessness, hunger, disease, racism, and sexism.

Finally, Vatican II declared the church to be in solidarity with the whole human family. However, Baum argued that the church was too identified with the wealthy and the middle-class and hardly at all with those people involved in emancipatory struggles for basic human dignity and rights.

Vatican II: Twenty-five Years Later

In 1990 the church celebrated the twenty-fifth anniversary of the closing of the Council. The celebration was muted, even somewhat neglected. There was praise and gratitude for all the successes mentioned above. After all, had not these movements, ideas, and actions been inspired by the Spirit?

On the other hand, several concerns were raised. The editors of *Commonweal* complained that the fierce resistance by the Roman curia to the thrust of the Council still survives and "has been given new life by Pope John Paul II and Cardinal Joseph Ratzinger."[2] (Ratzinger is the prefect of the Congregation of the Doctrine of the Faith [CDF], the Vatican office that oversees the integrity of the church's teachings on faith and morals.) Restorationists and reformers are painfully divided over the best way to deal with papal and episcopal authority, participation in the liturgy, collegiality, ecumenism, religious education, and the life of faith.

Archbishop Rembert Weakland of Milwaukee worried that the enthusiasm generated twenty-five years ago by the Council "has spun itself out." He hoped that the church would recapture the attitude that it is "but a humble partner, an imperfect society, engaging this world in dialogue." He regretted that "tensions have arisen between the role of the clergy and the laity. One simply has to admit that these tensions do exist and that the aspirations created by the Vatican II documents are not going to go away simply by edicts that reinforce the power of hierarchy" (Vidulich 1990).

The view that Vatican II's momentum had diminished was shared by the 431 American and Canadian theologians who, on December 8, 1990, endorsed a statement by a committee of the Catholic Theological Society of America that accused the Vatican of obstructing changes in the church.[3] The statement of twenty-four hundred words, titled "Do Not Extinguish the Spirit," claimed that the church's leadership has failed to carry out the changes called for by the Council in four areas that are of specific concern in North America: collegiality of the bishops, cooperation between the magisterium and theologians, ecumenism, and the development of legitimate public roles for women in the church. Concerning the latter, the theologians readily acknowledged "the insights on women shown in some teaching documents of this pontificate," but declared that there was still a glaring disparity between the roles of women and men in society and in the church. Feminism, then, was not being recognized as a sign of the times but was "consistently viewed with suspicion." Furthermore, "Candidates for the episcopacy are screened to insure their unqualified opposition to the ordination of women to the priesthood."

The last official promulgation of the church's traditional teaching prohibiting the ordination of women was the "Declaration on the Question of the Admission of Women to the Ministerial Priesthood," issued by the CDF on October 15, 1976. Despite this Roman teaching, the question of women priests has surfaced frequently in the postconciliar church. There are several reasons. First, those advocating the ordination of women reject the arguments of their opponents, particularly the arguments that it has not been done before and that the priests representing Christ to the community must be male. Advocates for women's ordination counter that the church's two thousand-year history of an exclusively male priesthood developed out of a patriarchal culture and that to further support this culture would tie the church's understanding of Christ and his church to one time and culture; and that all Christians should be other Christs. They also point out that several Protestant churches have been ordaining women as priests (since 1944) and bishops (since 1980). Many Catholics believe that the call to ordain women as priests is one of Christianity's great and historic transformations. Sandra Schneiders, an Immaculate Heart of Mary sister and professor of spirituality and Scripture, declared, "The last time there was such a ground swell that was not heeded was the Protestant Reformation" (Ostling 1992, 53).

In June 1992, almost thirty years after the opening of the Council, the question of women's ordination received public attention once more when 238 United States bishops met to discuss the draft of their proposed pastoral on women, "Called To Be One in Christ Jesus." This document, drafted several times over nine years, affirmed the equality of women, condemned discrimination as a moral and social evil, and emphasized the church's traditional teaching that only men can serve as priests (Goldman 1992; Steinfels 1992b; Vidulich and Fox 1992). However, the bishops were so divided over the contents of the document that they put off a vote until their November 1992 meeting. In November the 247 bishops present voted not to issue the pastoral. The vote (137 to 110) marked the first time since the modern bishops' conference was formed in 1966 that the bishops failed to reach a two-thirds majority consensus on a proposed pastoral letter.

Many bishops found the document incomplete and likely to alienate many women. It is reported that very few of the bishops who voted against the document wanted to see women as priests. Nonetheless, "the letter could not be read apart from its own history. Under Vatican prodding, later drafts adopted an increasingly guarded tone. The fourth draft warned, for instance, that 'to identify sexism as the principal evil' harming women socially would be 'to analyze the underlying problem too superficially'" (Steinfels 1992d). There is little doubt that the Vatican's insistence that women could not be ordained also influenced the deliberations of the bishops. What ultimately divided the bishops was their own teaching role. When should they stand firm and draw sharp boundaries and when reach out and advocate change? Many of those who voted against the document "concluded that a letter subordinating the new concerns of women to laying down sharp limits to the examination of church teachings would not only forestall dialogue but provoke a backlash against church teachings as well" (Steinfels 1992e).

The ordination of women as priests cuts into the very foundations of the church's institutional, devotional, and intellectual life. Most of the episcopal officeholders refuse to reform the institution's longstanding tradition; many women plead for leadership roles in the church's life, especially at the Eucharist, "the center and culmination of the whole life of the Christian community" (CD 30); and theologians struggle with the scriptural, cultural, and ecumenical dimensions of the question.

Conclusion

The preconciliar church offered Catholics a religion of beauty, order, and goodness, however imperfectly realized. At Vatican II—the decisive ecclesial event of the twentieth century—the Catholic Church emerged as a world church in a polycentric global culture. These developments brought necessary changes in the institution, in theology, and in spirituality. For example, the preconciliar spirituality was otherworldly, ahistorical, antisecular, and individualistic, whereas the Council moved Catholics toward a spirituality that is of this world, personal without being private, prophetic and countercultural without being partisan, and communal. The rest of this book examines how the church, in view of the signs of the times, reshaped its intellectual, devotional, and institutional life at and since Vatican II, and evaluates whether the changes have helped or hindered the church in clarifying its identity and fulfilling its mission.

4

The Identity and Mission
of the Church

The Council had several important goals, but it was primarily
concerned with the identity and mission of the church in the
modern world.

The Christian religion has a distinctive identity. It is a community of people who personally accept in faith, hope, and
love the good news that the eternal kingdom of God the
Father has been manifested in a special way in the life, death,
and resurrection of his son Jesus, and in the power, presence,
and gifts of the Spirit and with the church community.

Community is an analogous term; it has many definitions,
depending on concrete situations. Today it is used so widely
that it can refer to a family, a city, a political organization, a
voluntary association, a religious order, and other groups
(e.g., a college, blacks, Latinos, gays, lesbians). All these
groups are somewhat the same and yet entirely different from
one another. The church, too, is a voluntary association, a
society, a family, and an interest group. Nonetheless, it is *sui
generis*, because its source is Christ, its ground the Spirit, and
its goal the kingdom of God.

The New Testament narrates the complex stories of the
churches the apostles organized and left behind (R. E. Brown
1984). There was a great deal of variety, partly because the
churches had different needs and goals. Nevertheless, there

83

are four basic interrelated structures to all the church communities that form the one Church of Christ.

First, the church is a visible society or institution that mediates the risen Jesus and his Spirit. The institution has its own leaders, officeholders, laws, customs, rituals (especially baptism and Eucharist), and special doctrines or teachings. The institutional church is regarded as a means of grace; it is a conditional reality subordinated to the kingdom of God.

Second, the church is an interpersonal community or communion, bound together around the risen Christ and his Spirit. The community enjoys fellowship, prayer, goods in common, mutual concern, and love. The New Testament word for communion, *koinonia*, connotes a deep spiritual union, a nuance not captured by our word *communion.*

Third, the church is a missionary community. Led by the risen Jesus and his Spirit, it shares the good news and its life with the whole world.

Fourth, the church community is made up of individual disciples. Each makes his or her personal commitment in faith, hope, and love. Each has charisms (gifts) to be used to foster the church's identity and mission.

The Relationship of Identity and Mission

A fundamental theological question is the relation of identity to mission. Some claim that mission is a consequence of community; others that mission and community exist side by side as coequals. A third answer—one that reflects the facts both historically and existentially—is that not only is it impossible for identity and mission to be separated, but also that mission is constitutive of the community. The community was formed for its mission. The resurrected Jesus said: "As the Father has sent me, so I send you" (John 20:21). Eugene Hillman, a theologian, author, and missionary, suggests, "Instead of thinking of the church as having a mission to the nations, it is more helpful to think of the mission of Jesus Christ having a church as its instrument" (1989, 73; see also Moltmann 1975, 10).

The Church's Proper Mission

At Vatican II the church fathers declared, "The pilgrim church is missionary by her very nature" (AG 2). But this statement raises another theological issue: the extent of the church's mission. What is the church called to do? What is the church's proper mission?

Before Vatican II it was customary to teach that the church had two missions: one supernatural and the other natural, the latter subordinate to the former (Baum 1986a). The supernatural mission consisted in preaching the gospel (evangelization) so that nonbelievers would believe and enter the community and thus share its world view, participate in its worship, and spread its teachings. The natural or temporal mission was to contribute to the building of a just society by promoting justice on earth. An example of this point of view is found in a letter Pius XI wrote to a French priest: "It is necessary never to lose sight of the fact that the objective of the church is to evangelize, not to civilize. If it civilizes, it is for the sake of evangelization."[1] The teaching that the church had two missions, one supernatural and the other natural, flowed from the many dualisms between natural and supernatural, body and soul, profane and sacred, and church and world that characterized the preconciliar church and its neo-Thomistic theology and spirituality.

At Vatican II the church declared itself in solidarity with the whole human family and defined its mission largely in terms of service. Just as Jesus was servant, so the church was sent to be servant of the world. The bishops urged the faithful to "engage themselves in social action" (GS 9–10). They said there should be no dualism for Christians between their faith and their daily lives (GS 43). Nevertheless, Vatican II reiterated the preconciliar teaching of two missions. The bishops wrote that "Christ, to be sure, gave his Church no proper mission in the political, economic, or social order. The purpose which he set before her is a religious one" (GS 42).

Commenting on this statement, Richard McCormick, a Jesuit moral theologian, declared with justifiable frustration, "Terms such as 'proper mission' and 'strictly religious' cry out for clarification: for they are capable of yielding a very dualistic meaning which ends up restricting the mission of the church to instruction in the faith, liturgy, preaching and sacraments—in brief, a kind of 'sanctuary Christianity.' In this view those directly concerned in one way or another with righting unjust social structures would not be involved in the church's 'proper mission' or with something 'religious'" (1976a).

In addition to saying that the church had "no proper mission in the political, economic, and social order," however, the bishops also insisted that the church should not be relegated to the margins of society. This would be inconsistent with its unique religious mission because the church had "a function, a light and an energy which can serve to structure and consolidate the human community according to the divine law. As a matter of fact, when circumstances of time and place create the need, it can and indeed should initiate activities on behalf of all men" (GS 42).

The conciliar statements just quoted reflect a compromise between the two mindsets at the Council. The traditionalists, relying on the neoscholastic dualisms of church and world, and so on, insist that the church has no proper mission in the political and social order, while the progressives, relying on the new theology's rejection of the dualism of church and world, insist that the church's mission is to serve the world.

The decisive turning point in mission theology came during the international Synod of 1971, which addressed both priesthood and social justice. In the synod's famous document *Justice in the World*, the bishops declared: "Action on behalf of justice and participation in the transformation of the world fully appear to us as a constitutive dimension of the church's proclamation of the preaching of the gospel, or in other words, of the church's mission of the redemption of the human race and its liberation from every oppressive situation" (n. 6). The bishops went on to emphasize that "the mission of proclaiming the gospel in our times requires that we commit ourselves to man's integral liberation, here and now, in our earthly existence" (n. 35). At this historic meeting, the church acknowledged that it does indeed have a proper mission in the social, political, and economic areas.

Paul VI continued this theme in *Evangelii nuntiandi* (1975)—a document that reported on the Synod of 1974 on evangelization. He wrote that "the church is certainly not willing to restrict her mission only to the religious field and dissociate herself from man's temporal problems" (n. 34). He also discussed the church's one mission that embraced in an inseparable manner both evangelization and public witness to social justice. He took the two missions of the preconciliar theology and combined them as dimensions of one mission. John Paul II endorsed this teaching in his first encyclical, *Redemptor hominis* (1979). Both pontiffs reject the neoscholastic dualism of church and world and both "emphasize human dignity and love for humans as the link between evangelization and liberation. They refer to the transcendence of eschatology to show that evangelization should not be identified totally and exclusively with human progress" (Fiorenza 1982, 209).

However, is one mission with a twofold dimension a complete picture of the church's mission? Some theologians prefer to speak of one mission with a threefold dimension: not only evangelization and service for social justice, but also witness (McBrien 1981, 716; 1973, 140). These three—evangelization, witness, and service—are continuations of Jesus' threefold mission as prophet, priest, and servant-king.

At Vatican II the church highlighted its sacramental role. "The words 'testimony' and 'witness' (both as noun and verb) are found over 100 times in conciliar documents," notes Rene Latourelle (1988b, 408). Not only must the church teach the gospel and promote justice in the world, but it must exemplify this gospel and this justice within the community and for all to see. In other words, the church must practice what it preaches. Jesus did pray "that they may all be one, as you, Father, are in me and I in you . . . that the world may believe that you sent me" (John 17:21). The lifestyle of the first Christians had a major impact on the spread of the church: "See these Christians. How they love one another."

From Mission to Ministry

Since Vatican II, the meaning of the word *mission* has been broadened. Before the Council, *mission* was often understood in a narrow sense: it applied to those men and women who made a distant journey to teach the gospel to a foreign people. This understanding of *mission* is essentially heroic, denoting an extra thrust beyond normal Christian concern for the gospel. In the postconciliar church, *mission* is not regarded as something heroic or extra. Rather, every Christian shares in the threefold mission of Jesus and his church. The question is not *who* is called but *how* each is called.

Ministry is the word used to specify the outward reach of Christians. People are engaged in many ministries: liturgical, eucharistic, and ecumenical. In addition, there are special ministries to the divorced, the imprisoned, the sick, and the dying. There are also "parochial ministers," that is, nonordained people who direct parishes where there are no priests. It is interesting to notice a significant vocabulary change regarding the mission of priests. Vatican II spoke of a "ministerial priesthood" (LG 10), whereas the Synod of 1971 on priesthood had as one of its themes "the priestly ministry." Eugene Kennedy, writing in 1976, observed: "The most exciting religious awareness of this era centers on ministry as the vocation shared by all believers in virtue of their baptism. It is the theme that has been repeated by Pope Paul VI all through his years as head of the church, the notion he has underscored verbally and symbolically in a thousand different ways" (1976b).

Distinctively Catholic

All the Christian churches would agree, *mutatis mutandis*, that the four interrelated structures described above are what make a community distinctively Christian. The next question is: what makes the Catholic Church distinctively Catholic?

The word *catholic* can be spelled with a small *c* or with a capital *C*. *Catholic* with a small *c* designates a property of the one true Church of Christ, namely, its universality. *Catholic* with a capital *C* refers both to the Roman Catholic Church as a distinct Christian community and to a particular *type* or *style* of Christianity. The latter is what is being explained here.

Before beginning, however, it is necessary to state that the style that is distinctively Catholic is not found exclusively in the Roman Catholic Church. Some of the characteristics that describe Catholicism are found not only in some other Christian communities but also in some other religions, though not to the same extent.

We express our consciousness or sensitivity in language. The word *God*, for example, refers to that supreme being who is all holy, who is the originator and creator of all, and who is different from all persons and things (animal, vegetable, or mineral). Since human language denotes only persons or things, when we describe God, who is not a thing (but real) nor a person (but personal), we naturally have to use our imagination. On the one hand, we can say God is unlike any thing or person. For example, since God is not limited by time, he is eternal. This is a dialectical imagination. On the other hand, we can say God is like things (my wisdom, rock, star, lion) or persons (my father, king, shepherd, mother). This is an analogical imagination.

All Christians use both imaginations. However, Protestants tend to emphasize the ways the transcendent God is unlike us (dialectical imagination) and Catholics tend to emphasize the ways the providential God is like us (analogical imagination). It is that simple—but the implications are profound (Tracy 1981; McBrien 1978a; Kennedy 1988a).

This is not to say that there are no doctrinal differences that separate Protestants and Catholics. It does denote that the problems that separate the two groups are not primarily doctrinal but differences in the religious imagination.

To say God is like things and persons is to have a sacramental consciousness. Sacraments are signs and instruments of God. Catholics have a sacramental consciousness: every thing and person can be a sign and instrument of God's presence or love or judgment.

Hilaire Belloc (1870–1953), a Catholic apologist and author, wrote this little ditty: "Wherever the Catholic sun does shine/ There is music, laughter and good red wine. At least I've always found it so. *Benedicamus Domino*" (Greeley and Greeley Durkin 1984, 62).

Catholics enjoy good red wine and other alcoholic drinks. For this reason, Catholic Europe was bewildered when the United States prohibited alcoholic beverages in the 1920s. Several Protestant communities, including many Baptists, Methodists, and Mormons, discourage the use of alcohol. Catholics enjoy and encourage music and dancing. Some Protestants do not. Every so often there are reports in the media about groups of students and their parents who challenge school officials, and even the state and the federal government, about a ban on dancing in their schools. These bans, the students argue, reflect the Protestant fundamentalist opinion that social dancing is sinful, and therefore violate the constitutionally required separation of church and state.

An example of the difference between Protestant and Catholic imaginations is found in "Amazing Grace," an eighteenth-century Protestant hymn: "Amazing grace, how sweet the sound, that saved a wretch like me." Protestants highlight that, as sinners, people are quite unlike the all-holy God. A fundamental starting point of the Protestant reformation was the contrast between sin and grace. This hymn offends a Catholic sacramental consciousness, which proceeds from the assumption of harmony between nature and grace. In many Catholic hymnals the words are adjusted to read, "Amazing grace, how sweet the sound, that saved and strengthened me." The word *wretch* is seldom used in the Catholic vocabulary! But this does not mean Catholics deny their sinfulness and need for conversion and reform.

It must be admitted that contrasting the Protestant and Catholic imaginations and language in this way can lead to caricature. To give more perspective, perhaps it is necessary to hear from some mainline Protestant scholars about these matters. Martin E. Marty, a Lutheran minister and distinguished church historian, tells the story of his confirmation on May 12, 1941. It was the tradition that the pastor would ask surprise questions of each thirteen-year-old. He writes:

> I forget my three questions, but I must have passed. Ruth R. won the laurels for the day. We 13-year-old town-and-country kids knew all about animal sexuality, but our imaginations were dim when it came to human mischief. The pastor had to explain what adultery meant. It meant not dancing at Shady Oaks near Norfolk. Why that stricture? Our breed of Lutherans wasn't strict about everything. I recall seeing one pious grandfather through the blue haze of the Prince Albert smoke as he played cards until all hours, surrounded by fellow beer-drinking buddies. Still, no dancing: at Shady Oaks you might meet and marry a Catholic or, worse, the wrong kind of Lutheran. Shady Oaks was a "road house."
>
> Ruth, can you give an example of committing adultery? "It means when young people go dancing in outhouses." Oops! That was the only light moment I recall from the years of attending childhood confirmations (Marty 1989).

Paul Tillich (1886–1965), an influential Protestant theologian, is famous for constantly affirming what he called the "Protestant principle": "the divine and human protest against any absolute claim made for a relative reality." This very valid principle is rooted in a dialectical imagination.

In most dictionaries *catholic* is defined as universal. This definition is not quite exact. The Latin word for universal is *universalis*, yet when the church wanted to talk about being "all-encompassing" it preferred instead the Greek word *katholikos*. The etymological history of these two words is not clear in every detail. Nevertheless, universal is an inclusive concept. It suggests a circle that includes everything within it. However, it always carries the negative implication that everything outside the circle is excluded. *Katholikos*, on the other hand, is more positive. It means "throughout the whole" or "through the whole." Thus, *Catholic* means through or throughout everything, with nothing excluded.

Since Catholic means "throughout everything, with nothing excluded," then a sacramental consciousness will, indeed, include everything and everyone without exception. For Catholics, all of life is sacramental. Many scholars have listed and explained the characteristics of Catholicism.[2] According to Robert Imbelli, a sacramental consciousness has five dimensions and anything less fails of Catholicity (1982). The five characteristics are corporeal, communal, cosmic, global, and transformational, or what I call tradition-centered. These five terms, it seems to me, can be incorporated into one simple sentence: I am a body-person (corporeal) with others (communal) in this world (cosmic) of space (global) and time (tradition-centered).

A sacramental consciousness respects and appreciates everyone's corporeal reality. The body—the whole body—is good. Music, dancing, gambling, sexuality, drinking good red wine are all good. Catholics enjoy them, saying *"Benedicamus Domino."* As body-persons we have minds. Our body is animated and our soul embodied. A Catholic sacramental consciousness has always fostered the drive toward rationality. Faith is not blind, but is to be informed by reason. The Christian foundation for respecting each and every body-person is the fact that the Word of God assumed a full body and a full human mind in the person of Jesus of Nazareth, and the risen Christ pours out his Spirit on everyone. A sacramental consciousness opposes whatever dehumanizes the body-person: abortion, euthanasia, the death penalty, and every oppression: racial, sexual, political, economic, religious.

A sacramental consciousness is communal—each of us is a body-person with others. The community is a sign and instrument of God. Catholics maintain that Christ is encountered in the living community and the community can respond to him together.

Catholics believe in Jesus Christ, but *with* the Twelve and all those who joined them in passing on the faith. As we have seen, it is, perhaps, the vicars of Peter who have been the single most powerful force holding the community together. Catholics also revere the Scriptures, the Word of God in the words of men and women of the community. The Bible is the book of the community, interpreted in and through the community.

Furthermore, when Catholics assemble, it is often for music, dancing, and good red wine; but most frequently it is to celebrate some aspect of life or rite of passage by means of one or more of the seven sacraments, especially the Eucharist. The Christian foundation for the sacramentality of the community is the risen Christ's promise to be with the community until the end of time, especially when Christians discern the Spirit, serve the poor and needy, and eat the bread and drink from the cup. A communal, sacramental consciousness opposes individualism, moral relativism, elitism, divisions, and a privatized spirituality.

The cosmic aspect of a sacramental consciousness is well expressed in a quote by Gerard Manley Hopkins (1844–89), the English Jesuit poet. The created world, he said, is "charged with the grandeur of God." Francis of Assisi (1182–1226) wrote poetically of Brother Sun and Sister Moon. Again, everything can be a sign and instrument of God. Catholics are steeped in the earth's elements, using many of them in their liturgies: water, fire, oil, bread, wine, stone, light, darkness—and even ashes.

The Christian foundation for this cosmic dimension of a sacramental consciousness is the uniqueness of Christ and his relationship to the cosmos. The Scriptures proclaim that the Father chose us in his son before the creation of the world and God's plan is to unite all persons and things in the risen Christ (see Eph. 1:3–10).

Any abuse of the ecology is contrary to a sacramental consciousness. For example, just because some people drink a lot of beer and good red wine does not mean they have a sacramental consciousness. Actually, overindulgence indicates a lack of reverence for the body-person as well as the beer and good red wine.

Belloc described the global aspect of sacramental consciousness: "Wherever the Catholic sun does shine." The

Catholic sun shines everywhere. The church has always been global—at least in intent. The church goes out to every person and every culture (it is a world church). If a person has a sacramental consciousness, she or he spreads the gospel by teaching, witnessing, and serving others, in the tradition beginning with Peter and Paul and reaching to our day. Thomas Merton (1915–68), a Trappist monk, religious writer, and poet, said that even monks and nuns hidden away in monasteries are called to be everywhere by compassion.

The Christian foundation for this global dimension of the sacramental consciousness is the risen Christ's injunction to teach all nations in the power of the Spirit. Unfortunately, the church has not always been that Catholic. There have been solar eclipses, even arctic nights. We have had puritanical groups: Manichaeans, Jansenists, Albigensians. Today, it is obvious that the church is still too Western, too masculine, too clerical. Those with a sacramental consciousness oppose these misplaced emphases.

Finally, a sacramental consciousness is tradition-centered. The Catholic sun has been shining for two thousand years and over these years the church has been handing on the gospel from one generation to another, meeting new situations, new experiences, new questions. Catholics have an ecclesiastical order and process that helps the community understand the meaning of the gospel. This handing-on of the tradition has been accomplished by millions of faithful parents, hundreds of councils (twenty-one being ecumenical), hundreds of synods (ten international synods between 1967 and 1990), hundreds of popes, thousands of bishops, outstanding theologians in each century, and a countless succession of catechisms, books on spirituality, retreats, sermons, and so forth. The richness of the living tradition is staggering.

The Christian foundation for this tradition-centered, sacramental consciousness is the risen Christ's gift of the Spirit, who as Paraclete leads and defends the church. However, the church has not always been without fault in its interpretation of the gospel. For example, we have seen that the major theological achievement of Vatican II was the recovery of some of the tradition that was lost or blurred in post-Reformation and neoscholastic theologies.

At Vatican II the bishops expressed concern about the strength and depth of this sacramental consciousness among

Catholics when they noted that the "split between the faith which many profess and their daily lives deserves to be counted among the most serious errors of our age" (GS 43). Just as the papacy has been the single most powerful and visible force holding Catholics together at the institutional level, a sacramental consciousness has been at the core of the Catholic tradition at the devotional level. Even such aberrations as the Manichaean and Jansenist heresies are exceptions which prove the rule. The future identity and mission of the church depend upon a revitalized sacramental consciousness among all the disciples of Christ.

The Preconciliar Catholic Church

Christians believe in God's saving love manifested in the death and resurrection of Jesus and incarnated in his church through the Spirit. This multilayered and complex relationship is polycentric: Christians believe God's eternal, saving love, and kingdom (theocentric) is manifested in a special way in Jesus and his Spirit (christocentric) with and through the first disciples and apostles (ecclesiocentric). At various times the polycentric church has had different emphases. All three centers are always operative but, at different times, one center is underscored, often because of societal and/or ecclesial conditions and needs.

The institutional character of the Catholic Church makes it unique among the other Christian churches and the world's great religions. Most religions and churches have only minimal national or international organizations. In some Protestant denominations, the word *church* refers only to the local place of worship. The Catholic Church is a worldwide institution with an administrative apparatus that dwarfs those of most modern governments. The vast hierarchical machinery, besides supporting a vast network of public services like hospitals and schools, oversees the theological and devotional practices in thousands of dioceses and parishes.

In the preconciliar period, the institutional church was in a "state of siege mentality." As a result, the church was ecclesiocentric and the emphasis was on the church as an institution. The institution was conceived as an autonomous and sovereign society, one opposed to the rest of society. For example, when Pius XI issued his encyclical *Quas primas* (1925), in which he instituted the feast of Christ the King, he stated that as the church was divine in origin, its rights were inviolable, above and beyond the judgment of secular society.

The church's government was centralized and bureaucratic. Prized were clarity, unity, and order. The order was hierarchical—the Greek roots of this word means literally "priest-rule." Being hierarchical, the church is "an 'unequal society,' in which the members, located on different levels, know their place and through the interplay of authority and obedience serve the well-being of the whole. " (Baum 1989c, 725–26). The Catholic Church regards the papal-collegial structure of ecclesiastical government as of divine origin.

Pius XII, with the aid of the Jesuit theologian Sebastian Tromp, wrote *Mystici corporis* (1943), "the most comprehensive official Catholic pronouncement on the church prior to Vatican II" (Dulles 1989, 422). At first it seemed he was breaking with the overly juridical understanding of the church as a "perfect society" (n. 63), a notion dating to the Jesuit theologian Robert Bellarmine (1542–1621). According to Bellarmine, the church was perfect because it had everything it needed in order to achieve its ends and so it could (and even should) impose its "rights" over civil society. But the encyclical really protected the institutional nature of the church in all its dimensions.

Pius had two main points. First, he addressed those theologians who, in their efforts to highlight the church's supernatural or mystical qualities, were neglecting the visible, organized, and juridical institution. To counteract this approach, Pius tried to synthesize both dimensions by talking about "the doctrine of the Mystical Body of Christ, which is the Church" (n. 1). This identity of the Catholic Church with the Mystical Body meant that one had to be a member of the Catholic Church to belong to the Mystical Body. Christians not united to the visible institution were cut off from communion with Christ. Nevertheless, these Christians, if they were living by the grace of Christ and were in good faith (even in their "errors"), could be in communion with Christ by desire. Second, while underscoring the church as institution, Pius did not want the individual Catholic to be lost within the totality. He warned that the biological analogy for the church should not be carried so far that the totality was more important than the individual.

The encyclical evoked intense discussion in theological circles among liturgists, biblical scholars, canon lawyers, and ecumenists. The latter, for example, were embarrassed because the encyclical seemed to put other Christians in the same spiritual category as those who belonged to other religions.

The hierarchically ordered society has a purpose: it should stand in the service of the community and each individual in the community. Few have expressed this more clearly than Karl Rahner:

> In a chess club the main thing is that chess should be played well, and that masters of the game should be trained there. Everything else, the functionaries, the cashiers, the president, the club meetings and statutes are, indeed, necessary and cannot be abolished; but their true meaning is to serve playing chess. The true stars of a chess club are the best players, not the cashier or the president who may, indeed, be players who have failed. Exactly the same is the case in the Catholic church. . . . All presiding ministers of the church, from the pope and the bishops down to the parish priests and chaplains, exist only so that there may be Christians, that is, men and women who believe, hope and love, who bear their cross, who see light even in darkness, who firmly hope even against hope, men who have the folly and the courage to love in a loveless world. All sermons, all papal decrees, all canon law, all sacred congregations in Rome, all bishops—in short, the whole organization of the church exists only to assist the true Christian life in the hearts of men. Where this meaning is lost it becomes only man's ridiculous presumption before God (Rahner 1969, 18–19).

Few Catholics are opposed in any absolute sense to the church as institution. Institutions are indispensable to human development and order. Moreover, the church has changed its governmental structures over the centuries, from Jewish presbyterial government, feudal fealties, and monarchical nation-state. In all these forms the hierarchy has the responsibility to govern, legislate, and judge. What the faithful disapprove of is "a disproportionate sacrifice of individual freedom to collective discipline. . . . They disapprove despotism and absolutism" (Gaffney 1986).

The Conciliar Church

During the two decades preceeding the Council, extensive ecclesiological scholarship was taking place, especially in France and Germany. The so-called "new theologians" returned to the biblical and patristic sources where they found many images of the church that highlighted the life of grace and charity at the heart of the church rather than a juridical view of the church. Some argue that this shift from institution to communion by the progressive preconciliar ecclesiologists was "the single most important concept leading to Vatican II's reforms" (Doyle 1992, 140). The scholars produced studies on the church as Mystical Body (by Emile Mersch and Sebastian Tromp), as people of God (by Lucien Cerfaux and Joseph Ratzinger), as temple of the Spirit (by Yves Congar), as the sacrament of Christ (by Henri de Lubac, Otto Semmelroth, and Karl Rahner) and as a pilgrim people (by Rudolf Schnackenburg) (Dulles 1989, 425–29).

Vatican II did not make a sharp break with the official teaching of the recent past regarding the identity and mission of the church. It did make a substantial shift in emphasis. The preconciliar stress on the church as institution, while understandable at the time, did lead to institutionalism, one deadening effect of which was the creation of a wide gap between the faithful and the hierarchy. The latter were so identified with the whole church that it was not uncommon for the faithful to refer to the church as "they."

As a result of the "new theology" as well as the explosion of historical consciousness and the general trend in Western society toward freedom, equality, dialogue, community, and democracy, there was a desire to view the church more personally. At Vatican II the church shifted from an ecclesiocentric view of its identity and mission to a christocentric view. Recovered from the tradition was the presence of the risen Christ as the personal center of the church, and the church as the sacrament of his redemptive presence. The bishops wrote that it is the church's function "led by the Holy Spirit . . . to make God the Father and his incarnate Son present and in a sense visible" (GS 21).

Vatican II was a council by the church about the church. There were two major documents on the church: the

Constitution on the Church *(Lumen gentium)* and the
Constitution on the Church in the Modern World *(Gaudium et
spes)*. The former dealt with the identity of the church; the latter with its mission.

Volumes have been written about the shifts in emphasis
concerning the identity and mission at Vatican II. Summarized
here are six of the council's major ecclesiological themes.

First, the Council emphasized the church as sacrament or
mystery. In the preconciliar days, the church was regarded as
a plank of salvation for a shipwrecked humanity. At Vatican II
the church was described as the visible sign and instrument
(sacrament) of Christ's salvation of the whole world, that is,
for all those who did not belong to the community (LG 1).
This change from plank to sacrament more clearly explains
the identity and necessity of the church. It shows that God's
salvific will is universal and can be thwarted only when people make personal decisions contrary to it.

The theme of mystery was a favorite of Paul VI. In his
opening address at the second session (September 29, 1963),
he said, "The church is a mystery. It is a reality imbued with
the hidden presence of God."

Second, the Council moved to describe the church as the
people of God. The church is both an institution and a communion. The preconciliar church stressed the institution and
its hierarchical officers and specialists. Vatican II turned to the
image of the church as the people of God. In 1870 at Vatican I
the majority of bishops favored the hierarchical model but
there was a minority who advocated the communion model.
"What is certain is that the ecclesiology of the minority at
Vatican I was transformed into the majority at Vatican II"
(Anton 1988, 422–23).

Of all the images used at Vatican II, the bishops gave pride
of place to people of God. The second chapter of the
Constitution on the Church is devoted to exploring the ramifications of this image. Chapter 1 explores the mystery of the
church and chapter 3 discusses the hierarchical structures of
the church. Yves Congar called this sequence and placement
a Copernican revolution, because it radically moved from
identifying the church as an institution to identifying it primarily as a communion (ibid., 413). Communion became "the key
concept for interpreting the ecclesiology of Vatican II and the

one that best summarizes its results in ecclesiological doctrine and in the renewal of the church" (ibid., 416).

There are many reasons the Council chose the communion model. It focuses attention on the church as Christ's community; it avoids the controversy over whether the church is a mystical community or an institution of discipline and government; it highlights the historical and dynamic nature of the church as a pilgrim community gathered and led by Christ; and it is ecumenical, evoking an association with Israel, God's chosen people.

Third, the Council described the church as servant. The preconciliar church spoke of two realms: the church and the world. The church was a fortress of truth in an alien world. Vatican II, on the other hand, unambiguously established solidarity between the church and the whole human race, especially in the Constitution on the Church in the Modern World, the longest of the sixteen documents at 23,335 words.

The bishops declared that the church, while not bound to any particular form of human culture, nor to any political, economic, or social system, "should initiate activities on behalf of all men. This is particularly true of activities designed for the needy, such as the works of mercy and similar undertakings" (GS 42). All this activity the church does in imitation of the work of Christ himself who "entered this world to give witness to the truth, to rescue, and not to sit in judgment, to serve and not to be served" (GS 3).

Fourth, the Council portrayed the church as collegial. The preconciliar church stressed the universal church governed and directed by the papacy and the Roman curia. Vatican II said the church is realized and expressed not only at the universal level, but also the local level (LG 26; CD 11). There is a dialectical balancing between the church as a worldwide international community and the local congregation. Each exists only in the other.

The term *local church* encompasses parishes, dioceses, regions, and nations. In the Catholic tradition, each of these levels works together with their bishop(s) according to their proper roles for the common good of the church in its identity and mission. The local churches are church in the full sense and not as part of the universal church. The universal church is a communion of local churches and can act only in and through them. Collegiality, then, is the shared responsibility of pope and bishops for leading and governing the church.

Yves Congar commented on the church's rediscovery of the local church at the Council: "Universal is the opposite of particular or local, but Catholic is not the opposite of anything. A local church is Catholic, and even an individual is Catholic; a small community is Catholic, but it is obviously not universal. I believe that this rediscovery of the local church . . . is extremely important. Karl Rahner even thought it to be the most important part of all the council's work on ecclesiology" (Lauret 1988, 11).

Fifth, the Council also affirmed the church as ecumenical. The preconciliar Catholic Church declared itself the one true church of Jesus Christ. It alone possessed the marks of the true church—one, holy, catholic, and apostolic—and it alone had preserved the vicars of Peter. The other Christian communities had broken from the true church through schism or heresy.

Vatican II stressed what unites all Christian communities: the presence of the Spirit and the common belief that Jesus is Lord and Christ. The Council's perspective was christocentric. The other churches were addressed as separated brethren or sister churches, and not strangers or enemies. The elements that constitute the one true Church of Christ are distributed in varying degrees throughout the other Christian communities. Due to the presence of the Spirit and his gifts of faith, hope, and love, there is already an ecclesial communion among the Christian churches that is real, even if incomplete (LG 15; UR 3–4). The Council committed itself to ecumenism "so that the sign of Christ may shine more brightly over the face of the Church" (LG 15).

Sixth, the Council perceived the church as eschatological. The preconciliar church referred to itself as a perfect society and the earthly embodiment of the kingdom of God. Vatican II declared that the kingdom was already present in Christ but, as for the church, it was but the sacrament of Christ and the kingdom. Some theologians consider this shift from embodiment of the kingdom to sacrament of the kingdom the "single most significant reversal of ecclesiological perspective brought about by Vatican II" (Van Beeck 1985, 34).

The earthly church is the one true Church of Christ but in a pilgrim state and in constant need of reform. *The* one true Church of Christ will not be wholly one and holy until human history as we know it ends. "It is unreasonable to ask for perfect faith, hope undimmed, inexhaustible charity in the church. . . . The church is the flawed embodiment of faith, hope, and charity" (Hebblethwaite 1975, 238).

The Conciliar Images in the Postconciliar Church

The Council's images of the church as sacrament, people of God, and servant at first evoked considerable enthusiasm. Unfortunately, they could not capture the imaginations of people in a lasting way because of three factors: their ambivalence, the situation in the world, and the changes the church underwent after the Council.

The word *sacrament* suggested to some of the laity either "an impersonal reality, such as baptismal water; or a ritual action, such as anointing" (Dulles 1981). Also, the image implied a conspicuousness the church just did not have. Even in the United States, where the Catholic Church was some 20 percent of the population, the church had only a minor impact on the political and economic life of the country. Finally, there was some uncertainty about what the church as sacrament represented since the church was not a convincing sign of the unity, peace, justice, and love that the Council announced.

People of God, the favorite image of the council fathers, proved to be embarrassing for two reasons. First, it suggested that the rest of humanity was not included in God's love. Second, it proved difficult for Catholics to regard themselves as a people. The Jewish people had a religious, ethnic, and political heritage that made it easy for them to cherish the image people of God. Not so for the global and world church.

The servant model, when it specified the gospel injunction to make this a better world by healing, feeding, and reconciling in imitation of Jesus, met with less opposition than the other two images. However, in democratic societies like that of the United States, the term *servant* had taken on pejorative connotations. Today those who do the kind of menial tasks once done by servants are called "staff" or some other neutral term. In church parlance, the term *servant* was soon replaced by *stewardship* or *ministry*, words that evoke the notions of inventiveness and originality.

The Community of Disciples

After Vatican II considerable reflection and discussion was given to the models of the church, especially the five enumerated by Avery Dulles in 1974: mystical communion, herald, sacrament, servant, and institution.[3]

As is his style, Dulles explained the models most carefully and with balance. He did this by emphasizing these principles: the church is irreducible to any single image or model; no model should be absolutized; and the five models are sufficiently flexible to be mutually open and complementary. He went on to show that the five models can conflict with one another and so ecclesiologists should incorporate the major affirmations of each model without carrying over their distinctive liabilities. An ecclesiology would be truly adequate to the extent that it took into account the insights contained in each of the five models.

Something Dulles did not develop is the relationship of the five models to the four interrelated structures of the church. When the models are so related, they denote that the visible society (institution) is an interpersonal community (mystical communion) with a threefold mission: to teach the gospel (herald), to witness the gospel (sacrament), and to serve the needy and oppressed (servant).

Something else is lacking in Dulles's models: the personal dimension. At the beginning of this chapter, I indicated that one of the four essential dimensions of the church is the presence of individuals who personally respond to the God of Jesus in faith, hope, and love. This personal dimension is essential because at this level, although all men and women receive different gifts of the Spirit, all are equal in dignity and freedom. At this level, all women and men are followers and learners, all must embrace the cross of Christ, and all must appropriate their mission. *Gaudium et spes* stated that God probes the heart and awaits persons there. "There [a person] discerns his proper destiny beneath the eyes of God" (GS 14). The document also taught that "conscience is the most secret core and sanctuary of a man. There he is alone with God, whose voice echoes in his depths" (GS 16).

Karl Rahner wrote perceptively of the personal dimension of ecclesial life. He insisted that the nature of both the church and the person demanded that a legitimate private sphere be left for individual inspiration, initiative, and responsibility on the part of each member of the church. For example, the church cannot force prayer, faith, or vocation upon the unique individual member, nor can it decide upon the individual's moral standing in the sight of God. Finally, there is Rahner's oft-quoted prophecy: "The Christian of the future will be a mystic or he or she will not exist at all" (1964b, 217–34).

In 1979, John Paul II, in his first encyclical, *Redemptor hominis*, addressed the personal, mystical dimension of ecclesial life. He reminded his readers that membership in the church has its source in "a particular call" from Christ. The church "is the community of the disciples, each of whom in a different way—at times very consciously and consistently, at other times not very consciously and very consistently—is following Christ. This shows also the deeply 'personal' aspect and dimension of this society."

Dulles wrote an essay in 1981 about the church as a community of disciples. He outlined its biblical basis (e.g., Acts 6:2) and explained at length why this model is needed more today than in previous generations. He said that since we live in a world where atheism is pervasive, the world religions are attractive, and the lure of wealth, military power, and status are corrupting, then anyone coming to the church (or persevering in it) will be "obliged to hear a personal call and respond in a free, self-conscious manner, somewhat as the first disciples responded to the summons of Christ. The call, if it is to be efficacious, must be heard as coming not simply from the church but from the Lord of the church, so that Jesus himself is seen as the focal point of the Christian's life" (pp. 129–30).

Dulles appreciated the significance of the community-of-disciples model for our times. However, he never allowed this model to stand separately from the others. That is, Dulles believed this model was able to test and perfect the five he advocated. He said the discipleship model could only be adequately understood in light of the other five, "all of which were useful for illuminating different aspects of community and discipleship themselves" (1992, 50). While it is true that all the models are interrelated and shed light on one another, I contend that this sixth model is needed to complete the picture of the four basic structures of the church.

The Postconciliar Identity and Mission of the Church

We have seen that the conciliar theology was christocentric. This was manifested in the images of sacrament, people of God, and servant. We have seen that these images did not resonate fully with people's experiences. Are there any dominant images or models in the postconciliar church? Unfortunately, Vatican II largely ignored the symbol of the kingdom of God; "Any attempt to discuss the church in the world without spelling out the church's role in discerning, promoting and realizing the kingdom in the world is bound to be limited and frustrated" (E. McDonagh 1991, 111). It seems that many in the postconciliar church experienced this frustration and found the church's identity and mission based on the kingdom of God—the most important New Testament image. There has been a shift from christocentrism to theocentrism. Jesus said, "Whoever believes in me believes not only in me but also in the one who sent me." (John 12:44). As Eugene Hillman (1989, 56) explained, "A shift from christocentrism to theocentrism would conform more with the teaching Jesus. . . . Christo-centricism is not an end or a goal; it is a means or 'way' to theocentrism (John 14:6)" (see also O'Collins 1990).

Although neither Pope John Paul II nor Avery Dulles have highlighted the community-of-disciples image since the early 1980s, I would suggest that this model of the church's identity and mission captures the direction and spirituality of many in the postconciliar church (Osborne 1993). The church, the sacrament of the kingdom of God, is a world church of communities of disciples with a threefold mission, especially service and dedication to the poor. The implications of this view for liturgy, authority in the church, social justice, and morality is examined in later chapters.

The Synod of 1985

In order to promote collegiality between the pope and bishops, Vatican II recommended that international synods be held periodically (CD 5). Paul VI began them on a three-year cycle with the Synod of 1967 on the doctrinal and historical coherence of the faith. The seventh was held in 1983. On January 25, 1985,

John Paul II was in Saint Paul-Outside-the-Walls, presiding at prayers for Christian unity, just as John XXIII had done on January 25, 1959. John shocked the church by announcing the twenty-first ecumenical council; John Paul surprised the church by announcing the eighth synod—an extraordinary one—to be held later that year, November 25 to December 8, to mark the twentieth anniversary of the conclusion of Vatican II.

John Paul said that the Council "remains the fundamental event in the life of the modern church" and that for himself it has been "the constant reference point of my every pastoral action." He hoped the synod would revive the "extraordinary atmosphere of ecclesial communion" and "mutual sharing" expressed at the Council, would review the experience of the Council's application, and would continue to apply its insights "in the light of the new exigencies as well."

Commentators agreed that there were reasons this synod was needed. The sixteen conciliar documents were either poorly known or simply ignored. Also, the synod might be able to address two groups in the church: those who disapproved of the Council and those who believed the church had changed even more than the Council had mandated.

The synod assembled 165 bishops, 40 percent of whom had been at Vatican II and 60 percent of whom were from the third world—a sign of the world church. There were ten male observers from other Christian churches.

The synod produced two documents on December 9, 1985— a *Final Report* and a *Message to the People of God*—and offered four main recommendations: the completion of a code of canon law for the Eastern Catholic churches, a clarification of the status of episcopal conferences, a study of the principle of subsidiarity, and the preparation of a universal catechism.

Most synods get three years of preparation and last more than a month. This one opened ten months after its announcement and lasted two weeks. It had its shortcomings—for example, no women were invited (Schüssler-Fiorenza 1986). Probably its real achievement was its very strong affirmation of Vatican II. It correctly understood aggiornamento, which it described as "a missionary openness to the integral salvation of the world."

The history of the synod was written up in journals and books.[4] There was general agreement that three main tendencies emerged at the synod. Dulles called the first group "neo-Augustinian." Augustine (A.D. 354–430), one of the church's most influential theologians, wrote the *City of God*, which pictures Jesus as the one who redirects, reinvigorates, and regenerates human life, which has been corrupted by sin. Augustine identified the church with the kingdom of God, the heavenly city because the world, the earthly city, will one day pass away.

The neo-Augustinians—mainly curial bishops—viewed the church as mystery. By "mystery" they meant what it meant at Vatican II, especially in the constitutions on the church and revelation. That is, Jesus (and not the church) is the light of the world who not only mediates the very life of the triune God to the church but also "fully reveals man to man himself and makes his supreme calling clear" (GS 22). All Christians are invited to participate in this mystery of communion with God.

Robert Imbelli (1986), employing Von Hügel's triad, applauded the synod's stress on the mystical and its focus on the trinitarian and christocentric character of the church. He found that many pre-synodal articles made no reference "to Christ in the many expectations advanced and programs proposed. Management, not mystery, seemed the order of the day." He believed that, although Vatican II stressed the mystical element of the church, "much of the subsequent interpretation and implementation of the council was neglectful of it and concentrated upon the critical [intellectual] and institutional."

There are several conclusions that can be drawn from the theology of the church as mystery. The neo-Augustinians drew a pessimistic conclusion. For them the church was "an island of grace in a world given over to sin" (Dulles 1988a, 191). It was obvious, said these bishops, that the world of 1985 was not converging toward greater freedom, prosperity, or universal harmony, as the Council had said it was in 1965. Furthermore, those Catholics who seek friendship with the world easily fall into materialism, consumerism, and religious indifference. The bishops, influenced by Augustine's pessimism, insisted that the church must shun the secular world and must seek to arouse the sense of God's holy mystery. The world is so darkened by sin that it is only with the guidance of the church that it can attain truth.

The neo-Augustinians refused to let the church be reduced to an instrument for the rebuilding of secular society. They viewed the church as a divinely animated organism that directs people to eternal life. They were deeply convinced that special graces are attached to the church's officeholders, especially the pope. While approving of the accomplishments of the Council, they regarded the postconciliar period as one of turmoil. They strongly resisted all proposals to reform the structures of the church according to contemporary management theory. The church, in their view, was being excessively politicized. They observed that the very people who protest against the power of the papacy were seeking to gain power for themselves and their constituencies. True reform, these bishops maintained, is interior and spiritual, requiring humility, obedience, and respect for authority and tradition.

The second group, the bishops from Canada, Britain, and the United States, Dulles called communitarians. They viewed Jesus as servant of the world, declared that the church and the world have the same frontiers, and underscored the church as sacrament or communion of Christ. The final document said the "ecclesiology of communion is the central and fundamental theme of the council's documents."

In the opinion of these bishops the Council effected great progress, but the failure to achieve communion stemmed from those conservative prelates who failed to carry through the reforms. Some bishops had either resisted the reforms or had partly blocked them. The communitarians said, for example, that the laity still did not have an adequate sense of participation in and shared responsibility for the mission of the church. They said the church needed more development in its collegial and synodal structures. The communitarians wanted a church more internally diversified and, at the same time, one more involved in the promotion of peace, justice, and reconciliation.

The third group, bishops from Asia, Africa, and Latin America, Dulles labeled liberationist. Since these bishops viewed Christ primarily as a liberator, they envisioned a politically involved church that was confrontational and militant. The church must not retreat into itself, they held, but must fearlessly defend and promote authentic human values, such as personal dignity and freedom from oppression, including the right to life. This group favored a preferential option for the poor.

Dulles explained that the image of the church as sacrament was used to unify the diverse views of the three groups:

"Sacrament may be seen as a manifestation of mystery, as a source of communion, and as an instrument of transformation" (ibid., 195). He also believed that the "Final Report" captured all three groups in this "pregnant sentence": "The church as communion is the sacrament for the salvation of the world."

All the commentators on the synod agree that the "Final Report" is a compromise document, written so that no one of the three positions advanced at the synod would either be rejected or allowed to prevail. As Dulles put it, the synod "made it clear that the favorite themes of particular schools can and must be harmonized in the interests of depth, completeness, and unity." But is this true? Does not the sentence Dulles called pregnant reflect the communitarian view? The neo-Augustinians might have preferred the statement to read: "The church as sacrament of the world's salvation should be a strong communion that confronts the evil world." The liberationists might have preferred: "The church as liberator is a communion that itself must be a sacrament of the transformation it preaches." Dulles believed the synod's pregnant sentence leads to "depth, completeness, and unity." But is this true?

A compromise document is quite different from the actual life of the church. These mindsets are in tension and offer different views of the intellectual and devotional life of the church. The neo-Augustinians believe the church is still in a state of siege against a sinful world; that Christ is the light of the world; and that Catholics should be known for their life of prayer, humility, and obedience to the church's authority and tradition. The communitarians see the church as a communion or sacrament of Christ, who is the servant of the world; and believe that Catholics should take responsibility for the life and mission of the church and be involved in the transformation of society. To the liberationists, the church is a prophet of Christ's message of liberation and must confront society the way Jesus confronted the evils of his society, especially patriarchalism, violence, and greed.

Conclusion

The Acts of the Apostles narrates the struggles the early church experienced with its identity and mission, especially once the Jewish disciples began to accept gentiles. Since those days, identity and mission have been basic theological and practical issues, often causing confusion and even crisis.

Some believe that the present crisis of identity within the church is "probably the major theological issue of this century" (Mahoney 1990, 300). The postconciliar church is in turmoil because there does not seem to be a dominant image of the church in the imagination of the people and the clergy and because it is struggling to assimilate Vatican II and its consequences, especially its acceptance of modernity. There is a measure of truth in the judgment that the council documents, given their ambiguity and compromise, "helped to provoke postconciliar confusion. Therefore, the council itself cannot provide a sufficient criterion for the problems of the church [these many] years after the council closed" (Komonchak 1985, 456). Meanwhile, the three theologies of the identity and the mission of the church outlined in this chapter—preconciliar, conciliar, and postconciliar—exist in local churches throughout the universal church. As is clear from this survey of the Synod of 1985, these three theologies and spiritualities exist at the highest levels of the church. The three synodal tendencies are basically the three conciliar theologies. Instead of calling them preconciliar, conciliar, and postconciliar, Dulles labeled them neo-Augustinian, communitarian, and liberationist.

The bishops at the Synod of 1985 were divided. Yet they were able to work together reasonably well. Why? The answer to that question is probably what will help our divided local churches to live and work in harmony as true disciples of Christ. Perhaps the answer is found in the striking insight in the final paragraph of the synod's "Message to the People of God." The bishops prayed: "Finally, may there come in our day that 'new Pentecost' of which Pope John XXIII had already spoken and which we, with all the faithful, await from the Holy Spirit."

5

The Church and Authority

Authority is a sound and indispensable element in human growth. The word means at its roots "to make able to grow" or "to enable another to grow."

Today most Christian churches are experiencing an unprecedented crisis of authority. As Martin Marty explains, "The Christian church seems to have one great thing on its mind in each epoch. In one period it was the Trinity; in another, christology, and the two natures of Christ; in still another it may have been sacraments or the realization of grace. In our time it is authority. The fact that papal 'infallibility' and Protestant biblical 'inerrancy' came to be defended in the nineteenth century and used as weapons between the parties in the twentieth century is an indicator of their issue of authority" (1988).

The word *authority* is usually linked with two others: *power* and *leadership*. *Power* is "the ability to produce effects" (Provost 1989, 195). A person or group can accomplish something. *Power* also "describes the ability to compel others to do something, whether legitimately or not." (Rausch 1989a, 38). *Authority* is the legitimate exercise of power. A person or social unit can direct something to be accomplished. One possessing authority "can bring about some effect, whether of persuasion, definition, or compliance" (ibid.). *Leadership* is the actual leading of others in some direction, relying on one's credibility.

The Source of Church Power

The nature of power, authority, and leadership is less important than their source, exercise, and purpose. In Christianity, the source of power and leadership is the authority of the risen Christ. Only Jesus is Lord (Rom. 10:9) and no one else is to be called teacher, father (a rabbinic title), or master (Matt. 23:8–10).

The risen Christ is alive and powerfully present in human history with and through his Spirit. The Spirit, the personal center of the church, is the basis of the church's authority. Vatican II states, "The Spirit guides the church into the fullness of truth (cf. John. 16:13) and gives her a unity of fellowship and service" (LG 4).

The Scriptures do not provide a systematic theology of the Spirit. However, Scripture scholars discern five major activities of the Spirit as follows: it distributes charisms; it directs the church's mission; as the Paraclete in John's Gospel, it both defends the cause of Jesus against the world and guides each believing Christian; and it assists the church's officeholders (R. E. Brown 1985, 101–13).

John Paul II's fifth encyclical, *Dominum et vivificantem*, discusses the Holy Spirit. This long encyclical, published in June 1986, is not concerned with exegesis but with a philosophical reflection on the scriptural texts. While the letter does provide a sterling defense of human conscience laboring to carry out the work of the Spirit in the world, it has been judged an example of a pessimistic view of life because it one-sidedly portrays the main work of the Spirit as "convincing the world of sin" in a dramatic struggle with Satan (Hebblethwaite 1986c). It reflects a neo-Augustinian outlook on the relationship of church and world.

The thesis of this chapter is that the Spirit operates in the world through the signs of the times and in the church through seven interrelated bearers or voices of authority: papacy, bishops, tradition, Scripture, theologians, the community of the faithful, and each individual's conscience. What this means is that in the church there are not one or two agencies of authority, but rather "a plurality of complementary authorities" (Mahoney 1990, 172).

Each voice is distinct and not fully reducible to any other. Yet no one of them is autonomous and self-sufficient. Each has its limits (see Granfield 1987). To function properly, all depend on one another. For example, the faithful and hierarchy are interdependent. They are not antithetical, nor can one be understood without the other. Similarly, the faithful and theologians are interrelated. "Theological research examines, draws upon, challenges, deepens the faith of people—and therefore must interplay with, be available to, be tested by, make sense to those whose faith is involved" (McCormick 1986, 279).

The Exercise and Purpose of Authority

The improper exercise of authority is called authoritarianism. Authoritarianism demands uncritical, servile, or absolute obedience but offers no solid reasons for its directive or law (Kennedy 1988a, 1988b). The bottom line, therefore, is that those exercising proper authority must do so within the community and not above it.

The church is a hierarchical community with many levels of power, leadership, and authority. Without authoritative structures, the church would lapse into either narrow sectarianism (adhering to a factional viewpoint) or a vapid latitudinarianism (allowing complete freedom of thought and behavior). Presently, the United States is afflicted with a deadly individualism, which in its extremes, even within the church, denies the very notion of communal authority.

John Courtney Murray (1905–67), American Jesuit expert at Vatican II, wrote a seminal article in 1966 on authority in the church (1966b). He demonstrated that those in authority in the church have one function: to unify the church as an interpersonal and missionary community. The officeholders do this by dialogue and consultation. He added that the unitive function has two modalities. First, it is directive. The church is a faith community with its own tradition and so the officeholders should insure that the discipline and work of the community truly coincide with the true identity and mission of the church. Unity requires direction. Second, the unitive is also corrective. Since the church is a community of weak and sinful disciples, the officeholders should insure that nothing hinders the unity and mission of the church. Unity will require corrections.

Presently, authority is under attack in the Catholic Church. Disaffection with officeholders is widespread. Many of the faithful feel alienated, others apathetic, and many have withdrawn from the church. Eugene C. Kennedy suggests that the issuance in 1968 of the controversial encyclical on birth control, *Humanae vitae*, "will be noted one day as the event that killed authoritarianism in the church" (1976a, 248). Nevertheless, authoritarianism—the control of people's conduct—still exists, especially about sexual, marital, and feminist matters, both within and outside the church community.

There are seven interrelated agencies or voices of authority: the episcopacy, the papacy, tradition, Scriptures, theology, the sense of the faithful, and individual conscience. They are distinct, yet no one of them is an autonomous source of authority.

Bishops

Bishop Kenneth Untener of Saginaw, Michigan, wrote in 1984, "Our Western theology tends to start with the universal church and then see local churches as concrete realizations of this. Eastern theology, on the other hand, starts with the local church as the fundamental reality and then sees the universal church as a reality realized by the communion of local churches. The difference may seem subtle, but it can have a major effect on our theology." Vatican II declared that neither the universal church nor the local church has priority over the other because each arises out of the other. The Council declared that "each individual bishop represents his own church, but all of them together in union with the pope represent the entire church joined in the bond of peace, love and unity" and each local church is "a portion of the universal church" (LG 23).

Despite these clarifications, there is widespread confusion among the faithful about the authority and power of bishops in relation to the pope. Some imagine the church as a religious empire directed by an absolute sovereign or as a multinational corporation with the pope as the chief executive officer. The corporation's headquarters are in Rome, with bishops as branch managers around the globe.

This centralized view of the church is not the ancient and, therefore, traditional view of ecclesial authority (see Lauret 1988, 40–42). The existence of the Papal States aggrandized papal prerogatives to the detriment of collegiality. The centralized model received further impetus in the eleventh century under Gregory VII (1073–85), when the church appropriated great legal and political power. This model picked up theological support through Bonaventure (1221–74) and continued right up to Vatican II, when, with the idea of reversing the trend, "the relationship between pope and bishops was the primary item on the agenda" (Cooke 1989, 3).[1]

Bonaventure is an important figure in church history. This saintly Italian Franciscan was a theologian at the University of Paris, a cardinal, the general of the Franciscans (1257–74), and declared a doctor of the church by Sixtus V (1565–90). His theology tends to be pessimistic, especially when compared with that of his contemporary, Thomas Aquinas. Whereas Aquinas celebrated the universality of God's grace and the capacity of the human mind to know God and spiritual realities, Bonaventure stressed the universality of sin and distrusted the range of human reason in religious matters. Concerning the papacy, Bonaventure taught that the pope possessed the fullness of power, while bishops and priests only had power derived from the pope. Bonaventure defended this teaching by distinguishing between the power of orders and the power of jurisdiction. Bishops had the power of orders but this was of no avail to them until the pope granted them the power of jurisdiction, of which he possessed a monopoly. Bishops were, in Bonaventure's words, "vicars of the pope," that is, deputies empowered to implement his teachings. One of the reasons Bonaventure took this position was to safeguard the newly founded Franciscans and Dominicans from episcopal control.

Vatican II generally retrieved the traditional view. According to the Catholic tradition, each local church is distinct and equal as church; each local church is *an* entire church but it is not *the* church (LG 26). Every bishop is a "vicar of Christ" (LG 27). Bishops have full responsibility for their dioceses by exercising their offices of sanctifying, teaching, and governing. Bishops possess authority and power in virtue of the sacrament of orders and are not the pope's instruments and functionaries. They exercise pastoral authority within their dioceses based on the principle of subsidiarity. It was Pius XI who gave this principle a classic definition in 1931: "Nothing should be done by a larger and higher institution that can be done equally well by a smaller and lower institution." For example, today some would insist that if a bishop gives an imprimatur to a book and it is ordered withdrawn by the Roman curia, the bishop has both the right and responsibility to demand specific reasons. If the reasons given are not persuasive, the bishop should not withdraw the imprimatur.

Vatican II countered the notion that bishops are vicars of the pope, "for they exercise an authority which is proper to them, and are quite correctly called 'prelates,' heads of the people whom they govern" (LG 27). The bishops, as successors of the apostles, together with the pope, "govern the house of the living God" (LG 18). The universal church (the house of the living God) is a reality realized by the communion of local churches. The bishops, then, are neither independent of nor separated from the other bishops and the pope. Apostolic authority rests in the entire college of bishops in union with the pope. If a pope ever separated himself from the entire college of bishops, he could not claim to possess the fullness of apostolic authority. The same applies to an individual bishop or a group of bishops.

In conclusion, a bishop has three essential, interrelated relationships: to the pope, the bishop of Rome and head of the episcopal college; to the entire college of bishops; and to the people of his diocese.

Collegiality

Collegiality denotes the corporate responsibility of the whole body of bishops for the unity and mission of the whole church. The word indicates that the church is a community or college of local churches, which together make up the universal church. Collegiality is exercised in many ways, two of which are special: ecumenical councils and international synods.

Since the pope is "pastor of the whole church" and "has full, supreme, and universal power over the church" (LG 22), there naturally arises tension between the primacy of the pope and the power of the bishops. For example, Paul VI believed firmly in both papal primacy and collegiality. During the Council his speeches showed him "plainly struggling to hold these concepts in balance, unwilling to abandon either primacy or collegiality" (Hebblethwaite 1988a, 614).

In September 1965, Paul VI set up the international synods—but did not use the word *collegiality* (Dulles 1985). These assemblies are advisory to the pope. The bishops enjoy no deliberative powers. It is the pope who calls them and determines the agenda. Paul VI held five synods; between 1978 and 1990, John Paul II had called five.

Paul VI never let collegiality restrict his primatial powers. He went his own way on certain issues: he reinforced the teachings about priestly celibacy in 1967 and about contraceptive birth control in 1968. The theme of the Synod of 1969 was collegiality. This topic called for serious discussion in light of the aftermath of *Humanae vitae*. However, no practical directives came from the synod to make collegiality a more significant part of church governance.

John Paul II, too, continues to exercise the primacy in a highly personal style. For him the synods are "an instrument of collegiality." On a visit to Ireland in 1979, he called the postconciliar church "the synodal church," meaning synods have become part of the mainstream of the church's life. Nevertheless, for both these postconciliar popes, ecclesiastical authority resides in the pope and bishops, but especially in the pope, who makes use of the bishops at his own discretion.

Until the popes learn to deal collegially with the bishops, the authority tension will erode the identity and mission of the church. Brian Tierney, a church historian, wrote that the sixteenth ecumenical council, Constance (1414–18), tried to give the church a constitutional structure in accord with the church's own intrinsic collegial nature. But it failed. And the failure was disastrous for the church. "Now we live in the shadow of another great council. The doctrine of collegiality has been defined afresh. But the problem of constitutional structure remains quite open and unresolved. We have a second chance to solve it. And we have less excuse for failing than the men of the fifteenth century. We have not forgotten our history, and we are not condemned to repeat it," Tierney advised (1988, 237).

Episcopal Conferences
Bishops exercise collegiality through national or regional conferences. Such meetings have a long history in the church. Vatican II underscored and reinvigorated them on October 28, 1965, with this statement: "This most sacred synod considers it supremely opportune everywhere that bishops belonging to the same nation or region form an association and meet

together at fixed times. Thus, when the insights of prudence and experience have been shared and views exchanged, there will emerge a holy union of energies in the service of the common good of the churches" (CD 37).

The conferences serve a number of functions. First, they link the local churches to one another in mutual charity and care. Second, they become the occasion for the bishops to authoritatively teach the nation and set policy on moral and disciplinary issues. The United States bishops, for example, issued two masterful pastoral letters, "The Challenge of Peace" in 1983 and "Economic Justice for All" in 1986. In these letters the bishops distinguished between the church's social doctrine and the application of its principles to the concrete circumstances of the times. The applications, as prudential judgments, are not binding in conscience on the faithful. The bishops did ask Catholics to consider seriously the bishops' perspectives when forming their own opinions in the light of the gospel. Third, the conferences can also include doctrinal teachings. It seems clear that "within the church of Christ all pastoral activity has, or should have, a doctrinal basis" (Dulles 1983; see also Dulles 1990). Furthermore, the church's doctrines, customs, and disciplines can be adapted to meet the needs of the regional culture. Technically, this is called inculturation.

Paul VI decreed in 1966 that all nations (or regions) should have episcopal conferences. He even convened the extraordinary Synod of 1969 to discuss collegiality—but no solution was reached. By then, Paul had become wary of episcopal conferences because Vatican II had left their theological basis and power rather vague (see Dulles 1988a, 209–10). Some argued that the conferences tended to undermine the teaching authority of the pope; others feared that the conferences introduced an unnecessary nationalism into the church; and still others cautioned that they could conflict with the teaching authority of individual diocesan bishops.

Concerning inculturation—that is, making the church into a genuine world church by adapting the gospel to different cultures—Paul was at first open to it. In 1971 he made clear in his apostolic letter, *Octogesima adveniens* ("Call to Action"), that it is virtually impossible for himself as pope to specify in detail the relevance of the gospel for all the different cultural contexts in which the various local churches find themselves. "Such is not our ambition, nor is it our mission," he said. "It is up to the Christian communities objectively to analyze the situation which is proper to their own country, to shed on it the light of the gospel's unalterable words, and to draw principles of reflection, norms of judgment, and directives for action for the social teaching of the church." By the time of the Synod of 1974 on evangelization, he became cautious about inculturation, saying it would be "dangerous to speak of diversified theologies according to continents and cultures."

John Paul II, while he has encouraged regional meetings, maintains a highly centralized control over the church. He, too, is wary of inculturation. He prefers the phrase "the evangelization of cultures" and is reluctant to authorize regional liturgical innovations (see Dulles 1985). The pope's theologian, Cardinal Joseph Ratzinger, has written that "episcopal conferences have no theological basis" (Ratzinger and Messori 1985, 23; see also Lindbeck, Hellwig, and Higgins 1985).

The Synod of 1985 on Vatican II discussed episcopal conferences. The assembled bishops were unable to solve the theological debate and so mandated in their "Final Report" that "since bishops' conferences are so useful, indeed necessary in the present pastoral work of the church, a study of their theological standing is desired, and especially a clearer and more profound explanation of their doctrinal authority."

Such a study was undertaken and a draft statement titled "Theological and Juridical Status of Episcopal Conferences" was circulated in the spring of 1988.[2] The document offered essentially the same debate that took place during the Council. It declared that episcopal conferences have no theological basis, "have no competence to establish doctrinal and moral contents," and do not have the teaching authority that individual bishops have in their dioceses. The United States bishops reviewed the Vatican draft statement and criticized it for being "defensive, negative . . . and polemical." The editors of *Commonweal* wrote that the bishops also "found it deficient on historical, juridical, experiential, and thematic grounds. Taking a leading role within the universal college of bishops, they called for the complete revision of the document."[3] As of now, this issue remains unresolved.

Appointment of Bishops

In addition to the tension between the pope and bishops over synods and episcopal conferences, a third issue has become increasingly problematic: the appointment of bishops. The election of bishops by the clergy and people of their dioceses is a venerable and authentic Catholic tradition. However, the church's mechanisms for choosing bishops have changed numerous times, usually in response to changes in the secular world. At one time, kings and other national leaders had a decisive part in the appointment of bishops.

The present practice is that bishops are appointed by the pope (see Reese 1984). This practice is relatively recent, a product of the centralization that followed Vatican I.

There is a positive side to the system of Rome making the appointments: it makes bishops more independent of governments. In the past, many governments demanded a say in the appointment of bishops. However, today there is a measure of dissatisfaction with the present process in certain parts of the world. For instance, in Germany on January 27, 1989, 163 German-speaking theologians from Germany, Austria, the Netherlands, and Switzerland signed the "Cologne Declaration." These theologians—and their points were later ratified by a large number of Spanish, French, Italian, Belgian, and Brazilian theologians—complained that vacant episcopal sees were unilaterally filled without regard for the recommendations of the local church and without respect for their established rights. The Vatican's autocratic methods were declared in contradiction to the gospel spirit of brotherhood, to the positive postconciliar experiences of freedom, and to the collegiality of the bishops.

The catalyst in this case was the appointment of Cardinal Joachim Meisner as archbishop of Cologne, in opposition to the recommendation of the Cologne Cathedral Chapter. According to Bernard Häring, the theologians took this very bold step of publicly voicing their grievances because the bishops "seemed not to dare to play their role of collegiality and subsidiarity" (Windsor 1989).

The Papacy

The Catholic tradition has always recognized the centrality of the Petrine office. Nonetheless, Scripture scholars, historians and theologians agree that the papacy is an evolving institution in a living church (see R. E. Brown 1970, 1984; Brown, Donfried, and Reumann 1973; Tillard 1983; Miller 1983; Fiorenza 1984). Some of its authority and power is of divine design, hence permanent; and some of human design, hence changeable.

At Vatican I it was declared infallibly in *Pastor aeternus* of July 18, 1870, that Christ made Peter the "visible head of the church," and gave him "a primacy of true and proper jurisdiction," and "perpetual successors." Peter's successors have "full and supreme power of jurisdiction."

Such infallible statements are studied, explained, and interpreted by theologians. What did they mean in 1870 and what do they mean today? As a living community, the church holds onto its tradition by interpreting it for the contemporary situation. To simply repeat doctrinal statements without reinterpretation would freeze them into the language of one historical era, cripple the church's teaching function because she would be teaching in a language the people do not understand, and disallow any doctrinal development (see McCormick 1984).

The magisterium has officially taught that the Gospels are not biographies or lives of Jesus. The Pontifical Biblical Commission issued an *Instruction on the Historical Truth of the Gospels* in 1964, declaring that the Gospels contain the words and deeds of Jesus as theologically interpreted by Jesus' disciples, especially the four evangelists who edited, synthesized, and explicated the apostolic tradition that came down to them. For example, what specifically do the Gospels say about Peter during and after the ministry of Jesus? According to tradition, Peter founded the church in Rome and was its first bishop. But these "facts" are not found in the Gospels. How did they get into the tradition?

In 1973 the CDF published another landmark document, *Mysterium ecclesiae*. Here the church explained that there is a fourfold historical conditioning of all faith documents. These infallible statements are affected by the presuppositions of the authors, the concerns ("the intention of solving certain questions"), the thought categories ("the changeable conceptions of a given epoch"), and the available vocabulary of the times. In light of these principles, theologians examine the statements of Vatican I about the papacy, asking if they have biblical and historical limitations in view of the Vatican standards.

The consensus of Protestant and Catholic scholars is that in the New Testament "the image of Peter was adapted to meet the needs of the church after his death (R. E. Brown 1975a, 77–78). Peter became a symbol for those leaders who had to interpret the Christian and apostolic message for their times and churches. Futhermore, the "emergence of a single bishop, distinct from the college of presbyter-bishops, came relatively late in the Roman church, perhaps not until the second century. Leaders, such as Linus, Cletus, Clement, known to us from the early Roman church, were probably prominent presbyter-bishops but not necessarily 'monarchical' bishops" (R. E. Brown 1970, 53).

This brief historical account seems to suppose the possibility of continued adaptability of the papacy to meet church needs. Vatican I underscored the pope's jurisdiction over all Christians. Why? "Jurisdiction may have been a very appropriate expresssion for Petrine authority in the nineteenth-century-European context where the legitimate rights and claims of religion were trampled upon by the emerging national states" (R. E. Brown 1975a, 78).

Vatican II did not substantially change Vatican I's teaching on the papacy: "For in virtue of his office, that is, as Vicar of Christ and pastor of the whole Church, the Roman Pontiff has full, supreme, and universal power over the Church. And he can always exercise this power freely" (LG 22). Nevertheless, something new happened at Vatican II (Rausch 1986, 168). The Council shifted emphases, setting Vatican I in a new context and, therefore, making clear that there are limits to papal authority. First, the monarchical authority of the pope was tempered by collegiality, whereby all the bishops share responsibility for the identity and mission of the church. Second, the teaching that episcopal power was delegated by the pope shifted to sacramental theology, whereby episcopal power flowed from the episcopacy as a sacrament; in fact, "the fullness of the sacrament of orders" (LG 26).

With these shifts, the pope was more securely located within the church rather than over against it as its juridical head. In other words, the stress of Vatican I was on the church as a juridical institution with the rights of authority united in the pope at the very top of the church. At Vatican II the church's structure was viewed not from the top down to the bottom but from the people of God to the pope, with the pope called to use his supreme authority, extensive power, and charismatic leadership to unify and serve the "house of the living God."

Papal Authority

The pope has authority in three interrelated spheres. First, as the bishop of Rome, he, like other bishops, is responsible for his diocese. John XXIII, for example, convened a synod for his diocese in January 1960—the first in Rome's history—which made its own rules affecting only the diocese of Rome. Second, the pope is the "successor of Peter." Jesus made Peter "a permanent and visible source and foundation of unity of faith and fellowship" (LG 18). The pope is not the bishop of the world as though the world were all one diocese. But, in his role as the visible foundation of unity, the pope has the discretionary power to intervene directly into a particular diocese or in differences between bishops. Such interventions are proper only if they are necessary for the church's unity and mission. Third, as the vicar of Peter, the pope is leader of the college of bishops and the universal church. He can convene the bishops to implement what he believes is essential to the unity of the "house of the living God." The pope is the rock of unity and the strengthener of his brothers.

Papal Teaching

Church teachings are classified as either infallible or noninfallible. The former, always made with the consent of all the bishops (the extraordinary magisterium), comprise doctrines of the church to which the church irrevocably commits itself. These are divinely revealed truths and demand the assent of faith. In modern times infallible statements are very rare. The last three were Mary's immaculate conception (1854), the infallibility of the pope (1870), and Mary's assumption (1950).

Noninfallible teachings (ordinary magisterium) are the day-to-day interpretations by the magisterium of the church's faith and morals. These teachings are provisional and reformable. They are not necessarily inerrant. However, they are not to be treated lightly since the pope and bishops are Spirit-guided officeholders commissioned to teach in Jesus' name. In fact, at Vatican II, the bishops said the faithful should adhere to the teachings of the bishops in matters of faith and morals "with a religious assent of soul" (LG 25). Furthermore, "this religious submission of will and of mind must be shown in a special way to the authentic teaching authority of the Roman Pontiff, even when he is not speaking ex cathedra" (LG 25). Assent to and dissent from the ordinary magisterium have been hotly debated in the postconciliar church.

Interpreting Papal Teaching

Today the global church is struggling over two diametrically opposed interpretations of Petrine authority. One group regards some of the papal and curial pronouncements as historically and culturally conditioned documents open to investigation and, if warranted, even to dissent. The second group disagrees vehemently with this approach. They appeal "to a literal, ahistorical, and nonhermeneutical reading of papal and curial pronouncements as a sure bulwark against the tides of relativism, the claims of science, and other inroads of modernity" (J. A. Coleman 1989). This second group is labeled Catholic fundamentalists, or "integralists." Integralists assert "that Catholic orthodoxy is expressed in, and bound up with, a logically organized system of interconnected doctrines each of which goes to make up a divinely guaranteed whole" (G. Daly 1985, 776).

The term *integralists* has its origins around 1907, when Pius X condemned Modernism. At that time, as we have seen, the modernists were considered unfaithful to the church and especially the Petrine ministry. Those attached to the papacy and papal teachings in the manner described above called themselves "integral Catholics."

Some of the well-known organizations with an integralist perspective are the Catholics United for the Faith (United States), *The Wanderer* (a United States magazine edited by A. J. Matt, Jr.), Confrontatis (the Netherlands), Schönstadt (Germany), Communione e Liberazione (Italy), the Fraternity of St. Pius X (France and Switzerland), and Opus Dei, founded in Spain in 1928 by Josemaria Escriva de Belaguer (1902–75). Several of the European groups have chapters in the United States.

The integralists attribute inerrancy to all papal teachings. They emphasize that all teaching authority is in the final analysis papal teaching authority. Their litmus test for orthodoxy is uncritical adherence to papal and curial documents. They are quick to report any deviations from these norms on the part of priests, theologians, and bishops, or in religion texts, catechism classes, and liturgical practices. The conflict between the integralists and those who seek an integrated balance among the seven fonts or sources of the Christian faith has prompted essays about a "chill factor" in the church (see McCormick 1984) and about a "psychological exodus" from the church (see Windsor 1989).

John Paul II tends towards the integralist view. For example, the Cologne Declaration objected to the manner in which the pope sometimes teaches. There is a long tradition in the church to group teachings according to their importance for salvation. The technical expression is a "hierarchy of truths." Vatican II reminded Catholics "that in Catholic teaching there exists an order or 'hierarchy' of truths, since they vary in their relationship to the foundation of the Christian faith" (UR 11). The signers of the Cologne Declaration accused John Paul of violating this order of precedence, specifically when, in addresses to theologians and bishops, he "has connected the teaching on birth control with fundamental truths of the faith, such as the holiness of God and salvation through Jesus Christ." To give the ordinary magisterium the same prerogatives given the extraordinary magisterium is referred to by some theologians as "magisterial maximalism" or "creeping infallibility." These terms indicate that some believers will stretch the infallibility of the pope to such an extent that no dissent, even in the realm of fallible teachings, would be permitted. Integralists accuse dissenters of attacking fundamental cornerstones of Catholic doctrine.

Some wonder why John Paul teaches as he does. The answer may rest in his interpretation of Vatican II. We have seen that the Council insisted that a "religious submission of will and mind must be shown to the authentic teaching authority" (LG 25) of the pope, even when he is not speaking infallibly. Since Vatican II upheld this principle, John Paul adheres to it. Peter Hebblethwaite believes that for John Paul the Council "was an end and not a starting point; it settled questions rather than opened them up; it changed the vocabulary, but it did not result in any substantial change; it poured old wine into new bottles" (1979 b).

Tradition

Christians believe the church's long and rich tradition originated when the first apostles began to proclaim that God's saving love had been definitively revealed or manifested in the life, death, and resurrection of Jesus Christ and through his Spirit.

The origin and development of this tradition creates a tension between the past and the present, that is, between what the Father has done for our salvation in Jesus Christ and what the Spirit is still doing today. Since the two poles of the tradition "evoke each other and complement each other" (Schoof 1970, 197), both must be retained lest the church fall into primitivism (which accepts only the tradition of the apostolic church) or modernism (which rejects continuity over the ages). Both of these extremes lead to traditionalism: the attempt to freeze the living tradition at a specific stage of the church's history (see Pottmeyer 1992).

The nature of tradition and its relationship to both Scripture and the magisterium has been the subject of considerable study and development. In the preconciliar period the Tridentine explanation prevailed. Trent taught that Scripture and tradition were "two sources of revelation," the one written and the other unwritten. It also said that the living magisterium was the divinely authorized custodian and interpreter of both Scripture and tradition.

Unfortunately, during the preconciliar period many Catholic theologians interpreted Trent to mean that Scripture and tradition were two separate sources of revelation and that tradition was the final judge of the scriptures (McBrien 1981, 64–65).

At the first session of Vatican II, a document with this inadequate theology was presented to the bishops by Cardinal Ottaviani. In the debates of November 14–20, 1962, this draft met with severe criticism. The document emphasized that tradition consisted in an objective set of doctrines or precepts that came down from the first apostles and were passed on verbally, especially by the magisterium. Many bishops—almost two-thirds—judged this theology to be inadequate because its view of tradition was too static and unecumenical. These bishops wanted more emphasis on the subjective, dynamic, and nonverbal aspects of tradition, so that it would be identified with the total life and mission of the church. In other words, these bishops believed that all the disciples of Christ must be conscious bearers of the Christian tradition.

The debate became so heated that John XXIII intervened and appointed a new commission to prepare a different text for discussion. Yves Congar, whose masterly studies in the theology of tradition were published shortly before the Council, exerted a major influence on the Constitution on Revelation—a document that was finally promulgated in the last session of the council on November 18, 1965 (see Dulles 1992, 87–104).

For the purposes of this chapter, it is sufficient to point out two distinctions made in the conciliar document. First, it declared that tradition involves more than objective doctrines or precepts. It also involves a process whereby the sacred history of Jesus is revealed in the Scriptures and celebrated in the liturgy. From generation to generation the church hands on and perpetuates "all that she herself is, all that she believes" (DV 8) through worship, religious education, devotions, doctrines, saints, art works, and the Scriptures. Since Christianity is a distinct religion with its own beliefs about God, the world, community, and the individual, tradition consists of content about Jesus Christ and his church that is handed down consciously and purposefully from one generation to another. Each generation is its heir and continues the process by holding fast to the faith and bearing witness to it (DV 10). At Vatican II, for example, all the documents quoted not only the Scriptures but also previous councils, doctors of the church, and popes.

Both process and message are intrinsically interrelated. Schillebeeckx explained: "Christianity is not a message which has to be believed, but an experience of faith which becomes a message, and, as an explicit message, seeks to offer a new possibility of life experience to others who hear it from their own experience of life (1981a, 50). Rahner wrote that "revelation is an historical dialogue between God and man in which something happens, and in which communication is related to the happening, the divine action. . . . Revelation is a saving happening, and only then and in relation to this a communication of truths" (Nichols 1990, 221–22). The writings on revelation by Congar, Schillebeeckx, Rahner, and others were creatively synthesized right after the Council by Gabriel

Moran, presently at New York University. The thesis of his books on revelation and religious education—that revelation is a present, personal, social, and historical happening—revolutionized the intellectual and devotional lives of many United States Catholics (see Moran 1966a, 1966b, 1972).

Second, there is a distinction between tradition and traditions. Tradition is the living faith of the church that establishes the community's identity and mission; traditions are customary ways of doing or expressing matters related to the faith. The church is protected by the Spirit, who prevents it from deviating fundamentally from its life of faith and from the truth of the gospel. Traditions develop as each generation lives the faith within its cultural experiences in the Spirit. A rich variety of traditions has developed, for example, priestly celibacy, Mass in Latin, election of the pope by cardinals, and Marian devotions. Believers learn to select from these nonessential traditions and when to modify them. This process will continue over time and as "the church constantly moves toward the fullness of divine truth until the words of God reach their complete fulfillment in her" (DV 8). A perennial temptation in Christianity is to confuse nonessential traditions with tradition—and vice versa. It is tradition that is authoritative.

Scriptures

Tradition is logically and chronologically prior to Scripture. Both "are to be accepted and venerated with the same sense of devotion and reverence" (DV 9). The Scriptures are the living tradition of the first generation Christians written under the inspiration of the Spirit. These books bind the church so that it is in them she finds the meaning of her life and mission. Since these first-century texts were written for their respective churches, we cannot expect to find in them answers to such contemporary problems as nuclear war, for example. Nevertheless, they do provide Christian principles with which to evaluate our personal and communal problems. It is from the Word of God that the church draws "everything which it presents for belief as divinely revealed" (DV 10). It is the Scriptures that are the "soul of sacred theology" (DV 24).

The Bible, the book of the church, is interpreted in and through the church. The magisterium "has been entrusted exclusively" with the task of authoritatively interpreting the Scriptures, even as the whole church stands under and serves the word of God (DV 10).

Because the inspired books are historically and culturally conditioned, the magisterium should interpret them in association with the scholars trained to do so, namely the theologians, exegetes, and historians. The collaboration of the magisterium and theologians in interpreting the Scriptures has not been a smooth relationship during the twentieth century. For instance, at the heart of the Modernism crisis was the question of authority—the authority of the hierarchy to interpret Scripture versus the authority of scientific and historical scholarship.

In fact, the magisterium, tradition, and Scripture are interrelated voices of authority. The Council addressed this point: "It is clear, therefore, that sacred tradition, sacred scripture, and the teaching authority of the Church, in accord with God's most wise design, are so linked and joined together that one cannot stand without the others, and that all together and each in its own way under the action of the one Holy Spirit contribute effectively to the salvation of souls" (DV 10).

Theology

The Christian faith does not exist in some "pure" state. As soon as the Christian experience of God and his intentions is brought to expression by explanation, interpretation, and questions, theology begins. Theology, in the classic expression of Anselm of Canterbury (1033–1109), is "faith seeking understanding."

In the medieval universities, theology was honored as the "queen of the sciences." Its intellectual methods and criteria compared well with the methods of other sciences. With remarkable intellectual courage, theologians engaged the theories and challenges of their contemporaries. In doing so, they did not simply repeat magisterial teaching. Rather, they also used the new philosophical and historical resources recovered from the ancient world to reinterpret the tradition. They knew that without dialogue about contemporary philosophical and historical problems, their theology would be conducted "from deep within the hinterland of faith, safely but irrelevantly" (Hebblethwaite 1975, 114). Theologians worked within and for the church and without need of an ecclesiastical mandate.

Today there is a Vatican view of theology that is clearly at odds with the traditional understanding. The Vatican, continuing the policy of Pius XII in *Humani generis* (1950), urges theologians to show how a truth of faith or a theological statement is grounded in Scripture and the tradition of the church. For example, John Paul II in his first encyclical, *Redemptor hominis*, stated that theologians are called to "serve the magisterium, which in the Church is entrusted to the bishops." While "a certain pluralism of methodology" is legitimate, theology may not depart from "fundamental unity in the teaching of faith and morals." "Close collaboration by theology with the magisterium is indispensable." Nobody "can make theology, as it were, a simple collection of his own personal ideas." From this, one might conclude that John Paul II would describe a theologian as "a person who is formally authorized to teach what the church teaches and to do so in the name of the church" (Komonchak 1987).

Why this radical shift from the traditional view to the present Vatican understanding of the work of theologians? There are two causes (ibid.). First is the advent of modernity. With the rise of modern science in the seventeenth century, the church lost much of its power, leadership, and authority in society. Science promised to enhance human life by providing social, economic, and political advantages. As described earlier, the official church reacted negatively and adopted a siege mentality whereby it became a countersociety, centralized and bureaucratic. Within this defensive context, theology's main function became the defense and explanation of the official teachings of this countersociety.

Second, once Vatican II accepted the positive values of modernity, theology was free to take many creative directions. In bringing the church out of its countercultural and anti-modernity mindset, Vatican II inaugurated many changes in the life of the church and in its relations to both society and the other religious communities. Uniformity and centralization were undercut when local and regional churches were encouraged to adapt the gospel to their various cultural circumstances. These changes in doctrine and discipline involved changes in theological methodology. Following the lead of the Council, many theologians abandoned the language and methods of neoscholasticism. New theologies developed: political, liberation, feminist, black, and process. Encouraged by the Council's concern for such issues as the needs of the modern world, atheism, and ecumenism, theologians addressed these and other public issues.

The effects of Vatican II on theology, as just described, are ambiguous. Some rejoiced with the changes brought by new theology; others did not. For instance, Jacques Maritain (1882–1973), a renowned Catholic philosopher, believed that the theological developments and controversies that arose after the Council were so terrible that, by comparison, the crisis of Modernism was only a mild case of hay fever. Similarly, George A. Kelly vehemently argued (1982) that the chief responsibility for the ongoing difficulties of the postconciliar Catholic Church in the United States rested not with this or that bishop, but with the body of the United States bishops. Kelly charged all the bishops with disloyalty to the pope and "appeasement" of the theologians. He was convinced that the majority of United States theologians and Scripture scholars fully intend to "dismantle the Catholic church."

Cardinal Ratzinger, prefect of the CDF, also interpreted the postconciliar years as disastrous for the church. The church, he said, had passed from "self-criticism to self-destruction."[4] The unity the Council expected had not materialized because many went beyond what the Council recommended. Theologians and others invoked a false "spirit of the Council" to justify their teachings and practices. Ratzinger called for a return to the Council's letter and true spirit. He called for a "restoration," by which he meant that the church must now "search for a new balance after all the exaggerations of an indiscriminate opening to the world, and after the overly positive interpretation of an agnostic and atheistic world" have been considered (Ratzinger 1985, 37). This search involves a turning back "beyond the preconciliar attitudes to an earlier, pre-modern vision of the faith." His vision comes from Bonaventure, the noted thirteenth-century Franciscan, whose theology was outlined earlier in this chapter.

To achieve this restoration, Ratzinger has fostered a series of actions: greater recourse to the new Code of Canon Law; a reassertion of Vatican authority; the appointment of bishops favorable to a centralized view of church authority; and the censuring of theologians considered harmful to the church. It should not come as a surprise that some fear that "restoration" is simply a code word for undoing the deeper thrust of the postconciliar renewal and reform (see Lernoux 1989).

Doctrinal Control and Dissent

At Vatican II the bishops declared that "the task of authentically interpreting the Word of God, whether written or handed on, has been entrusted exclusively to the living teaching office of the church, whose authority is exercised in the name of Jesus Christ" (DV 10). Since the church is a community of disciples, theologians should assist the hierarchical magisterium with its teaching. However, it is obvious that there is going to be a measure of tension between them. At Vatican II when the hierarchy was unduly exalted (as the quote above indicates), the result was "a certain downgrading of other teachers in the church. Unlike the scholastic theology manuals, Vatican II made no allusion to the scholarly magisterium of theologians" (Dulles 1985, 401). Nevertheless, theologians believe there is room for dissent by an individual or a group from the church's authoritative, noninfallible teachings.

There is tension between the magisterium and theologians because the Christian tradition, even though Spirit-guided, is ambiguous—fundamentally it is to be trusted, but it is ever in need of self-reform, self-correction, and self-clarification because all human knowledge that is concerned with specific human actions is imperfect and contingent. Despite the continuity it often claims for its teachings, the hierarchical magisterium has struggled with this ambiguity and frequently changed its explanation and/or attitude in many of its theological pronouncements and disciplinary practices. The following are three modern examples: (1) Pius XII identified the Mystical Body of Christ, *the* church, with the Roman Catholic Church, but Vatican II did not; (2) John Courtney Murray was silenced for his teachings on religious freedom in the 1950s, but Vatican II endorsed and promulgated his foundational ideas; and (3) in the early church, priests administered confirmation, but in the preconciliar church, the authoritative teaching and common theological opinion was that only bishops could administer this sacrament; Vatican II restored the practice to priests (OE 13).

Paul VI and Theology

Paul VI, in keeping with his two most constant concerns—prudent change of church life and discipline, and a faithful safeguarding of the papal office—made great efforts to smooth the relationship between the magisterium and theologians. On December 6, 1965, two days before the closing of the Council, he changed the name of the Holy Office to the CDF. His motive was to encourage sound doctrine. At the first of the international synods, the Synod of 1967, he set as the topic of discussion the doctrinal and historical coherence of the Catholic faith. In 1969 he set up an International Theological Commission to assist the CDF. In 1971 the CDF instituted new procedures for the examination of doctrinal cases of alleged errors. During his pontificate the CDF issued a number of instructions on controversial issues: Incarnation and Trinity (1972), infallibility (1973), sexual ethics (1975), and the ordination of women (1976). Most of these instructions were theologically incisive; some, like the one on the ordination of women, evoked controversy and dissent. As we will see in chapter 10, despite Paul VI's efforts to work with theologians, his 1968 encyclical on birth control evoked worldwide dissent. He was profoundly shaken by the critical international reaction to it during his last ten years in office.

John Paul II and Dissent

The pontificate of John Paul II has been marked by a series of well-publicized confrontations with dissenting theologians and by the publication of a major document in 1990 that banned public dissent.

The confrontations began in earnest once Cardinal Ratzinger was appointed prefect of the CDF in November 1981. Since then the CDF has silenced many famous theologians, removed them from their teaching or editorial posts, or condemned their books. Censured were Jacques Pohier (France) (see Jossua 1987); Edward Schillebeeckx (Holland); Hans Küng (Germany); Leonardo Boff (Brazil); Jose Maria Castillo, Juan Antonio Estrada, and Benjamin Forcano (Spain) (see Goslin 1988); and Charles Curran and Matthew Fox (United States).

The case histories of these men make interesting but disturbing reading, especially of the two that received international media attention: Charles Curran and Hans Küng. Curran's case is discussed in chapter 10. A review of Küng's case follows.

Hans Küng, a priest born in Switzerland in 1928, has been in controversy with the Vatican ever since his doctoral dissertation from the Sorbonne was published in 1957. In this ecumenical work he argued that Luther's doctrine of justification as explained by the prominent Swiss Reformed theologian, Karl Barth (1886–1968), was fundamentally the same as the Council of Trent's. Küng subsequently produced books, some of them best-sellers in Europe, in which he questioned such teachings as papal infallibility, the virginal conception of Jesus, and Mary's title as Mother of God. On December 18, 1979, the Vatican informed him that he "can no longer be considered a Catholic theologian or function as such in a teaching role." The immediate occasion of the Vatican's action was Küng's attack on the doctrine of papal infallibility (see Swidler 1987; J. J. Hughes 1971, 1980a).

In the past when theologians fell into severe disfavor with Rome, they "were either censured, silenced, made to recant, suspended from priestly office, excommunicated, burned at the stake—or all of the above" (Swidler 1987, 198). Küng suffered none of these punishments. The quasi-silencing of Küng was something new. It did result in the loss of his membership on the Catholic theology faculty at the University of Tübingen. Nevertheless, since he enjoyed tenure in the German (state) university system, he remained at Tübingen as professor of ecumenical theology and the director of its ecumenical institute. As such, his position was unconnected with the Catholic theological faculty.

Another conflict between theologians and the Vatican erupted over "Instruction on the Ecclesial Vocation of the Theologian," a twenty-eight-page document issued by the CDF on May 24, 1990. This instruction was addressed primarily to bishops and through them to theologians. It encouraged bishops to "maintain and develop trust with theologians in the fellowship of charity." Avery Dulles called the document "quite good," saying, "I've never seen a Vatican document give so much attention to the difficulty theologians have in accepting certain authoritative teachings."[5]

The instruction said some positive things about theology. It said, for example, that theology is a valid "scientific" pursuit, and should use history and other human sciences as well as the surrounding culture as instruments for understanding the mysteries of faith. On the other hand, its points about the mission of the magisterium and the ban it placed on public dissent prompted alarm and even furor in some places. In Europe, Küng, Schillebeeckx, and others responded with the so-called Tübingen Declaration of July 12, 1990, which accused the Vatican of attacking the legitimate freedom and autonomy of theologians in a repressive and dictatorial fashion. A *Commonweal* editorial said the instruction "may be the prelude to further steps that could provoke—we choose our words carefully—forced schism, forced apostasy, or widespread hypocrisy."[6] Charles Curran promptly declared that the instruction was "akin to Rome's denunciations of Americanism and Modernism" (Feuerherd 1990). Then, more than a year later, Richard A. McCormick and Richard P. McBrien argued at length that the document attempted to impose "the privatization of theological reflection." By privatization they meant that the document restricted theology's critical and creative function to the hierarchical magisterium and theologians and thereby removed theology from the scrutiny of the public and the rest of the believers in the church community (McCormick and McBrien 1991). What did the document say to provoke such strong criticism?

The document explained the important mission the magisterium has in the church. The church, the people of God, has been gifted with God's own infallibility. However, the people can participate in this infallibility only under the guidance of the magisterium, "the sole authentic interpreter of the Word of God." The "magisterial teaching, by virtue of divine assistance, has a validity beyond its argumentation." The magisterium's mission is threefold: "to affirm the definitive character of the Covenant"; to "protect God's people from the danger of deviation and confusion"; and to guarantee them "the objective possibility of professing the authentic faith free from error."

Theologians, the document said, should "submit loyally" to all the teachings of the magisterium. If a theologian has difficulties with a teaching, he or she "has the duty to make known to the magisterial authorities the problems raised by the teaching in itself." In any case, the theologian should avoid turning to the mass media. Dissent is forbidden. "One cannot speak of a 'right to dissent' in the church." Dissent in opposition to and in competition with the church's magisterium only creates "a kind of 'parallel magisterium' of theologians." If dissent occurs, the magisterium has the right and duty to intervene by taking serious measures to guard the integrity of the faith. In doing so, the church condemns intellectual positions publicly taken, not the individual theologians. "The fact that these procedures can be improved does not mean that they are contrary to justice and right."

There was widespread disagreement with this integralist document, which equated dissent with disrespect for, and even rejection of, the hierarchical magisterium. Many questions were raised. Why was nothing said about the episcopal magisterium? The document's exclusive concern was with the papal magisterium (Hebblethwaite 1990c). "How far can the magisterium bind the faithful (including theologians) in matters that are not of faith?" asked Ladislas Orsy (1990). Why were the theologians not treated with trust? Why were they presented as troublemakers who challenged the magisterium, did not love the church, and had sold out to worldliness? And why were the theologians cast, at best, as supercatechists, and at worst, as mouthpieces for approved Vatican theology?

The Function of the CDF

How effective is this attempt by the Vatican to mediate theological disputes through the CDF? On the one hand, some see its positive side. Jeffrey Gros, a Christian Brother and ecumenist, argues it can be healthy. The church's having a centralized body oversee its teachings attests to "the church's intellectual vitality, its commitment to seriousness in discerning God's truth in Jesus Christ, and its healthy dialectic between continuity and change" (1990). Edward Cuddy, historian and political scientist, writes in a similar vein: "The church needs her rebels. But rebels also need the church. Her living tradition, nourished by many intellectual currents, often provides the vision underlying their commitment. Church authorities are the friction points which force dissenters toward greater intellectual clarity and intensity. Catholicism provides a structure to harness creative energies and a living community to test and assimilate (however painfully) new ideas" (1979).

On the other hand, some have been deeply disturbed by the silencing of theologians. The Cologne Declaration was written to express "solidarity with all Christian women and men who are scandalized by the latest developments in our church." Gregory Baum pointed out that John Paul II has as the key concept in several of his encyclicals the individual as a "subject," that is, the individual person as a responsible agent in society and in all relevant institutions. For example, in 1987 in *Sollicitudo rei socialis*, the pope wrote: "No social group—for example, a political party—has the right to usurp the role of sole leader, since this brings about the destruction of the true subjectivity of society and of the individual citizens, as happens in every form of totalitarianism. In this situation, the individual and the people become 'objects,' despite all the declarations to the contrary."

Baum commented on this passage by saying that "we have then the curious contradiction that at the very time the Vatican tries to return to centralization, control and authoritarian rule, the church's magisterium affirms the divinely grounded human destiny to be 'the subject of society and its institutions.'"[7]

Sidney Callahan's critique was even more trenchant: "We also appear absurdly hypocritical in preaching freedom of conscience to the world when we do not live by those same standards within our own community. Who will stay in a church that seems to demand that the free assent of conscience needed to enter the church will be the last free decision one will ever make?" (1986).

The Theology of Dissent

Dissent from official church teachings has always had a place in the church (see Fauss 1989). Since Vatican II, and especially since *Humanae vitae* in 1968, dissent has had more notoriety, partly because of the media. Charles Curran was sensitive to this fact and admitted that on the eve of the impending 1968 encyclical he himself was alarmed at the crises of conscience he anticipated for both priests and laity. He said, "I was convinced that most Catholics and priests did not even know about the right to dissent from authoritative noninfallible, hierarchical teachings" (Cuddy 1979, 497).

In 1968, shortly after the encyclical was issued, the United States bishops were forced to propose norms for theological dissent. They did so in their pastoral letter "Human Life in Our

Day." They set down three conditions: "The expression of theological dissent from the magisterium is in order only if the reasons are serious and well-founded, if the manner of dissent does not question or impugn the teaching authority of the church, and is such as not to give scandal." Some writers have delineated principles that permit dissent. First, since critical theology involves the interpretation of the faith for its own times, dissent about what the faith means today is inevitable. However, dissent as such is not the problem. The problem is how to use it for the unity and growth of the church's identity and mission. Dissent is the church's self-correcting source of reform and renewal.

Second, "since [theology] is of the public, with the public and for the public, it must be done in public," argues Richard McCormick (1986, 279). The media can actually assist in this process. Moreover, theologians should be able to engage in their task with freedom so that there is room for trial and error and mutual criticism. "In a pluralistic society, a non-pluralistic church would be an anachronism" (Modras 1979). Where the self-correcting processes of theological debate do not suffice, the hierarchy should intervene. This should begin at the local or regional level and only later at the Vatican level.

Third, since theology is an academic discipline, the signers of the Cologne Declaration asserted that judgments against theologians must rest on legitimate reasons and be substantiated in accordance with recognized academic norms.

And finally, since there is a major difference between infallible and noninfallible teaching, it is wrong to expect the same kind of uncritical and unqualified obedience for noninfallible teachings as is expected for infallible teachings. Canon 752 says official magisterial texts do not require an assent of faith in the area of noninfallible teaching, but, rather, a *religiosum obsequium* of intellect and will. The English translation reads "a religious respect of intellect and will." Bernard Häring believes the respect expected has two dimensions. First, out of religious loyalty a believer will honestly and sincerely endeavor to understand and appropriate the teachings. Second, again out of religious loyalty, a believer will "examine the teachings critically and, should the situation arise, assert those reservations which seem necessary without rebellion against authority" (Häring 1987, 238).

The Sense of the Faithful

The sense of the faithful *(sensus fidelium)* means that the people have a certain existential affinity or "connaturality" or "a deep sure-guiding feeling" with the realities of the faith so that they can spot what is true (orthodoxy) and what is wrong (error or heresy). This idea has a long and varied history in the Christian tradition. At Vatican II the bishops reaffirmed this ancient doctrine: "The body of the faithful as a whole, anointed as they are by the Holy One . . . cannot err in matters of belief. Thanks to a supernatural sense of the faith . . . it manifests this unerring quality when . . . it shows universal agreement in matters of faith and morals. For, by this sense of faith which is aroused and sustained by the Spirit of truth, God's people accepts not the word of men but the very word of God (see 1 Thess. 2:13). It clings without fail to the faith once delivered to the saints (see Jude 3), penetrates it more deeply by accurate insights, and applies it more thoroughly to life. All this it does under the lead of a sacred teaching authority to which it loyally defers" (LG 12).

Many were disappointed with the Council's explanation of the sense of the faithful. For example, the last sentence in the above quotation actually downgrades the *sensus fidelium* because nothing is said about how, in its own way and as directed by the Spirit, it is a separate source of Christian faith.

Today, because we are perhaps more conscious than previous generations of the social, historical, and psychological conditioning of human ideas, we have several questions about the way the sense of the faithful has and does function. For instance, can we name a significant doctrine (e.g., Mary's immaculate conception or assumption) that has truly had a universal consensus? Can we credit the faithful over the past two thousand years with the kind of scriptural and theological expertise that go into explaining even the two Marian doctrines just mentioned? Can we gauge the motivation of the faithful in their assent to certain doctrines? Were they impelled by prayerful familiarity with the gospel or were their opinions shaped by prejudice or passion or ideology?

Despite these theological questions, Dulles points out that we must ultimately rely on a prayerful discernment of the Spirit: "If we have identified the word of God, it serves as a criterion for recognizing God's people, and if we know who God's people are, we have a clue for ascertaining the word of God" (1986).

In conclusion, it seems impossible to overestimate the importance of the community of disciples in fostering the faith century after century. Their authority rests in the quality of their witness. John Henry Newman (1801–90), a priest, cardinal, and the leading Catholic apologist of the nineteenth century, was asked how truth is maintained in society. His answer applies to Christ's communities of disciples. The truth, Newman wrote, "has been upheld in the world not as a system, not by books, not by argument, not by temporal power, but by the personal influence of such men [and women] as . . . are at once the teachers and patterns of it."[8] At Vatican II the bishops declared that "we can justly consider that the future of humanity lies in the hands of those who are strong enough to provide coming generations with reasons for living and hoping" (GS 31). The ninth international synod, the Synod of 1987 on the laity, addressed this perennial problem of active witness when the bishops appealed to Catholics to become more active participants in church and social matters. However, despite all the talk of shared responsibility and equality based on baptism, the bishops never really offered an adequate theology for understanding the role of the laity in either the church or the world. The same can be said of *Christifideles laici,* the document issued in late January 1989 to follow up the synod. John Paul admitted that this apostolic exhortation adds little to the teaching on the the laity found in Vatican II.

Individual Conscience

According to Christian tradition, the grace of Christ is *not* made available to individuals primarily in prayer, rituals, readings, and laws. It is true that these are important for helping a person focus upon the reality and meaning of the Christian life. Nevertheless, they remain secondary occasions of grace. It is in the common and ordinary events of daily life when people obey or disobey the dictates of conscience that the grace of Christ is primarily available. Conscience is a permanent natural disposition that summons us to seek the good and to avoid evil. It is not an impersonal oracle that confirms or negates our decisions. Rather, it is the result of hard, honest, and practical thinking about a particular decision. Conscience is human reasoning applying to individual situations both moral principles and the teachings coming from the other six complementary authorities discussed above. Vatican II called conscience "the most secret core and sanctuary of man. There he is alone with God, whose voice echoes in his depths" (GS 16).

The Christian tradition has always respected the autonomy of conscience, declaring that it is the ultimate judge in decision-making. This teaching was reiterated at Vatican II: "In all his activity a man is bound to follow his conscience faithfully, in order that he may come to God, for whom he was created" (DH 3). The present crisis in the church over conscience and dissent "comes down to disagreement over how an integrated human personality functions and how the Holy Spirit works within individuals and within the church" (S. Callahan 1986).

In the preconciliar church the hierarchy's moral authority was quite direct. Individuals were told what they should and should not do. The truth content of a teaching was assumed. Teaching "was a disciplinary issue, calling for a response of will rather than intellect" (Vacek 1983). Those who disagreed were simply being disobedient.

With Vatican II the magisterium did not stop trying to educate the consciences of the faithful, but it stopped directing them with the same force. The Council acknowledged that "a sense of the dignity of the human person has been expressing itself more and more deeply on the consciousness of contemporary man. And the demand is increasingly made that men should act on their own judgment, enjoying and making use of a responsible freedom, not driven by coercion but motivated by a sense of duty" (DH 1). The bishops also said, "Let the layman not imagine that his pastors are always such experts, that to every problem which arises, however complicated, they can readily give him a concrete solution, or even that such is their mission" (GS 43).

The Council also agreed that "the truth cannot impose itself except by virtue of its own truth, as it makes its entrance into the mind at once quietly and with power" (DH 1). This means that religious leaders have to present their moral teaching so that their basic authority lies in the truth of the claims they make. The truth has its own authority and can command assent to itself. The teachings of the hierarchy will have authority to the extent that they illumine the doctrinal and moral issues they address.

Conclusion

This chapter has surveyed Von Hügel's triad from the perspective of authority or control. The institutional church was given new directions in its authoritative structures by Vatican II when it called upon the pope to work more closely with the bishops within the principles of collegiality and subsidiarity. Unfortunately, neither Paul VI nor John Paul II have decentralized the papacy within the episcopate. Both popes kept a tight grip on the universal church by issuing encyclicals, by approving CDF documents, by controlling the international synods, by overseeing episcopal conferences, by appointing bishops receptive to the Vatican policies, and by silencing theologians. Even John Paul's numerous overseas pilgrimages, while they help to symbolize the church as a world church, do keep the focus on papal power and jurisdiction.

It is no secret that there is widespread dissent from official teachings among many of the faithful, clergy, and theologians. Many of the faithful are hard-pressed to know where to turn. A certain relativism has crept into the church—many simply go their own way, making decisions that are pragmatic, utilitarian, and individualistic. Although conscience is the ultimate judge in decision-making, it is not autonomous and each Christian must always decide in the context of faith and the faith community. According to the Catholic tradition, the authoritative voices in the faith community include the pope, the bishops, Scripture, tradition, theologians, and the whole body of the faithful. Consequently, all Christian disciples are teachers and learners. Until these perspectives are taken, the institutional, intellectual, and devotional life of the church will be in disarray.

Finally, it has been explained that all members of the church should also learn from society by scrutinizing the signs of the times because, as is now clear, the world's joys, hopes, griefs, and anxieties are the joys, hopes, griefs, and anxieties of the church (GS 1). Vatican II reminded the faithful about dialogue with society: "In fidelity to conscience, Christians are joined with the rest of men in the search for truth, and for the genuine solution to the numerous problems which arise in the life of individuals and from social relationships" (GS 16).

One dialogue that has become increasingly important in today's global village is interreligious dialogue. The presence and vitality of so many other religious traditions has forced the interpersonal and missionary church to clarify the identity and mission of Christ and his church. Missiology—the theology of missionary activity—is the subject of the next chapter.

6

The Church and the Other Religions

At the heart of the Catholic tradition is Christ's command to teach all nations. Right from the first generation of disciples when Peter, Paul, and the other Jewish Christians discussed the evangelization of the gentiles, this mission has been a daunting and controversial enterprise. Today, since we live in a polycentric, global culture, many agree with David Tracy's remark that "there is no more difficult or more pressing question on the present theological horizon than that of interreligious dialogue" (1991, 27). In light of Von Hügel's triad, it is clear that the existence of many vital religions challenges the church in a way that no other issue can to clarify its identity and to explain its understanding of the person and mediatorship of Christ and its devotion to him.

In the history of humankind, there have been thousands of religions. These can be classified either as indigenous or as "world religions." An indigenous religion originates within a culture and, for the most part, is identified with that culture. When the culture dies out, so does the religion. A religion becomes a world religion when it has a universal message that it both adapts to and incarnates within other cultures. The major religions—Christianity, Buddhism, Hinduism, Judaism, and Islam—have been especially good at this.

Christianity is confessed by about 33 percent of the world's people, of whom 18 percent are Catholic. The Christian mission to the other 67 percent of humankind is a major challenge for several reasons. First, "for an increasing number of people today, the chief obstacle to being fully convinced of the truth of Christianity is not a scientific view of the world that has no room at all for religion, but the existence of rival religions" (Allen 1990, 22). Second, it has become clearer today that the mission to spread Christianity through interreligious dialogue is inextricably related to two other issues: cultural pluralism and global social justice.

How can the church witness to Christ, who said, "I came so that they might have life and have it more abundantly" (John 10:10), and not address the legion of problems (e.g., hunger, genocide, militarism, sexism, and war) that prevent people from living a wholesome life? In view of the poverty and suffering present in so many developing lands, Michael Riley wrote that missionaries "will have to place work for justice and material sufficiency at the heart of [their] agenda, even, perhaps, before the name of Christ is mentioned" (1978; see also Riley 1979).

Cultural Pluralism and Ethnocentrism

Culture denotes the set of customs, rules, institutions, and values inherent in the way of life of a community, which express the aspirations of the society and the norms for the interactions of people and groups in that society. The church always expresses its faith in cultural forms. The modern church acknowledges, especially now that it is a world church, that it should never be identified with one particular culture. Joseph Fitzpatrick, a Jesuit sociologist, wrote that "*the* fundamental problem of the church from its very beginning to the present has been its reaction to culture" (1978).

Most missionaries in the preconciliar church believed they were conferring in God's name both the true religion and a better culture when they imposed their own culture as a precondition for admission to baptism. Believing one's own culture and people to be superior to others is called ethnocentricism. Fortunately, not all missionaries were so psychologically insensitive and sociologically exploitative. There were some significant and heroic attempts to respect the autonomy of foreign cultures. For example, in the seventeenth century, the Jesuit missionaries Matteo Ricci (1552–1610) in China and Roberto de Nobili (1577–1656) in India believed that Christ's grace was available outside the church and respected the non-European cultures they entered. Ricci adopted the lifestyle and clothing of a Chinese scholar and accepted into the liturgy the honors paid to Confucius and the dead. His liturgical efforts were squelched by Rome.

A modern illustration of the problems created by cultural pluralism and ethnocentricism is the controversy in 1987–88 that centered around the beatification of Junipero Serra (1713–84). This Franciscan missionary built nine of the twelve California missions and baptized thousands of Native Americans. When John Paul II's scheduled visit to Monterey, California, on September 17, 1987, had been planned, he was supposed to celebrate a mass of beatification for Serra. However, this ceremony never took place. It was reported that the process of verifying the two miracles required for beatification had been slowed down. Others said the change was due to the protests of the Native Americans who considered Serra a brutal conqueror. One Indian elder said, "You cannot make a statement about the richness of our culture and then in the next breath hold Junipero Serra up as a model."[1]

The overall effect of mission rule on the indigenous people is debated. Some church historians portray the results in idyllic and romantic terms; some anthropologists compare the mission compounds to concentration camps; some theologians decry Serra's beatification as a legitimization of a system of racism and paternalism. It is an indisputable fact that European diseases such as measles and syphilis reduced the Indian population during the mission period from approximately 130,000 to 83,000. The nomadic Indians were forced into menial labor at the missions, and those who escaped or were caught stealing were flogged, often by order of the priests, including Serra. Serra's beatification finally took place in Rome on September 25, 1988. At the celebration, John Paul said that in his dealings with the Indians, Father Serra "was well aware of their heroic virtues" and that he "sought to further their authentic human development on the basis of their newfound faith as persons created and redeemed by God."[2]

The Popes and Missiology

Benedict XV

During the pontificate of Benedict's predecessor, Leo XIII, the global church developed significantly: 248 new dioceses were established outside Europe, including twenty-eight in the United States. However, World War I created many problems in the mission fields. Benedict, who is often called "the pope of the missions" because of his landmark encyclical, *Maximum illud* (1919), set forth three principles for missiology. He called for the promotion of the formation of native clergy. He told missionaries to renounce nationalism—they must seek the good of the people among whom they worked and not the imperialist interests of their own country of origin. He urged missionaries to show appreciation for the cultures among which they worked. Benedict's vision had an important effect on Vatican II: many of the bishops from Asia and Africa were natives of their own countries. The seeds of the world church germinated during Benedict's pontificate.

Even before Benedict's encyclical, missionary endeavors had been underway in the United States. For example, in 1911 two priests, James A. Walsh (1867–1936) and Thomas Price (1860–1919), founded the Catholic Foreign Missionary Society, popularly designated Maryknoll. This was the first American group designed uniquely for mission work in foreign lands. The first Maryknollers went to China in 1918. In 1912 the Maryknoll Sisters were founded by Mary Joseph Rogers (1882–1955). Their first mission took place in 1921, when six sisters went to China.

Pius XI

Pius XI was ardently involved in overseas missions, even requiring religious communities to get more involved. He continued Benedict's call for native priests and cultural adapation in his encyclical *Rerum ecclesiae* (1926). That year he personally consecrated the first six Chinese bishops and in 1927 a Japanese bishop. He also ordained numerous native priests from India, southeast Asia, and China. He founded a faculty of missiology at the Gregorian University and a missionary museum in the Lateran. Theresa of Lisieux (1873–97), a French Carmelite nun whose autobiography captured the attention of so much of the world, was canonized in 1925 and declared patroness of the missions.

Unfortunately there is a negative side to the efforts of Pius XI. He was intolerant of other Christian communities and other religions. His belief was that the other Christians should be absorbed within Catholicism and the other religions should be conquered.

Pius XII

His first encyclical, *Summi pontificatus* (1939), had as its theme the evil of aggressive nationalism. Pius included in his discussion of this theme long passages about missionaries respecting all that is good in other peoples' cultures and traditions. In *Evangelii praecones* (1951), an encyclical on the overseas missions, he reiterated the themes of Benedict XV and Pius XI about respecting the culture and traditions of the indigenous peoples. Pius XII was progressive about this issue. For example, he published a decree in December 1939, tolerating the honors paid to Confucius and the dead that were promoted by Ricci in the seventeenth century. His decision was certainly historic—but one tragically and disastrously too late for China and the rest of the East. More than 50 percent of the world's population lives in Asia but only about 3 percent is Christian.

Pius' encyclical *Mystici corporis* (1943) contained an important sentence about the relation of those not Christian to the Catholic church. These persons, although not explicitly united to the church, can be related to the Mystical Body of the Redeemer "by an unconscious yearning and desire" (n. 103).

Despite this concession in the encyclical, an unfortunate controversy broke out in the United States over the necessity of the church for salvation. Leonard Feeney (1897–1978), a Jesuit from Boston and a respected essayist and poet, took the church's infallible statement "outside the church there is no salvation" and taught it literally. He insisted that all are lost who do not belong explicitly to the Catholic Church.

In a letter to Boston's Archbishop Richard Cushing, dated August 8, 1949, the Vatican explained that, although the church is a necessary means of salvation, actual membership in the church is not required in all circumstances. What is required is that a person belong "at least in desire and longing. . . . When a man is invincibly ignorant, God also accepts an implicit desire, so called because it is contained in the good disposition of soul by which a man wants his will to be conformed to God's will." The letter maintained that these points had been clearly taught in the 1943 encyclical. When Father Feeney persisted in his position, he was dismissed from the Jesuits in 1949 and excommunicated in 1954. He returned to the church before his death.

The Feeney case did force theologians to retrieve the infallible statement "outside the church there is no salvation."

Today this doctrine is interpreted as follows: The redemptive action of God among the thousands of religions prefigures and prepares for the church. The triune God cannot be separated from the church. Wherever grace is given, therefore, it is given in view of the church—and in this sense there is no salvation apart from the church (see LG 16). In other terms, instead of insisting that "where the church is, there is Christ," Christians say, "Where Christ is, there is the church." Whoever is graced by Christ belongs to the church.

John XXIII

His encyclical on overseas missions, *Princeps pastorum* (1959), commemorated the fortieth anniversary of Benedict XV's letter and covered the same area. But John also did the groundwork for a multicultural church by acknowledging that the church was not bound to any culture, even the European and Western culture to which it was so closely linked over history.

While John was an apostolic delegate in Turkey, he was instrumental, following the instructions of Pius XII, in saving thousands of Jews from the Nazis. He liked to repeat Pius XI's teaching that "spiritually, we are Semites." It is not too surprising, then, that on Good Friday in March 1959, John dramatically interrupted the liturgy, ordering then and there that the phrase "the perfidious Jews" be deleted. The adjective "perfidious" implied that Jews were a people without faith or were guilty of a deliberate breach of faith.

Paul VI

On Pentecost Sunday, May 1964, he created the Vatican Secretariat for Non-Christian Religions. The purpose of this office was "to search for methods and ways of opening a suitable dialogue with non-Christians," so that both sides will come to know and esteem one another's teachings and life. This dialogue can take place without the church compromising its faith in Christ.

Three months later, Paul published his first encyclical, *Ecclesiam suam.* This letter picked up the themes associated with the Secretariat for Non-Christian Religions, especially the desire of Catholic Christians to join with the other religious communities "in promoting and defending common ideals in the spheres of religious liberty, human brotherhood, teaching and education, social welfare and civil order." However, Paul VI reiterated that Christianity is the one true religion and he hoped everyone would acknowledge this belief.

In the 1960s missionaries were describing one of their major tasks with the term *pre-evangelization*. This term was popularized by the Jesuit missionary Alfonso Nebreda both at the international catechetical meeting held in Bangkok in 1962 and through his book *Kerygma in Crisis?* The term meant people had to be prepared to hear the gospel; that is, missionaries had to meet people's physical needs first. Often, said Nebreda, the culture and lifestyle of the indigenous peoples were too pagan, primitive, or poor to permit them to be receptive to Christianity. These social, religious, and economic obstacles had to be removed before the people could hear the gospel and celebrate the sacraments. In short, pre-evangelization was concerned with humanization.

In *Evangelii nuntiandi* (1975), the follow-up document to the Synod of 1974 on evangelization, Paul brilliantly eliminated pre-evangelization as a viable term. He declared that all actions that fostered human growth and dignity—education, health care, freedom, food—were already evangelization, albeit in "its initial and incomplete stage. . . . The church promotes the human by evangelizing, and the church evangelizes by promoting the human." Humanization, therefore, is itself a dimension of salvation and not simply a tactical prelude to teaching the Christian gospel. Paul also broadened the scope of evangelization by indicating that it should be directed not simply to individuals but also to cultures. He wrote that "the split between the gospel and culture is without doubt the drama of our times" and that "every effort must be made to ensure a full evangelization of culture, or more correctly, cultures."

Vatican II
The Council produced two documents that dealt with the church's relationship to the other religions. The Declaration on Religious Liberty affirmed religious freedom as a human right (see chapters 7 and 9 below); the Declaration on the Non-Christian Religions called for interreligious dialogue. The history of the latter document began in June 1960. At that time

John XXIII decided that the Council should make a statement on Jewish-Catholic relations. In September he turned this project over to Cardinal Augustin Bea, prefect of the Secretariat for Christian Unity. Robert Graham, a Jesuit and Vatican historian, observed that "between that beginning and the outcome there is perhaps the most dramatic story of the council" (1966, 656). Thomas Stransky added: "To those of us who were directly involved in the preparations and the four sessions of Vatican II, no draft had a more unplanned, tortuous and threatened journey than did *Nostra Aetate*, especially no. 4 on the Jews" (1986b).

The document that became the Declaration on the Non-Christian Religions was at first part of the Decree on Ecumenism. Later the bishops voted that a separate document on Jewish-Catholic relations be published. Finally, the scope of the proposed document was expanded to include the other world religions in order to give it a global view. On October 28, 1965, the day of the promulgation, the final vote in favor was impressive: 2,312 to 88 (see Oesterreicher 1969).

Originally, John XXIII wanted the Council to address ecumenism: the Catholic Church's relations with the other Christian communities. His subsequent concern for interreligious dialogue—called wider ecumenism—"may prove to be, because of its far-reaching implications, the council's most revolutionary act" (Hillman 1989, x). The implications of this wider ecumenism profoundly enriched the self-understanding of Christians and also encouraged the extensive transformation of the church's missionary outreach.

The Declaration on the Non-Christian Religions *(Nostra aetate)* is a compact and clear essay, the shortest of the sixteen documents at approximately 1,120 words. It has three major points. First, it affirms that all peoples share much in common: all have a single origin and a final goal, and constitute a single community. It also points out that people ask the same religious questions about the nature of the human, the meaning and purpose of life, and "that ultimate and unutterable mystery which engulfs our being."

John Oesterreicher (1904–93), a convert from Judaism who became a Catholic priest and a consultant to the Secretariat for Christian Unity from 1961 to 1968, was one of the authors of *Nostra aetate*. He explained that Vatican II marked the first time in history that an ecumenical council acknowledged the search for the absolute by whole races and peoples, and honored the truth and holiness in other religions as the work of the one loving God (1969, 1).

Second, in its brief reflections on Hinduism, Buddhism, and Islam, the document says the church "rejects nothing that is true and holy in these religions," which "often reflect a ray of that Truth which enlightens all men." This is an ancient teaching reaching back to the Gospels (see John 1:9) and the Church Fathers. The apostle Paul challenged the Athenians to worship Jesus Christ, the one he explicitly identified as the one they worshiped unknowingly (Acts 17:23). Similarly, in the second century, the apologist Justin Martyr wrote that Christ is Logos, or the wisdom of God imprinted in the mind of humanity. As such, "whatever has been uttered aright by any men in any place belongs to us Christians."

In our times it is Karl Rahner who defended and developed the ancient teaching that all people have been saved in Jesus Christ. He explained that the church is faced with two teachings that are hard to reconcile. On the one hand, the church must preserve the belief that we are saved only in Jesus Christ (Christian exclusiveness). On the other hand, it must teach at the historical and practical level that salvation takes place outside of Christianity (God's universal love). Rahner brought these two teachings together by coining the term "anonymous Christianity." While Rahner's term never appeared in the council documents, it is his theology that Vatican II espoused. Its influence is clear in one of the bishops' more famous sentences: "For, since Christ died for all men and since the ultimate vocation of man is in fact one, and divine, we ought to believe that the Holy Spirit in a manner known only to God offers to every man the possibility of being associated with this paschal mystery" (GS 22; see also LG 16, NA 2, AG 7).

Rahner used the term *anonymous* to indicate that the "first beginnings of Christianity are already given, but have not yet grown to the real fullness of their nature, have not yet attained their historical and social specificity and tangibility" (Rahner 1966). A person may already possess the grace of Christ even before he or she has explicitly come into contact with Christianity. The life of Jesus of Nazareth indicated that he was a man who accepted his existence as drawn and claimed by God, who loved his neighbor, who hoped for the future in spite of circumstances that suggested fear or even despair, and who accepted his death not as the victory of emptiness but as an openness to life. People who freely accept these attitudes or dimensions of human existence are at the beginning of faith in Christ who is the goal and crown of God's plan for human history.

Rahner's thesis met with some opposition. Theologians like Heinz Robert Schlette said his explanation was filled with the same old Christian imperialism that had long been a barrier to authentic interreligious dialogue (1976; see also Maloney 1970). Rahner's response to this objection speaks for itself: "The non-Christians may think it superfluous that the Christian attributes all that is good and whole in every man to the fruit of the grace of his Christ and regards the non-Christian as a Christian who has not yet found himself. But the Christian cannot do otherwise. And actually this seeming superiority is the way in which his greatest humility is expressed, both as regards himself and his church. For it lets God be greater than both man and the church" (1969, 86).

Third, the declaration also discussed Judaism, declaring that Christianity has its beginnings in the faith of Abraham. Jesus, who was a Jew, "reconciled Jew and Gentile, making them both one in himself (see Eph. 2:14–16)" (NA 4). The document repudiated the persecution of any people and deplored all forms of anti-Semitism (NA 4). It also disavowed the thesis that the Jewish people are guilty of the death of Jesus and reiterated the Pauline teaching (Rom. 11:28–29) that God's covenant with the Jews perdures even to this day. Oesterreicher observed, "It [was] the first time that the church [had] publicly made her own the Pauline view of the mystery of Israel" (1969, 1).

Mission Theology Today

The church has always been missionary. She has gone forth at Christ's command and the Spirit's direction to evangelize and baptize all nations. She has proclaimed to all men and women the gospel of Jesus and the belief that he is the principle of eternal life and "the key, the focal point and the goal of all human history" (GS 10).

One of the results of the Declaration on Non-Christian Religions is that mission theology is very concerned with two major weaknesses in preconciliar mission activity and theology. First, missionaries brought the Christ of their own culture to the peoples they were evangelizing without adapting their religion to the new culture. The church lacked an appreciation of cultural pluralism and was not a world church in a fully official way. Second, missionaries strove to convert all nations and all religions to Christianity, based on the conviction that Christianity was true and the other religions were incomplete or false. Judaism was incomplete and had been superceded and invalidated by Christianity, and the other world religions were "merely natural at best, satanic at worst" (Hillman 1989, 46). The church lacked a theology of religious pluralism.[3]

Before proceeding, a word of caution is necessary. These changes in the theological understanding of the uniqueness of Jesus and the validity of the other religions have occurred so recently and so rapidly that they have barely had time to enter the mainstream of Catholic life. In fact, there is evidence that the search for some resolution to the two central problems of missiology—cultural and religious pluralism—while ongoing, is very much in an early phase of discussion. Cardinal Bea, knowing the importance of the conciliar document on the other religions, declared that "it is an important and promising beginning, yet no more than the beginning of a long and demanding way towards the arduous goal of a humanity whose members feel themselves truly to be sons of the same Father in heaven and act on this conviction" (Oesterreicher 1969, 130).

Christ and Cultural Pluralism

Evangelization is the activity whereby the church proclaims the gospel in order to awaken living faith among those who do not know Christ. Today there is considerable discussion about the methodology of evangelization. In the past there was widespread disregard for the autonomy of each culture. When missionaries went from the West to the East, it was understood that they brought the Western image of Christ and the church to the foreign culture, creating their own type of society artificially rather than respecting the values and traditions of the

culture they were entering. The Christ whom Western missionaries taught was a replica of the Christ they knew in their own
culture. This ethnocentric approach became, unfortunately, a
sign that the Catholic Church, far from being a world church,
was essentially bound to the civilization of the West.

Today there is a greater appreciation of inculturation, the
process of discovering and developing those Christian values
that are already present in a culture. Like Christ who bound
"himself, in virtue of his incarnation, to the definite social and
cultural conditions of those human beings among whom he
dwelt" (AG 10), so the church must incarnate itself in each culture. Not only can Western Christianity be enriched by the
incorporation of the customs and traditions of a foreign culture, but the missionaries' relationship to Christ can be
enhanced as they discover Christ and his Spirit already present
to the people and their culture (Ranly 1977). If, in the past,
missionaries thought they had much to give and teach, they
now acknowledge that they have much to receive and learn
about diverse ways of being human, religious, and holy.

It should be noted that this inculturation process is actually a
manifestation of greater changes taking place throughout the
world as a result of several manifestations of historical consciousness: communication technology is improving, nationalism
is on the rise, and people are becoming aware of the obstacles
in their society that prevent them from assuming responsibility
for themselves (conscientization). For example, the countries of
the third world have challenged the success of the first world in
placing themselves at the center of the earth, for controlling the
greater share of the earth's resources, and for understanding
human history and culture along an axis that passes through
their own immediate past. Langdon Gilkey remarks, "I do not
think this new sense of rough equality among religions comes
from any new and sharper *dogmatic* critique of Christianity, for
instance, of its christological claims," but rather because "the cultures have become roughly equal." Since the cultures "are now
perceived *on both sides* as equal, so the religions of the cultures
are perceived differently than they were" (1989, 380–81).

Christ and Religious Pluralism

In recent times a Christian theology of other religions has
moved through two paradigms to a third in its understanding

of Christ's relationship to the world religions.[4] These changes pivot around Vatican II and are usually labeled preconciliar, conciliar, and postconciliar.

Roman Catholic missiology has moved to new plateaus because new consideration has been given to some of the most basic concepts of evangelization. It will be possible to understand the postconciliar missiology after examining the changes that have taken place in the understanding of four interrelated areas: salvation, the mediatorship of Christ, conversion, and true and false religion.

Salvation

All men and women have found themselves in a state of alienation from self, others, nature, and God. Salvation delivers us from the restraints that bind and alienate us from ourselves, the human community, and divine love and life. The Catholic tradition holds that Jesus of Nazareth brought universal salvation through his life, death, and resurrection, and his salvific grace and life are found in his Catholic Church.

The preconciliar view of salvation held that members of the Catholic Church had available to them all the means of salvation. Membership in the visible church was the ordinary way to be saved. The duty of the church was to preach Jesus' message of salvation to all people so that they could be converted and saved. If followers of other religions remained in their religion, they could be saved if they practiced their religion sincerely and honestly. However, their salvation did require the extraordinary intervention of God.

At Vatican II, the church moved away from this ecclesiocentric view and acknowledged the salvific value of the other religions (LG 16). It declared that God and his Spirit have been working through these religions and not in spite of them. The other religions were legitimate and had a proper place in God's salvific plan (1 Tim. 2:4–6). In the postconciliar period theologians like Heinz Robert Schlette and Hans Küng proposed that the world religions were the normal and ordinary way of salvation and that Christians, being so overwhelmingly outnumbered during the thousands of years humans have been on earth, had been given the extraordinary grace of knowing Christ. Christians should be a sign that all people are saved in Christ (O'Grady 1977).

The postconciliar understanding of salvation for those not Christian is much more radical than the conciliar view. It developed in part because there was a certain uneasiness and even dissatisfaction with Rahner's theology of the anonymous Christian. When Christian theologians, mystics, and missionaries started using Rahner's phrase in interreligious dialogue, Jews and Muslims found it offensive. For them, Jesus is simply a prophet; to consider him divine is idolatrous. Hindus and Buddhists found the term incomprehensible because they believe that all humans are destined for nirvana and not a personal relationship with a fellow human being. Foisting anonymous Christianity on the other religions would be like whites trying to express esteem for Martin Luther King, Jr. by saying that he was anonymously a white man—or for men to say that women are virtually as good as men. Furthermore, it seems that to read Christian ideas into the world religions does not do justice to the distinctiveness of these faiths. What we encounter in each religion is a different faith and different patterns of behavior; different standards and ideals of ultimacy, happiness, and salvation; and different claims to the truth about God, the universe, and the nature of humanness.

Faith is the basic foundation of each religion. Each religion has its own identity and autonomy because of the specific epistemological nature of faith; because of the certitude that faith confers upon the believer concerning the content of her or his religion. When a Muslim, for example, makes an act of faith, he or she stands in a relationship to Allah which is in no way less immediate than that of the Christian to the Trinity.

We have also learned to distinguish faith from beliefs, and this very important distinction provides a means for ecumenical encounter. While each religion has different beliefs and practices that are culturally fashioned and historically circumscribed, common to all religions is faith. Faith is the most basic and dynamic feature of each religion. This explains why all the religions of the world may be understood as communities of faith.

The postconciliar theology of salvation states that the gospel of Jesus Christ is only one way of salvation. The preconciliar view of salvation was ecclesiocentric and exclusivist: salvation was to be found in the Catholic Church alone. The conciliar view was christocentric but inclusivist: salvation is found in

Christ alone. The postconciliar view is theocentric and pluralistic: salvation is found in God who works in the heart and history of each person and in all the religions. This position is so radical that John Hick did not hesitate to call it "a Copernican revolution in theology" (1973; see also D'Costa 1984).

Theology has taken this theocentric position for two reasons: the church is relative to the kingdom of God, and the mission of Jesus is relative to the work of the Father. In other words, our theology of salvation first shifted its focal point from the specifically Roman Catholic to the total Christian community—and, now, to the entire human family. The reason for this shift is the retrieval of a basic fact about Jesus: he calls all people to be totally open to their humanity so as to receive the grace of his Father. Jesus says all people are of infinite worth to the Father and it is his kingdom which is absolute. "Neither historical Christianity, nor the church, nor Jesus himself, are absolutes. The historical vocation of churches is not the maximum extension of Christianity itself, but rather—in dialogue with other religions and spiritual families—to bear witness to the kingdom of God anticipated in the paths of history" (Geffre 1989, 394).

From the theocentric theology outlined here one can conclude that the statement "Jesus is the principle of eternal life, the meaning of history, and the perfect man" is a faith conviction that can be made only through the power of the Spirit. There does not seem to be any way in which these claims to Jesus' absolute uniqueness can be objectively verified. Eugene Hillman points out that there is no objectively reliable evidence for any religion to make "sweeping generalizations concerning its answers to life, death, and salvation" (1989, 52–53).

Some question this theology of religious pluralism. It certainly seems like a form of indifferentism. It also smacks of relativism (a denial of the primacy of Christ) (see Gorday 1989) and reads like a capitulation to those secularists who say that the Christian belief that Jesus is the universal savior is both arrogant and imperialist. This is not so. First, Christian evangelization need not be interpreted as some kind of religious imperialism or a betrayal of open dialogue: "To discuss one's firmly held beliefs with non-believers is not the same thing as trying to impose such beliefs upon them" (Hillman 1989, 58). Second, Christians evangelize knowing that every religion affects the quality of a person's personal and communal life. Missionaries tell those of other religions how Christian life is distinct from their religious life. The adherents of other religions learn that Christianity creates a transformation of consciousness whereby a person acquires a new and distinct awareness of self, others, the world, and God. They learn also that Christian life consists in living with and for Christ as one lives with and for others. Third, a theology of religious pluralism directs missionaries to free the adherents of other religions for a saving contact with the best of their own religious traditions. The missionary helps these people solve their own problems, humbly, genuinely, openly, and with respect for their traditions and a willingness to learn about God from them.

The Mediatorship of Christ

The church teaches that Jesus is the world's unique savior. There is salvation in no one else (Mark 16:15–16; John 14:6; 15:5). He is the mediator, the representative before God in the process of atonement. In the preconciliar church, the missionary taught that Jesus founded the Catholic Church—the one true church—and this is where he is present, mediating the Father's kingdom and sending his Spirit. There was a radical discontinuity between Christianity and the world religions. Jesus was the exclusive savior of the world (Acts 4:12).

At Vatican II the bishops refocused their view of the Scriptures. They began to see Jesus as the fulfillment of the religions of the world (1 Tim. 2:5; Acts 17:23). The authentic seeds of the gospel are contained within the other religions. Christianity is not discontinuous from the world religions, but the leaven in all of them. The relation of the church to the other religions of the world is not one of competition, nor an effort at substitution. It is one of sublimation. The mission of the church is to take what is holy and true in the other religions and show its fulfillment in Christ. He is constitutive of these religions.

Postconciliar theology still teaches Christ's universal and decisive mediatorship even while respecting other religions (Watts 1989). This is a difficult balance, since a theology of religious pluralism accepts a diversity of mediators and avatars (earthly mainfestations of the deity) whose relationships to

God are equal to Christ's in a way that had not been thought possible before now. Postconciliar theology retains Christ's universal and decisive mediatorship by pointing to the fact that the crucial decision regarding the divine is made by people in their relationship to the human community (Rom. 13:8–10). The Gospels say that in the human community people are open to the Spirit, are addressed by the Spirit, and can commit themselves to the Spirit. When missionaries teach people to love all people, especially one's enemies, they are actually evangelizing them.

Postconciliar theology's identification of Jesus as the normative mediator may seem to be no more than another version of the "exclusive mediator" of preconciliar theology. The difference is that postconciliar theology views Jesus as normative because he is the one who illumines for the missionary "other ways in which God has saved and is saving people" in other religions. In other words, Jesus is the touchstone by which other religious experiences are examined and related (Redington 1983).

Conversion

Conversion involves a transformation of the person and his or her worldview; that is, a person makes a total change from one way of living to another. Christian conversion entails a commitment of faith, hope, and love to Jesus Christ, the sacrament of the Father and the source of the Spirit. This conversion has intellectual, moral, and ecclesial dimensions.

Preconciliar missiology sought overt conversion to Catholic Christianity as its goal. At Vatican II the Catholic Church adopted a policy of "mergerism." Since the other religions prepared the way for Christianity and since they possessed elements that could be fulfilled in Christ, the bishops' dream was for a gradual convergence of all religions into Catholic Christianity.

This theology was hardly acceptable, especially to those not Christian, because it really entailed a union by absorption. Postconciliar theology holds greater respect for the autonomy of each religion, and, in view of the tenacious persistence and steady numerical growth of many religions, an increasing tendency to accept religious pluralism as part of the divine dispensation. The primary conversion that the missionary tries to effect is to convert each believer within the framework of the religion she or he already professes. The initial task of the missionary is to help believers live their religion more integrally and honestly.

True and False Religion

Religion pertains to the relationship of God with humans. Every religion declares that God has revealed himself through its sacred persons, signs, and symbols. Each religious group thinks that it is the true way (Cox 1988b). Many religious groups have little use for the other religions. Historically, Christianity has probably made the strongest claims that it is the one true faith.

In preconciliar theology, the Catholic Church professed to be the home of the one true religion. It could point to the "marks of the church" as the sign of its veracity. It alone was one, holy, catholic, and apostolic. The other religions were considered to be natural, imperfect, and, ultimately, erroneous. Missionaries attempted to prove the superiority of Christianity over the other religions against the measurement of the "marks" of the true church.

In conciliar theology, the church moved from an ecclesiocentric to a christocentric position in which it acknowledged some truth in the other religions. This truth had its source in Christ. If these religions developed their principles to their logical conclusions, they would naturally culminate in Christianity.

Postconciliar theology shifted the concept of true or false religion from measurement (special criteria of validity) to function or value. Paul Knitter suggests "that many religions may have equally meaningful and valid messages for mankind and that it may be the case that no one religion has *the* final or normative word for all the others" (1990). A corollary to this position is the conviction that true religion humanizes and reconciles people, whereas false religion dehumanizes and fragments the human community. This is a theocentric approach to religion. It begins with the fact that God incarnates himself in every human person, above every religious barrier.

Jesus taught a theocentric religion. He said that people do not relate themselves to God in worship (a religious practice) and then, as a second step, seek the right relationship to their brothers and sisters (Matt. 5:23–24). Rather, as people relate to the human community, they also relate to the Father. The Father is love and anyone who does not love his brother and sister does not know God (Matt. 25:31–46). The ultimate test between true and false religion, then, is the reconciliation of people in community. Anything in the church that hinders human community is false religion.

This understanding of true and false religion does not demand that the members of another religion become Christian. When missionaries help people overcome whatever fosters egotism, hatred, and injustice, they are evangelizing. Perhaps, then, a common ground for interfaith dialogue is the goal of liberating the countless people in the world who suffer poverty and injustice (Collinge et al. 1986). In fact, this is the thesis of Paul Knitter who suggests that since there has been "an evolution from ecclesiocentrism to christocentrism to theocentrism, it is now time to move on to soteriocentrism" (1986, 135).

The Parliament of the World's Religions held two meetings in Chicago, the first in 1893 and the second in 1993. It is possible to see the dramatic shifts that have taken place in interreligious dialogue by comparing the purposes and goals of these two significant meetings.

The 1893 meeting—the first time the major religions met together in a public forum—was largely a Protestant Christian undertaking. The great majority of the four hundred official delegates representing forty-one religious communities were Christian. Although there were appeals for the end of religious fanaticism and warfare and for respect for the essential dignity of each person, the "purpose was more evangelical than ecumenical" (Briggs 1993). Christian missionaries hoped to become better acquainted with the other religions in order to more easily convert them to Christianity.

The 1993 Parliament met for eight days beginning on August 29. It drew six thousand delegates and represented over 120 religions. Present were not only representatives of the major religions, but also self-styled "neo-pagans" and goddess worshipers. The underlying theme was not theological unity but unity for peace and justice in a world marked by violence and war, much of which had (and has) religion at its core. The delegates agreed that unless humans were guided by an overarching global ethic, the future of the planet and the human race would be bleak (Stammer 1993). Approximately 250 religious leaders signed *The Declaration of a Global Ethic*, a five thousand-word document that expresses such an ethic.

Hans Küng was the principal writer of this document. He did not use the word *God*, a step necessitated, said Küng, to respect Buddhism and other faiths that are nontheistic (i.e., they accept a spiritual dimension to reality but not the personal involvement of a divine creator in their lives). Küng said he took this position because the religions are not ready to talk about unity of religion. "I talk about peace among religions. That would be enough."

Küng also stated that "we have to answer questions that Jesus or Moses never thought about. We are at a transformation of consciousness with regard to nature." He also admitted that the declaration offered a "minimum ethic," but one to which all religions could hold themselves and others accountable (Steinfels 1993b).

Although the declaration professes to be, in Küng's words, "a minimal, fundamental consensus concerning binding values, universal standards and moral, fundamental attitudes," nevertheless, it makes firm statements about religious leaders who incite fanaticism and violent and bloody conflicts; the misuse of religion "for purely, power-political goals, including war"; and sexual discrimination, "one of the worst forms of human degradation." In short, the document affirms the religious wisdom of the ages and declares that much of it should be applied to modern circumstances. The document is also a clear indication that interreligious dialogue can have a certain measure of success if it begins with soteriology, that is, if it begins with our need for salvation from whatever alienates us from one another, the created world, ourselves, and God.

Recapitulation

Is Jesus indispensable for salvation? To this crucial question there are five different answers. First, a relativist approach maintains that there should be no Christian missionary activity because this is an age of religious pluralism. Jesus is one of many ways to God and not the universal mediator. Jesus is not indispensable for salvation.

Second, the Orthodox, evangelicals, and some other Christian communities view dialogue with other religions as an affront to the centrality of Christ. These groups insist that missionary activity directed toward conversion to Christ is absolutely necessary because Jesus is *the* way, and none of the other religions are salvific. The Scriptures declare that Jesus alone is savior (Acts 4:12; John 14:6).

Third, the preconciliar position holds that Jesus is the exclusive way to salvation, yet God in his compassion can and does save others.

Fourth, the conciliar position maintains that Jesus is the inclusive savior. The other religions are united anonymously to Christ and his final and unsurpassable salvation.

Fifth, the postconciliar position holds that Jesus is the normative savior. This pluralistic view accepts that God has manifested himself to others, but Jesus' salvation is universal and decisive. One significant nuance is that, while for the Christian, Jesus is the indispensable and normative way to God and the meaning of life, this faith position cannot be the basis of ecumenical dialogue. Such a faith claim would seriously obstruct the dialogue.

Christianity can never drop its belief in the universality of the salvation brought by Jesus. Nevertheless, it so happens that many are letting go of both the exclusivist and inclusivist understandings of that universality.

The church can never cease its missionary activity. The postconciliar missiology of religious and cultural pluralism explained here states that, from one point of view, Christian evangelization has three dimensions: human, religious, and Catholic Christian. The missionary evangelizes on any or all of these levels, depending on the circumstances and the needs of the people.

The church evangelizes on the human level when it teaches Christian values and lifestyle—when it urges people to accept their humanity and to treat others lovingly and justly as their brothers and sisters. To repeat what Paul VI said in *Evangelii nuntiandi* in 1975, "The church promotes the human by evangelizing, and the church evangelizes by promoting the human."

The church evangelizes on the religious level by teaching that any religion is true to the extent that it contributes to humanization, liberation, and reconciliation (James 1: 27), and any religion is false to the extent that it contributes to fear, superstition, injustice, and exploitation.

The church evangelizes on the Catholic Christian level when it teaches that people can know Jesus Christ through a living tradition that is guarded by a community of disciples, and people can respond to Christ through and with this community of disciples.

John Paul II

The relation of the Catholic Church to the other religions is important to John Paul. He has written about missiology in two major encyclicals, attended an unprecedented day of prayer with representatives of other religions, and has had multiple contacts with Jews.

In 1979, he issued *Redemptor hominis,* his first encyclical and the first papal letter since *Humanae vitae* in 1968. He recommended activities that can bring Catholics closer to followers of other religions: "dialogue, contacts, prayer in common, investigation of the treasures of human spirituality in which . . . the members of these religions are indeed not lacking." The pope also insisted again and again that Christ is united to each person without any exceptions whatsoever. Commenting on the letter, Gregory Baum declared, "What is new and startling in the encyclical is the emphasis, many times repeated, on the redemptive presence of Jesus Christ to the entire human family—to people everywhere, to every single human being in his or her concrete, historical situation" (Baum 1979a; see also Hillman 1980).

On October 27, 1986, John Paul met at Assisi, Italy, with one hundred representatives of religions from around the world for a day of prayer, fasting, and silence for world peace. The pope called these leaders together because "the challenge of peace, as it is presently posed to every human conscience, transcends religious differences." One fear—that of papal dominance—haunted the preparations for the gathering. However, John Paul promised, "I shall be at Assisi as a brother among brothers and sisters" (Crow 1986).

John Paul's relations with the Jews have been very uneven, however. Critical headlines greeted the presence of a Carmelite convent on the site of the Auschwitz concentration camp, and the visit to the Vatican by President Kurt Waldheim of Austria, a man accused, but never tried for nor convicted of, Nazi war crimes.[5] These political events did not ultimately impede Jewish-Christian dialogues. However, one political position does—the Vatican's persistent refusal to recognize the state of

Israel until the Palestinian question is settled (Baum 1988). Nevertheless, during the summer of 1992, the Vatican approved the establishment of a bilateral, permanent commission aimed at achieving normalized relations between the two states.

The Vatican has made other positive contacts with Jewish groups. For instance, John Paul always acknowledges the spiritual relationship Christians have with Jews. The God of Abraham and the prophets is the God of Jesus Christ. On April 13, 1986, John Paul visited the central Roman synagogue. This was a meaningful and historic occasion for Catholicism because it was the first recorded appearance at a synagogue by a pope since Peter. The pope said, "With Judaism we have a relationship which we do not have with any other religion. You are our dearly beloved brothers and, in a certain way, it could be said you are our elder brothers."[6] Some Jewish leaders had hoped John Paul would recognize Israel, but he did not address politics except to express his abhorrence of anti-Semitism and to condemn the Holocaust.

On October 28, 1985, John Paul met with a group of Jewish leaders to celebrate the twentieth anniversary of the Council's Declaration on Non-Christian Religions. This document declared that the Jews as a group could not be held responsible for the death of Jesus and it deplored anti-Semitism. A rabbi told John Paul, "October 28, 1965, was both a historic and revolutionary date. It marked a turning away from eighteen centuries often characterized by both misunderstanding and persecution" (Dionne 1985). Finally, in December 1990 the pope received an international delegation from Jewish organizations to endorse their "Prague Statement." This candid document, drawn up in September, acknowledged that some aspects of Catholic teaching and practice had fostered anti-Semitism and the church should repent for this (Steinfels 1990e).

John Paul addressed mission theology in his eighth encyclical, *Redemptoris missio* ("Mission of the Redeemer"), published on December 7, 1990—the twenty-fifth anniversary of Vatican II's Declaration on the Church's Missionary Activity. This long document of 153 pages represents the first major papal statement on missionary work since 1959.

John Paul wrote this encyclical "to clear up doubts and ambiguities" regarding missionary activity both within and outside the church (Steinfels 1991). Within the church, said the pope, there are semantic confusions around the word *mission* and he deplored any move toward a God-centered rather than a Christ-centered understanding of interreligious dialogue. Christ, the Word of God made man for the salvation of all, has, he wrote, "an absolute and universal significance, whereby, while belonging to history, he remains history's center and goal" (n. 9). However, some theological trends seem to dampen missionary activity, motivation, and vocations. Furthermore, some so stress interreligious dialogue and involvement in political and economic struggles that they neglect spreading the faith and seeking converts to Christianity. Indifferentism is widespread. Also, missionary activity is waning, whereas it should be the concern of all Christians. Evangelization is the "primary service" of the church to the world. The duty of the church is to proclaim without fail wherever there is no local church that Jesus Christ is the source of salvation. Catholic Christians should be concerned that millions of people live in ignorance of God's love as manifested in the life and death of Jesus Christ. In fact, the number of people who do not know Christ has doubled since 1965.

The pope also complained that some Middle Eastern, African, and Asian countries refuse entry visas to missionaries and that some Islamic countries forbid converts and any cult that is not Muslim.

In light of the explanation of preconciliar, conciliar and postconciliar missiology outlined here, it is clear from John Paul's two encyclicals that his perspective is conciliar. He states that the church alone possesses the fullness of the means of salvation; that conversion and the planting of new churches throughout the world is required of the church. Needless to say, missionaries and theologians with a postconciliar missiology object to these views of the church's missionary activity (Balasuriya 1991).

Conclusion

In his 1991 book on the religions of the world, Huston Smith writes, "When historians look back on our century, they may remember it most, not for space travel or the release of nuclear energy, but as the time when the peoples of the world first came to take one another seriously" (p. 7). This chapter has reviewed the ways in which the conciliar and postconciliar church has taken seriously the other religious communities.

Any contact with the other religions will focus on christology and Christ's role as universal mediator (Acts 4:12). We have seen that, although interreligious dialogue is still in its early phase, it is complicated. For example, there are five approaches to the indispensibility of Jesus for salvation: relativist, fundamentalist, exclusivist, inclusivist, and pluralistic.

Catholic theologians have developed different understandings of the other religions. In the preconciliar days most Catholics judged the other religions to be false, that is, futile attempts to reach God. However, when missionaries and mystics came into close contact with the world religions, many soon learned that this judgment was not true. For example, Bede Griffiths (1906–93), the trailblazing Camaldolese Benedictine from England, spent some thirty-eight years in India defending Eastern spirituality and trying to bridge Christianity and Hindu and Buddhist traditions. As early as 1954 he wrote in *The Golden String*, his autobiography about his conversion to Catholicism in 1932 and his entry into the Benedictine community, that all Christians should recognize "all that is valid and true in all the different religious traditions."

In the conciliar period, there was a shift in theology: members of other religions were called anonymous Christians, a term which ultimately they themselves rejected. In the postconciliar period there was another theological shift: some Catholics regard the world religions as autonomous bodies, as valid ways to God, and as sources of new religious awareness.

Pope John Paul does not favor the postconciliar view. In the Catholic Church, then, this discussion between the magisterium and the theologians and missionaries will continue. For now, the suggestion of Ralph D. Mecklenburger, a rabbi from Michigan, deserves serious consideration: perhaps the best attitude Christians can have toward the other religions is to call them "honorary Christians." "Think of a foreign visitor being declared an 'honorary citizen' of a city; the term connotes appreciation, fondness, respect" (1979). Certainly, this world would be a much more peaceful place if every Jew, Muslim, Buddhist, and Hindu were considered an honorary Christian and every Christian considered an honorary Jew, honorary Muslim, honorary Buddhist, and honorary Hindu.

7

The Church and the Other Christians

Applied to the Christian religion, Von Hügel's triad reveals a religion in disastrous disarray. Christianity is like a precious mirror that has been shattered into thousands of pieces. The Christian churches hardly honor one another. They are deeply divided over identity, mission, authority, theology, interreligious dialogue, the role of women, moral issues, and other issues. This chapter investigates the whole Christian church and ecumenism: the efforts to restore visible unity to "the one and only Church of Christ" (UR 24). Ecumenism, acknowledged as one of the signs of the times (UR 4), was one of the purposes of Vatican II (SC 1).

Most Catholics living in the West know only the Catholic churches of the West united with Rome. What they often overlook is that the church originated in the Middle East and then spread from the mother church in Jerusalem to such centers as Antioch, Alexandria, and Damascus. Even today there are churches in such countries as Greece, Egypt, Syria, Russia, and Ukraine that are united with Rome and called Eastern Catholic churches.

Eastern Catholics have their own institutions, disciplines, theologies, liturgies, and spiritualities, all rooted in their own cultures and traditions. The Catholic Church has always had this diversity-in-unity. Unfortunately, the Eastern churches have lived under a twofold shadow: their separation from their Orthodox mother churches, and their administrative and cultural domination by Rome. Because of the latter, Eastern Catholics have often been overlooked or slighted by the West. For example, Pius IX placed them under the Propagation of the Faith in 1862. On May 1, 1917, Benedict XV corrected this insult by establishing an autonomous office, the Congregation for the Eastern Churches. Similarly, the Eastern churches allow married men to be ordained as priests. Once a man is ordained he may not marry and if a married priest loses his wife through death, he may not remarry. Pius XI decreed in 1929 that in the United States married men cannot be ordained to the priesthood of the Eastern churches. He believed American Catholics would find this scandalous. Needless to say, the Eastern churches find this restriction of an age-old tradition unjust. Finally, at the first session of Vatican II in 1962, the Eastern patriarchs were given seats behind the cardinals; later they sat opposite them.

Vatican II promulgated a document on the Eastern Catholic churches on November 21, 1964. It solemnly declared that "the churches of the East, as much as those of the West, fully enjoy the right, and are in duty bound, to rule themselves" (OE 5; cf. UR 16). It also affirmed the equality of the eastern and western traditions of Christianity (OE 3) and the importance of preserving the spiritual heritage of the East (UR 14–15).

Jesus prayed that his community of disciples would be one so "that the world may believe that you sent me" (John 17:21). Throughout its history, however, the church has not been "the seamless robe of Christ" (UR 13). The conciliar bishops noted that "from her very beginnings there arose in this one and only Church of God certain rifts (cf. 1 Cor. 11:18–19; Gal. 1:6–9; 1 John 2:18–19)" (UR 3). In 1054, however, there was a major rift between the church of the West and the East; and in 1517, a devastating division within the churches of the West. These divisions are a shameful contradiction of the nature of "the one and only Church of Christ" and a stumbling block to its mission. A divided church scandalizes the world and divided Christians become unconvincing messengers of peace and fellowship. Ecumenism is "the holy task of reconciling all Christians in the unity of the one and only Church of Christ" (UR 24).

Eastern Schism: Leo IX and Michael Cerularius

Pope Leo IX (1049–54), a man of spirituality, gentility, and courtesy, was a reformer and disciplinarian. This able pope was more a spectator than an actor in the great schism of 1054 because he was already dead when it occurred. Nevertheless, since his legates were acting in his name, the East-West division is attributed to his pontificate.

Leo IX wanted the churches of the East to help him control the growing power of the Normans. He appealed to the Patriarch of Constantinople, Michael Cerularius (1043–58), for help, but the patriarch refused to get involved in the pope's political problems. The patriarch then added fuel to the estrangement by imposing the Eastern rite on Latin churches in Constantinople and by condemning several Western practices. To seek reconciliation, Leo sent legates to Constantinople under the leadership of Archbishop Humbert. By all reports, Humbert was a fiery competitor with little charity of spirit. He hated Greeks and could not communicate adequately in their language.

Michael Cerularius was an arrogant, ambitious, yet popular leader who hated Latins and was concerned for the ecclesiastical supremacy of Constantinople. With their sophisticated liturgy, theology, and spirituality, the Greeks felt superior to Rome. When Cerularius and Humbert met, the two very irreconcilable personalities clashed. In addition to linguistic and cultural differences, the Latins and Greeks were divided over disciplinary practices; for example, the Greeks fasted on Saturdays, used leavened bread in the Eucharist, and allowed married men to be ordained as priests. However, it was at the level of theology— especially that of the Holy Spirit and the nature of the church— that their differences were more significant.

The Greeks taught that "the Spirit of Truth . . . proceeds from the Father" (John 15:26). This was the wording in the ancient creed adopted by the ecumenical Council of Chalcedon (451). The Latins, relying on Augustine and a local council held in Toledo, Spain, (589), said the Spirit proceeds from the Father *and* the son (*filioque*). Rome adopted the *filioque* theology around the year 1000 without consulting the Greeks and without reference to Chalcedon.

Filioque is theological theory. Who can ever know about the inner life of the triune God? Are not all descriptions of God analogical? *Filioque* might be a better explanation than the one based on John 15:26, but it is still the refinement of an idea and does not belong "in a creed intended to express the common faith of the East and West" (Kilmartin 1979, 57–58).

Beneath the cultural and theological differences lurked the ecclesial problem of authority. Who can authoritatively explain the nature and mission of the Spirit? The Spirit is central to Christian Scriptures, church doctrine, and creeds. However, the creeds say little about the Spirit. These theological and historical facts prompted Raymond Brown to say "with permissible exaggeration" that the Spirit "has been the most divisive feature in the history of Christianity" (1985, 102).

The authority issue also involved the interrelationship of conciliar and papal authority. The Greeks questioned the extent of papal jurisdiction, arguing that ecumenical councils were the one sure source of inspired doctrinal authority. Their model was the church's first council in Jerusalem as related in Acts 15. After deliberation, the Jerusalem Church announced its understanding of its mission in consultation with Peter, James, and Paul: "It is the decision of the Holy Spirit and of us. . . . "

The above account of the personal, political, and theological differences among the delegates is the background to the heated exchange that took place between Humbert and Cerularius in full view of the congregation in the Santa Sophia on July 16, 1054. Humbert placed on the altar a decree, excommunicating the patriarch and his supporters. Cerularius responded with his excommunication on July 24.

Conventionally, if somewhat inaccurately, the East-West division is dated 1054. Actually, some of the successors of Leo IX attempted reconciliation with the patriarchs. Most of the patriarchs of the East were better disposed toward Rome than toward Constantinople. But two events solidified the division. In 1098, the Greek patriarch of Antioch was expelled from the city and replaced by a Latin patriarch. There still may have been reconciliation, but the ruthless sack and pillage of Constantinople by crusaders in 1203 ended all hopes of reunification.

The Eastern churches that were excommunicated are called *Orthodox*, a term which means "right praise" or "holding the correct faith." Presently, the Orthodox number some ninety million, as compared to the twelve million Eastern Catholics.

The Reformation: Leo X and Martin Luther

Leo X (Giovanni de'Medici) was a polished yet devious politician. This Renaissance pope (1513–21) was immersed in literature, the arts, and music, and, consequently, was generous to artists and scholars because of his interest in furthering humanist culture. Nevertheless, he damaged the papal finances by his lavishness. To recoup his treasury and in order to build Saint Peter's, he permitted the sale of indulgences and sold church offices, even cardinal's hats.

Leo was unconcerned about the church's spiritual welfare; unaware of the intellectual ferment brought on by the printing press; and insensitive to the widespread desire for reform of the corruption, ignorance, and doctrinal confusion in the church. When Luther was first brought to Leo's attention, he dismissed the controversy between Luther and the sellers of indulgences as "a monkish squabble." He eventually condemned Luther in 1520 and excommunicated him on January 3, 1521.

In the twentieth century the possibility of lifting the excommunication has been discussed several times. In 1970, a group of German Lutheran bishops stated that the excommunication had already become history and that historical facts could not be abolished retroactively by formal legal acts. In 1980, when Cardinal Joseph Ratzinger was archbishop of Munich, he concurred with the Lutheran view, saying that he was "in principle against such posthumous cleansings of history."[1]

Martin Luther (1483–1546), a German Augustinian monk, was a man of violent temper, rough manners, and coarseness of language. At the same time, this complex man was a well-educated, intelligent, honest, and devout priest with extraordinary powers of persuasion, both written and oral.[2]

In his personal twofold search for certitude about his salvation and for a gracious God, Luther found in the Scriptures, especially Rom. 1:16–17, the answers he needed. Today his theology is often summarized as follows: humankind is saved (justified) by the grace of Christ alone through Scripture alone, appropriated by faith alone. This theology brought Luther into conflict with the popular theology of the day and its misplaced emphasis on works (e.g., the selling of indulgences), the authority of popes and councils, the acquisition of merit, and the excessive veneration of saints and Mary.

Luther challenged this theology by posting his ninety-five theses of protest on the church door at Wittenberg on October 31, 1517. These were quickly printed and disseminated.

As in the 1054 controversy, the deeper issue was authority, especially that of the Spirit and the papacy. How does the Spirit of truth function in the church, its officeholders and the Scriptures? The Catholic Church has consistently taught the infallibility of the church—that Christ delivered the truth about himself to the church, which is infallibly protected when discerning the truth collectively. This teaching was reiterated at Vatican II: "The body of the faithful as a whole, anointed as they are by the Holy One (cf. 1 John 2:20, 27), cannot err in matters of belief" (LG 12). Edward Norman, an Anglican priest and historian, believes that it is the Catholic understanding of the infallibility of the church itself "which is the major difference between Catholics and Protestants" (1991, 459). The Catholic tradition also maintained that the pope and bishops are the official interpreters of the Christian faith and Scriptures. The Spirit does not speak through the Scriptures in such a way that individual readers could indiscriminately challenge the teachings of the officeholders.

Protestant Christianity divided further over the theology of the Spirit. Although both Luther and John Calvin (1509–64) taught that "the Spirit speaks through the Scriptures *in the church,*" some of their followers later taught that the Spirit speaks "so *individually* in the heart of every Christian that the Bible read in a personal way, without church tradition or church setting, is an adequate guide" (R. E. Brown 1985, 103).

The conflict between Luther and Rome started as a protest in the name of the Scriptures and salvation. Because of a whole series of factors—some political, some economic, some the result of ignorance, stubbornness, and poor communication—the church of the West was divided beyond the imagination of any of the participants. Luther never intended to shatter the church of the West. His revolution is probably the most devastating event in the history of the church. The devastation continues as new denominations spring up weekly, "adding to some 22,190 separate ones estimated in 1985" (Marty 1988). Ernst Käsemann, a Lutheran Scripture scholar, has indicated the very ambiguous role the Scriptures play in the one Church of Christ: "The New Testament canon does not, as such, constitute the foundation of the unity of the church. On the contrary, as such, it provides the basis for the multiplicity of confessions" (Toolan 1982).

Ecumenism

Thomas Stransky, a Paulist priest who served on the Vatican Secretariat for Promoting Christian Unity from 1960 to 1970, wrote in 1986 that "the main flaw in the present ecumenical movement . . . is a lack of vision . . . of what ecumenism is" (1986a). A faulty understanding of ecumenism can only create fear and further divisions.

Ecumenism is the quest by Christians for full visible unity for mission through personal and church renewal and reform. The Greek root of the term means "the inhabited world." Ecumenism, then, points to the whole world and wholeness. This meaning prompted Arie Brouwer (1935–93), a former General Secretary of the National Council of Curches, to state that ecumenism "is the shaping and nurturing of the whole person committed to the whole ministry of the whole gospel through the whole church for the whole world" (1986).

My phrase, "full visible unity," assumes that since all Christians are disciples of Jesus Christ, a real but imperfect union already exists among them. However, this view of unity can point to an invisible and spiritual union, whereas the union should also be visible and juridical. Christians should have the same altar, a shared life, a common worship, and a single mission.

Two developments have taken place to deepen the understanding of unity. First, the Catholic Church and the Russian Orthodox Church, two communities that emphasize catholicity, have become more substantially involved in the ecumenical movement since Vatican II. Second, "many ecumenists are realizing afresh that the ground of unity is the apostolic faith" (Deschner 1986). The result of these two developments has been a striking emphasis on apostolicity and catholicity alongside unity as primary ecumenical themes. There can be no unity unless the churches are grounded in the apostolic faith. Similarly, this apostolic faith must be articulated in such a way that it will be "open to the pluralism, the mutual surprise and joy of discovery which belongs to an adequately diversified unity" (ibid.).

This unity should occur for the purposes of mission. Thomas Stransky defines ecumenism as "a commitment to the unity of the church-in-mission." Mission is "the obligation of the whole church to proclaim, by word and act, the whole gospel to the whole world" (Stransky 1986a). Stransky fears that our ecumenical pedagogy is weakest at the point of mission: "Few Christian persons or groups enter the ecumenical movement because of a commitment to the unity of the church-in-mission" (ibid.). Most get involved in specific common ministries (e.g., social justice projects, Bible study), but in doing so they often miss the wider implications of their specific projects: "the vision of Christ's revelation for the whole church in the whole world" (ibid.).

Renewal and reform are conditions for the possibility of unity. Christians cannot bring about the one and only Church of Christ by their own efforts. This is the work of the Spirit. Yet, all Christians are obliged to work with the Spirit for unity, until it is fully accomplished by the Spirit. This work, which should be a priority, requires the "continual reformation" of the church (UR 6) and, said the council fathers, takes its rise and grows toward maturity with "a change of heart" (UR 7). The bishops called a change of heart and holiness of life, along with public prayer for the unity of Christians, "spiritual ecumenism," and regarded it as "the soul of the whole ecumenical movement" (UR 8).

The ecumenical movement has achieved a measure of success. However, most Catholics of this generation have escaped the scars of religious bigotry. They do not realize how much fear, hatred, and ignorance of Catholics existed in many countries, including the United States. Most modern Catholics are tolerant of other Christians and other religions. Thus, they are puzzled or shocked to read of public insults to the pope. For example, in 1988, when John Paul was in Strasbourg to address the European Parliament, he was interrupted by militant Northern Ireland Protestant leader Ian Paisley, who, while holding up a placard that read, "Pope John Paul II—Antichrist," was yelling, "I renounce you and all your cults and creeds."[3]

They are also shocked to read of conflicts among other Christian communities. For example, in January 1990, at a week of prayer for Christian unity held at Westminster Cathedral, a group of Welsh Presbyterians protested the services, presided over by the Anglican Archbishop Robert

Runcie of Canterbury. They said, "We wish to defend our Lord and Savior, Jesus Christ, against the blasphemy and idolatry of the papist Mass and the treachery of Dr. Runcie. We believe the ecumenical movement comes directly from hell."[4]

The Papacy and Ecumenism: Leo XIII

The preconciliar church had developed a "state of siege mentality." Orthodox and Protestant Christians were regarded as schismatics and heretics who had broken from the true church. Nevertheless, Leo was the first pope to speak of these other Christian communities as "separated brothers" and in his encyclical *Praeclara* (1894), he invited both communities to return to Rome (J. Kelly 1986, 312).

The Armenian and Chaldean churches did return. Leo had no success with the other Orthodox communities, especially the Russian Orthodox, mainly because of his insistence on obedience to the Holy See and because they did not want to be latinized (Murphy 1981, 28–29).

Leo's encyclical *Ad anglos* (1895) revealed special interest in the reunion of the Anglican churches with Rome. That same year he appointed a commission to investigate the validity of Anglican ordinations of bishops and priests. After receiving a negative report, he declared in September 1896 that Anglican ordinations "have been and are absolutely null and utterly void."

Modern theologians and historians have argued over the accuracy of the "proofs" presented to Leo by his expert commissioners. Francis Clark, a British theologian, defended the papal decision in his book *Anglican Orders and Defect of Intention* (1956), while John Jay Hughes disagreed with both Leo XIII and Clark in his 1970 publication *Stewards of the Lord: A Reappraisal of Anglican Orders* (see Fichter 1988b). When the Vatican archives were opened in 1978, new sources of information became available. It seems that Leo's commission of eight experts was evenly split on the issue. However, Cardinal Rafael Merry del Val (1865–1930) drafted the final report. Upon investigation, many historians have criticized the way he handled history to support his arguments.

John Jay Hughes, the church historian cited above, was ordained an Anglican priest in 1954, became a Catholic in 1960 and a Catholic priest in 1968. His ordination (not reordination) in 1968 was performed *conditionally* by the then-bishop of

Münster and later Cardinal of Cologne, Joseph Hoffer. Hughes and Hoffer were convinced that today's Anglican orders are no longer identical with those declared invalid in 1896. Their judgment is based on their rejection of a sacramental theology of orders, which is based on the names in a bishop's table of succession—the theology of apostolic succession favored by Rome. In this view, bishops form a "continuous chain" back to the twelve apostles. Nevertheless, in Hughes' case, the Episcopalian bishops who had ordained him "had in their tables of succession consecrators whose orders are recognized by Rome as valid" (J. J. Hughes 1980b).

Today, most Catholic and Anglican theologians prefer a sacramental theology of ordination that attaches greater importance to the faith and sacramental life of the ecclesial communities in and for whom bishops and other ministers are ordained. In this view, there is "functional succession": the bishops carry on the special apostolic mission of founding and leading churches. As of now this issue has not been resolved and it continues to block ecumenical relations.

Despite the debacle of 1896, Leo's overall perception of ecumenism was honorable. In a discourse on March 9, 1895, he said, "Our eyes will never see the union of the churches that we are working for, but let us not be so fainthearted as to regard this unceasing effort as a fanciful dream. Such a sentiment would be unworthy of a Christian" (Tavard 1960, 113). During Leo's pontificate, there were no major ecumenical efforts as such on the part of other Christian communities. There were stirrings, however. The most significant initiative came from Patriarch Joachim III of Constantinople, who in 1902 sent to all the Orthodox churches an encyclical expressing concern about possible rapprochement among those who believe in God as Trinity so that the union of all Christian churches might eventually come about. The patriarch hoped for two things: a union of Orthodox churches and programs whereby the Orthodox could make contacts with other Christian churches.

Pius X

His goals were religious rather than political or ecumenical. One of his actions offended Christians, especially in the

United States. In 1910, former President Theodore Roosevelt was in Rome to lecture at the Methodist church there. When he requested a papal audience, he was refused because he was a Protestant.

It is ironic that during the pontificate of this unecumenical pontiff, "spiritual ecumenism" began in the United States (in 1908) and the actual ecumenical movement was organized by an American (in 1910).

Spiritual ecumenism began through the efforts of Paul Francis Wattson (1863–1940) and Lurana Mary White (1870–1935). They were Anglicans who in 1898 founded in Garrison, New York, the Society of the Atonement, a Franciscan community of friars and nuns with a special ecumenical dedication. This little group was corporately received into the Catholic Church on October 30, 1909.

In 1908, they had initiated eight days of prayer—from January 18 to 25—for church unity. They called this the Church Unity Octave. For some time, this octave focused firmly on reunion with Rome. The prayers were rather sternly phrased. For example, on January 20, prayers asked for "the submission of Anglicans to the authority of the Vicar of Christ." On January 22 the prayers asked "that Christians in America may become one in union with the chair of St. Peter."

Pius X approved the octave in 1909, and Benedict XV extended its observance to the universal church in 1916. In 1934, Paul Couturier (1881–1953), a priest active with the Orthodox in Lyons, France, suggested that prayers simply be offered for "the unity Christ wills by the means he wills."

In the early 1960s, the name of the week of prayer was changed to the Chair of Unity Octave. Finally, in 1966, in keeping with a greater ecumenical awareness, the present name was given: the Week of Prayer for Christian Unity. The title changes are significant for two reasons: Catholics had learned to pray with others and not simply for them; the emphasis was no longer church reunion but Christian unity.

It is plausible to date the beginnings of the modern ecumenical movement to the World Missionary Conference at Edinburgh, January 13–23, 1910. There were twelve hundred delegates from the Protestant missions from around the world, except Latin America and Africa (Desseux 1983, 46). The main concern of the delegates was their common task:

the evangelization of the world. One of the conference's eight commissions was designated to study cooperation and the promotion of unity. Several speeches alluded to the regrettable absence of Roman Catholic and Orthodox representation.

The organizer and president of the conference was the American Dr. John Raleigh Mott (1865–1955), a Methodist layman, who later received the Nobel Peace Prize in 1946. In his first address he asked, "Has it not humbled us increasingly as we have discovered that the greatest hindrance to the expansion of Christianity lies in ourselves?" Nonetheless, the meeting was an optimistic and unanimous affirmation of their task to evangelize the world.

During the conference, Bishop Charles Brent (1862–1929), a Canadian Episcopal bishop in the Philippines, was disturbed because questions of faith and church order were considered to be outside the competence of a missionary conference. He argued that Christians could not be content with cooperative efforts. In addition to cooperation, a forum was needed so the churches could study the causes of division with the purpose of removing them. Brent was to be the chief instrument in bringing about the Faith and Order Movement. A committee was approved, eventually set up in Geneva, and the first world conference was held in 1927.

Benedict XV

Like his predecessors, he dreamed of reunion with the Orthodox. As a way to achieve this very goal, he moved to strengthen the ties between Rome and the Eastern Catholics, especially when "the outbreak of the Russian Revolution made him think that the moment for this [reunion] had arrived" (J. Kelly 1986, 316). He created the Congregation for the Oriental Churches in May 1917 and set up the Pontifical Oriental Institute in Rome that October.

The Orthodox themselves became involved in ecumenism. On January 10, 1919, under the leadership of Patriarch Germanos of Constantinople, they called for all Christian churches to form a "league of churches." They "became the first church to call for a permanent organ of fellowship and cooperation between the churches" (Rusch 1985, 27).

In January 1920, they sent an encyclical to all the churches of the world, calling for the formation of an ecumenical council of churches (Visser't Hooft 1982, 1–2). The encyclical recognized both the new opportunities and the dangers of the times. It underscored the need for discussions at the practical level, insisting that doctrinal differences did not doom the enterprise to failure. By taking common action, it was stated, the churches would gain mutual knowledge, eliminate prejudice, and create a spirit of trust that would militate against disagreements and distrust. Unfortunately, the document did not receive wide circulation. Yet it was a significant contribution.

Meanwhile, Protestants were organizing an interchurch and international forum to examine doctrinal causes of disunity. In May 1919 they sent a delegation to Benedict to invite him to attend. He politely declined, but said he would pray for the success of the conference and, especially, that "those who participate in it may, by the grace of God, see the light and become reunited to the visible Head of the church, by which they will be received with open arms" (Tavard 1960, 117; Jay 1978, 299).

On July 4, 1919, the Holy Office forbade Catholics to participate in ecumenical congresses organized by other Christians, unless by express permission of the Vatican.

Pius XI

Pius had little sympathy for the other Christians other than as potential returnees to the Catholic Church (Murphy 1981, 56). The Orthodox gave little response to his calls for reunion. On the other hand, he did approve the conversations between Catholics and Anglicans held at Malines, Belgium, from 1921 to 1926 (J. Kelly 1986, 318).

In 1927, Protestant emissaries preparing for the first ecumenical conference on Faith and Order to be held at Lausanne, Switzerland, visited the pope, seeking his blessing and cooperation in the search for Christian unity. Pius declined any interest in the "distinctive witness" they sought to bring intact into "the coming great church." Rather, the pope politely reminded them that their search could be immediately finalized right there on the spot by a return to the Catholic Church.

After the visit, the Holy Office announced in July 1927 that Catholics could not take part in the Faith and Order Conference at Lausanne. Just after the Lausanne conference, Pius issued his encyclical *Mortalium animos* (January 1928) in which he denounced ecumenical congresses, meetings, and addresses because they led to indifferentism. Catholics could not take part in these assemblies, he wrote, nor should they encourage or support them, since "the unity of Christians can come about only by furthering the return to the one true Church of Christ of those who [had] separated from it." Furthermore, since the other Christians are themselves so divided in belief on many points, the encyclical wondered how, with their wide variation of opinions, they "can open up the way to unity of the church when this unity can be born of but one single authority, one sole rule of faith, and one identical belief."

Finally, during Pius's pontificate another Protestant conference was organized: Life and Work. Its actual origins go back to 1919, followed by a preparatory conference at Geneva in 1920. Nathan Söderbloom (1866–1931), Lutheran Archbishop of Uppsala, Sweden, was the organizer and leader. This outstanding Christian was to receive the Nobel Peace Prize in 1930.

The purpose of Life and Work was to relate the Christian faith to the social, political, and economic problems of society. They believed the churches should first unite and then discuss doctrines. Their motto: "Service unites; doctrines divide."

Their first meeting was held at Stockholm in 1925, with six hundred delegates from thirty-seven countries. Some consider it *the* first ecumenical conference because it was composed entirely of delegates who were representatives of their churches (Visser't Hooft 1982, 10).

Pius XII

The ecumenical movement that began among the Protestant churches in 1910 reached a major landmark in 1948 during the pontificate of Pius XII. Within both the Faith and Order and the Life and Work movements there grew an awareness that their concerns were so intertwined that they needed to be brought together in a single council. In 1937, these councils met at Edinburgh and Oxford, respectively. Both recommended unity in a World Council of Churches (WCC). A provisional WCC was set up at Utrecht, Holland, with Willem A. Visser't Hooft (1901–85) as its general secretary. He gave the council its name and is considered "the supreme architect of the ecumenical movement" (Thompson 1985a).

World War II prevented the WCC from holding its first meeting until August 22–September 4, 1948. The meeting in Amsterdam attracted 351 delegates from 147 churches from 44 countries. Visser't Hooft was elected the first general secretary, a post he would hold until 1966. Geneva was chosen for their headquarters.

Their theme was "Man's disorders and God's design." Right from their first meeting, concern for church unity and for social questions were inextricably linked; they are two sides of the same ecumenical coin. For example, the most controversial statement made in the Amsterdam assembly was its criticism of laissez-faire capitalism and Marxist communism. "The Christian churches should reject the ideologies of communism and laissez-faire capitalism and should seek to draw men away from the false assumptions that these extremes are the only alternatives. Each has made promises which it could not redeem."

At Amsterdam, the delegates committed themselves to stay together, having defined themselves as "a fellowship of churches which accept our Lord Jesus Christ as God and savior." The last two words in the statement were never defined. Incarnation and atonement were underscored, but each church was free to interpret them in its own way.

The WCC does not pretend to be or become a "super church." It is an instrument for the union of the churches; only particular churches can choose to unite with others. The WCC provides a forum for speaking and acting together, hoping to create the conditions for the possibility of visible union. The WCC "is not a church but a confederation of independent churches, each of which remains free to disassociate itself from any WCC position or statement" (Rausch 1985).

In December 1949 in *Ecclesia sancta*, Pius XII relaxed his predecessor's negative views of the ecumenical movement by formally recognizing it and by permitting Catholic scholars to dialogue with other Christians on matters of faith and morals. He even allowed that such meetings could begin and end with shared prayer. This permission came as a very considerable shock to moral theologians and ecumenists because in the previous year Pius had reiterated the church's position that any sharing in worship with those not Catholic was "entirely forbidden."

The second WCC assembly was held in Evanston, Illinois, in August 1954. There were 502 delegates from 161 member churches. Their theme was "Jesus Christ—the hope of the world." They committed themselves not only to stay together (as had been agreed at Amsterdam) but also to grow together. They stressed service to the world and said less about evangelization and missionary activity than had been said at Amsterdam.

On June 24, 1985, the seventy-fifth anniversary of the World Missionary Conference, a meeting was held in Edinburgh with some five hundred delegates present. The meeting was not a triumphalist celebration. A delegate from Nigeria reminded the assembly that "there were Christians in Africa before they were in Edinburgh." Emilio Castro, secretary general of the WCC, did not spare his predecessors. He criticized the way they had married missionary activity with colonialism, and noted the irony that by 1914 the armies of the missionary countries were killing each other. Finally, he observed that the regions whose representatives dominated Edinburgh in 1910—the United Kingdom and western Europe—had reached the point in 1985 where they now needed re-evangelization. In fact, to the dismay of many, neither the Church of England nor the Church of Scotland had sent delegates (A. H. Jones 1985).

John XXIII

One of the chief concerns of Vatican II was the restoration of unity among all Christian churches. In John's first encyclical, *Ad petri cathedram* (June 29, 1959), he greeted the other Christians as "separated brethren and sons." However, his ecumenical theology echoed that of his predecessors. He invited the other Christian churches "to take or resume that place [in the Catholic Church] which is yours, which for many of you was your father's place."

In June 1960, John created the Secretariat for Christian Unity. This office was given responsibility for inviting leaders of Christian churches as official observers at Vatican II and for initiating interchurch dialogues.

The original members of the secretariat included Cardinal Augustin Bea and Monsignor (later cardinal) Jan Willebrands, and two staff members, Thomas Stransky (later Superior General of the Paulist Fathers) and Monsignor Jean-Francois Arrighi. This team won the respect of ecumenists worldwide. Bea was the first president (1960–68) and Willebrands succeeded him (1968–89). The current president is an Australian, Cardinal Edward Idris Cassidy (Hebblethwaite 1989h). On March 1, 1989, the Secretariat was renamed the Council for Promoting Christian Unity and subordinated to the CDF.

During John's pontificate there were two important developments: the founding of another ecumenical organization and the third assembly of the WCC. On December 4, 1960, at Grace Episcopal Cathedral in San Francisco, Eugene Carson Blake (1906–85), stated clerk of the (then) United Presbyterian Church, gave a landmark sermon, "A Proposal Toward the Reunion of Christ's Church." This sermon marked the tenth anniversary of the National Council of Churches in the United States and attracted such nationwide attention that it rated Blake a spot on the cover of *Time*. Blake's sermon called for a church "truly catholic, truly evangelical, and truly reformed" (Thompson 1985b; see also Radano 1985), and launched the Consultation on Church Union (COCU).

COCU "is not a denomination but a movement created by the nine denominations that participate in it. Its one task is to hammer out theological underpinnings and practical details of a possible united and uniting church" (Penfield 1980). Its foundation document, "The COCU Consensus," sets out areas of theological agreement and has been approved by eight of the nine member denominations.

In December 1989, the member churches voted unanimously to adopt a second document, "Churches in Covenant Communion." The thesis of this one hundred-page document is that churches in covenant are not at an interim step on the way toward joining one big church but the covenanting process *is* a new form of church union. In its outline of ways for churches to achieve unity without structural merger, it focuses on mutual recognition of ministers and also shared communion, membership, and mission. By mission they mean the churches should work together on projects that enhance the social, political, and economic life of the community. By June

1993 (ecumenism is a long, slow process), three of the churches had endorsed the plan and the remaining six churches are scheduled to act on the document between 1994 and 1995.

The WCC held its third assembly, at New Delhi in 1961 with 577 delegates from 197 member churches. Its theme was "Christ, the Light of the World." The delegates affirmed their intention not only to stay together and to grow together, but also to assume new tasks together. They revised their self-definition as presented at Amsterdam: "The WCC is a fellowship of churches which confess the Lord Jesus Christ as God and Savior according to the Scriptures and, therefore, seek to fulfill their common calling to the glory of the one God, Father, Son, and Holy Spirit."

Four Orthodox churches—Russian, Romanian, Polish, and Bulgarian—became members. This gave the Orthodox more influence in ecumenism. Their presence, said Visser't Hooft, did not make the ecumenical task easier, but did enrich it. John XXIII approved Roman Catholic observers at the New Delhi meeting, leaving Cardinal Bea to choose the delegates.

Vatican II

The Council produced two documents that dealt with ecumenism: a Decree on Ecumenism and the Declaration on Religious Freedom. Paul VI signed the ecumenism decree on November 21, 1964. In the final count, it received only eleven negative votes. From what has been reported about the preconciliar popes, it should come as no surprise that this decree was not based on experience in ecumenical matters; actually, it became the source of a new tradition. It marked the beginning of Catholic openness to ecumenism. Wider horizons and urgent tasks would become clearer as the church's involvement developed.

The decree is new because it acknowledged that both sides were responsible for the divisions and because it overcame the simple identification of "the one and only Church of Christ" with the Catholic Church, as had been claimed by Pius XII in *Mystici corporis* (1943). Nevertheless, the Council reaffirmed the special claim of the Catholic Church to be *the* Church of Christ: "For it is through Christ's Catholic Church alone, which is the all-embracing means of salvation, that the fullness of the means of salvation can be obtained" (UR 3). But then the Council went on to add significant qualifications: (1) It recognized the unity already created by baptism, faith, hope, and love, and spoke of "obstacles to perfect ecclesiastical communion"; (2) it acknowledged the ecclesial character of the other Christian communities—until the publication of this conciliar decree, other Christian churches, with the exception of the Orthodox, were officially referred to as "societies" and not churches; and (3) it stated that the Church of Christ "subsists in" the Catholic Church (LG 8; see UR 3–4).

The phrase "subsists in" has been controversial since the Council. In March 1985, the CDF, in criticizing a book by Leonardo Boff, argued that the authentic meaning of "subsists in" was that "only elements of the church" exist outside the "visible structure" of the Catholic Church. In May 1987, Cardinal Jan Willebrand, president of the Secretariat for Christian Unity, questioned this interpretation.[5] Avery Dulles concurred, insisting that "subsists in" is quite different from "is" and that the phrase "subsists in" was "an expression deliberately chosen to allow for the ecclesial reality of the other Christian communities" (1989, 430). Gregory Baum had already written along these lines in 1972: "Whoever speaks of the Catholic church as the one true church must qualify this doctrine by the complementary teaching that the one true church transcends the Catholic church and cannot be simply identified with it" (1972b).

The Declaration on Religious Freedom was the most controversial council document because it raised the question of doctrinal development. Pius IX's *Syllabus of Errors* (1864) had rejected religious liberty. But the experience of religious pluralism in the United States—perhaps the greatest contribution the United States has given to world civilization—made its impact on the development of doctrine and policy at the Council, thanks to the brilliance of John Courtney Murray. This conciliar document was the distinctive contribution of the United States to the Council. During the Council it was this document that "had become a Protestant litmus test of the sincerity of the council's ecumenical resolve" (R. M. Brown et al. 1987a, 178). The declaration received a final approval by a vote of 2,308 to 70.

Despite the controversy, it is generally acknowledged that Vatican II marked a fundamental shift in Catholic appreciation of the other Christian communities. Before the Council, Catholics emphasized what divided the churches. The other churches were strangers or enemies. The Council underscored what united Christians: all are brothers and sisters baptized in Christ and exist for one another. All Christian communities belong to the one Church of Christ. This new perspective reflected a shift from an ecclesiocentric to a christocentric theology—instead of unity through return to the Catholic Church, there should be unity by deeper and more explicit regrafting into the "one and only Church of Christ," especially as this is manifested in the Roman Catholic Church.

Later Evaluations of the Council

Writing in 1979, Richard McBrien judged ecumenism "almost dead in the water, at least at the officially approved levels." He based his judgment on two points: many bishops ignored reports from bilateral consultations and there was hardly any positive action being taken about intercommunion and the mutual recognition of ordained ministers.

In 1983, Kilian McDonnell wrote that the conciliar decree was cautious, reticent, and even fearful. It gave a careful answer to the realities of 1964 when the question was about how the church could take part in ecumenical meetings, he explained. But in the meantime, the question had changed. Ecumenists asked how the unity of the church could become a reality. How can unity be manifested today? The decree had no answer to this question.

In 1986, Thomas Stransky highlighted some of the surprises in ecumenism since the Council. The Council had recommended interchurch dialogues. The extent and pace of the dialogues, both bilateral and multilateral, had far exceeded all expectations. The Council also recommended that "the ecumenical dialogue could start with the moral application of the gospel." When this statement was made, the bishops were not unaware of the sharp and serious differences between Catholics and other Christians about moral matters. A real surprise is that twenty years after the Council, the personal and social ethical issues would be more divisive than they were in the 1960s (Stransky

1986a). However, after a look at the list of issues, it is easy to see why there is so much division. Part of the long list includes abortion, birth control, the death penalty, euthanasia, divorce and remarriage, and active homosexuality. As Thomas Rausch, a Jesuit ecumenist, observed, the moral issues now constitute "the Achilles' heel of the ecumenical movement" (1989b).

In 1986, Stransky was disappointed with the reception of ecumenism. "Authentic ecumenical thinking, attitudes and practices have entered the bloodstream of only a minority of Catholics," he remarked (1986a). A few years later, Thaddeus Horgan was more optimistic. He stated that since the Council, "the church has wholeheartedly committed itself to the ecumenical quest, particularly in its leadership at the international and national levels" (1990).

In another 1990 assessment of ecumenism, Thomas Rausch wrote, "Perhaps the greatest obstacle to ecumenical progress remains the fact that far too few Christians really long for reconciliation. The churches today seem content to live in peace as they follow their separate paths. There is a new level of mutual respect. Occasionally they cooperate on practical matters . . . But for the vast majority, Christians in different churches remain strangers to each other."

Paul VI

Paul VI and Patriarch Athenagoras of Constantinople met in Jerusalem on a common pilgrimage, from January 5 to 6, 1964, praying that "this meeting may be the sign and prelude of things to come for the glory of God and the illumination of his faithful people." On December 7, 1965, the day before the closing of the Council, the two leaders mutually lifted the excommunications of 1054. Since the Council had Christian unity as one of its goals, this act was a dramatic symbol of the intent of the institutional church. In 1967, the two leaders exchanged visits, July 25 in Constantinople and October 26 in Rome. These religious encounters helped smooth the way for many productive Catholic-Orthodox dialogues.

Paul visited the WCC in Geneva on June 10, 1969, a visit unthinkable in 1948. The visit proved his esteem for the work of the WCC, and yet he made it clear that the Catholic Church was still reluctant to enter fully into the organization.

There are several reasons for this reluctance. First, the Catholic Church is so hierarchically and solidly structured and organized that it would be very difficult to diffuse its identity and independence of action within another organization. Second, there are theological and jurisdictional problems that must be considered, especially those concerning the future role of the papacy. Third, the sheer size of the Catholic Church is such that it would so overwhelm the WCC as to call into question its very identity.

The WCC held two general assemblies during Paul's pontificate. Its fourth assembly was held at Uppsala, Sweden, in July 1968, with Eugene Carson Blake as general secretary (1967–72). The assembly met against the background of the many challenges of the 1960s: the ambiguity of new scientific and technological progress, the growing gap between poor and rich nations, and racism. Its theme was "Behold I make all things new" (Rev. 21:5). There were 704 delegates from 235 churches and 84 countries, one-third from the third world. The largest group of delegates came from Orthodox churches. The Catholic church sent fourteen observers and also had two firsts: nine theologians joined the Faith and Order Commission and Roberto Tucci, a Jesuit theologian and editor of *Civilta Cattolica*, gave a major address to the assembly. In his talk he referred to the possibility of the Catholic Church joining the WCC.

The fifth assembly was held in Nairobi in 1975 (J. R. Nelson 1976; Gibeau 1976a). There were 676 delegates from 285 member churches. The general secretary was Philip Potter (1972–84). The delegates agreed that in addition to staying and growing together, they would struggle together. Their theme was "Jesus Christ frees and unites." The delegates declared that faith in the triune God and socio-political engagement, conversion to Jesus Christ, and active participation in changing economic and social structures belong together and condition one another. They wrote a major amendment into their constitution, declaring that the churches are called "to the goal of visible unity in one faith and in one eucharistic fellowship expressed in worship and in common life in Christ, and to advance toward that unity in order that the world may believe."

New Delhi (1961) had called for the unity of all in each place, and Uppsala (1968) had underscored the depth and extent of catholicity. Nairobi (1975) complemented those two meetings by acknowledging there can be unity-in-diversity and diversity-in-unity.

John Paul II

On October 17, 1978, the day after his election, John Paul committed himself to the work of ecumenism without reservation. He expressed hope that with common effort "we might fully arrive at full communion." On June 12, 1984, he visited the WCC headquarters in Geneva, symbolizing that the search for unity was still among Rome's pastoral priorities. Among his ecumenical overtures were visits with the Orthodox. In 1979, when John Paul visited Turkey, he and the Patriarch of Constantinople attended each other's liturgies—without, however, sharing communion. Some commentators believed this visit signaled John Paul's keen interest in the East, so much so that he seems to have relegated dialogue with the West to second place (Hebblethwaite 1980a, 1980c).

It is natural for John Paul to be drawn more to the East than the West. First, he is a Slav. His fourth encyclical, *Apostles of the Slavs* (1985), commemorated the two Greek missionary brothers to the Slavs in the ninth century, Cyril and Methodius, and appealed for spiritual unity between eastern and western Europe. Second, Peter Hebblethwaite suggests that the Orthodox tradition confirms many of John Paul's own concerns: his insistence on high christology, sacramental piety, Marian devotion, monasticism, a "sacred" view of the priesthood, and resistance to "secularizing" trends (Hebblethwaite 1980d).

Nevertheless, those involved in Catholic-Orthodox dialogues admit that their concerns are just as demanding and complicated as those that engage Catholic-Protestant dialogues. For example, it is unthinkable to hope for a successful dialogue with the Orthodox unless claims to universal papal jurisdiction are reconstituted and the papacy functions mainly as a quasi-sacrament of unity for the whole church. Also, Orthodox-Catholic union is impossible until the churches first work out how it will be possible for Eastern Catholics and Orthodox to exist in communion. Finally, as long as Eastern Catholics are treated as second-class members of the Roman Catholic Church, Orthodox churches will suspect and disregard the Catholic Church's declaration to be a sister church to the Orthodox.

Some of the deep-seated problems between the Orthodox and Catholics surfaced in 1991 when John Paul II called a special synod of European bishops to discuss "a new evangelization of Europe" in light of the collapse of communism and the sudden fall of the Iron Curtain. About 137 bishops gathered in Rome from November 28 to December 14. In addition to the European bishops, the pope invited episcopal observers from different continents and also Protestant and Orthodox church leaders. The synod got off to a poor start when concerns raised by the Orthodox leaders took center stage as five Orthodox churches rejected the papal invitation to attend. The Russian Orthodox Patriarch Alexsei II declared that the Catholic Church had created "rival missionary structures" in Soviet territory by appointing bishops in regions where there had been none before and by conducting a proselytizing campaign of "conversion."

The meeting, although tense at times, ended with attempts at reconciliation. Both sides agreed that more ecumenical dialogues were needed so that unfortunate differences such as the one that disrupted this meeting would not erupt in the future. And the concluding document stressed the valiant testimony to Christ exhibited by the Orthodox churches under decades of communist regimes (Cowell 1991; Rosato 1992; Weakland 1992).

Pope John Paul paid comparatively less attention to United States Protestants when he visited the United States for a week in 1979 (October 1–7). During this historic visit, the pope never met with Protestant leaders, nor did he learn about the ecumenical progress taking place in the United States, but he did give a talk to ecumenists at a prayer service in Washington on October 7. In his address, John Paul referred to such topics as intercommunion and the deep division over moral and ethical matters. He said, "The moral life and the life of faith are so deeply united that it is impossible to divide them." Some Protestant leaders were disappointed with the visit, but most agreed that while the visit did not further ecumenical relations, neither did it hinder them (Winiarski 1979b).

On September 11, 1987, during his second visit to the United States, John Paul prayed with evangelical Protestants in Columbia, South Carolina. This was a highly public approach to this group, especially the Southern Baptists, who at thirteen million are the second-largest denomination in the United States. Since the Southern Baptists have not participated with the National Council of Churches, the visit was "a step toward bringing evangelical Protestants more comfortably into pan-Christian discussions" (A. Jones 1987). On the negative side, "a number of perceptive Protestants . . . see Pope John Paul II as being more concerned with reasserting the identity and integrity of the Roman Catholic church as a worldwide community" than with ecumenism (Rausch 1985). It is not that John Paul is unecumenical; he is ecumenical in his own way.

Contacts between Rome and Anglican leaders have increased since Geoffrey Fisher, Archbishop of Canterbury, met with John XXIII in 1960. Archbishops Michael Ramsey (1961–74) and Donald Coogan (1974–80) met with Paul VI in 1966 and 1977, respectively. Archbishop Robert Runcie (1980–91) met John Paul five times between 1980 and 1989. In the last visit, Runcie announced that the papacy had to be more than a symbol of unity: "Today the divisions among Christians require that the primacy of the Bishop of Rome should also be a primacy of action and initiative in favor of that unity for which Christ so earnestly prayed" (Hebblethwaite 1989e).

In response, John Paul acknowledged his ecumenical mission but also honestly pointed to differences between Rome and Canterbury. He said, "Events in recent years have seriously aggravated the differences between us, making the work of unity more difficult" (Hebblethwaite 1989g). John Paul was referring to the Anglican consideration of ordaining women as priests, and even bishops, a practice rejected out of hand by the institutional Catholic Church.

This issue surfaced again when, on November 11, 1992, the mother church of the Anglican community voted by a narrow margin to ordain women to the priesthood. The Vatican's reaction was quick and uncompromising: "This decision by the Anglican Communion constitutes a new and grave obstacle to the entire process of reconciliation."

Rome's relationship with evangelicals in Mexico has been less than cordial. In May 1990, John Paul made his second visit to Mexico. This predominantly Catholic country has had a rapid growth of Protestant denominations, especially among such fundamentalist churches as the Assemblies of God, Pentecostals, and Seventh-day Adventists. The Catholic hierarchy in Mexico pejoratively refers to them as "sects." On the occasion of the pope's visit, the local hierarchy refused to invite them to an ecumenical meeting with the pope. One Mexican bishop was quoted as saying, "You do not have dialogue with bandits."

In one of his homilies John Paul noted that some Catholics had "broken the link of saving grace, joining the sects." "No Catholic in Mexico can consider himself exempt" from the obligation to bring defectors back to the church. He continued, "I would like to meet with you one by one to tell you: come back to the fold of the church, your mother" (Rohter 1990).

During John Paul's tenure, two major documents were produced and an assembly of the WCC was held. First, in January 1982, the Faith and Order Commission of the WCC met in Lima, Peru, and by a unanimous vote accepted its document "Baptism, Eucharist and Ministry" (called BEM, or the Lima document). BEM is unique in the history of the ecumenical movement. It is probably the most significant ecumenical document to appear since the Decree on Ecumenism of Vatican II. It represents fifty years of development in the Faith and Order Commission. "The next chapter of the history of the ecumenical movement may well be written on how the churches respond to this statement" (Rusch 1985, 31).

It is not possible to give a lengthy summary of this thick text (see World Council of Churches 1982; Benjamin 1984; Dulles 1982; and Heim 1986). Some significant points are the following. The statement on baptism maintains that the difference between infant and adult baptism becomes less sharp when Christians recognize "that both forms of baptism embody God's own initiative in Christ and express a response of faith made within the believing community." The section on the Eucharist states that Christ's presence in the Eucharist is real, living, active, and unique, and should be celebrated "at least every Sunday." The statement on ministry singles out the threefold ministry of bishop, presbyter, and deacon. Those churches with this ministry "will need to ask how its potential can be fully developed for the most effective witness of the church." Those churches without this threefold ministry "need to ask themselves whether the threefold pattern as developed does not have a powerful claim to be accepted by them."

BEM has become a part of church life at the local and denominational levels. The Vatican is preparing a response, based on the reflections of international episcopal conferences. By 1986, some 300,000 copies of the document were in print around the world. It has evoked a new level of interest and involvement in ecumenism at the grass roots. There are, however, some concerns and reservations. Many in the United States argue that the document should have dealt with the ordination of women in a more positive and forthright way. Also, some churches without the threefold ministry expressed some reluctance to endorse such a ministry, mainly because of uncertainty about how these categories—especially that of the episcopate—are to be understood.

The second major document dealt with Anglican and Catholic relations. On March 26, 1966, Paul VI and Michael Ramsey, Archbishop of Canterbury, announced their intention "to inaugurate between the Roman Catholic Church and the Anglican Communion a series of dialogues that, founded on the gospels and the ancient common tradition, may lead to that unity in truth for which Christ prayed."

In 1967, a preparatory commision on Anglican-Catholic unity was established. By 1968, the commission issued its "Malta Report," which noted that there were large areas of agreement between the two communities and three areas of disagreement: the Eucharist, ministry and ordination, and authority in the church. The authority differences were particularly concerned with the role of the papacy.

The first Anglican-Roman Catholic International Committee (ARCIC I) met in 1970, studied these areas of disagreement and twelve years later (March 12, 1982) published its "Final Report." This document has been called "the most dramatic achievement toward Christian unity in the realm of international ecumenical consultations" (A. Cunningham 1986, 69). In the report the theologians of ARCIC I declared that they had reached "substantial agreement" on major doctrinal issues concerning authority, Eucharist, ministry, and ordination. They believed the report was "consonant with the faith" of both communities.

The CDF praised the report in its initial response in 1982 for "the quality of doctrinal rapprochement achieved," but sharply criticized it as being ambiguous or inadequate on several key points. The CDF said it had reservations because the Anglicans explicitly acknowledge that they cannot accept such Catholic teachings as infallibility, the Marian dogmas, eucharistic adoration, and the primacy of the bishop of Rome (Tavard 1980; McDonnell 1982). The CDF sent its initial eleven-page response to the international episcopal conferences for their responses. The Vatican's response evoked surprise, since the Catholics on the committee had helped produce and consented to the "Final Report."

In 1988, the Anglicans accepted the committee's document. The Vatican's long-overdue response came on December 5, 1991. It began enthusiastically, saying that the report achieved "points of convergence and even of agreement which many would not have thought possible." It commented on the "notable progress toward a consensus" on the Eucharist and on the ordained ministry. It saw "convergence" but "no substantial agreement" on authority in the church, the Marian dogmas or Roman primacy. It also noted that "convergence has eluded ARCIC I on such issues as papal infallibility." And it concluded with these words: "The objection may be made that this reply does not sufficiently follow the ecumenical method. . . . It must, however, be remembered that the Roman Catholic Church was asked to give a clear answer to the question: Are the agreements contained in this report consonant with the faith of the Catholic Church? What was asked for was not a simple evaluation of an ecumenical study, but an official response as to the identity of the various statements with the faith of the church."

The Catholic Church appears to be asking that the ARCIC I report express a theology that is identical (rather than consonant) with its own teachings. But if either church community requires that the other conform to its own theological formulations, further progress will be hard to achieve. Both churches need to concentrate on "the substance of the ancient deposit of faith"—the message of John XXIII at the opening of Vatican II.

ARCIC II was convened in 1982 by Archbishop Robert Runcie and John Paul II. It must deal with these documents and the differences that surfaced so that the debilitating division of these two international communions will be healed.

The WCC held its sixth assembly in Vancouver, July 24–August 10, 1983 (see Geyer 1983; Moore 1983; Lyles 1983; Misner 1983; and Rausch 1984). There were 847 delegates from 301 member churches from one hundred countries. Twenty Roman Catholic observers, including six bishops, were approved by the Vatican. The theme of the assembly was "Jesus Christ—the life of the world."

The WCC has been a controversial body because it deals with controversial issues in which theology and ethics impinge on political, economic, and social policies. Its Vancouver meeting was as faithful as previous assemblies had been to the ecumenical pioneers who emphasized the importance of the work of Christian unity not in a political or social vacuum, but in relation to the continuing worldwide struggle for a greater measure of justice, peace, and human dignity. The delegates were reminded that peace and justice belong together with baptism, Eucharist, and ministry. These two strains must mutually reinforce one another rather than become parallel tracks which might split apart. Keeping them together is no easy task.

In 1984, Emilio Castro of the Evangelical Methodist Church of Uruguay was elected the fourth general secretary of the WCC (Howell 1984). He presided over the seventh assembly, which met in Canberra, Australia, February 7–20, 1991. The 842 voting delegates from one hundred countries represented 311 churches—a major increase over the 147 churches present in 1948. In 1983, 31 percent of the delegates were women; in 1991, women constituted 35 percent. Present also were twenty-three Vatican-delegated observers.

For the first time the theme focused on the Spirit: "Come, Holy Spirit, renew the whole creation" (Ryan 1991). This was also the first time the theme was formulated as a prayer.

The assembly was held while the Persian Gulf War was being waged and it affected the deliberations. For example, Emilio Castro, disappointed that all could not celebrate one Eucharist, hoped all the delegates would unite at the eucharistic table at the next assembly in 1998, the fiftieth anniversary of the founding of the WCC. He asked how the presidents of warring countries could ever unite in peace if the churches could not unite around the Eucharist. This plea raised the perennial question: Is the Eucharist the expression of unity or a means to unity?

Some of the ecclesial questions that were debated included theological perspectives (particularly that of northern nations versus that of southern nations), the relation of men and women (and women's ordination), the cultural limitations of biblical language (particularly the dominance of male metaphors for God), and the inevitable tension between ecumenists and social activists. The former focus on the nature of God and church unity; the latter emphasize peace and justice. However, this tension reached a most critical point at Canberra because "it became apparent that the quest for Christian unity, and so issues of faith and order, were no longer the major concern of many of the delegates. If this is true as well of the churches they represented, then something significant has happened in the ecumenical movement" (Putney 1992, 633). Orthodox participants were disturbed by some of the presentations, which seemed to equate the Holy Spirit with the spirits of nature, ancestors, or social movements. They warned that they might withdraw from the organization if it deviated from basic Christian beliefs.

Finally, it should be noted that Konrad Raiser was elected the fifth general secretary of the WCC and assumed office in January 1993. An ordained minister in the Evangelical Church in Germany and a professor of ecumenical theology, Raiser had been deputy general secretary of the WCC from 1973 to 1983.

A Multifaceted Unresolved Issue

In terms of Von Hügel's triad, the Christian churches have a long way to go to solve the institutional, intellectual, and devotional problems that divide them. One significant issue— the way churches evaluate one another's ordained ministry— impinges on such debatable issues as the authority of the papacy, women priests, married clergy, and intercommunion. Thomas Rausch maintains that "while authority and ordained ministry are not synonymous, it is precisely the different understandings of the nature and authority of the ordained ministry which are at issue between the churches" (1989a, 74).

Paul VI remarked to the Secretariat for the Unity of Christians on April 28, 1967, that the papacy "is undoubtedly the greatest obstacle in the path of ecumenism." This sentence is often taken out of context. It was not intended to reflect the pope's own conviction, but was an observation. He was "entering sympathetically into the minds of other Christians" (Hebblethwaite 1980d).

The bishop of Rome has a special ministry: to serve and symbolize the unity of the church universal. At Vatican II, the bishops asserted that the bishop of Rome "presides over the whole assembly of charity and protects legitimate differences, while at the same time [he] sees that such differences do not hinder unity but contribute to it" (LG 13). A restructured papacy that would provide more legitimate diversity, collegiality, and subsidiarity than presently exists would further the ecumenical movement. Furthermore, many voices call the Catholic Church to study other dimensions of ordained ministry. Presently the Vatican rejects the idea of women priests and married clergy, and does not recognize the priestly ordination of most Protestant ministers.

Indeed, Harvey Cox believes "the real ecumenical issue is the women's issue" (Rausch 1990, 220). There is considerable evidence that women had public ecclesial roles in the early church. These roles were later subordinated in patristic teaching. Today, based on developments in the theology of charism and a concern for justice, several Protestant communities ordain women. The Catholic Church supports full equality for women in the workplace and in political life, but not the priesthood. But, it must be noted, that even in some of those churches that ordain women, many problems remain. Some do not permit women into higher levels of ministry, allow them little decision-making power, and are still guilty of sexism in other ways.

Efforts are underway to correct these injustices, especially sexism. Recently many Protestant churches adopted an inclusive language lectionary. Rosemary Radford Ruether expressed the thought of many women (and men) when she wrote that "such a lectionary is needed because women in contemporary churches are suffering from linguistic deprivation. . . . They can no longer nurture their souls in alienating words that ignore or systematically deny their existence. They are starved for the words of life, for symbolic forms that fully and wholeheartedly affirm their personhood and speak truth about the evils of sexism and the possibilities of a future beyond patriarchy" (Ruether 1985, 4–5; see also Ruether 1987, 279–83).

The acceptance of married clergy is another dividing concern. The issues of sexism, women priests, married clergy, and the mutual recognition of ordained ministry coalesced in a recent development in the Catholic Church: the acceptance of married Anglican clergy into the Catholic Church as priests. When the CDF announced this process in March 1981, it made it very clear that "this exception to the norm of celibacy in favor of individuals should not be taken to imply a change in the thinking of the Church about the value of priestly celibacy, which remains the norm even for future priestly candidates emerging from this group" (Hebblethwaite 1981a).

The history of this policy change has been clearly chronicled by such scholars as the Jesuit sociologist Joseph Fichter (1988a, 1988b). In 1974 and 1975, female deacons in several Anglican communities in the United States were ordained to the priesthood, much to the distress of many Anglicans. Then in July 1976, the General Convention of the Episcopal Church ratified women's ordination to the priesthood. This move was protested by a large minority of laity and clergy. In the fall of that year, a group of married Anglican priests opened discussions with Archbishop Jean Jadot, the Apostolic Delegate to the United States, about joining the Catholic priesthood. Jadot asked the United States bishops to discuss this request, which they did in 1978 and 1980. The bishops tentatively accepted the request and forwarded it to Rome, subject to the approval of the pope.

In June 1980 the CDF granted the request, with specific conditions. One limited the married clergy to educational ministries for the first five years of their Catholic ministry. Also included was the stipulation that if the priest's wife died, he could not remarry.

Rome's acceptance of married priests transferring from another Christian church is not without precedent. Pius XII accepted a number of married Lutheran clergy in Europe in the 1950s, and Paul VI allowed a married Anglican priest to carry on his priestly ministry in Australia in 1968 (Gaine 1991).

By early 1990, approximately seventy Episcopal priests had become Catholic priests in the United States. The first

Anglican priest was received into the Catholic Church in September 1981 in New York. It was required that he receive the sacrament of orders at the hands of a Catholic bishop. This condition was a clear repudiation of the previous ordination by an Anglican bishop. It recalled the controversy in 1896 when Leo XIII declared Anglican orders "null and void." This reordination was perceived as a real threat to agreements reached in extensive ecumenical dialogues between Anglican and Catholic experts. For instance, in September 1981, the final report of the Windsor meeting of ARCIC I stated, "As God calls all the faithful to lifelong discipleship, so the gifts and calling of God to the ministers are irrevocable. For this reason ordination is unrepeatable in both our churches."

Intercommunion or eucharistic hospitality still fails to be an area of unity. As soon as Catholics and Protestants joined in social concerns, they discovered in such activities how much of the gospel they shared. Yet the Eucharist kept them apart. Robert McAfee Brown expressed his dismay: "It seems a mockery to deny our oneness in Christ at the very point where he intended us to show it forth more clearly" (1972, 66).

Two extremes have to be avoided in practicing intercommunion: anti-doctrinal carelessness, which permits indiscriminate intercommunion; and pre-ecumenical rigidity, which denies any intercommunion.

Catholic and Protestant churches regard Eucharist differently. Catholics regard the Eucharist as a sign of an already existing unity in ecclesial life, apostolic tradition, and mission. For many Protestants, the Eucharist is a sign of a growing unity and a means to its fulfillment.

Vatican II set forth two principles for intercommunion. These principles are somewhat in conflict. First, since Eucharist is a sign of unity, then intercommunion is not recommended on a regular basis. Second, since Eucharist is a means of grace, then intercommunion is to be encouraged (UR 8). Intercommunion is appropriate on special occasions, for example, when friendship, cooperation, and ecumenical understanding will grow.

In May 1972, the Secretariat for Christian Unity published instructions concerning cases when other Christians may be admitted to the Eucharist. (Nothing was said about Catholics taking communion at a Protestant service.) The three conditions:

they should be spiritually well-disposed and should ask for communion; they should share the eucharistic faith of the Catholic Church; they should be allowed to receive only if there are no ministers of the would-be communicant's own church available. In short, only in cases of "urgent necessity" may Catholics share the Eucharist with others.

These Vatican directives do not rise above pre-ecumenical rigidity. Their inhospitality upset many committed ecumenists. Some, no doubt, were alienated further from the institutional church by its obviously ideological pronouncements. Gregory Baum explains, "A church that makes its institutional elements, even if divinely given, the sole norm of its practice and worship is in danger of becoming an obstacle, a wall, standing between men and women" (1972b).

The Future of the One Church of Christ

In the preconciliar times other Christian churches were asked to return to the Catholic Church. This course of action was dictated in good measure by the church's siege mentality and its ecclesiocentric theology. At Vatican II there was a shift in perspective. The church acknowledged that the other Christian communities belong to the one Church of Christ. This was based on historical consciousness and a christocentric theology. The bishops declared that, since the Church of Christ subsists in the Catholic Church, the true church, other communities were invited to be regrafted into the Catholic Church.

Today, the focus of ecumenical theology for many is the mission of the church to proclaim, manifest, and expand the kingdom of the Father of Jesus Christ. This mission should be directed to all, especially the poor. There are two principles that should govern all proposals for Christian unity for mission. First, unity should be visible, with the spiritual dimensions incarnated in the church's forms and structures. This means that all the Christian churches should unite to manifest the holiness of the triune God and to worship this God. Unfortunately, the reports of too many ecumenical meetings read "like negotiations waiting for concessions rather than accounts of meetings seeking common worship" (Van Beeck 1985, 70). Second, visible unity should be such that each church can maintain its distinctive identity, and none would be absorbed by others or all leveled into a synthetic hybrid. There is growing support for the model of church unity advocate by Cardinal Ratzinger and others: reconciled diversity (Hebblethwaite 1993a; Rusch 1985, 118).

No one knows what form the one and only Church of Christ will take. In the search for visible unity, paradigms have been proposed by the Vatican, the WCC, COCU, and Lutherans,[6] and by theologians like Oscar Cullmann (1988), and Heinrich Fries and Karl Rahner (1985). It is obvious that the churches have a long way to go before any one form of visible unity can be implemented, much less accepted by all.

Conclusion

At the end of this review of the nature and history of ecumenism, several conclusions are in order. First, the Christian religion is composed of many vital communities around the world. However, in view of the deeply entrenched divisions of this religion into Protestant, Orthodox, and Catholic branches, it is clear that the religion's principal elements—the institutional, intellectual, and mystical—need radical renewal and reform. This renewal and reform depends in great measure on the response of the churches to the Holy Spirit. No one has addressed this point more pointedly than Raymond Brown (1984, 61–74).

In an explanation of Luke-Acts, Brown points out that "the distinguishing feature" of Luke's ecclesiology is "the overshadowing presence of the Spirit." He explains that the Acts of the Apostles is the story of the many interventions of the Spirit. For example, the Spirit directed Peter to the house of Cornelius, inspired Paul and Barnabas to seek out gentile converts, helped the church reach a decision about circumcision for gentile converts, and led Paul to decide he must go to Rome. But Brown wonders if this account of the many interventions of the Spirit leads easily "to a *deus ex machina* concept of Spirit," especially with regard to ecumenism. He agrees that the ecumenical movement—from 1910 to 1948 to 1962 to 1982 to the present—is the work of the Spirit. But he points out that we cannot "assume that the Spirit will bring the work to a triumphal conclusion." Brown shows that the Bible is filled with stories of how the people of God failed to respond to God and paid the price for their failures (e.g., the twelve tribes were reduced to two; religious institutions such as the monarchy and priesthood failed; and "Israel learned more about God in the ashes of the Temple destroyed by the Babylonians than in the elegant period of that Temple under Solomon"). He then concludes with this disturbing question: "If in the next two decades the churches do not seize the opportunity, if a union between two major churches does not take place as a sign of what may be possible, and if consequently Christianity enters the third millennium much more divided than it entered the second millennium, is it not possible, and even likely, that the opportunity will never come again?" (ibid., 72–73).

Second, since the unity of church-in-mission is so central to the very nature of the one Church of Christ, ecumenism is more than a duty, it is a way of being Christian. A valid litmus test of a Christian's devotion to the one Church of Christ is his or her involvement in ecumenism.

Third, the ecumenical movement has made great strides at the executive levels, especially through the many inter-church dialogues and such outstanding documents as BEM and those produced by ARCIC I. More work has to be done at the parish and congregational levels. For some ecumenists the parish level is "the most crucial area for future development of ecumenical life. . . . Ultimately it is here that Christian unity will or will not happen" (Horgan 1990).

Fourth, since there is only one prayer for Christians—the prayer of Christ as he gives himself to his Father—it is unfortunate that Christians cannot join together with Christ at the Eucharist. More dialogue is needed about intercommunion. The next chapter investigates the eucharistic life of the Catholic Church and its bearing on the other Christian churches, other religions, and the world.

8

The Church and Eucharistic Worship

Von Hügel wrote that a religion is as strong as its three principal elements: the institutional, the intellectual, and the mystical or devotional. This chapter and the one that follows explore the mystical or devotional dimension of the church's life, and the contribution of Vatican II, the popes, the people of God, and theologians to its development.

The official, public worship of the church is called liturgy. It is expressed in such rituals as the Mass, the sacraments, and the divine office. This chapter will not cover the whole liturgical system but will be restricted to a study of the eucharistic liturgy, the heart of the whole liturgy.

Christian life begins for individuals when they are baptized into the life, death, and resurrection of Christ. In the Catholic tradition all the sacraments are celebrations of and participations in the baptismal faith. However, the sacrament most frequently celebrated in the world church is the Eucharist. It is the Eucharist that draws the disciples together for worship, providing nourishment, support, healing, and hope, and from which they go forth to their threefold mission. The bishops at Vatican II reiterated the church's ancient tradition: The church "constantly lives and grows" through the eucharist (LG 26) and the eucharistic celebration is "the center and culmination of the whole life of the Christian community" (CD 30).

Distinctive Characteristics of Christian Worship

There is an ancient saying in the church: *lex orandi, lex cre-dendi*—the "law of worship is the law of belief," implying that worship shapes belief. This aphorism declares that correct belief follows the practice of correct worship, not vice versa. "The way people worship tells us more about their view of the sacred than any other activity. The prayers we use, the clothing we wear, the attitudes we adopt, the buildings we put up—all these are a living source of implicit theology" (Hebblethwaite 1975, 25).

First of all, Christian worship begins as a communal response to God's many initiatives. The Father creates, covenants, loves and saves, and still speaks through the Scriptures, the community, and the signs of the times. The community responds to the Father's unconditional love with praise, thanksgiving, and supplication with Jesus Christ in the power of the Spirit (Rom. 8:26). There is an exchange of gifts: the Father gives us his Son and we in turn join with Christ, the only "holy and perfect sacrifice," as he gives himself back to his and our Father.

Second, Christian worship is sacramental. Just as the Word became flesh, so the word of God comes to us through bread, wine, words, oil, stone, and water, and so on. The word of God speaks to us through the interplay of all these symbols. We, in turn, use the symbols to communicate with God. The worship should reflect the lived and unique social experience of each community.

Third, in Christian worship the church most fully appears as a sacrament of Christ. Gathered around the altar, the community expresses and intensifies what God has done for all people in Jesus Christ. The church "reveals itself most clearly" in the celebration of the liturgy (SC 41). The community not only joins with Christ's commitment of his whole self to his Father but it also recommits itself to its vocation to promote and expand the saving presence of God in family, church, and society by promoting justice, mercy, and compassion.

The Tridentine Rite

The church made its official response to Luther's reformation through the ecumenical Council of Trent, shakily begun under Paul III in December 1545 and successfully concluded under Pius IV in December 1563. At Trent the bishops solidified the dogmas and disciplines of the church. In 1570, Pius V (1566–72) approved a Mass structured according to the aims of Trent. This one liturgy, which Pius V decreed should be prayed "in perpetuity," came to be called the Tridentine rite, or the Roman Canon. It could be celebrated as "solemn" or "high" or "low." Nevertheless, there was little variation within each of these forms.

The Mass was said in Latin. The altar was in the very front of the church and there the priest (the celebrant) prayed the Mass with his back to the people. The priest followed detailed instructions (rubrics) about standing, genuflecting, and making innumerable signs of the cross over the objects on the altar. There was always the danger of ritualism, the mere continuation of the external actions without much internal faith.

The Mass had two kinds of prayers: the "ordinary," certain prayers repeated every day of the year; and the "proper," the prayers and readings that changed each day to observe particular feasts.

The scriptural readings played a secondary role. The three most important parts of the Mass began after the sermon: the offertory, consecration, and Communion. The congregation received Communion by approaching a rail that separated them from the altar. Here the people knelt and waited for the priest to place the consecrated bread on their tongues.

Aside from moving to and from the Communion rail, the people were silent and passive spectators who either watched the sacred drama enacted at a distance or spent the time in personal prayer, often to Mary or a favorite saint.

The church buildings were, by today's standards, often gaudy. The altar was decorated with candles and flowers. Around the church were many side altars and statues where people could pray and light candles.

For those who attended with a prayerful attitude, there was a sense of mystery, wonder, and holiness created in part by the silence, the special language, and the decor. People knew they were on holy ground in the presence of the almighty triune God.

The Papacy and Eucharistic Worship: Pius X

The popes of the twentieth century were devoted to the Eucharist. Each in his own way underscored the importance of Christian worship, especially attendance at the Sunday liturgy. Leo XIII, for example, not only wrote several encyclicals on the Eucharist, but also instituted a feast of the Holy Family in 1893 and consecrated the entire human community to the Sacred Heart of Jesus in 1900.

Pius X is hailed as a pioneer of the modern liturgical movement because his creative initiatives had far-reaching consequences for the rest of the century. On November 22, 1903, scarcely four months in office, he issued an instruction on the "Restoration of Sacred Music." Pius, formerly a seminary choir director, offered Gregorian chant as the model for all worship and he used for the first time the liberating words "active participation of the faithful." He wrote that his concern was for "the holiness and dignity of the temple in which our people assemble for the purpose of acquiring that spirit from its first indispensable source, namely, their own active participation in the sacred mysteries and in the solemn public prayer of the church." In 1905, he issued numerous decrees enjoining frequent, even daily, reception of the Eucharist. He pleaded for people to shed their Jansenist hesitations and scruples about worthiness. (Jansenism was a seventeenth- and eighteenth-century movement in Europe that discouraged frequent Communion because its adherents believed only the very holy were worthy of the sacrament). In 1910, he lowered the age for receiving one's first Communion from twelve or thirteen to seven or eight, so that the young would have the benefit of receiving the grace of the Eucharist at an early age. Finally, in 1914, he initiated a revision of the Sunday liturgies so that they would have the precedence they deserved over the feasts of saints.

During Pius's pontificate, the liturgy was being studied intensely in Benedictine monasteries and in academic circles by theologians who investigated the scriptural, historical, and pastoral dimensions of the liturgy. The beginning of the modern liturgical movement is attributed to Dom Lambert Beauduin (1873–1960), a Belgian Benedictine priest who specialized in ecclesiology and ecumenism. In 1909, he read a paper titled "The Full Prayer of the Church" at a congress at Malines, Belgium, in which he pointed out that in the early church the Mass was the act of the whole Christian people. Active participation of the faithful, he said, was important for the vitality of the people and for the whole church (Sheppard 1967; Dwyer 1985, 367). Another theme of his writings was the unity of life and liturgy. He urged Catholics to bring their sacramental union with God to every action of daily life.

In addition to Beauduin, many other liturgists and theologians were active in the liturgical renewal in the preconciliar period.[1] These scholars contributed to several influential liturgical journals, such as *La Maison-Dieu, Irenikon,* and *Liturgie et Paroises.* The latter, for instance, was read at one time by one of every four priests in France and Belgium (K. Hughes 1991, 149). These scholars also held study weeks to discuss liturgical matters. The First International Congress of Liturgical Studies was held in 1951 at Maria Laach, the famous Benedictine monastery in Germany. About forty-five scholars from Germany, France, and Belgium attended to discuss topics like the Easter vigil. In 1952 a congress was held at Strasbourg with nine nations represented. In 1953 a congress at Lugano, Switzerland, included eight Americans in attendance. These meetings, as well as those held at Louvain (1954), Monserrat (1958), and Munich (1960), prepared the church for Vatican II.

In the United States, the liturgical movement was promoted by such pioneers as H. A. Reinhold (1897–1968), Michael Mathis (1885–1960), Gerald Ellard (1894–1963), Reynold Hillenbrand (1905–79), Martin Hellriegel (1890–1981), Godfrey Diekmann (1908–) and Virgil Michel (1890–1938). It is the Benedictine Virgil Michel who is credited with launching the liturgical reform in this country. He was sent to Rome and Louvain to study philosophy for two years (1924 to 1925) but the liturgical movement sweeping across Europe captivated him and he brought the movement back to the United States.

Michel was troubled by the many problems wrought by industrial society and he sought to transform society through Christian values. He claimed that the root of our social ills were found in individualism and a complacent bourgeois spirit. As a remedy, he proposed greater awareness of human solidarity, the retrieval of the image of the church as the people of God, and the practice of such Christian virtues as sacrifice, simplicity of life, and concern for others. For Michel, liturgy meant community and a concern for others. For him, "the labor encyclicals of Leo XIII and the liturgical reforms of

Pius X did not just by accident happen within one generation, but were responses to cries of the masses for Christ who had power and gave good tidings. They belonged together."[2]

Michel considered the worldwide economic depression of the 1930s as a judgment on capitalism. He opposed racism and supported both organized labor and the agrarian reform movements. He insisted that the liturgy provided an instrument of social reform. Michel believed that the Mass could counteract the destructiveness of individualism because of its communal emphasis. At the Mass, class barriers were transcended since all were admitted equally to the celebration, prayers were said that those in positions of power in society would act justly, and money and goods were collected for the needy and the sick. At the Mass, also, the faithful heard the biblical injunctions to live in solidarity with the poor and to shun a materialistic lifestyle. "But Michel also saw that to accomplish these, the liturgy had to be reformed. It would have to expel clericalism and promote active lay participation, symbolize an authentic community, and inspire service to the world at large" (K. S. Smith 1988).

To foster these ideas, Michel established The Liturgical Press in 1926 and published the influential journal *Orate Fratres*. He was assisted in 1933 by his pupil and fellow Benedictine, Godfrey Diekmann. When Michel died suddenly after a brief illness in 1938, Diekmann became editor-in-chief. As editor for twenty-five years (1938–63), he gave outstanding leadership to the movement. In 1951, when *Orate Fratres* was in its twenty-fifth year, Diekmann realized how incongruous it was for a journal in the forefront of promoting vernacular worship to have a Latin name. After wide consultation, the name *Worship* was selected.

The United States Benedictines also began a series of study weeks called The Liturgical Week. The inspiration to hold these meetings came from the very successful seminars conducted by their confreres in Belgium. The first was held in Chicago in 1940. Approximately 1,260 people attended from across the country. These congresses continued until 1968. The impact of those held before Vatican II was uneven, due to the war, policy differences among the administrators, and changing times. Nevertheless, they prepared many in the United States for the Council's reforms.

Pius XI and Pius XII

Pius XI initiated the feast of Christ the King in 1925. Commentators see this move as an attempt to counter secularism. Pius believed that the church, the perfect society, should predominate in both the secular and religious spheres since it represented the kingdom of Christ on this earth. Secular society could not bring about the peace and prosperity required for the well-being of the world. Only the Catholic Church could. Christ was the true sovereign over all people. Francis X. Murphy judged this thinking to be "a direct throwback to the absolutist claims of Gregory VII and Boniface VIII at the height of the Middle Ages" (1981, 44).

Pius XII published his encyclical *Mediator Dei* in 1947, the first encyclical ever to concern itself completely with Christian worship. He commended the "dialogue Mass," in which the faithful participated by making the oral responses that would otherwise have been made by the server. He issued two other encyclicals on liturgy: *Sacred Liturgy* (1947) and *On Sacred Music* (1955).

In 1951, Pius XII reformed the entire Holy Week liturgy, especially the Easter vigil. In 1957, he changed the rules of fasting before reception of the Eucharist. Instead of abstaining from food and drink from midnight, one had to fast only an hour before reception. He also allowed evening Mass on feastdays. (Some suggest that Pius's motive might have been to check the exodus from the church rather than to initiate the faithful more closely into liturgical life [Falconi 1967, 284].)

In 1956, European liturgists organized the Assisi Congress as a tribute to Pius XII during his eightieth year. This congress gave the liturgical and pastoral leaders of the world the chance to express their gratitude to the pope for his leadership in making the liturgical movement " a *pastoral*-liturgical apostolate" (K. Hughes 1991, 161). Present were six cardinals, eighty bishops, and twelve hundred participants from all over the world. Pius XII gave a closing address to the congress in which he referred to the liturgical movement as a sign of God's providential care of his church.

Diekmann and Mathis organized the large United States delegation. According to Diekmann, the real highlight of the meeting was a talk by Bishop Wilhelm van Bekkum, "The Liturgical Renewal in Service of the Missions." The bishop addressed the need of adapting the liturgy to the customs and cultures of peoples (ibid., 165). Since his thesis that the church should act like a world church was advanced three years before the announcement of Vatican II, it caused a sensation. There is little doubt today that this talk paved the way for the Council and its reforms, liturgical and otherwise.

Vatican II

John XXIII started some liturgical reforms before the Council. Specifically, he approved a new code of rubrics in July 1960, which greatly simplified the liturgical calendar and the celebration of the Mass. John said he made these changes because they "should no longer be put off" until the Council. When the Council convened, liturgy was the first topic discussed. Vatican II was also the "first council to try to think out the liturgy from basic principles" (Hebblethwaite 1975, 31). For many of the bishops it was clear that sacramental reform was indispensable to the renewal of the church.

Two Americans, Godfrey Diekmann and Fredrick McManus, professor of canon law at Catholic University, were invited as consultors to the liturgy committee and as *periti* to the Council. They found themselves in the midst of Vatican politics and the tug of war between the traditionalist and the progressive viewpoints. It took the committee more than a year of discussion and debate to resolve such questions as the restoration of a deep love and reverence for the Scripture, cultural adaptation of the liturgy, reform of the breviary, and the adoption of the vernacular. The most controversial of these issues was the proposal to permit the recitation of much of the Mass in the vernacular. The traditionalists favored the retention of Latin. They maintained "that Latin is the link that brings all men together in worship. It [was] their contention, too, that in continents with many languages, a babel would result from a vernacular Mass" (Dugan 1962a).

The Constitution on the Liturgy was the first text promulgated by the Council. It was approved on November 22, 1963, by a vote of 2,158 to 19 (Jungmann 1969). Of the sixteen documents, no other had such a direct and dramatic impact on the life of Catholics. The document incarnated the spirit of the Council, and its reforms enfleshed the Council's dream of aggiornamento. It made the Council a part of the ordinary life of Christians. Liturgy, it declared, is "the summit toward which the activity of the church is directed; at the same time it is the fountain from which all her power flows" (SC 10).

As can be seen from its many footnote references to Trent and Pius XII, the document is in continuity with the preconciliar teachings. The bishops wanted sound tradition retained and yet called for legitimate theological, historical, and pastoral progress. Its general objectives were to make the liturgy more dynamic, simple, intelligible, and participatory.

To make the liturgy more dynamic, no "rigid uniformity" should be imposed upon it. The Council wanted to maintain "the substantial unity of the Roman rite" and yet provide for future "legitimate variations and adaptations to different groups." This formal embrace of the principle of cultural adaptation (and hence of cultural pluralism) was a major innovation within the church (Searle 1988). Once the liturgy was based on community response rather than rubric, then certain ideas that Vatican II did not foresee surfaced. How far could cultural adaptation stretch? "It is perhaps the fundamental flaw of the Constitution on the Liturgy that it did not address this question in sufficient depth" (Keifer 1975).

To be more simple and more intelligible, the bishops said, the rites "should be short, clear and unencumbered by useless repetitions; they should be within the people's powers of comprehension, and normally should not require much explanation" (SC 34). The Council said the Latin language was to be preserved, but the competent, territorial ecclesiastical authorities could allow the use of the vernacular.

In the preconciliar church, the priest and the bread and wine were the dominant symbols of the presence of Christ. The Council said greater intelligibility would be achieved by rehabilitating the other sacred signs that symbolize the presence of the risen Christ, such as the assembly, the altar, and the Scriptures. "Paramount importance" is to be given the Scriptures. The Scriptures should be explained in the homily, which "should be highly esteemed as part of the liturgy itself." Those who objected to the liturgical reforms sometimes called them "Protestant" because of the shift from Latin to the vernacular and because of the retrieval of the Scriptures from a minor role to a place of importance (Irwin 1986, 14).

The bishops ageed that the symbolism of Christ's death and resurrection would be more intelligible if the faithful "receive the Lord's body under elements consecrated at the very sacrifice." Communion can be received under both the bread and wine when the bishops think fit. Similarly, the two parts of the Mass, the Liturgy of the Word and the Liturgy of the Eucharist, "are so closely connected . . . that they form but one single act of worship" (SC 56). The faithful will have to be taught "to take their part in the entire Mass." Since every Mass celebrates the memory of Christ's death and resurrection, the feasts of the saints and even of Mary should not "take precedence over the feasts which commemorate the very mysteries of salvation."

The liturgy has to be more participatory. The church "earnestly desires that all the faithful will be led to a full, conscious, and active participation in liturgical celebrations" (SC 14). All the reforms calling for more dynamism, simplicity, and intelligibility have as their purpose more active participation.

More active participation can develop out of a renewed understanding of the role of the priest. Before Vatican II the priest was called the celebrant. After the Council he was called the president of the assembly. Bernard Cooke explained that as presider, the priest "has a distinctive and perhaps indispensable role: he voices the people's faith and prayer and symbolizes the link between a given community and the liturgy of the world-wide church. He does this as a member of the community and not as a mediator between the community and God. Christ himself is present as the mediator and member of the community" (1990).

The document said the people "should not be there as strangers or silent spectators" (SC 48). Some studies show, unfortunately, that most Catholics do not have living in the parish their five closest friends. Some have only one or two close friends there. What this means is that when people greet one another with the sign of peace, it is given to a virtual stranger (P. J. Palmer 1986). This puts a strain on participation.

Finally, there is another problem that affects participation. In fact, Joseph Champlin wrote in 1989 that the "most pressing and difficult issue facing pastoral leaders in the church today" is how to respond properly to those Catholics who rarely participate in liturgy yet want to do so on special occasions. He had in mind inactive engaged couples who desire marriage at a Mass and inactive Catholic parents who seek baptism for their child (1989a, 1989b).

Paul VI

Paul VI signed the Constitution on the Liturgy and then set about the task of implementing it. His numerous accomplishments were so outstanding that he will go down in history with Gregory the Great (590–604), Pius V, and Pius X as one of the great reformers of the liturgy.

In 1964, the Tridentine Mass was declared no longer the official rite of the Catholic Church. Paul organized a commission to look into liturgical matters. In 1966, the priest and altar were moved to face the people and churches were renovated. Most gaudy churches soon gave way to spare, uncluttered churches with the altar as the focus of attention. The removal of the altar rail allowed the people to move closer to the altar and their involvement increased when they helped plan the services, read aloud part of the service, and served as eucharistic ministers. In most parish churches communicants now receive the Eucharist in their hands and feed themselves.

In 1965, Paul issued *Mysterium fidei*, an encyclical about liturgical reform and traditional eucharistic doctrine. He reiterated the teachings of Trent about the Eucharist as sacrifice and as the true substantial presence of Christ. Although his terminology is very different from the Constitution on the Liturgy, he made a good defense of the Eucharist as mystery. He urged that eucharistic worship continue "to be the point of convergence of all other forms of piety."

Other musical instruments besides the organ were officially approved in 1968. That year three new canons were introduced as alternatives to the Roman Canon (eucharistic prayer number one). On April 3, 1969, a new Mass order was published that scraped off the stiff crust of rubrics. The 1570 missal of Pius V had no directions for the people. This one did—the first time in the history of the church that the role of the congregation was spelled out. The liturgical year was also revised with emphasis on the central saving actions of Christ and with excessive attention to Mary and the saints tempered.

In March 1970, it was ruled that the Sunday Eucharist could be anticipated on Saturday evening. Also, the scriptural readings were updated. Instead of a one-year cycle of Sunday readings, the new lectionary contained a three-year cycle of readings. Priests were instructed to preach regularly on the Scriptures.

Finally, the council fathers, while in the process of retrieving the Catholic tradition, called for the restoration of two ancient traditions: the catechumenate for adults (SC 64) and the permanent diaconate (LG 29). Both were restored during the pontificate of Paul VI.

On January 6, 1972, in what "represents the most dramatic chapter in the liturgical revolution wrought by the council," the Rite of Christian Initiation of Adults (RCIA) was promulgated (Bokenkotter 1985, 169). One of those who had led the efforts to restore the catechumenate and to establish the RCIA was the Belgian liturgist and educator Christiane Brusselmans (1931–91) (Parker 1992).

The RCIA is the process by which people become members of the Catholic Church. Since the process aims at the total formation of the person into the faith community, it covers doctrinal, liturgical, and apostolic matters. At the Council the bishops explained that the catechumenate is not "a mere expounding of doctrines and precepts, but a training period for the whole Christian life" (AG 14). The RCIA culminates in the celebration at the Easter vigil of the sacraments of initiation—baptism, confirmation and Eucharist (Mainelli 1986; Duffy 1987).

Several motives led the bishops to their decision to restore the permanent diaconate: to recover the full range of ordained ministries and to alleviate the priest shortage in mission territories. The bishops listed the pastoral, educational, and eucharistic responsibilities of the deacons. Regarding the latter, they said the deacon is the "custodian and dispenser of the Eucharist," can read the sacred Scripture to the faithful, can bring Viaticum to the dying, and can instruct and exhort the people (LG 29).

Paul VI promulgated the norms for the restoration of the permanent diaconate in 1967. He stated that the diaconate "is not to be considered as a mere step toward the priesthood but is so adorned with its own indelible character and its special grace" that it is to be considered a "permanent" vocation. The United States bishops approved the restoration in 1968. In

1993 in the United States alone, there were about 10,000 deacons and nearly 4,000 candidates for ordination.

The Liturgical Reforms Evaluated

Reforms such as the RCIA and the diaconate have revitalized the intellectual and devotional life of the church, especially at the parish level. How effective have all the conciliar reforms been? Periodic evaluations have been made. Here are some examples.

Ten years after Vatican II, Ralph Keifer wrote that our liturgy is in a state of crisis. "The roots of our present crisis is a failure to put the gospel and conversion at the top of our list of liturgical priorities" (1975). According to Keifer, the major liturgical problem is one of spirituality and not the changes in ritual. "The most serious failure . . . has been the failure to develop, articulate, and make pastorally applicable the theology of the paschal mystery which animated liturgical reform in the first place, and which permeates the new rites." The new rites are built around the high Johannine and Pauline christology and ecclesiology, as well as Augustine's theology of grace. But our hymns and homilies, said Keifer, are pervaded with an optimistic humanism that depicts Jesus merely as an ethical example. "There is virtually no connection between the 'community celebration of life' almost totally at the mercy of the celebrant and the corporate Pauline proclaiming the death of the Lord until he comes or the Johannine entry into the liturgy of the heavenly court."

Twenty years after the Vatican II document, Patrick Collins wrote that "no person or single group of persons has all the answers to the problems and questions of liturgical experience." Nevertheless, he went on to say that "what is still needed is a team effort by persons of several disciplines and skills, persons who are experienced in *doing* liturgy's most appropriate languages: image, symbol, story, and ritual action. Such persons are called artists" (1984).

Liturgy is an art. The Mass is a ritual, a dramatic symbolic action of Christ's death and resurrection specified by words. This ritual should be an aesthetic creation designed to set up the conditions for the possibility of religious experience. God is present in and through the people and materials (the sacramental principle). Christians are present at liturgy to encounter God through his Son and in the power of the Spirit. In the Eucharist God heals, teaches, and empowers, sending Christians back to their everyday life to transform the world into the kingdom of God. The Sunday Eucharist should not be an isolated entity, but a bridge to Christian worship and service throughout the week.

Today many complain that the liturgies lack a sense of mystery. Collins and others (Dinter 1989) admit that the Tridentine rite evoked a sense of mystery—in part because of the special language, the silence, the decor, and the sense of a great distance between God and the people. On the other hand, these liturgists also believe there was a good measure of mystification and misunderstanding. Christ's presence was narrowed to the sacramentality of the priest and the eucharistic species. In the postconciliar church the sense of mystery can be retrieved without losing participation, simplicity, dynamism, and intelligibility by creating better rituals and by appreciating that the eucharistic mystery has been relocated: Christ is directly present in the midst of his people. At Vatican II, "the liturgy became the immediate expression of the church as the gathered community" (Hebblethwaite 1975, 33). In other words, the experience of the sacred can be found in the community of disciples as they listen, forgive, celebrate, speak, sing, share the bread and cup, and share the gospel with the world, especially among the poor and where there are injustices.

Writing in 1988, Mark Searle explained at length that "the liturgical life of the American church is pretty much in the doldrums" (p. 620). He offers several reasons for his judgment. First, he cites symbolic minimalism. The Eucharist for Communion is often taken from the tabernacle, the cup is not always available, gospel processions are rare, and the music, while singable, is not suited to the actual liturgy. Second, people still lack a sense of the identity and purpose of the parish or church. On the one hand, a significant number of parishioners do not know the liturgy should promote an organic union among the community, and on the other hand, many still "thought that celebrating the liturgy was the most important thing their parish did." Third, in many places the liturgy is still too clerical. It is supposed to be the action of the whole community, but priests still dominate the scene. The community can become subject to his idiosyncrasies or to those of whoever else is in charge.

Mark Searle was convinced that the principal motive for the reform—active participation—was not understood and rarely promoted. Participation, he insisted, does not mean just "joining in." True participation has been overshadowed by attempts to get people to sing. To take part by singing, listening, responding, and offering the sign of peace do not "of themselves constitute the 'active participation' the council had in mind." These activities are intended to "promote" participation. Active participation involves two things: sanctifying action and a social dimension (SC 59). The sanctifying action is a conscious and willed encounter with the risen Christ as he gives himself totally to his Father. The social dimension suggests that this worship should manifest itself in social justice. There is an intrinsic link between worship and justice. The liturgical spirit should radiate from the altar to all of life.

To help people participate, said Searle, we need better community and better education. It is at the grass-roots level that the renewal of liturgy must begin again. Surely, the time has come "to relaunch the liturgical movement." As of now, "there is nothing—or perhaps precious little—in the actual experience itself that suggests to the imagination fascination, wonder, surprise. In the absence of fascination, there is no illumination. . . . Liturgical renewal, I submit, has not even begun. Attempts to use the liturgy to educate, to indoctrinate, to transform character will only postpone the day of authentic renewal of the eucharistic story."

John Egan also wrote about the Council twenty years later. He contended that the connection between liturgy and social justice "was entirely missed" by the Council. He pointed out that the Constitution on the Church in the Modern World "utterly omits any mention of the place of the liturgy of the church as source and summit of its mission for all humanity." According to Egan, then, the "relationship between liturgical celebration and the practice of justice is probably the most significant question calling for liturgists' attention today" (1983).

While both Egan and Searle agreed that the liturgy should radiate from the altar to all the world, especially where there is injustice, they differed about the link made by the Council between liturgy and justice. In his presentation, Searle referred to paragraph 59 of the liturgy constitution. However, paragraph 59 does not use the word justice. It says the sacraments dispose the faithful "to practice charity."

Twenty-five years after the Council, Andrew Greeley echoed the judgment of those liturgists who judged that the liturgical renewal has yet to begin. Greeley argued that the symbolism was wholly inadequate. For one thing, the eucharistic meal should resemble a common meal. Also, instead of a ritualized relic that needs constant explanation, the Mass had to become a fascinating story (1990b).

Finally, as of 1990, an aspect of the liturgical reform that had yet to begin is liturgical inculturation, that is, the attempt to integrate significant and acceptable cultural values and symbols within liturgical expression. We have seen that both Paul VI and John Paul II were (are) very reluctant to encourage liturgical inculturation. Although Paul VI encouraged the African bishops to think about how they might "bring to the church [their] unique gifts of Blackness," and although John Paul urged the Native Americans in Arizona to "preserve and keep alive [their] culture, language, values, and customs," neither pontiff encouraged these people to integrate their cultural values and symbols into the liturgy.

To address this issue, a major meeting was held in Rome in November 1990. The meeting was sponsored by the North American Conference on Cultural Awareness in Liturgy because liturgists "have few clues as to how to go about creating effective inculturation programs in their dioceses" (G. W. Brown 1990; see also Empereur 1992).

John Paul II

The pope is not unaware of the positive and negative results of the conciliar reforms. For example, he directed the Synod of 1983 to address the sacrament of reconciliation with the theme "Reconciliation and Penance in the Mission of the Church." Since the Council, there has been a noticeable abandoning of the sacrament of reconciliation. One reason for the decline is that the Sunday Eucharist is for many a special moment of forgiveness and renewal at the deepest level of their lives. The synod addressed the ancient practice of individual confession and its infrequent use today, but with little success. There has been no noticeable increase in participation in this sacrament since the synod. Similarly, in an apostolic letter of thirty-seven pages addressed to the world's bishops and priests to mark the twenty-fifth anniversary of the liturgy constitution (May 13,

1989), John Paul insisted that the liturgical reforms must now concentrate on giving Catholics a "deeper grasp" of the meaning of the liturgy, and must now "root out" abuses and "outlandish innovations."[3] He insisted that it is wrong for priests to compose their own eucharistic prayers or to substitute "profane readings for texts from sacred scripture."

To date, there have been two serious problems that have dominated John Paul's pontificate: the priest shortage and the schism of Archbishop Marcel Lefèbvre in 1988.

The Priest Shortage

Vatican II produced two decrees on the priesthood. These documents underscored both the pastoral (rather than cultic) roles of the priest and the close union between priests and bishops. The documents did not address the priest shortage. In fact, there is only a footnote reference to this issue in the decree on the formation of priests (OT 2).

Nevertheless, the priest shortage in the global church is alarming. Between 1969 and 1985, as a result of both withdrawals and deaths, the number of priests dropped from 425,000 to 399,000 (Gaine 1991). The priest shortage might be the most serious problem facing the institutional and devotional church, and, given the steady decline in the number of seminarians, there is no solution in sight. Nevertheless, the priest shortage is not that new. We have seen that the reason Pius XI called for the development of Catholic Action in 1922 was the priest shortage.

The real issue is not the total number of priests but the number of priests relative to the entire Catholic community. For example, since in the United States the Catholic population has been growing steadily, "the peak year for the availability of priests was 1942 and since then the ratio of priests to people has declined" (Castillo 1992). In 1942 the priest-to-laity ratio was 1 to 617, according to Castillo; in 1962, 1 to 771; and in 1990, 1 to 921. The United States bishops have predicted that by 2005 the ratio will be 1 to 2,200. The ratio is (and will be) much higher in other parts of the world.

At the international Synod of 1990 on the priesthood, the delegates discussed the formation of candidates for the priesthood, as well as the "identity crisis" and "burnout" said to be afflicting many priests. "But church leaders have made clear that a few fundamental aspects of the problem are off-limits to debate, notably the Catholic requirement of priestly celibacy and the prohibition against ordaining women and married men" (Haberman 1990b; see also Haberman 1990c). Nevertheless, the possibility of ordaining women and married men continues to be discussed.

Edward Schillebeeckx, an internationally-known Dominican priest and theologian, addressed the priest shortage in 1981 in a book that brought him into conflict with Rome (1981b). His principal contention—based on the fact that the right of the faithful to have the Eucharist is absolutely fundamental—was that local communities have both the ability and the responsibility to appoint their own presiders in cases where a serious lack of ministers occurs.

The CDF directed the Dominicans to investigate the book. A group of Flemish and Dutch Dominicans found Schillebeeckx's thesis "dogmatically possible and pastorally necessary" (Willems 1987). Rome was not satisfied, declaring that Schillebeeckx's conclusions were not in agreement with Vatican II.

At any rate, the problem persists, even intensifies. Some groups have boldly made public their solution: they have allowed nonordained to preside at a liturgy—not only Catholic men and women but even persons not Catholic (Timmerman, Zahn, and Baldovin 1988).

The growing phenomenon of a priest shortage and Sundays-without-Eucharist prompted several episcopal conferences to petition Rome for guidelines for Communion services conducted by nonordained Catholics. Four guidelines were issued in the fall of 1988 by the Congregation for Divine Worship. (1) Only one such service can be held each Sunday. (2) The service must be led by a deacon. If a deacon is not available, the service can be conducted by a lector or acolyte. (3) No Sunday Communion service may be held if a Saturday vigil Mass is celebrated. (4) Local episcopal conferences have the option to deviate from these standard procedures if local customs so require.

This Vatican document has temporarily alleviated the serious situation. Several issues, however, continue to receive discussion because, given the present low pool of priestly candidates, this is a problem that is going to get worse.

First, the relationship of the "ministerial or hierarchical priesthood" (based on ordination) to the "common priesthood of the faithful" (based on baptism) needs greater clarification. At the Council the bishops said both are interrelated, but "they differ from one another in essence and not only in degree" (LG 10). Second, many people often cannot tell the difference between a Communion service (the reception of the Eucharist at a worship service) and the eucharistic celebration (when the bread and wine are consecrated at a Mass). Communion services are sacramental, but they are not eucharistic celebrations. At the Eucharist the fourfold action of taking, blessing, breaking, and sharing of the bread and wine is the symbolic representation of Christ's death. The distinctive dimension of eucharistic worship is to unite one's whole heart and being with the risen Christ, who is forever fixed in the act of redeeming us. If the distinction between a Communion service and the eucharistic celebration is not maintained, Catholics could very well be unwittingly holding worship services similar to those of evangelical Protestants. Their services are neither sacramental nor eucharistic. Rather, they focus on a very personal spirituality: a personal conversion to Jesus as savior, a personal but prayerful interpretation of the Scripture, and group services of enthusiastic singing with fervent preaching.

Third, often (and unfortunately), some Sunday Eucharists at which priests preside actually move in the direction of Communion services (Huck 1989). This occurs when the eucharistic prayer is not the central deed of assembly and presider together, and when the bread that some or all the people share in Communion is previously consecrated bread taken from the tabernacle and not what the priest and people prayed over. Vatican II called this latter procedure "the more perfect form of participation in the Mass" (SC 55).

The priest shortage is a serious problem. However, Sunday-without-priests points to the deeper and more crucial issue: Sunday-without-Eucharist. Devoid of the Eucharist, Christian community makes no sense. The conciliar bishops declared: "No Christian community . . . can be built up unless it has its basis and center in the celebration of the most Holy Eucharist. Here, therefore, all education in the spirit of the community must originate" (PO 6).

Archbishop Marcel Lefèbvre

Lefèbvre (1905–91), a soft-spoken but stubborn Frenchman, became famous when he publicly denounced Vatican II and Paul VI, and then John Paul II. He became a thorn in the side of Paul VI, accusing him of "philo-Lutheranism" and "Masonic behavior." John Paul was forced to announce his automatic excommunication in 1988.

The career and teachings of Lefèbvre are worth reviewing because they touch on every major issue in the previous chapters: modernity, tradition, Vatican II, the identity and mission of the church, papal and conciliar authority, religious freedom and pluralism, ecumenism, and liturgical inculturation.

Lefèbvre obtained doctorates in both theology and philosophy before his ordination in 1929 as a member of the community of the Holy Ghost Fathers. He served in French colonial Africa for thirty years, during which time he was consecrated the archbishop of Dakar, Senegal, in 1955. He resigned from the diocese in 1962 to become superior general of his religious community and, as such, participated in the four sessions of Vatican II. He refused to sign several conciliar documents: those on the church, the church in the modern world, and religious liberty (White 1979).

His term as superior general concluded in 1968, when the general chapter of the Holy Ghost Fathers, embarrassed by his views about Vatican II, did not renew his mandate. He then began actively to oppose the reforms of the Council, especially in liturgical and ecumenical questions, and in 1970 founded his own organization of priests, the Fraternity of St. Pius X, with its own seminary in Econe, Switzerland.

The Fraternity was given canonical approval on November 1, 1970, but this was withdrawn in May 1975 after Lefèbvre refused to obey Paul VI's request that he stop his bitter denunciations of Vatican II and stop advocating private celebrations of the Tridentine rite. In June 1977, he was suspended for unauthorized ordinations to the priesthood. Between 1974 and 1979, he illegally ordained eighty-nine priests.

In 1984, the Vatican approved limited use of the Tridentine rite. This decision was seriously criticized by most liturgists and bishops because it both gave support to those who have resisted liturgical renewal and violated the collegial sense of the world-wide episcopate. At that time, 98 percent of the bishops had expressed the view that allowing the Tridentine rite was unnecessary (Hebblethwaite 1984c).

On June 30, 1988, the day Lefèbvre ordained four bishops at Econe, he was automatically excommunicated in accordance with church law (see canon 1382). He said, "I prefer to be in

the truth without the pope than to walk a false path with him."
Lefèbvre's schism—a word that literally means "to set up a
rival altar"—was the first since 1870, when the Old Catholics,
many of them French, Dutch, and German, left the church
after Vatican I had adopted the doctrine of papal infallibility.

The four bishops were also excommunicated, although they
were legally bishops in the eyes of Rome. The other followers
of Lefèbvre, including some 250 priests, were told they would
be excommunicated only if they "knowingly" embraced the
archbishop's schismatic practices. Since then, the Vatican policy of leniency and flexibility has led many of Lefèbvre's followers to return to Rome.

As mentioned earlier, John Paul wrote an apostolic letter of
May 13, 1989, marking the twenty-fifth anniversary of the
Council's document on the liturgy in which he reprimanded
those on the left who composed their own eucharistic prayers
and introduced unauthorized readings. However, the real target of the letter was the right: Lefèbvre and his priests who
regarded "religious practice as a private affair" and who
rejected "fuller and more active participation" in the liturgy
(Hebblethwaite 1989d). Lefèbvre and his followers promoted
private celebration of the Tridentine rite. John Paul said "private" liturgical acts had no validity. The liturgy, he stated,
belongs to the whole church and is regulated in its name by
the hierarchical authority. John Paul declared that no one has
permission to say the Tridentine Mass privately.

In general, Lefèbvre opposed the advances initiated by and
following after Vatican II. As just discussed, Lefèbvre canonized the Tridentine Latin rite, insisting it is the one and only
Mass for all times, in keeping with Pius V's decree that the rite
must be maintained "in perpetuity." Lefèbvre called the new
rite of 1964 "a bastard rite" and a "Protestant rite" that failed to
convey the eucharistic doctrines of the church as formulated
by the Council of Trent (Dinges 1988).

It has been pointed out that the liturgy was "the medium,
not the cause, of his ongoing conflict with Vatican authorities"
(ibid., 602). Lefèbvre's real argument was not with the so-
called abuses, distortions, or misrepresentation of the Council.
Rather, it was the official church's acceptance of modernity.

Lefèbvre extolled not only a Counter-Reformation ecclesiology but also the political and social system of France before
the Revolution of 1789. Lefèbvre had never accepted the

Protestant and French revolutions, "those twin progenitors of secularization, pagan nationalism, scientific humanism, and the apotheosis of the 'rights of man'" (ibid.). According to Lefèbvre, the false principles—Protestantism, liberalism, and modernism—of these two revolutions were assimilated into the church at Vatican II. Lefèbvre asked a reporter, "Why should I submit to modernists and liberal-communist conciliar reforms?" (Hebblethwaite 1979a).

Since 1965, Lefèbvre had repudiated the Council in lectures, homilies, and a 1976 book, *I Accuse the Council!* In a 1970 profession of faith, he declared, "We refuse, and have already refused, to follow the Rome of neo-modernists and neo-Protestant leanings. These are quite obvious in Vatican II and in the reforms that followed that council. . . . It comes from heresy and will finish in heresy, even if in all its stages it is not formally heretical" (Hebblethwaite 1987c; see also Hebblethwaite 1980b).

Lefèbvre also questioned the identity of the postconciliar church, which he called false. He claimed that his Fraternity was the true church, a faithful remnant holding fast to the church's true identity. The Roman Church was rampant with error and heresy and made up of many of its enemies—such as the Freemasons, whom Lefèbvre believed were responsible for many of the Council's reforms.

Authority was another issue that divided Lefèbvre from Rome. He repudiated the exercise of authority by popes and a universal council. He taught that his view of the Catholic Church was the only acceptable alternative to the church of Vatican II. In short, Lefèbvre created a sect. And, as in the case with all sectarian virtuosi, Lefèbvre presented his actions as something pristine and uncorruptable—proclaiming that he, and he alone, had continuity with the true church and the authenticity of the faith. Ostensibly, Lefèbvre challenged Vatican II's most visible reform, the new liturgy. Ultimately, his conflict with the Vatican was not first and foremost a battle over which rite is right. The archbishop challenged "not the factual wisdom of Roman practice, but rather the very principle of whether Rome [had] the authority to legislate in liturgical and doctrinal matters."[4] Lefèbvre failed to realize that the church's tradition is not a set of answers found in books. Rather, it is an experience embodied in the living community of the church and in the bishops who, collegially, are entrusted with its oversight. He thought he was orthodox because he appealed to long-dead popes, like Pius V, against living ones, specifically Paul VI and John Paul II.

Lefèbvre also opposed interreligious dialogue and ecumenism. He rejected universal religious liberty, since it denies a privileged position to the Catholic Church. He declared that both the regular and wider ecumenisms lent credibility to "false" religions. Being an integralist, he declared collegiality an error. He believed all of France's problems, especially liberalism, socialism, communism, and modernism, originated with the French Revolution (Reese 1988). These three—religious liberty, ecumenism, and collegiality—were in Lefèbvre's view the religious equivalents of the French Revolution's tripartite slogan "Liberty, equality, fraternity." Lefèbvre once said, "Vatican II is 1789 in the church" (Steinfels 1989).

John Paul II was seriously disturbed by his open conflicts with Lefèbvre. In his traditional "state of the church" address at the end of 1988, John Paul listed the many good things that had happened during the year and then said there were "two shadows" that caused him "deep hurt." The second was the weak resistance of the Anglican Archbishop Ronald Runcie to the ordination of women as priests and even bishops. The first was the schism of Lefèbvre (Hebblethwaite 1989a). When Lefèbvre died on March 25, 1991, John Paul prayed for his well-being, entrusting him "to the mercy of God" (Greenhouse 1991; see also Hebblethwaite 1991b).

Conclusion

The Eucharist makes the One Church of Christ visible and is the occasion for the community of disciples to celebrate its mission. The resurrected Christ, the source of the church, is present. Unfortunately, all Christians do not share the Eucharist at the same altar. Catholics, too, are divided in their appreciation of the Eucharist. On the one hand, many do not participate on a regular basis. Many who do attend are not pleased with the style of the ceremonies and the substance of the homilies, or they regret that women are excluded from ministry in the full sense. In a word, many agree that the liturgical reform "has yet to begin." On the other hand, many Catholics participate regularly and grow spiritually. The eucharistic liturgy grounds their lives and solidifies their connection to the community and its mission. At the Eucharist they experience great joy, love, peace, and healing, have a deeper sense of community, and attain a clearer understanding of their involvement in what contributes to a more just world.

Since the church is so divided over liturgical theory and practice, the task of fostering the liturgical life of Catholics in a world church will occupy the church for years to come.

9

The Church and Social Justice

Previous chapters have shown that the identity of the institutional church is seriously marred if it does not provide its members the very same justice it teaches the world: that modern theology cannot afford to overlook the terrible injustices suffered by the Jews in the Holocaust; that action on behalf of justice is a constitutive dimension of the church's proclamation of the gospel; that interreligious dialogue is inseparable from cultural pluralism and global social justice; that ecumenists seek Christian unity within the struggle for justice; and that perceptive liturgists like Virgil Michel called for reform of the eucharistic celebration within the context of social justice. This chapter explores the history, theology, and spirituality of social justice in the Catholic Church of the twentieth century.

Human Rights

The Catholic tradition, based on its sacramental consciousness, holds that God made a rational and ordered world, and that we humans are graced, moral agents responsible for the ethical character of our social, political, and economic existence. Unfortunately, from our very beginnings, we humans have been perverting our relationships and our world.

Human rights are usually coupled as civil-political and social-economic. The former include such rights as equality with no discrimination based on race, sex, or religion; freedom of assembly, speech, and movement; and no arbitrary arrest, torture, or unfair public trial. The latter include the right to access such needs as food, shelter, basic health care, education, a living wage, and private property, and the right to form labor unions.

Today, injustices abound as people's basic rights are violated. The gap between the poor and rich, both individuals and nations, continues to widen. Every minute the nations of the world spend millions on arms; every hour thousands of children die from hunger-related causes; every day a species becomes extinct; every month the world's economic system adds more billions of dollars to the unbearable debt burden already resting on third-world shoulders.[1]

These injustices fly in the face of the Christian belief that all people have dignity because they are created by God and redeemed by Christ. The Creator gives all people both their essential dignity and their existential originality. The presence of the risen Christ to all people means that all persons are sacred. When Christians respect and serve others, especially the poor, imprisoned, and the hungry, they serve Christ himself (Matt. 25:40).

One reason there are so many problems related to human rights is that there is disagreement about their origin. There are several theories.

First, some regard rights as God-given. The Declaration of Independence of 1776 asserted that the inalienable rights to life, liberty, and the pursuit of happiness were God-given. The first nine amendments to the Constitution—the Bill of Rights—were added to the Constitution on December 15, 1791, to provide adequate guarantees of individual liberties. The justification for these universal human rights is that all humans have dignity and fundamental value.

Second, totalitarian governments claim to be the source of rights. The state grants and denies them. Under the infamous Nazi government of Adolf Hitler (1889–1945), those judged worthless (the disabled, homosexuals, the aged) were eliminated.

Third, humanists such as John Locke, John Stuart Mill (1806–73), Jean-Jacques Rousseau, as well as the twentieth-century philosopher John Rawls (1971) ground rights and justice in social-contract theories. According to this theory, rights belong only to individuals. It is assumed that people exist primarily and most importantly as individuals and each person has a domain within which she or he is sovereign. Individuals can consent to share with others when it is in their self-interest. Any forced sharing violates human rights. A society will have peace and order rather than suffering and disorder only if the people opt for a system in which all citizens sacrifice some of their personal benefits in favor of others.

Fourth, many contemporary philosophers believe human rights are grounded not in God, governments, or social contracts but in our relationships to one another. These thinkers regard the contract theory (whereby justice and rights are based on grudging agreements entered into by self-interested parties) as inadequate. Justice in these terms "is no longer a positive good but only a necessary evil" (Di Ianni 1989). Furthermore, contract theory ultimately denies the inherent social nature of people. It supposes that humans are political by choice and not by nature. Many contemporary philosophers also point out problems with the Christian recourse to creation and redemption. The latter give us no rights in the presence of impersonal nature: a hurricane does not do a person an injustice if it deprives him of his home or his family or even of his life; nor do creation and redemption give a person rights if no one else is present. As the noted philosopher Robert O. Johann explained, "If I were the only person in the world it would not be the case that I *had* rights but no one was around to respect them. I would not have rights at all. Other persons are not therefore required simply to do justice to rights already constituted" (1967, 43; see also Johann 1968, 137–39).

Johann goes on to explain that the obligation to be just is identical with our nature as essentially relational beings. Humans are rational agents who by nature respond to other beings in terms of what they are and do. In the presence of another person, a person is obliged to treat the other person as a person. Injustice is present when people deliberately hurt others or are indifferent to their presence—that is, act in their presence as if they were not there. The injustice is not done by the mere fact that a person's reality as a person is ignored, or things are taken away from the person. Injustice is done only because a person refuses his or her obligation to be responsive to the personal character of the other person. In short, the foundation of human rights is our mutual obligation to be responsive to others as persons. Injustice is in the person who fails to be responsive to the personal character of others. This is the New Testament view of justice, as exemplified in Jesus' story of the Good Samaritan (Luke 10:30–37) (Allen 1989, 26–27). The Samaritan treated the man who "fell victim to robbers" with compassion, a word accurately defined by Matthew Fox as "love-justice" (Fox 1979, 3).

Justice

The general description of justice is captured in the ancient phrase *suum cuique*—to each what is due. Justice demands equality and fairness. There are three complementary forms of justice: commutative, distributive, and social. Commutative or individual justice concerns private claims between individuals or groups. It entails such things as fidelity to agreements, contracts, and promises. Distributive justice specifies that all persons have some share in those goods that are essentially public or social, such as education, housing, health care, and the right to earn a living wage. Social justice concerns the realization of distributive justice. Both are based on the assumption that people are social by nature. Social justice directs all citizens to aid "in the creation of patterns of societal organization and activity that are essential both for the protection of minimal human rights and for the creation of mutuality and participation by all in social life" (Hollenbach 1977, 220). For example, all citizens should contribute to the common good by paying taxes, performing jury duty, and by opposing structures that abet racism, classism, and sexism. In view of this description, social injustice is the structured exclusion of people from access to those things required by their dignity as human beings (Baum 1986a, 22).

Liberal Capitalism

During the twentieth century, two visions of how society should be organized politically and economically have dominated: capitalism and Marxist socialism. Capitalism is characterized by the private ownership of both property and the means of production. It is based on individual initiative, competition, supply and demand, and a profit motive. It believes that the free market, operating according to the law of supply and demand, can assure the well-being of society and raise the standard of living of the vast majority. People, then, function autonomously in their economic lives. Society and the privately controlled market are extensions of this private autonomy. Political, cultural, and market institutions do not function autonomously, but form one interlocking structure in the service of private capital accumulation. For example, the above-named institutions depend upon the military, the secondary labor market, and race and gender role assignments.

Capitalism arose in the eighteenth century with the Industrial Revolution. At that time, the economic, cultural, and social structures of society moved from countryside farms to urban factories. It also began with some clear presuppositions: individuals are (and always will be) fundamentally selfish and destructive; there is conflict between the individual and society; this conflict can be moderated by individuals working to produce a healthy, harmonious social unit (Greeley 1982b). The state is established by individuals out of enlightened self-interest because only institutional force can keep individuals from destroying one another. Otherwise, a political community is neither essential nor intrinsic to the human condition.

In theory, capitalism glorifies the freedom of the individual and views society not as organic or corporate, but as composed of discrete individuals. An example of this viewpoint is found in the thought of John Locke. He taught that humans are by nature aggressive competitors, each one a threat to all neighbors. People are essentially isolated and are selectively social in limited ways. Given this situation, individuals must protect themselves and their rights from the control of others. Rights in society belong to the individual. No one, including and especially government, can deny individuals their rights. Government is necessary to provide minimum security, but it is the people themselves who, by means of a formal contract, create a democratic state to protect their rights. Too much power should not be given to government.

The term *liberal capitalism* denotes a system wherein the free market is the one essential mechanism for regulating the production and distribution of goods (Baum 1989a). At the end of the eighteenth century, those who advocated liberal capitalism argued that a free market would increase economic development, generate enormous wealth, and eventually raise the material well-being of the entire society. Poverty and unemployment are basically individual social problems due to a temporary malfunctioning of the market, or to forces outside the economic system, such as ignorance, laziness, prejudice, and the disturbances of free exchange by labor unions or government interference (Hobgood 1989, 170).

There are many criticisms of liberal capitalism. Two interrelated ones are the following. First, liberal capitalism creates a wealthy class over against a large group that lacks access to the market or dignified participation in society. This extreme centralization of power in the hands of a wealthy elite "is the fatal flaw of capitalist society" (Greeley 1981, 48; see also Greeley 1990a, 289–309). Second, liberal democracies pride themselves on fostering civil and political rights. However, they neglect social and economic rights since explicit promotion of these rights seems to contradict the nature of capitalism. Communists judge capitalism's defense of civil rights as an ideological disguise of its refusal to honor the rights to life, adequate health care, a decent home, food, a job, and other needs.

At this point, a postscript about Protestantism and society is in order. In general, Protestant social theory, while based on the dialectical imagination, is similar to that of Locke and Marx insofar as it begins with the presupposition that the individual and society are in conflict or competition. They usually maintain that there is a dialectical relationship between the individual over and against the person as a social being. The individual strives for freedom and independence; society strives to constrain the independence of the individual for the common welfare.

Communist Socialism

Socialism advocates collective or government ownership and management of both the production and distribution of goods. Karl Marx (1818–83) constructed his version of socialism as a reaction to some of the results of the Industrial Revolution and capitalism that deeply disturbed him. He was particulary disturbed by the struggle of the workers (proletariat) with the property-owning class (bourgeoisie or capitalist class). Marx was angry because the capitalist institutions—whether social, political, or economic—produced hierarchies of race, class, and sex that enhanced the profit intake of corporate business. There is no way, Marx observed, that private profit can be made without exploiting the working people. Social solidarity, Marx maintained, is undermined as the people are pushed into individualism and competitiveness.

Like capitalism, socialism begins with some presuppositions: individuals tend to be selfish but they do not have to be this way; the individual and society are in conflict (as Marx found in capitalist society); and human nature can be changed so that the rational economic person can be produced, the person who not only contributes to society according to his or her means but also receives from society what he or she needs to live with dignity. This will happen once the contraints of the present economic and social class structures are eliminated.

In theory, communism glorifies the importance of the individual's obligations to society. Individuals are considered units isolated from a massive and perhaps highly structured society. This is the same kind of atomistic individualism we noted in capitalism. Society is not an organic or corporate body. Power is centralized in the party. Human rights originate from the state. "The inseparability of personal freedom and social solidarity is the cornerstone of Marxist social philosophy" (Hollenbach 1979, 21). The individual is essentially social. He or she gets individual meaning and rights from the people, the nation, and the state. An isolated individual can achieve only stunted growth.

Finally, communism claims to protect the social and economic rights of individuals. A major criticism of communism over the years has been not only that existing systems never really enhanced the social and economic right of its citizens but also that, for all practical purposes, it denied people their civil and political rights. The breakup of communist rule in eastern Europe in 1989 and of the U.S.S.R. on December 21, 1991, when eleven of the twelve republics formed a new commonwealth, was due in part to the wastefulness of the cold-war arms race and to the demand of the people for social, economic, civil, and political rights.

Catholic Social Teaching

Despite the fact that the church has had to adjust to emperors, tribal chiefs, kings and queens, feudal systems, and democracies, it has fundamental social teachings. These teachings have developed in stages and, especially since 1968, have taken notably different directions, "not in [their] basic truths and values but in the practical implications for the life of the church" (Dorr 1983, 263). What concerns us here are these basic truths and values.

Catholic social teaching is based on "a pre-Protestant, pre-capitalistic, and pre-Marxist view of society" (Greeley 1981). It begins with two insights, one theological and the other political. First, God's presence to humans and their history as revealed in the human life of Jesus tells us human life is good and should be of quality for all. Second, self and society, viewed from a sacramental consciousness, are not necessarily opposed but, rather, are interconnected. In fact, the formation of a state or a political community is a natural and necessary law of survival and maturation for humans (Maguire 1986, 20–21).

The most basic principle of Catholic social thought is the dignity, worth, and inviolability of the individual. It opposes collectivist tendencies or systems that leave individuals, especially the poor, vulnerable to oppression of any kind. Its aim is the growth of a fully integrated human being.

Catholic social teaching places the dignity of the individual within the context of society, which it views as an organic, supportive network of overlapping and interlocking yet hierarchical relationships that work toward social well-being or "the common good." The common good is the result of reponsible citizens acting in a way that leads to mutual respect for rights and dignity. When the council fathers discussed the common good, they declared, "Catholics should try to cooperate with all men and women of good will to promote what is true and just, whatever is holy and worth loving (cf. Phil. 4:8)" (AA 14). "The common good, since it is founded on mutual dignity, is not in opposition to human rights, but rather their guarantee" (Hollenbach 1979, 61).

Traditional Catholic teaching reasoned that the common good of society encompassed more than the sum of the private goods of individuals. The common good embraces the institutions, laws, and values that regulate in terms of justice the interaction of individuals and groups in society and protect them from exploitation or oppression by the powerful and resourceful. In this perspective, the private good of individuals is subordinated to the good of the whole society. Personal freedoms have their clearly defined limits. The task of government is to enhance the common good by protecting the common values, institutions and laws, and by resisting any individualism that would elevate an individual's own private good over the common good (Baum 1979b).

This organic and supportive society is also decentralized. Healthy societies need to be built upon strong neighborhoods and local communities. Villages, towns, and cities have formal political and social power and authority. The principle of subsidiarity holds that choice is of the essence of human freedom, so basic political choices must be left in the hands of those most affected by decisions.

This organic and decentralized society is also pluralistic. A plurality of cultures is necessary since there are many valid ways through which an individual can pursue wholeness.

Finally, the Catholic tradition is unwilling to separate civil and political rights from social and economic rights. It teaches that all four rights are indivisible and that violations of any of these rights are due to selfishness and greed. Right order and social justice can be reestablished in society if each and every person undergoes an intellectual and moral conversion to greater love, accepts the norms of justice, and strives to serve the common good.

At times the institutional church has not always been true to its own social teachings. For example, when the nineteenth-century popes condemned economic, religious, and political liberalism and, at the same time, denied civil rights, they were out of harmony with the Catholic tradition. Their justification was their belief that liberal political philosophy undermined the social cohesion of traditional society, total freedom of religion promoted indifferentism, and economic liberalism exploited the poor.

Vatican II did not endorse the unconditional rejection of modernity by the church of the nineteenth century. Yet, there was some validity to the stance of the nineteenth-century popes. Classical liberalism did promote individualism and undermined social solidarity; it did relativize, even trivialize, the question of the truth of religion; and it did legitimize the free-market economy since it demanded that the government allow maximum freedom of production and trade.

Leo XIII

The future Leo XIII became an archbishop and nuncio to highly industrialized Belgium at the age of thirty-three. There he saw the smelting furnaces and the factories in the Meuse River valley. There he rode his first steam train and, in a letter home, wrote, "It is part of a miracle. . . . We came from Brussels to Namur in three and a half hours, rushing over a distance of 64 miles."

He also saw the poverty and despair of the industrial workers. They lived in Dickensian slums and worked long hours while their children roamed the streets uncared for.

When he went to Perugia as bishop of the diocese at the age of thirty-six, he worked with the poor. He conducted schools, established orphanages, set up free kitchens—and even a savings bank (Lamboley 1979, 37).

His predecessor, Pius IX, was preoccupied with church doctrine and the Papal States and so lost sight of the religious decline of the working class in the cities. Leo "fully grasped the importance of arresting this process, even if it was too late to reverse it" (Cheetham 1983, 272).

Leo was very aware of Catholic social theory and of his responsibilities to promote and defend human rights and the common good in a world situation made more complex by the diversity of social, cultural, economic, and political styles and theories. This is not to say that he (or his successors) had any more competence than the economists and politicians to offer specific solutions and programs that would make the complex industrial economies of societies function equitably for individuals and the common good.

Leo inaugurated the modern church's struggle for social justice in 1891 with his famous 70,000-word encyclical *Rerum novarum* ("The Condition of Labor"). The historical setting for this encyclical was the Industrial Revolution in Europe and the United States. In 1891, approximately 77 percent of all Catholics lived in the industrialized world of the north and 23 percent in the countries now called the third world. Factory workers, many of them women and children, crowded into the cities where they either worked fifteen or more hours a day, seven days a week, at less than subsistence pay, or were unemployed. Employers tolerated no interference in the way they operated their businesses. The law of supply and demand regulated hours, wages, and working conditions.

The official church's response to these intolerable conditions and slave-market practices was, in general, extremely conservative, even reactionary. There were some outstanding exceptions: Felicite de Lamennais and Frederic Ozanam (1813–53) in France, Bishop Wilhelm von Kettler (1811–77) in Germany, and Bishop Gaspar Mermillod (1824–92), president of the so-called Fribourg Union.

At Fribourg, Switzerland, Catholic leaders from Germany, Austria, France, Belgium, and Italy, met annually for a week from 1885 to 1891 to study social problems. This group was open to progressive liberalism, which faulted classical liberalism for its excessive individualism, its failure to understand the quasi-organic nature of society and its inability to appreciate the radically social nature of human nature. One practical conclusion from these social-psychological premises was that government had the right and duty to intervene in the life of society, especially its educational and economic life. The Fribourg school favored the new democratic procedures over the prevailing Catholic paternalism and authoritarianism. For the workers, they advocated separate unions, instead of the joint unions of employers and workers favored by more conservative Catholics. They defended the right to work, to earn a living wage, and to have insurance against sickness, accidents, and unemployment. They also favored state intervention to protect the rights of workers. Their ideas and policies offered a powerful alternative to both liberal capitalism and Marxist socialism.

Lawrence Cunningham argues persuasively that *Rerum novarum* owed more to the social and economic developments in the United States than to Europe, especially because of the efforts of Cardinal James Gibbons (1834–1921), who worked closely with both the labor movement in this country and with curial officials in Rome (1986, 144–45). Gibbons was a bishop for fifty-three years, forty-four of them (1877–1921) as archbishop of Baltimore.

The liberal views of both the Fribourg Union and Gibbons were opposed by other Catholics who believed those policies, especially government intervention, would lead to socialism and other errors. For them, the remedy to the social problems was Christian charity.

Rerum novarum was intended to be a major intervention in defense of the poor and to correct the dehumanizing impact of industrialization on the dignity and rights of workers. Leo endorsed the Fribourg Union's arguments for government intervention, for the right of workers to organize unions of their own, and for the principle of a just wage. Against the socialist and Marxist idealization of the state, Leo defended the right to private property and insisted that the family is the basis of society and not the state. Leo had a "passionate concern for the plight of the working class" (Dorr 1983, 53). He did not mention liberal capitalism as such, but he did condemn abuses in the marketplace. For example, he complained that too few people controlled the production of goods and that the greedy laid on the poor "a yoke little better than that of slavery itself." He urged his readers to look on the whole of material existence from a Christian perspective, reminding all that "God himself seems to incline to those who suffer misfortune."

Rerum novarum is primarily moralistic in tone—it calls for a change of attitude rather than structural changes in society. Also, it focuses on the economic situation within the typical industrialized country of the West. Nevertheless, it represents a major achievement. "While rooted in tradition, it offers an opening to the new situation, including the emergence of democratic governments, the reality or threat of political revolution, and the development of an industrial proletariat ground down by poverty. It is not surprising, then, that Leo's teaching has remained the basis of the official Catholic position on social issues" (ibid., 51).

Leo's successors, Pius X and Benedict XV, made few notable advances in the understanding of Catholic social teaching. The former, the least socially enlightened of this century's popes, was preoccupied with Modernism; the latter with World War I and with a church still hobbled by a lingering anti-Modernism and suspicion of new thinking on social issues. Benedict addressed these issues in 1914 in his encyclical *Ad beatissimi* ("Appeal for Peace").

Pius XI

His pontificate was dominated by three social developments with extensive political consequences—the worldwide depression of the 1930s, the expansion of Soviet communism, and the emergence of fascism in Germany and Italy.

Fascism is a philosophy of government that opposes both democracy and socialism and that glorifies the nation-state at the expense of individual human dignity. In 1931 Pius denounced the state absolutism of the Italian Fascists in *Non abbiamo bisogno* ("We Have No Need"). His response to the Nazis in Germany was very uneven. At first he negotiated a concordat with Hitler in 1933, moved, it seems, by a fear of communism and by trust in Hitler's assurances. The concordat temporarily enhanced the prestige of the Nazis. However, from 1933 to 1936, Pius frequently had to protest the Nazi oppression of the church. Finally, on March 14, 1937, he issued the encyclical *Mit brennender Sorge* ("With Burning Concern"), condemning the Nazis for violating the 1933 concordat by harassing church members and damaging church property.

Some commentators thought it deplorable that Pius never condemned the Nazis for their violations of the natural law (for example, their denial of the human dignity of Jews, homosexuals, and the mentally and physically disabled), their crimes against liberty, and their tyranny and oppression of every kind (Falconi 1967, 207). It has been reported that the German episcopate opposed Hitler from the beginning. When, on September 14, 1930, the National Socialist party secured sixteen million votes and 107 seats in the parliament, the bishops exhorted the faithful to examine their consciences (ibid., 193). But this is not the whole story of the German church's relationship with Hitler.

Concerning communism, the future Pius XI (Ratti) had first-hand experience of it when he was nuncio to Poland for three years (1918–21). At that time the country was under the dictatorship of the socialist Marshal Josef Pilsudski. Ratti's tasks were to help rebuild the church in Poland, negotiate a concordat, and secure information about the thousands of Polish Catholics who had been deported to Siberia by the Russians. In the summer of 1920 the communist army laid siege to Warsaw. Ratti remained in the city and saw with his own eyes the might of the Russian armies that enforced communism.

On March 19, 1937—five days after the encyclical against Nazism—Pius declared in his encyclical *Divini Redemptoris* that communism was intrinsically wrong and the greatest of all evils. He said no one should collaborate with communism in any way if Christian civilization would be saved, because it promotes class struggles and relies on the working class for leaders in its "dictatorship of the proletariat."

With regard to the problems of the working class, Pius, like Leo, had to evaluate two opposing schools of Catholic social thought. The *Sozialpolitik* school basically accepted the capitalist system but believed that its harsher features could be alleviated by various forms of social welfare, for example, by a strong social insurance system. Like Leo XIII, they advocated unions and insurance against sickness, unemployment, and old age.

The other group—the *Sozialreform* school—wanted to revamp capitalism. They denounced its many deviations from traditional Catholic social teachings, especially its exaggerated individualism, which promoted both greed and an unjust distribution of wealth. They also urged harmony between the classes and denounced the call of the socialists for revolution. To achieve harmony between workers and management, they advocated industry councils on local and national levels in which employers and employees would determine local and general economic policy. They also advocated government intervention when the public good demanded it.

In 1931, on the fortieth anniversary of *Rerum novarum*, Pius issued *Quadragesimo anno* ("On Reconstruction of the Social Order"). This major encyclical was written by Oswald von Nell-Breuning (1890–1991), a Jesuit theologian, economist, and social scientist (Murphy 1991). In this document, Pius sided with the *Sozialreform* school and criticized the capitalist system not only as it had developed since the pontificate of Leo but in its essential nature. He wrote, "Free competition has destroyed itself; economic domination has taken the place of the open market." He rejected capitalism because its central principle—free competition—was affirmed as the determining factor in the economic order, regulating prices, profits, and wages. Furthermore, materialistic capitalism breeds greed and, in its single-minded quest for profits, pushes aside human compassion.

Some argued that Pius XI was proposing an alternative socioeconomic system, one that would replace socialism and capitalism. This is a debatable issue, but it does not seem to be the correct interpretation of his call for a reconstruction of the social order. *Reconstruction*, as Pius used the term, meant renovating old structures. Furthermore, what he was doing was laying down fundamental principles of social morality. On the basis of these principles, he ruled out "the acceptance of socialism in any form and of capitalism both in its basic ideological principle and in its actual historical development" (Dorr 1983, 63). Pius proposed "a free-enterprise system which would be more or less equivalent to capitalism without its abuses and without its ideology" (ibid., 143). Finally, Pius declared that charity alone will not solve the problems of the poor. The economic structures that cause "the open violation of justice" have to be restructured. Perhaps we can say he advocated a limited free-market economy—capitalism with a human face.

Quadragesimo anno was a classic expression of Catholic social teaching, as described above. Its common themes were solidarity, smallness, cooperation, and subsidiarity, which entail both decentralization and respect for the existing networks of workers, families, and neighborhoods. The encyclical gave classic formulation to the principle of subsidiarity, some form of which "can be found in nearly every major social document of the tradition since *Rerum novarum*" (Hollenbach 1979, 157). Pius said it is "both a serious evil and a perturbation of right order to assign to a larger and higher society what can be performed successfully by smaller and lower communities." The basic reason for this principle was to prevent members of the social body from being destroyed or absorbed by society.

Thomas Bokenkotter said Pius XI's "prescriptions were so vague and indefinite that his plan was given a bewildering variety of interpretations" (1985, 362). Andrew Greeley, on the other hand, declared that the "fundamental weakness of *Quadragesimo anno* and the Catholic social theory that it articulates formally is not it has been tried and found wanting, but found hard and not tried" (1981, 48).

During the preconciliar period, many Catholics—liturgists, college professors, priests, and so forth—heeded the papal teachings on social justice. Two notable examples were John A. Ryan (1869–1948) and Dorothy Day (1897–1980).

Ryan, a priest and political scientist, taught at Catholic University and was an adviser to both government officials and the bishops on such issues as prohibition, women's suffrage, and child-labor laws. He wrote *A Living Wage* (1906), in which he emphasized the obligation of employers to pay wages sufficient to maintain a worker and his family in decent comfort. The source of his ideas was *Rerum novarum*. "Indeed, the whole book can be read as an application of that encyclical to the American situation" (Gustafson 1978, 24). He later argued that *Quadragesimo anno* "supported the New Deal [of Franklin Delano Roosevelt] in the United States" (ibid., 133).

Dorothy Day was probably the most influential Catholic of her time. A convert to Catholicism from the Episcopal Church, she was a woman of prayer and deeply devoted to the institutional church. In collaboration with Peter Maurin (1877–1949), a philosopher, poet, social visionary, and a former Christian Brother from France, she published the first issue of *The Catholic Worker* on May 1, 1933. Their paper was a direct challenge to the communist paper, *The Daily Worker.*

Day and Maurin are credited with the first major expression of radical social criticism in United States Catholicism. They took literally the gospel challenge regarding peace, nonviolence, and voluntary poverty. Together they challenged the church's social conservatism, which, with its focus on the hereafter, thwarted the development of a social conscience, especially when the church reinforced the conventional wisdom concerning such issues as war, civil disobedience, and taxes. Day and Maurin challenged the economic and political structures of the day as well, both national and international, because they failed to make a world where "it is easier for people to be good." One of their major efforts was to move society from the impersonalism of urban-industrial society to the personalism of rural-agrarian society. Their newspaper and houses of hospitality continue today.

Dorothy Day also influenced Vatican II. She went to Rome to lobby for her causes, especially nonviolence. She convinced the council fathers by her words and actions (a ten-day fast) to insert a paragraph (n. 80) in *Gaudium et spes* calling for the unequivocal condemnation of the indiscriminate destruction of cities (MacEoin 1991b, 61–65).

Pius XII

Pius XII, whose motto was "Peace is the work of justice" and who wrote forty encyclicals, never produced a social encyclical equal in importance to those of Leo XIII and Pius XI. Nevertheless, his many pronouncements on social issues, many broadcasts on radio or television, are similar to his predecessors'. In accordance with the Catholic tradition he condemned the omnipresent threats to the dignity of the person and families, called for respect for basic human rights, and offered support for democratic political structures.

Concerning capitalism, his writings seem to accept it as the only feasible alternative to communism, nazism, and fascism.

During his pontificate the church gave strong religious and ideological support to those who opposed socialism and communism at all levels—international, national, and local. Pius was almost paranoid about communism in the Soviet Union, the first organized state in the history of the world to be openly atheistic. Inasmuch as he had joined the papal diplomatic service in 1914, Pius had intimate knowledge of the communist revolution in Russia on November 7, 1917, and the Soviet Union's relentless and ruthless rise to world dominance. The millions of Catholics in communist countries— some fifty million at the time of his death—were one of his main concerns. On June 30, 1949, he issued a decree denying the sacraments to those Italians who voted communist and excommunicating those who professed its "materialistic and antichristian" teachings.

Leo XIII and Pius XI had advocated economic justice within each nation. The teachings of Pius XII had a wider focus: he taught what would later be labeled "international social justice" (Hehir 1981). Pius was led to this level by at least four factors. First, before becoming pope, he had spent almost his entire career in the papal diplomatic service. He had been Pius XI's secretary of state from February 1930 until 1939, when he was elected pope. In 1944 he made himself secretary of state when his secretary, Cardinal Luigi Maglione, died. Second, he was aware that around the globe people were subject to grave injustices not only from totalitarian governments but also from the development of large bureaucratic industries and governments. Third, six months after his election, the world suffered through its second world war, this one more tragic and disastrous than the first. That war came to a climactic end when the United States dropped atom bombs on Japan. Since then the world has lived under the menace of nuclear war. Pius eloquently warned about such a war: "There will be no song of victory, only the inconsolable weeping of humanity, which will gaze upon the catastrophe brought on by its own folly."[2] Fourth, after the war the nations of the world looked for international order, especially through the United Nations. In 1948, this body issued its Universal Declaration of Human Rights, a document that was not a binding treaty subject to the full strictures of international law, but nevertheless one that did serve as a "standard of achievement" for the nations of the world. Pius clearly understood the postwar changes in the social and economic spheres and the emergence of a truly global international system. In his addresses he focused on the political-legal meaning of international order (Hehir 1991). When Pius died on October 9, 1958, the *New York Times* report of his death was subtitled "All of world ills were his concern."

John XXIII

In 1961, John wrote the encyclical *Mater et magistra* to honor the encyclicals of 1891 and 1931. In it he broke with the tradition of using rational arguments drawn from natural law. This tradition had been adopted in order to develop a public discourse of universal validity. Instead, John proposed and defended his social teachings with arguments drawn from Scripture. Christians should be commited to justice and freedom in society because of Jesus and his gospel. Furthermore, a "natural" view of humans as a source for moral reasoning is inadequate. Christians do not view nature as "pure nature." Rather, everyone always lives within the enduring offer of the grace of God and has a supernatural origin and destiny.

Within this context, John adhered to the Catholic tradition of defending individual human dignity and integrating the individual and society. However, John wrote to meet a new range of problems, especially the growing interdependence among nations. He lamented the widening gap between rich and poor nations, and asked for greater concern for the "international common good." While respecting the principle of subsidiarity, he believed that the common good actually required more government intervention. He even suggested greater need of government ownership, espousing a "welfare state model," which requires society and the state to assume responsibility for the public's well-being by remedying poverty and deprivation. He also stated that the right to private property was not an absolute, since God had given the world to everyone.

Regarding capitalism, John seemed to be optimistic about its future development. He never repudiated the condemnations of it made by Leo XIII and Pius XI, yet "he seemed to believe that before too long and without too much trouble the system could be effectively humanized" (Dorr 1983, 92).

Regarding communism, John mitigated his predecessors' hostility to it by arguing that, despite its false philosophy about the origins and purpose of human existence, it had good elements that could be used carefully in social analysis. The implications of this encyclical were so radical that the church came to have new allies and new opponents. For instance, in the United States, conservative Catholics felt betrayed and cried, "Mater, si, magistra, no" (Buckley 1961, 88).

Pacem in terris (1963) was issued after Vatican II finished its first session and within the context of the nuclear arms race and the Cold War. It marked the first time in history an encyclical was sent to "all men of good will" and not just to the Catholic bishops of the world. The document drew from specifically Catholic sources, yet appealed in its vision and sense of moral urgency to thoughtful men and women outside the Catholic community. Most people agreed with its most quotable sentence: "It no longer makes sense to maintain that war is a fit instrument with which to repair the violation of justice." All did not agree, however, with John's call to ban nuclear weapons.

The encyclical was built on the Catholic vision of society: humans function best when there is order, solidarity, and peace on earth. Force, coercion, or fear destroy both individuals and society.

John addressed communism in this encyclical as well. He once more distinguished between a philosophy with false ideas about "the nature, origin and destiny of the universe and of man" and "the economic, social, cultural and political programs" which issued from it and which one had to contend with in the historical order because they "contain elements that are positive and deserving of approval" (n. 159). For some Catholics, these ideas were blatant heresy. Even Peter Hebblethwaite, that otherwise most liberal of interpreters, declared John was not that clear: "The link between theory and praxis in Marxism is allegedly such that one cannot drive a wedge between them, and this is one of the originalities of Marxism" (1975, 150).

David Hollenbach considered this encyclical "the most powerful and thorough statement of the Roman Catholic understanding of human rights in modern times" (1979, 41). In his encyclical John eradicated an argument about human rights that had befuddled the church's approach to human liberty for over a thousand years. The traditional axiom was "error has no rights." This proposition had been used by the Inquisition (1542) and other heresy-hunters. John insisted that only human persons have rights. Made in the image of God, every individual is entitled to live in peace and freedom for the pursuit of truth, justice, and love. This freedom had to be respected by church and state alike. In practical terms, John's teachings called for respect for the inviolability of the person-hood of all, even those in error. He also said people are not to be forced to act in a fashion contrary to their beliefs, thus giving support to conscientious objectors to war. Finally, he condemned every type of discrimination, racial, sexual, national and religious (Murphy 1990).

Vatican II

In a radio address on September 11, 1962, one month before the opening of the Council, John said he hoped the Council would present the church "in the underdeveloped countries as the church of all, and especially of the poor." In 1965, the Council addressed social morality in two documents, the one on the church in the modern world (*Gaudium et spes*) and the other on religious freedom.

Gaudium et spes is by far the longest conciliar document. It is a synthesis of Catholic social teaching from Leo XIII to Paul VI, especially in sections 23 to 32 and 63 to 72. It declared that the church cannot stand by, indifferent to the world and its changes. While the church has no mission in the political and economic world, it does have "a function, a light, and an energy which can serve to structure and consolidate the human community according to the divine law. As a matter of fact, when circumstances of time and place create the need, it can and indeed should initiate activities in behalf of the people" (GS 42). It also recommended that "some agency of the universal church" be established in order to "stimulate the Catholic community to foster progress in needy regions and social justice in the international scene" (GS 90).

The bishops affirmed the dignity of the human person and acknowledged that the demands of human dignity are historically conditioned. It stated that the basis of the church's social ethics is personalism (the needs and rights of the person) rather than natural law (see GS 26). It also affirmed historical consciousness by acknowledging that people are more and more conscious of building "a better world based on truth and justice. Thus we are witnesses of the birth of a new humanism, one in which man is defined first of all by his responsibility toward his brothers and toward history" (GS 55). The bishops declared that "among the signs of our times, the irresistibly increasing sense of solidarity among all peoples is especially noteworthy" (AA 4). Finally, the Council did make one condemnation, against "total war" (GS 80).

There have been many evaluations of *Gaudium et spes*— too many to synthesize here. A point made by Richard McBrien concerning the new understanding of social justice in the church deserves special attention, in part because it supplements the discussion on the proper mission of the church discussed in chapter 4. McBrien pointed out that before the Council the church's social teaching was regarded primarily as a subdivision within moral theology. With the Council the focus shifted from moral theology to ecclesiology. Social justice activity was perceived by the council fathers not only as a way of practicing the virtue of justice, but also, and now primarily, as a way of fulfilling the mission of the church. The Council taught that the demands of social justice are an obligation upon the whole church to serve the world based on truth and justice (1978b).

The Declaration on Religious Freedom was the most controversial of the sixteen conciliar documents, in good part because Pius IX had condemned religious freedom in his

Syllabus of Errors (1864). Paul VI described the document as "one of the major texts of the council" (Abbott 1966, 674). Mainly the work of John Courtney Murray, it was approved on December 7, 1965, by vote of 2,308 to 70 (Murray 1966a).[3] The bishops grappled with this issue in order to "develop the doctrine of recent popes on the inviolable rights of the human person and on the constitutional order of society" (DH 1).

The document affirmed religious freedom as a human right. It also taught that all governments ought to recognize religious freedom and "show it favor" so that all "citizens and religious bodies" can enjoy it. Finally, it declared that "freedom of the church is a fundamental principle in what concerns the relation between the church and government and the whole civil order."

This declaration had many implications for church life. No more would the church seek to impose itself on any government or another religious body. This retreat from imperialism would improve ecumenical dialogues. Similarly, Rome would have trouble accusing any national local church of trying to be different from the rest of the church. An accusation, such as that of Americanism, for example, will not stand up because "the council recognized and called for the constitutional recognition and legal implementation of those fundamental human rights which validate all democratic governments" (Linnan 1986, 177). Finally, the Council reaffirmed the most basic principle of Catholic social teaching: the dignity of the responsible person in society. It is this principle, declared David Hollenbach, that is "an important key to the problem of the foundation, interrelation and institutionalization of human rights" (Hollenbach 1979, 76).

Paul VI

During the pontificate of Paul VI, significant developments in the church's social teachings resulted from his writings, from the gathering of bishops at historic episcopal conferences and the Synod of 1971, and from the rise of political and liberation theologies.

In 1967, Paul published *Populorum progressio* ("On the Development of Peoples"), building on John XXIII's theme of the international common good. Paul acknowledged that while there were many "situations whose injustice cries to heaven," nevertheless, he said he believed positive change was coming throughout the whole world and that a well-balanced society would soon break through. He urged the developed nations to achieve this social order by fostering the full self-development of the poor nations on every level—economic, social, political, personal, and spiritual. Development, he warned, cannot take place as long as liberal capitalists neglect their social obligations. Paul rejected liberal capitalism because it considers "profit as the key motive for economic progress, competition as the supreme law of economics, and private ownership of the means of production as an absolute right that has no limits and carries no corresponding social obligation" (n. 26). Is it any wonder that these strong words prompted the *Wall Street Journal* to call the encyclical "warmed-over Marxism"?[4]

Philip Scharper was probably more on target when he said the encyclical's "major flaw" was its call "to rich nations and persons to share the problems of poverty and injustice. . . . Effective altruism—rare enough in individuals—is seldom found in nations or groups possessing wealth and power" (1978).

In 1967 Paul VI followed up on the Council's recommendation (GS 90) by setting up the Pontifical Commission of Justice and Peace to assist in the establishment of the international common good. This office "is certainly the outstanding institutional consequence" of *Gaudium et spes* (E. McDonagh 1991, 109).

Latin American Episcopal Conferences

Vatican II reinvigorated episcopal conferences; Paul VI ordered them to meet regularly. The Latin American bishops, prompted by Pius XII, had held their first conference (CELAM is the acronym for *Conferencia Episcopal Latinoamericana*) in 1955 in Rio de Janeiro. Inasmuch as it preceded Vatican II, it was ecclesiocentric. For example, it lamented the shortage of indigenous priests and condemned both Protestantism and communism. Vatican II rendered it obsolete.

On August 24, 1968, the bishops gathered for CELAM II at Medellín, Colombia, to discuss the role of the church in the actual transformation of Latin America in the light of the Council. Medellín had been approved by Paul VI in 1967, who even suggested that it take place when he could be present. Paul had already planned to be in Bogotá for the International Eucharistic Congress. It worked out that Paul inaugurated CELAM II in Bogotá and, thereafter, it met for two weeks in Medellín.

At Vatican II, the Latin American bishops (there were 531 present) introduced the term "church of the poor." This phrase denotes a church that denounces impoverishment caused by sin and injustice, preaches and lives spiritual poverty, and binds itself to material poverty as a commitment. Not all 531 bishops were enthusiastic about the term and its consequences. For those who were, many of the questions so fiercely debated during the council—religious freedom, ecumenism, and doctrinal development—seemed like "European" questions. For instance, Dom Helder Camara, archbishop of Recife in northeast Brazil, declared that development was indeed the number one problem—but not doctrinal development. The development he was concerned with was "the social and economic development of peoples" (Hebblethwaite 1989c).

Medellín became the "new Pentecost" for the Latin American church. It was the bishops' opportunity to apply Vatican II to Latin America. It produced sixteen documents of uneven quality and without a unified conclusion. Nevertheless, the conference surpassed the Council in many respects. Summarized here are five of its principal themes.

First, the bishops agreed that, contrary to the view expressed earlier by Helder Camara and *Populorum progressio*, economic development was not the solution to their problems. The era of development was actually over because the attempt to make the undeveloped countries of the south like the developed nations of the north was impossible. Nothing had changed: the developed nations continued to prosper at the expense of the poorer ones. The organic networks of society had broken down. The rich and poor were in a serious conflict, and the bishops identified the main areas of oppression: "a situation of injustice that can be called institutionalized violence"; "internal colonialism" whereby a rich minority (oligarchy) dominate power; and an "external neocolonialism" of powerful, foreign nations. The true solution is liberation for the poor, the voiceless, and the oppressed. The bishops questioned the church's traditional alliance with wealthy, oligarchical establishments, and called for radical structural changes. Vatican II had declared a change of heart (inner, personal transformation) as the way to achieve social justice. As people grow in virtue, political commitment would emerge and social justice will follow, they believed. Medellín, on the other hand, called for both a transformation of individuals and a transformation of the structures of society. However, some of the bishops said transformation of society must come first. Evil societies must be overcome first. In fact, they said, personal growth and holiness truly occur when people combat evil. Also, without the transformation of structures, the transformation of persons is extremely difficult. In the end the bishops compromised and called for both transformations because they were divided over which would be more appropriate for the different countries of the continent (Baum 1984a, 85).

Second, the bishops encouraged conscientization—helping people understand that they become responsible for injustice if they remain passive. That is, if people out of fear of the personal risk involved do not take courageous and effective action to bring about necessary changes, they, by their passivity, perpetuate the injustices.

Third, the bishops declared that evangelization cannot take place except within the context of a commitment to the struggle against the systems of domination.

Fourth, Medellín condemned social sin, something never mentioned at Vatican II. The bishops reinterpreted the classic doctrine of sin by stating that people need liberation not only from their personal sins but also from the social sin of oppressive social structures. Social sin has a powerful hold on people. It results from past personal choices for injustice that form into systemic institutions of socioeconomic and political oppression and deprivation. Social sin has to be identified and eliminated.

Fifth, the bishops declared that personnel and resources within the church must be redistributed so as to give effective "preference to the poorest and most needy sectors." This expression would be rephrased as the "preferential option for the poor" at CELAM III in 1979.

The preferential option for the poor is not exclusive, but it does require two commitments from the church: to look upon society in all its dimensions from the perspective of the poor, and to give public witness to the church's solidarity with the poor. It is through criticizing injustices that the church can express in a practical way this solidarity. This criticism should never be expressed through violence.

The phrase "preferential option for the poor" has evoked considerable controversy. Donal Dorr noted that it "became the most controversial religious term since the Reformers' cry, 'Salvation through faith alone'" (1983, 1).

The church has always taken care of the poor, particularly through almsgiving (see 1 Cor. 16:1; Gal. 2:10) or through monks and nuns who commit themselves to serving the poor and sick. Also, concern for the involuntary poor pervades the Scriptures, which portray God as being on the side of the oppressed and the outcasts. A paradigm of God's care for such people is the exodus of the Hebrew slaves from the clutches of the pharaohs, and God's electing them his chosen people. The Jewish prophets challenged the priests and people to care for the sick, orphans, and widows; they also announced messianic promises. Jesus is also paradigmatic. He was poor and fulfilled his mission among the marginalized, oppressed, and poor. His life as critic of injustices brought him persecution and death. However, his resurrection is a sign of God's promises of wholeness and life.

While the church always cared for the poor, it never proclaimed a preferential option for the poor. Why was this call not heard in the past—or why was it not heard in the same way as at Medellín (Baum 1986b)? There are several reasons. The first concerns the scriptural basis of this stand. The phrase "preferential option for the poor" is not found as such in the Bible. It is grounded in biblical teaching, but was formulated by interpreters who presuppose historical consciousness—that humans are the subject of their own history. In today's world there is massive suffering and oppression; many people do not have access to many of the basics of human life.

Modern hermeneutics proposes that written texts can be interpreted in two ways: with the historical-critical method, which tries to discern the author's intended meaning, or with the critical method, which suggests the text's implications for today's world. The critical method, as David Tracy explained, is based on the belief that "once one has written a work, the work lives on its own. The author becomes another reader—

with some privileged knowledge of what she or he once meant, but with no hermeneutical privilege at all in interpreting what the text really says. For that latter task, for better and for worse, the work alone speaks" (1990, 903).

A second reason why the idea of a preferential option for the poor moved to the forefront is due to the way theology developed after Vatican II. Until the Council, the church had a state-of-siege mentality. It withdrew from direct engagement with the social, economic, and political orders, viewing itself as separate from the world. The popes protested injustices, but the effect of their teachings often gave a measure of legitimation to the status quo. This defensive posture was captured in the phrase "in the world but not of it."

With Vatican II Christians found themselves "released from the world for the world." This perspective sees the church as part of the world but aware of its evils. The church must be released from the pretensions, delusions, and sin of the world, but at the same time it "should be released for the world *as it really is*: arbitrary, contingent, ambiguous, loved by God and by the Christian" (Tracy 1981, 48).

Involvement with the world, especially the world from which Christians must be released, entails interpretation. It is impossible to take a neutral position. Everyone views history, the historians inform us, from a particular value perspective. The Medellín bishops read history from the perspective of the involuntary poor. They wrote "people history." They realized that the conflict between the powerful rich and the powerless poor was one of the world's major problems, especially in Latin America. The bishops realized that their people had to be released from the deadly evil of the violence of poverty. The opponents of the bishops accused them of reading history with a Marxist perspective. But choosing for the poor is not Marxist. Marx promoted a preferential option for the workers, the industrial proletariat whose toil fueled the economy. Marx believed the unemployable had no destiny in society. He called them *Lumpen*, the German word for "hoodlum."

Gregory Baum maintains that the church's commitment to a preferential option for the poor is definitive and irreversible. This preference was adopted and developed by the Synod of 1971; by CELAM III and IV; by national episcopal conferences, including the United States bishops in their pastoral letters of

1983 and 1986; and by both Paul VI and John Paul II. Baum regards the turn to the poor begun at Medellín "as an extraordinary happening, possibly of world historical importance" (1986b, 30). It has made a major impact on Catholic social teaching. Instead of viewing society as an organic network of interlocking relationships, Catholic social teaching now evaluates society from a critical, conflictive perspective. This perspective sees that society is divided by structures of oppression, and believes that the church should ally itself with the poor, the workers, and the unemployable. By struggling together with the poor, the church can transform the social order (Baum 1984b). Eventually, and ultimately, the transformation sought would reflect the Catholic ideal: an organic, supportive, decentralized, and pluralistic society characterized by peace and freedom.

The Medellín documents represent compromise; not all the bishops favored the preferential option for the poor. One group that was fiercely anti-communist favored the establishment of a neo-Christendom, that is, a society and culture, aided by the moral and material support of the state, ruled by the Catholic tradition. These bishops insisted that society's principal enemy is the secularization encouraged by the growing industrial developments. Latin America is in danger of losing its soul and so must defend its homogeneous culture against secularization by becoming industrialized, but without following the example of the West. These bishops maintained that the primary task of the church, therefore, is to promote a cohesive Latin American culture, adapted to the requirements of industrial society yet faithful to its original values, including the Roman Catholic faith. The primary thrust of the church's pastoral projects is religious. Concern for justice will follow from the transformation of people.

The other group—the bishops who dominated at Medellín—viewed the Latin American scene differently. They believe injustice and oppression are the principal social evils in Latin America. Furthermore, they claim that a homogeneous Latin American culture has never existed, and that the concept is an ideology that disguises the structural injustices in Latin American society (Baum 1983b).

Twenty-one years after Medellín, some seventy-five academics and social activists met at the University of Notre

Dame in March 1989, to review Medellín. They concluded that the church had made advances and retreats since 1968. Among the advances was "the unravelling church-state entanglements when the church began to prefer the poor." One serious retreat: the appointment of "conservative bishops inclined more to pasteurizing doctrine and less to succoring those in desperate need" (Gibeau 1989).

Paul VI: *Octogesima adveniens*

In 1971 Paul published *Octogesima adveniens* ("Call to Action") to mark the eightieth anniversary of *Rerum novarum*. It also "may be understood at least partly as a response by Pope Paul to all that Medellín came to stand for" (Dorr 1983, 157).

This apostolic letter (it was not an encyclical) moved the church's socioeconomic concerns to another level, namely, that of transnational issues (Hehir 1981, 585). This is not to say that the national issues of economic justice (e.g., the unionization of workers) or the international social questions (e.g., the disparity between rich and poor nations) had even approached resolution. However, by 1970 there emerged on the international scene in a qualitatively new way transnational actors (multinational corporations) and transnational problems (e.g., debt, pollution, over-population, hunger) that placed new constraints on many nations, further complicating international relations.

Paul acknowledged the difficulties inherent in establishing a just social order and did not himself provide detailed moral norms for transnational relations such as Catholic thought had developed for national issues of social justice (Henriot 1988, 11). Nevertheless, he insisted that the complexity of our world makes the search for the common good even more important than in the past. He said that social justice problems, "because of their urgency, extent and complexity, must, in the years to come, take first place among the preoccupations of Christians" (n. 7). Paul pointed to the role local Christian communities could play in this pursuit. At this level people can come together "to analyze with objectivity the situation which is proper to their own country," pray and reflect on their situation in the light of the gospel and the church's social teachings, and then take appropriate action.

In addition to his critique of the transnational capitalists' placing new constraints and problems on the poorer nations, Paul continued his warnings against Marxism. He admitted that Marxism has various elements—it is a philosophy of history, a political movement, and a form of social analysis. As "a rigorous method of examining social and political reality" it also attracts some adherents. He warned, however, that even revisionist statements of Marxism demand careful discernment. Ultimately, Paul rejected both Marxist socialism and liberal capitalism because they deny dimensions of personal and social development that are integral to human dignity.

Political Theology

This term is ambiguous. It goes back to the Stoics who used it "to justify theologically the primacy of politics and the absolute claims of the state" (Metz 1970). Actually, political theology is almost as old as recorded religious experience. For example, the Bible addresses the history and politics of ancient Israel, especially in the prophets' reproach of kings, priests, and people for their failures to fulfill the covenant and their warnings about Israel's precarious future as a political entity.

Johann Baptist Metz retrieved the term in an attempt to apply the gospel to today's society. Political theology is not a complete system. Rather, it is a critique of both modern society and modern theology that aims to correct them. Metz explained it as follows: "I understand political theology first of all to be a critical correction of present-day theology inasmuch as this theology shows an extreme privatizing tendency (a tendency, that is, to center upon the private person rather than public, political society). At the same time I understand this political theology to be a positive attempt to formulate the eschatological message under the conditions of our present society" (1969, 107).

Political theology developed in Germany and in other parts of the world in the late 1960s. Advocates of political theology included Metz, Jurgen Moltmann (1967) and Dorothee Sölle (1967). This account focuses on the writings of Metz, a priest-theologian and student of Karl Rahner.

The inspiration for this theology is threefold. First, it grew out of the Marxist-Christian dialogues of 1965 through 1967.

Marx had declared that the task of philosophy is not to interpret the world but to change it. Metz realized that this observation challenged Christian life and theology. Christian
theology had to abandon its emphasis on the next life, an
emphasis that had dominated Christian spirituality for centuries. Rather than staying aloof from society, Christians
should commit themselves to changing it.

Second, political theology opposed the dominant spiritualities of pietism and existentialism. Pietism arose in the seventeenth and eighteenth centuries as a reaction to the cold
objectivity of much of the prevailing theology, preaching, and
prayer. In both Protestant and Catholic forms, pietism fostered
a religion of the heart and feeling, and a deep and intimate
relationship with God. It also stressed personal salvation and
personal sins. Metz showed that this privatizing trend, once
vital and imaginative, now left little room for the social dimension of the Christian message. Christianity in its privatized form
had actually "been distorted by the modernity it claimed to be
confronting since the Enlightenment" (McDade 1991, 432).
Similarly, the existentialism of such influential biblical scholars
as Rudolph Bultmann (1884–1976) underscored a personal
relationship with God. The gospel, said Bultmann, is a call to
individuals now as they make important decisions about their
individual lives. Existentialism had its roots in the
Enlightenment, which shattered the unity of religion and society. Christianity was reduced to the status of one particular
phenomenon in a pluralistic world. Once religion and society
were separated, the social dimension of the Christian gospel
descended to secondary importance (Fiorenza 1975, 8–9).

Metz opposed pietism and existentialism because they privatized the gospel message and limited Christian faith to individual decision, private virtue, and apolitical individual
encounters with the Wholly Other. Religion and society, said
Metz, must stand in tension. After all, the Scriptures promise
liberty, peace, justice, and reconciliation—values that are necessarily social.

Metz's theology also developed in response to that of his
mentor, Karl Rahner. Rahner's theology—called transcendental
Thomism—highlighted the individual as a graced, self-tran-
scendent subject. Rahner wanted to close the distance
between grace and nature as set forth by the neo-Thomists.

Humans, said Rahner, have a supernatural origin and destiny. God's grace is always present. It is not added to nature, or separate from it, or offered only intermittently in certain privileged times and circumstances. Based on this theological anthropology, Rahner insisted that the aim of theology is not to pump religion into people but "to find the art of drawing religion out of" a person. Metz, while he found this focus significant, said it ignored a very essential dimension of human existence, namely, the sociopolitical.

Political theology articulates a theocentric spirituality with a nuanced understanding of three central concerns of Christian theology: God, Christ, and church.

Christians have always acknowledged the transcendence of God. According to Metz, biblical faith points to a God who is oriented towards the future, a dimension that has been unduly separated from transcendence. Metz emphasizes that God's transcendence is temporal. "God revealed himself to Moses more as the power of the future rather than a being dwelling beyond all history and experience. God is not 'above us' but 'before us'" (1969, 88). This orientation toward the future is also fundamental to the New Testament. The proclamation of the death and resurrection of Jesus "is essentially a proclamation of promise which initiates the Christian mission. This mission achieves its future insofar as the Christian alters and innovates the world toward that future of God which is definitely promised to us in the resurrection of Jesus Christ" (ibid., 89). To talk about God is to talk about his coming kingdom. Political theology is a theology of hope.

Metz emphasized Jesus' proclamation and manifestation of the kingdom of God—the liberating presence and power of God's unconditional love. Jesus' proclamation was not "strictly religious." Rather, Jesus fulfilled his mission among the oppressed and poor. His ministry was in the political, economic, and social order. For "inciting the people" (Luke 23:5) with his criticisms of the establishment and his association with sinners and the outcasts of society, Jesus was persecuted and crucified. But his resurrection anticipated the final promises of the kingdom: peace, justice, love, and life. Thus, Metz speaks of the disturbing and dangerous legacy of Jesus Christ, who summons people to greater love and holiness gained by working to promote and expand the kingdom of God (1980, 80–99, 200–204).

The preconciliar view of church and society held the church above and outside politics, angelically judging a sinful society for whose sins it shared no blame and for whose problems it had all the answers. Metz countered that if Christianity flees from the world and retreats into an isolated fortress, it will be condemned to the periphery of society because it ignores the hopes and needs of modern people. The justification for the church's mission to the world is the coming kingdom of God. To herald the advent of this kingdom, the church should be an institution of creative criticism of society. As such, it should also be the sacrament of hope; embodying, however imperfectly, people's aspirations toward greater freedom, peace, justice, and reconciliation. The task of political theology is to alert people to the structures of oppression and to prevent the political order from becoming a false absolute. The message the church offers in its creative criticism of society will be dangerous, subversive, disrupting, and disturbing.

By 1981, Metz had linked his political theology to Latin American liberation theology by endorsing the base-community churches as models of solidarity with the people, replacing the acculturated Christian churches of the West and their religious and economic individualism.

Liberation Theology

Political theology helped many Catholics move from a privatized to a political spirituality. Its direct political influence is not easy to gauge. Peter Hebblethwaite believes Metz's theology "remained rather notional. He gestures towards the marketplace without appearing to spend much time there" (Hebblethwaite 1975, 109). Metz and Moltmann are accused by liberation theologians "of writing endless prolegomena (introductions) to an action that never takes place. Their insistence that all political systems fall under the judgment of the gospel is dismissed as 'idealistic,' the strongest term of abuse in liberation vocabulary" (Hebblethwaithe 1976). A similar criticism was made by John McDade, an English Jesuit theologian, when he wrote that political theology in Europe "still has the character of a university-based project, lacking real contact with a faith-community actively searching for a theological understanding of its social experience. It is overwhelmingly 'critical' in character, but it has been able to do little more than fulminate against the 'privatized' and 'bourgeois' character of contemporary Europe; this judgment is more a comment on the complexity of constructing a 'contextual' theology in capitalist Europe than on the inadequacies of its political theologians" (1991, 433).

These negative judgments do not seem to apply to Dorothee Sölle, a poet-theologian, who views herself as "living within the belly of the Beast." Instead of developing a theology of liberation, she speaks of "a theology of resistance." She uses the analogy of the resistance fighters during World War II to urge Christians to resist our all-encompassing and overwhelmingly unjust socioeconomic and political systems.

Liberation theology spends a lot of time examining the marketplace, consciously attempting to change history through a struggle for justice because it originated, developed, and culminated in response to social, political, and economic injustices. Liberation theology began to emerge in Latin America, Africa, and Asia at the same time in the 1960s and for the same reasons—because liberation theologians were involved in the lives of the poor, and Vatican II's concern for the poor had a positive influence on many bishops, priests and nuns (Ferm 1986, 1988). The following sections highlight Latin-American liberationist thought.

Liberation Movements

Before liberation theology was written in the late 1960s, there were liberation movements. The most famous example is the case of Camilo Torres (1927–66), a young and charismatic Colombian priest and social activist. He abandoned the clerical state and in early 1966 joined a guerrilla movement, only to be killed a few weeks later (February 15) in his very first skirmish with the army. His death had a profound symbolic impact. It was an unmistakable sign of a new mood in the Latin American church.

The cause of liberation has continued. Hundreds of thousands have been martyred as they struggled in the name of Christ against injustice. Most go unnamed and unnoticed. Nevertheless, some of the murders have been reported worldwide, drawing attention to the ruthlessness of the military rule in some nations. In El Salvador's civil war, for example, there have been shocking assassinations of church people. On March 24, 1980, Archbishop Oscar Romero (1917–80) was shot while presiding at the Eucharist. Four women missionaries from the United States were brutally raped and murdered on December 2, 1980: Jean Donovan and three nuns, Dorothy Kazel, an Ursuline; and Maura Clarke and Ita Ford, both of Maryknoll. On November 16, 1989, six Jesuit priests, their housekeeper, and her teenage daughter were ruthlessly tortured and executed. The two army officers responsible for this crime were sentenced to thirty years in prison on January 24, 1992. The civil war ended a week later on January 31, 1992.

Liberation Theology Is Pluralistic

Liberation theology is a term that covers, sometimes rather loosely, a variety of theologians and activists. What they share is a common starting point and an ultimate vision.

Vatican II replaced the official neoscholatic theology with the perspectives of the "new theologians." The point of departure of the conciliar theology was modernity and the social locus of the developing countries of the West. This theology directed the church into the modern world in order to connect with its scientific and technological enterprises for the promotion of human, political, social, and economic development. However, Leonardo Boff explained that the conciliar theology evaded "the basic question, the question of the profoundly unequal relationships that prevail among nations and between classes, and the price others have to pay for the benefits of accelerated development in the central countries." Liberation theology's point of departure is "the people, the social locus of the popular, oppressed classes. It strives for the liberation of these classes and seeks to win them a voice in the historical process" (1989, 54).[5]

The ultimate vision shared by liberation theologians is of a salvation that achieves total liberation from both personal and social sin. Beyond this shared goal, there are many differences among liberationists, differences that are conceptual and strategic. For example, some denounce class conflict because it can lead to armed violence and guerrilla warfare.

Some of the leaders include Gustavo Gutiérrez of Peru, Juan Luís Segundo of Uruguay, Hugo Assmann and Leonardo

Boff of Brazil, Enrique Dussel and Jose Miguez-Bonino of Argentina, Segundo Galilea of Chile, Jose Miranda of Mexico, and Jon Sobrino of El Salvador.

The most famous of the group is Gutiérrez. This priest-theologian is often called the "father of liberation theology" because he first proposed the term in July 1968 (Molineaux 1987), and because of his 1971 book, *A Theology of Liberation.*

Many see Gutiérrez as a deeply spiritual man who teaches and inspires them as they face the overwhelming task of helping the poor. His critics attempt to portray him as a man who foments violence in society and infidelity to the church. There have been Vatican attempts to censure him, but to date he has not been silenced. He does not take this harassment that seriously, commenting wryly, "The Vatican has devised a new form of torture. They have made me defend what I have written. I have had to reread my writings three times!" (T. Fox 1988, 2).

Liberation Theology Is *New*

The word that dominates liberation theology is the word *new.* This theology originates in a new experience of God that results in a new spirituality that is explained and guided by a new theology. It also offers a new self-understanding, new social structures, and a new future.

Liberation theology begins with a new experience of God, one which Gregory Baum believes "differs from other religious experiences which Christians have treasured over the centuries" (1983a).[6] Those who have this new experience are either Christians "born into subjection" or Christians who recognize this struggle for freedom and self-determination as the significant sign of the times and believe they cannot grasp the Christian message apart from this. They see that the poor are "inhumanly poor precisely because the rich are so inhumanly rich" (Scharper 1978, 397). They experienced God on their side in solidarity with them, summoning them to justice. Christ is encountered as the divine liberator and protector of humanity who blessed "those who hunger and thirst after justice."

The new experience of God moved people beyond their privatized and pietist spirituality, a spirituality that had dominated the church during the nineteenth and twentieth centuries. Conversion took on new dimensions. A change of heart had to affect more than one's personal relationship with God. It also should include entry into a critical perception of society, especially an awareness of the existence of the structures of sin. The response to God requires a response to others.

Sorrow for sin encompasses more than repudiation of one's personal transgressions, according to liberation theology. What also must be taken into account is social sin, those structures of oppression that are the consequences of personal sins. Pietist spirituality taught salvation in terms overly individualistic and overly otherworldly. Liberationist spirituality revealed the illusion of individualism, created "a sense of solidarity with others, especially the poor, and [made] people aware that they [were] imbedded in a conflictual social matrix, the liberating movement of which is part of the mystery of divine redemption" (Baum 1987, 126).

Christian spirituality is built on faith. The new experience of God modifies the three traditional components of faith: conviction, commitment, and confidence (trust). Love and hope have always been acknowledged as dimensions of faith. Faith as commitment borders on love; faith as conviction borders on hope. But since love and hope have a justice dimension, the liberationists recognized that faith and justice are joined in an indissoluble way. The God who calls us to conviction, commitment and confidence also calls us in the poor and their unjust situations. A "faith that does justice" not only makes people critics of the present order, but it also promotes the cause of liberation and justice. "Faith, therefore, is more than intellectual assent, more than hope in what God will do without us; it is also a present participation in the work that God is doing—that is to say, in the task of bringing forth justice to nations" (Baum 1984a, 77).

In many Latin American countries, but particularly in Brazil, this faith-justice spirituality is lived out in base communities (*comunidades de base*) (Welsh 1986; Hewitt 1986). These communities actually grew out of the liberation movements in the 1960s and so they had a parallel but distinct history of development with liberation theology (McGovern 1989, 588).

For Christians, the base-community churches are a new way of being church. As a matter of fact, such churches are as old as Christianity—the so-called "house-churches" of the primitive church. But they are a new structure in this era.

These "popular" churches differ from the "hierarchical" churches or parishes, but like them they should serve as sacraments of the coming kingdom of God. In these base communities the gospel is proclaimed from the perspective of the poor in order to convert the rich and the powerful. The members serve the world by denouncing injustice and promoting social transformation. Together the members study the Bible and celebrate Eucharist. The Eucharist is "de-privatized" because it is no longer perceived simply as spiritual food for individual disciples on their journey. Rather, it creates community among the participants; it is a symbol of the banquet where all will have enough to eat; and it is the presence of Christ the liberator, himself oppressed and killed but now vindicated by God (Baum 1987, 115–16). Finally, the murder of Archbishop Romero and thousands of other Christians indicates that martyrdom is also new in Latin America. In the past when martyrs refused to renounce their faith in Christ, they were imprisoned and killed soon after; in Latin America men and women face the threat of death at any moment for their commitment to the struggle for Christ's peace and justice.

Liberation Theology and Marxism

The new experience of God, the new liberationist spirituality, and the new faith and justice movement have been explored and guided by a new theology, liberation theology. Theology's primary task is to interpret "the Christ event in dialectical correlation to an interpretation of the situation" (Tracy 1981, 340). We have already seen that the liberation theologians read the Bible through the eyes of the poor. What was also new is that they critically used certain terms derived from Marxist or neo-Marxist social theory. Thus it is that liberation theology connects "the biblical idea of the deliverance of those who are in bondage or suffering and the Marxist hope for freedom from class oppression" (Kolden 1984, 123). But why the atheist Marx? When Gutiérrez was asked that question he promptly replied, "Because the people do."

Some Marxist teachings are at odds with Christianity. For example, Marxism encourages armed revolution, teaches the inevitability of class conflict, neglects the poor, and singles out the economic conditions as the significant factor responsible for the transformation of society. Liberation theology not only rejects these teachings but it also ultimately (and ironically) attacks Marxism and any form of atheism "that perpetuates social structures which deform the image of God in human beings" (McDade 1991, 437).

On the other hand, Marxist social analysis also has several strengths. Marx explained the existence of ideologies. Liberation theology realized that traditional theology can be ideological. It can, for example, legitimize injustice and inaction. The Old Testament prophets denounced the ways in which religion was used by some priests to support unjust kings (Jer. 5:31).

Marx showed that evil is systemic. There can be no reform within an unjust system; the whole system has to be changed. For example, impoverished women are the most oppressed group in society and the church. This situation will not change until the machismo ideology and the patriarchical structures that pervade both society and the church are transformed.

For Marx, humans are creative workers. He analyzed industrial or manual labor as the source of multiple alienations for workers and denounced it. He said labor caused a threefold alienation. First, it alienated a person from nature because the factory treated the worker's body like a machine, making the worker's own body feel like a stranger to him. Second, it alienated a person from himself because it removed the product of his hands from him. Third, it alienated the worker from his fellow workers because his relationship to others was completely determined by his place in the industrial process (Baum 1975, 21–39).

Finally, Marx had challenged the Aristotelian understanding of the process of gaining knowledge: first theory, then application. This is the order used in the physical sciences. First medicine is studied in a theoretical manner, then it is applied to the sick. According to Marx, the relation between theory and practice (praxis) should be different for the human sciences. Marx believed that commitment and solidarity precede the true perception of reality and, in turn, this true perception of reality leads to action that transforms society (Baum 1976). Praxis is too often understood as mere practice. Actually, praxis is the critical relationship between theory and practice whereby each is dialectically influenced and transformed by the other. Furthermore, praxis reminds us that theoretical activity is itself a praxis—and one to be tested by the practice it serves (Tracy 1987b, 10).

The liberation theologians make praxis the touchstone of truth or authenticity. They say the Christian faith must be lived before it can make any kind of theological sense. Solidarity with the poor is the presupposition for the authentic grasp of the gospel. You know you are a disciple of Christ if you are in solidarity with the poor. This theory of knowledge is captured by the following paradox: we get our most objective knowledge by subjective participation.

Many critics of liberation theology focus on its use of Marxist ideas and its espousal of socialism (Novak 1975, 12; Novak 1987; Sigmund 1990). From the previous paragraphs it should be clear that many of the works written in the 1970s did indeed use Marxist social and economic-political analysis. Moreover, the fact that some liberationists did use Marxism imprudently made it easy for the critics of liberation theology to link them with the criticisms leveled at radical groups. For example, Dom Helda Camara reported, "When I feed the poor, I am called a saint. When I ask why they are poor, I am called a communist." Similarly, it is true that the late 1960s and early 1970s were a time of great revolutionary ferment and some liberation theologians called for a revolutionary overthrow of the military dictators who kept themselves unjustly in power. For many of these theologians it seemed an obvious right and duty to rise up against them. However, books on liberation theology in the 1980s hardly contain any treatment of Marxist social analysis. This is not to imply, argue Arthur F. McGovern and Thomas L. Schubeck, two United States Jesuit priests, that the earlier writings can be labeled their "Marxist phase" (1988). Even in the early 1970s, Gutiérrez and others distanced themselves from Marxist options and warned against christianizing any revolutionary ideology (Kirk 1986). In February 1988, McGovern and Schubeck began a three-month study of liberation theology in Latin America that took them to eight countries. They found liberation theology working in a new context and taking new directions. There was some use of Marxist critique of capitalism "but liberation theologians used its concepts only at a very general level to describe exploitation by wealthy owners, the dominance of northern capitalist countries in the world economy, and the use of ideology to maintain and justify the tangentially status quo" (1988). In a two-week course in Peru under the direction of Gutiérrez, the two Jesuits said they heard no mention of Marxism in any of the talks they attended. Finally, McGovern and Schubeck report that the liberation theologians are quite aware that classic Marxist analysis does not adequately deal with the problems of indigenous peoples, racism, and the oppression of women.

The Effectiveness of Liberation Theology

Its results are mixed. On the negative side, its direct political significance remains small. Even in Brazil where its force seems greatest, its impact comes more from the strength and leadership of the episcopal conference, which constitutes a strong voice in that country. Liberation theology enjoyed some influence early on. Now it seems that "the present historical situation in Latin America eliminates any hope for the success of liberation movements . . . [It may have to] moderate its aims and work together with the progressive sector of the bourgeoisie to stabilize civilian, democratic rule and assure the protection of civil liberties" (Baum 1989b, 123).

On the positive side, liberation theology has drawn the attention of the world to the plight of the poor, has drawn Christians to find in the Bible a God who favors the poor, and has drawn the institutional church to commit to a preferential option for the poor. Liberation theology has also contributed immeasurably to the one Church of Christ in two interrelated ways: it has advanced the ecumenical movement and it has given theology a postmodern focus.

Liberation theology has advanced ecumenism even though not all Catholics and Protestants have accepted this theology. Nevertheless, it "is the first common theological movement of Catholics and Protestants since the sixteenth century Reformation. . . . In a real sense, this marks the end of the Reformation and Counter-Reformation; and it is significant that it originated in and has taken deepest roots in Latin America, Asia and Africa, regions for which the Reformation as a European historical phenomenon was irrelevant" (MacEoin 1984, 12). This means that liberation theology, which began as a movement *in* the church, is now almost a new movement *of* the church, albeit a minority movement.

Liberation theology has given theology—both Protestant and Catholic—a postmodern focus. Since we live in a world in which most people neither know Christ nor are Christian, traditionally theologians have written to and for these people. For example, in 1976, Hans Küng discussed the two great challenges for Christianity as he perceived them: the world religions and secular humanism (pp. 25–116). Küng's analysis is very helpful and accurate in many ways. In the past, theology has addressed three groups: those within the church, in order to help them clarify their faith; those who belong to other religions and churches, in order to dialogue with them about the God revealed in Jesus Christ; and those indifferent or antagonistic to religion, in order to dialogue with them about the ultimate meaning of life. Today, however, liberation theologians and theologians influenced by them—Harvey Cox (1980), Schubert Ogden (1980), Philip Scharper (1978), and Robert McAfee Brown (1978, 1980)—have gone beyond Küng.

These theologians do not deny the serious challenge from the world religions and secular humanism, but they argue that there is a more primary challenge, namely, the call of God to us through the poor, the oppressed, and the hungry. Millions of people live a life that is so minimally human that Gutiérrez referred to them as "nonpersons," that is, "people who are not considered human in our society" (Gibeau 1976b). Schubert Ogden explains the term more clearly: a nonperson is "one who, being excluded from the existing order in one or more respects, is to that extent unfree, a passive object of history instead of its active subject" (1980).

Why this shift from Küng's nonbelievers to liberation theology's nonpersons? The reason is that nonbelievers question our religious world, but usually share our socioeconomic outlook. Like us they have a deep regard for human life and yet, at the same time, they contribute to the plight of the poor by being part of the power elites. Like us they foster the dominant, unchristian ideologies of our society. On the other hand, the poor and the oppressed challenge not only our religious world but our socioeconomic and political worlds as well. Their poverty and hunger challenge our consumerism, racial and sexual prejudices, and comfortable lifestyle. In short, liberation theology says there is a specifically Christian way to view society and to do theology—from the viewpoint of the nonpersons. The poor need a chance to live authentically.

Synod of 1971

In addition to the rise of political and liberation theologies and Paul VI's own encyclicals, the other important event that occurred during his pontificate was this synod. On September 30, 1971, the bishops met to discuss social justice. As we have already seen, Vatican II called for social justice. It reminded the faithful that a free social order is "founded on truth, built on justice, and animated by love; in freedom it should grow every day toward a more humane balance" (GS 26). The bishops also observed that "in our times a special obligation binds us to make ourselves the neighbor of absolutely every person" (GS 27).

The bishops at the synod reiterated the conciliar teachings but, influenced by political and liberation theologies, did so more explicitly. The beginning of the most quoted sentence from its document, *Justice in the World*, insists that "action on behalf of justice and participation in the transformation of the world fully appear to us as a constitutive dimension of the preaching of the gospel."

This sentence evoked a great deal of discussion. The point of contention centered on the word *constitutive*. The bishops meant that social justice is neither incidental to the mission of the church nor does it take second place to more "spiritual" or "religious" matters. For example, some maintain that evangelization is primarily a spiritual enterprise. Those who question the word *constitutive* prefer the word *integral*, that is, something not absolutely essential to the church's mission but which pertains to its fullness (Dorr 1983, 188). But the writings of both Paul VI and John Paul II indicate that the church would fail to be true to its very identity if action on behalf of social justice was absent.

The 1971 Synod also went beyond Vatican II's analysis of social justice. The council fathers said justice would flow from a change of heart, a transformation of persons; the synod said justice would be achieved with the transformation of social structures. A conversion of heart is a great step but it does not change the context of people's lives. There are networks of domination and oppression that stifle freedom, truth, justice, and love, and prevent a greater part of humanity from sharing in the building up and enjoyment of a more just world. These sinful structures need to be eliminated.

John Paul II and CELAM III in 1979

John Paul II has been extremely active in the cause of social justice in society. Through his writings and charismatic presence he has forcefully denounced injustice and advocated justice around the globe. For example, during the Persian Gulf War in 1991 he made more than fifty appeals for peace. By June 1992, John Paul, a restless man, had made fifty-five visits to Catholic communities outside of Italy. In January 1979, the attention of the world was focused on Mexico for the pope's first visit to that nation. There he toured the country for a week, delivering twenty-eight speeches. It is reported that he adjusted some of his prepared texts once he saw at first hand the massive poverty. But his main reason for the visit was to open CELAM III at Puebla (MacEoin and Riley 1980; Eagleson and Scharper 1979).

In his speech to the bishops on January 28, 1979, John Paul did not use the term liberation theology, but he did speak of liberation. "The church," he said, "feels the duty to proclaim the liberation of human beings; the duty to help this liberation become fully established; but she also feels the corresponding duty to proclaim liberation in its integral and profound meaning, as Jesus proclaimed and realized it." He reminded the bishops that Jesus "identified with the deserted," was committed "to the neediest," and was "never indifferent to the imperatives of social reality."

The address "was couched in abstract, traditional and highly nuanced language" (Brockman 1979, 180–83). The *New York Times* interpreted some of the pope's sentences about liberation and "political involvement" as a rejection of liberation theology.[7] However, most commentators believed he rejected extreme forms of liberation theology, particularly the kind that made "the gospel into political ideology" or which called for "all-out class warfare, and even [Fidel] Castro-style revolution, as the only way to achieve social justice" (Peerman 1979).

After his address, John Paul left the city, allowing the bishops to meet from January 28 to February 13, to make the pastoral decisions necessary for the good of the church in their region. Their theme—evangelization in the present and future of Latin America—had been proposed by Paul VI, who had planned to inaugurate the meeting just as he had done at Medellín.

The first thing the bishops reflected on was the socioeconomic conditions of their countries. They reported that, unfortunately, the social situation had severely deteriorated since Medellín in 1968. Most Latin American countries had become more impoverished, more debt-ridden, and more repressive. A surprising reversal had also taken place between 1965 and 1990 in most Latin American countries. In 1965 most countries had a 70 percent rural population; in 1990, most were 70 percent urban (F. McDonagh 1990).

The bishops produced a lengthy and rich final document with five major parts, each with chapters and subsections. This document reaffirmed the direction set by Medellín. Four of their principal points are described below.

First, Medellín, they declared, "adopted a clear and prophetic option expressing preference for, and solidarity with, the poor." "Preferential option for the poor"—the title of one of the chapters in their document—became the catchword of Puebla and captured its spirit. The bishops expressed concern for many groups—the poor, youth, elderly, and ill-housed city-dwellers; and those involved in liturgical, educational, and social services. All of these persons or groups are to be viewed in light of the option for the poor. This means the preferential option for the poor "is not itself optional—it is not one of several theological or pastoral tendencies among which Christian ministers or constitutions may pick or choose."

Second, the bishops expressed appreciation for the base communities and encouraged their growth. In 1979 there were some forty-one thousand in Brazil alone.

Third, the bishops explained the crucial difference between evangelization and partisan politics, and they denounced violence of every kind.

Fourth, the bishops called attention to the problems of two exploited groups: the indigenous people and the women of Latin America. Medellín did not discuss either of these two groups. By focusing on them, the bishops indicated that gender and ethnic differences are aspects of the rampant poverty and oppression.

In March 1979, John Paul sent the Latin American bishops a letter with a ringing endorsement of their conclusions from the conference.

The Encyclicals of John Paul II

John Paul has written three encyclicals specifically about the church's social teachings. With *Laborem exercens* ("On Human Work") in 1981, he marked the ninetieth anniversary of *Rerum novarum*. This newer letter dealt with oppression and exploitation in the industrialized world of the North. In it the pope argued, as no other church document had ever done, that humans should be defined as workers, and that it is through labor (by which he means society-building) (Baum 1986a, 19) that people constitute their world and in doing so, constitute themselves as persons. Humans differ from animals because they work. Only humans have to create the conditions of their survival by labor. Nature does not sustain human life unless it is transformed by work.

Despite his Marxist language, what the pope did was develop a non-Marxist critique of liberal capitalism. He called for "the solidarity of labor and with labor." He offered the principle of "the priority of labor over capital" as central to a just society. Both communism and liberal capitalism operate out of the principle of the priority of capital over labor. Workers, the pope declared, are entitled to ownership and participation in decision-making regarding the work process and the use of the capital they produce. Both liberal capitalism and communism exclude workers from this kind of participation. Both make labor alienating and the situation unjust because people are treated like cogs in a huge machine.

John Paul differed from the style and substance of previous popes in that he called upon people to struggle for their own emancipation. His encyclical promoted the solidarity of workers and the poor in a joint struggle that included confrontation in order to ensure the common good. Leo XIII and other popes challenged men in high offices to reform society and improve conditions of the poor and workers. John Paul called on all those who love justice—and he included the church—to be in solidarity with workers. Solidarity, explains Donal Dorr, "is an *attitude*, a commitment on the part of those who form community, to participate in the life of that community in a way that promotes the common good" (1989, 151).

In an extended and otherwise very favorable commentary on the encyclical, Gregory Baum pointed out two oversights in it. The pope was insensitive to the self-understanding of women, and he did not ask whether his principles that intended to protect "the subject character of human beings" were operative in "the Catholic ecclesiastical organization" (Baum 1982).

In a 1987 encyclical *Sollicitudo rei socialis* ("Social Concerns") John Paul commemorated Paul VI's *Populorum progressio*. In 1967 Paul VI had called for true development to occur in human terms, including the personal and spiritual dimensions of life, in order to close the gap between rich and poor nations. His best-remembered sentence was "Development is the new name for peace."

Asserting that little or no development had occurred since 1967, John Paul tried to impress upon the world how insufferable were its economic inequities. He identified the failure of development in global terms. He pointed out that in fact the gap between the developing North and the slowly developing South had widened. In this encyclical the pope examined the world from the perspective of the poor, particularly the third-world nations. He indicated that there were two principal causes for the ever-widening gap, one economic and the other political. The capitalist economic systems of global interdependence, he said, continued to allow the rich nations to reap the greater benefits. The political situation was dominated by the continuing rivalry between the two superpowers, each claiming universal validity. The developing countries got caught between these two powers of the north. They were forced to choose one—so that their "development" got defined by either liberal capitalism or Marxist collectivism, two false economic understandings of development.

The world, the pope stated, was marked by hunger in the South, by arms production and sales in the North, and ecological damage on the entire globe. The common good of the universe was so disregarded that civilization was "oriented toward death rather than life." The way out of these crises situations was through interdependence and solidarity based on love and justice. "Peace is the fruit of solidarity."

John Paul repudiated both liberal capitalism and communism as ideologies and as economic systems. He placed both on the same level of iniquity: both are "imperialisms," one of power and the other of profit. Nevertheless, he never advocated their abolition. Rather, on the one hand, he asked capitalism to reconstruct its free-market inheritance into "some form or other of ethically-steered, mixed economy welfare capitalism;" on the other hand, he asked communism to transform its socialist heritage in order to "become more responsive to the economic initiative of individuals" (Baum 1989a, 87). He offered no social theory or "third way" to which all must conform. His goal was to offer critical reflection in the name of the gospel so that the existing economic systems would take a more humane direction.

The encyclical received considerable praise. Yet there were some negative criticisms. First, "conservative" Catholics in the United States found it extremely radical. However, said Gregory Baum, both they and the pope needed a broader perspective. The encyclical did not convey "full realization that the capitalist economic system *has achieved global proportions*, that even the communist countries, including the Soviet Union, trade with the West and hence to a considerable extent depend on the global capitalist system, and that it is therefore the orientation of this global system that largely determines the economic well-being of the world population" (ibid., 75).

A second critique came from Maria Riley, a Dominican sister and social analyst. She said the encyclical was blind "to the essential contribution that feminists, both women and men, are making to the development debate. . . . It is becoming clearer that 'women's issues' are not marginal; they are central to the search for the kind of development in which people matter" (1989, 200).

In 1991, John Paul published his third encyclical, the centenary of *Rerum novarum*, which dealt with the topic of social justice. He commemorated Leo's landmark encyclical with his own, *Centesimus annus* ("The Hundredth Year"). This letter was signed on May 1, 1991, the feast of St. Joseph the Worker.

This encyclical of twenty-five thousand words reviewed one hundred years of Catholic social teaching in light of the collapse in 1989 of Marxism in the Soviet Union and Eastern Europe, and reaffirmed the option for the poor. John Paul insisted that major new efforts were required to meet the needs of the poor. For example, he argued that money and goods would be available if the huge military machines were dismantled.

The pope severely criticized Marxism for its economic inefficiency, for stifling the national rights of countries, and for its atheism, which brings on a "spiritual void" in human affairs.

Capitalism (sometimes called "market," "free," or "business" economy by John Paul) received both positive and negative critiques in the encyclical. The collapse of communism prompted John Paul to ask whether capitalism should now be considered the model to be proposed both to European countries seeking to rebuild their economies and societies, and to the countries of the third world. His answer was yes, insofar as by capitalism one meant "an economic system which recognized the fundamental and positive role of business, the market, private property and the resulting responsibility for the means of production, as well as free human creativity in the economic sector." Capitalism, he agreed, has the potential for increasing freedom and dignity. The free market is the most efficient instrument for utilizing resources and for effectively responding to needs. However, capitalism must maintain a moral core by not exploiting the poor and by repairing injustices within its own system.

On the other hand, the pope warned that capitalism is not the best model for countries trying to rebuild and develop "if by capitalism is meant a system in which freedom in the economic sector is not circumscribed within a strong juridical framework which places it at the service of human freedom in its totality, and which sees it as a particular aspect of that freedom, the core of which is ethical and religious." Capitalism has its own inadequacies and these are especially visible in the "domination of things over people." The pope also warned against consumerism which leads nations and people to believe they can achieve material satisfaction without relying on spiritual values. Consumerism reduces humanity to the sphere of economics and the satisfaction of material needs.

Again, John Paul did not propose any specific "third way" between communism and capitalism. On the contrary, he warned that "the church has no models to present." In the end it is up to Christians, taking their cue from the social teachings of the church, to be creative and inventive in devising and introducing models that are ever more just and democratic.

There were diverse reactions to the encyclical. Feminists were quick to point out that the document contains only one sentence referring to the special economic problems encountered by women. After noting that the elderly, the young, and those "part of the so-called Fourth World" can be marginalized if they do not keep up their skills in a rapidly changing, technological world, the encyclical simply states, "The situation of women too is far from easy in these conditions" (n. 33).

Two groups maintained that the encyclical reinforced their position: proponents of the free market and those who advocated more government control of the markets. The former overlooked what John Paul said about the inadequacies of capitalism and the latter overlooked what was said about the excesses of the welfare state (Windsor 1991; Neuhaus 1992; McBrien 1992).[8] Finally, others viewed the encyclical not only as a strong challenge to much recent United States economic and social policy but also as a call to "renew the effort to overcome the increasing marginalization and poverty of vast numbers of people who are left out of the market economies that are shaping the future of the globe" (Hollenbach 1991; see also McBrien 1993).

John Paul II and Liberation Theology

Catholics have different views of the interrelationship of church and society. Some believe that Christians, as individuals and together as church, must be involved in politics and economics if they are to fulfill their mission to be peacemakers and to hunger and thirst after justice. Others find the church's involvement in economics and politics difficult to understand because their spirituality does not have a social dimension, one that demands that they go beyond personal piety to concern for the poor and oppressed. Others believe the church is "too political," meaning that the church is becoming primarily or even solely political.

John Paul has consistently warned Catholics that their commitment to liberation must not be understood in primarily political and economic terms. For example, in addressing priests in India in 1986, he said priests should give "humble service to all, including those who are not poor," and authentic love for the poor can only "spring from a deep experience of God."[9]

Listed in chronological order are some of the statements or actions of John Paul relative to liberation theology.

In 1984 the CDF issued an instruction, "On Certain Aspects of the Theology of Liberation." It warned of dangerous trends in liberation theology, particularly "an insufficiently critical use" of Marxism. This can undermine the church's unity and the integrity of the Christian faith, the CDF warned. Some found the instruction not only a caricature of Marxism but also based on the unbelievable thesis that those who accept certain aspects of Marxism inevitably assimilate, whether they like it or not, the entire Marxist system (Baum 1987, 104–5).

In February 1985, Leonardo Boff, a Brazilian Franciscan, was silenced. Cited in the notification that he was prohibited from teaching, speaking, or writing was his book *Church: Charism and Power.* This book had been a best seller in Brazil when it was first published in 1981. Boff wrote about the church's abuse of power. He thought the way of the future for the church was in the base communities, which he advocated as an alternative to the existing system of parishes and dioceses. It should be noted that this point is a doctrinal issue not specific to liberation theology.

Since Boff had wide personal support with the Brazilian episcopal conference, his punishment angered many Brazilians (Lernoux 1985).[10] His case was followed with keen interest by some Protestant scholars in the United States, who found his ecclesiology very helpful (R. M. Brown et al. 1986; Cox 1988a). Boff accepted the Vatican's "reservation" and voiced his intent "to walk with the church rather than walk alone with my theology." The censure was lifted eleven months later. However, in May 1991, Boff was forced to resign as editor of a Catholic magazine published in Brazil. His removal came after the publication of a series of articles that urged the Vatican to change its policies on several issues, such as its refusal to allow priests to marry. When John Paul II made his second visit to Brazil in October 1991, he admitted that the ratio of priests to people was low—one priest per 9,306—but said the ordination of married men was "not acceptable."

In July 1992, Boff resigned from the priesthood, complaining bitterly of the Vatican and Franciscan censorship and oppression he experienced over a twenty-year period. He blasted the Vatican as an "oppressive regime, which like a bat, fears the light." In choosing to leave the priesthood and his Franciscan community, Boff said his intent was "not to be free of the church, which I love and will never abandon, but to be free to continue working without impediments" (Hebblethwaite 1992a).

In April 1986, the CDF, with the approval of John Paul, issued another instruction, this one titled "On Christian Freedom and Liberation." It never mentioned liberation theology or Marxism. Its five chapters covered the Western history of freedom and the church's understanding and practice of liberation.

The document had several controversial areas. It seemed to undercut the Puebla phrase "a preferential option for the poor" by substituting "a love of preference for the poor." This is an awkward phrase which has not caught on. Regarding the base communities, the instruction supported them as "a source of great hope" and "a real expression of communion." However, it warned that they only serve these purposes to the extent that "they really live in unity with the local church and the universal church." Those familiar with base communities and their attachment to the universal church thought this proviso unnecessary.

Aside from these minor criticisms, the general reaction was that the instruction supported liberation theology in Latin America and elsewhere. Alfred Hennelly thought the instruction so profoundly integrated liberation themes into the mainstream of Catholic social teachings that it should have been written as an encyclical, "which would have given its teaching even greater weight on the world theological scene" (1986). Gutiérrez praised it as a "relaunching" of the liberation movement and insisted that "it closes a chapter; a new, more positive period is beginning" (ibid., 428).

In spring 1986, John Paul wrote the Brazilian bishops a letter in which he praised liberation theology. He wrote, "We are convinced, we and you, that the theology of liberation is opportune, useful and necessary." Not only did he take for granted the existence of base communities but he even praised them as the ordinary way of the church in that country. The letter brought great relief. The background for the letter goes back to July 1980, when John Paul made his first visit to Brazil. At that time he told the 372 assembled bishops, the largest episcopal conference in the world, that they should not substitute base-community churches for the parishes. But the bishops had built their entire pastoral policy on base communities. Why this change of mind between 1980 and 1986? The pope said he was now able to rectify the long and painful misunderstanding between himself and the bishops due to a "new and deeper form of collegiality, thanks to which the pope and his collaborators now know better the realities of the Brazilian church" (Hebblethwaite 1986b).

John Paul II and CELAM IV

This meeting was held October 12–28, 1992, in Santo Domingo, Dominican Republic. The time was chosen to mark the fifth century of evangelization in the western hemisphere. The place was chosen because here the first Catholic diocese in the western hemisphere was established. In announcing the conference, John Paul declared that this meeting should pay particular attention "to a renewed evangelization of the continent, which will penetrate deeply into the hearts of individuals and into the culture of peoples." The theme of the conference was "New Evangelization, Human Advancement and Christian Culture."

During the preparations for the conference two interrelated concerns surfaced. First, active defenders of the option for the poor among Latin American bishops were now in a minority since many bishops appointed by John Paul since Puebla were chosen because of their fidelity to John Paul's ideological and ecclesiological guidelines. Those who had attended Puebla had fond memories of the successes achieved there but they were "not expecting great things" (MacEoin 1991a). Rome still favored a preferential option for the poor but it claimed also that "part of the problem is that the poor lack a work ethic" (MacEoin 1992a).

Second, there were rumors that there would be a shift in focus regarding the process of evangelization: from the poor to "the Catholic culture" of Latin America. This shift was deemed necessary, it was said, because in many Latin American countries, Pentecostal and evangelical churches had grown rapidly. For example, in Guatemala in 1991, the evangelical churches claimed 30 percent of the people in this traditionally Catholic country. In Brazil, 88 percent of the people identified themselves as Catholic in 1980, but in 1991 the number was less than 80 percent. When John Paul had visited Brazil in October 1991, the Brazilian bishops addressed these words to the pope: "We look forward to this conference in Santo Domingo and are glad to join with the church in this call to evangelization. But we would like to know who will be evangelized, how they will be evangelized and who will do the evangelizing" (Piccolino 1991). Many Latin American bishops feared that "Catholic culture" was simply a code word for the reimposition of a European model of church. These bishops insisted that the poverty of millions of their people should remain the starting point for their reflections on the theme of new evangelization.

John Paul was in Santo Domingo for six days, October 9–14. His schedule—which was originally planned to include stops in Jamaica, Nicaragua, and Mexico—was cut back to include only the Dominican Republic because he had undergone abdominal surgery in July. In his homilies and lectures he reiterated the preferential option for the poor: "We must feel other's poverty as our own and become convinced that the poor cannot wait." He praised the Latin American women for being the guardian angels of Christianity in their countries. Although he chided activist priests and nuns not to be blind to their primary religious role, he encouraged them to take up the program of Christ's beatitudes, especially as it affects the poor and the downtrodden. He declared that the evangelical churches were like "rapacious wolves . . . causing division and discord in our communities." Finally, depite the fact that he was aware of the bitter disputes over Columbus's legacy, he thanked God for "the abundant fruits of the seeds planted over the last 500 years by [the] intrepid missionaries" (French 1992a; see also Steinfels 1992c; Stahel 1992).

John Paul inaugurated the episcopal conference attended by 307 voting bishops from twenty-two nations on October 12. In his lengthy address, he asked pardon for the church's offenses, past and present. Nevertheless, he stressed that the Catholic Church had acted as the "untiring defender of the Indians, the protector of the values that existed in their cultures and supporter of their humanity in the face of the abuses committed at times unscrupulously by the colonizers." He also called for continuity with the Medellín and Puebla meetings, especially their preferential option for the poor (Wirpsa 1992a).

The sixteen-day conference was marked by serious debate about the future of the church (Wirpsa 1992b). The two most important issues were poverty and the indigenous cultures. The bishops acknowledged that the major problem facing the Latin American church was the growing poverty. During the pope's visit, protesters had called Columbus "the exterminator of a race" and they denounced the "500 years of hunger and massacre" (French 1992b). The bishops also acknowledged that in many of their countries "races and cultures [were] reasserting themselves—indigenous, blacks, mestizos—many of them impelled by spiritualities far older than Christianity that came to them across the water."[11] The majority of the bishops believed that the gospel can flourish in a variety of cultures. Other bishops, however, talked about spreading and deepening the Christian culture, which they viewed "as a monoculture, European style" (Peerman 1993, 184). The bishops who opposed this direction for evangelization did so "not only because of its recolonizing content, but also because it relativizes and reduces to a subordinate position the many cultures of the hemisphere, indigenous, African-American, mestizo, all of them with multiple variations" (MacEoin 1992b).

The bishops produced a sixty-one-page document, "Jesus Christ, Yesterday, Today and Tomorrow." It breaks very little new ground in its sections on such topics as human development, new evangelization, Christian culture, and neoliberal economic policies. It does contain a strong statement on ecology, an emphasis missing from the 1968 and 1979 documents. It reaffirmed both the Christian base communities as a new way of being church and the "irrevocable but not exclusive" option for the poor. The bishops emphasized the "new faces of poverty." Special attention, they maintained, must be paid when the rights of "children, women and the poorest groups in society—peasants, Indians and Afro-Americans—are violated." By linking these people to ecological issues, the bishops manifested their sensitivity to the relationship between the oppression of the poor and the abuse of natural resources.

The impact of CELAM IV will probably not be realized for years to come, but it represented another major step by the institutional church to oppose, in the name of Christ the Liberator, the social, political, and economic forces that dehumanize everyone, especially the poor.

John Paul and Communism

John Paul is the only pope who spent most of his life under a communist government. He is knowledgeable of Marxism. Marxism has as one of its starting points the elimination of religion. Marx considered it a source of alienation. Vladimir Lenin (1870–1924), the major force behind the founding of the U.S.S.R., called religion "a sort of spiritual booze, in which the slaves of capital drown their human image, their demand for a life more or less worthy of man." Lenin supposed that communism would create a new species of man—an atheistic, homogeneous Soviet man—freed of religious, ethnic, or nationalist attachments.

During the course of the twentieth century, the popes, *mutatis mutandis*, condemned communism in words that echoed Pius XI's declaration that "communism is intrinsically wrong and there can be no collaboration with it in any field on the part of those who want to save Christian civilization."

John Paul has written and spoken extensively against communism. He has done whatever he could to defeat it. For example, his visit to his native Poland in 1979 gave the people the self-confidence to found Solidarity and eventually defeat the communist regime by peaceful means. Writing in 1992, Peter Hebblethwaite declared that "history will judge this [support] to have been John Paul's greatest achievement" (1992b, 6). Francis X. Murphy added that John Paul "is likewise credited with the spread of the 'Polish contagion' to Hungary, Czechoslavakia, East Germany and eventually to all the Soviet satellite lands" (1990).

In June 1988 John Paul made contact with President Mikhail Gorbachev through a letter delivered by Cardinal Agostino Casaroli, his secretary of state from 1979 to 1990, in which he expressed his concern for the welfare of Soviet Catholics. In January 1989, in his annual speech to the diplomatic corps attached to the Vatican, John Paul directly challenged the Soviets to follow up on their promises of greater religious freedom by taking some concrete steps. Beginning in February, the Soviets began to permit the restoration and appointment of bishops.

President Gorbachev traveled to Rome to see the pope on December 1, 1989—the first personal exchange between a Soviet president and a pope. Gorbachev knew that Lenin was wrong, because even "after seven decades of Communist rule, the ties that bind religious faith to ethnic culture and nationalist sentiment [were] stronger than ever" (Murphy 1990). On the eve of the meeting, Gorbachev said that the Soviet Union had erred in long rejecting religion and now needed its moral force to help his plans for a restructured society to work (*perestroika*). Gorbachev's words represent a major break with the Marxist-Leninist tradition: "We have changed our attitude on some matters, such as religion, for example, which admittedly we used to treat in a simplistic manner. Now we not only proceed from the assumption that no one should interfere in matters of the individual's conscience, we also say that the moral values that religion generated and embodied for centuries can help in the work of renewal in our country, too. In fact, this is already happening" (Haberman 1989).

At their meeting Gorbachev promised full religious freedom in the Soviet Union and invited John Paul to visit Russia. John Paul agreed to resume official ties with Moscow, broken in 1917, and to support *perestroika.* John Paul concluded this historic summit by remarking that "providence prepared the way for this meeting," one that put an end to decades of fear, anger and oppression (Woodward, Nordland, and Coleman 1989, 11).

On September 26, 1990, the Soviet parliament decreed freedom of religion.

On September 4, 1993, John Paul launched the first papal visit to the former Soviet Union when he landed in Lithuania. This pilgrimage—his sixty-first oversees visit— was the start of a week-long tour of the Baltic states: Lithuania, Latvia, and Estonia, countries that were occupied by Soviet forces in 1940. Just five days before the pope's arrival, Moscow withdrew the last of its troops from Lithuania, removing a possible friction during the papal visit. The president of Lithuania called this departure of the troops "a very significant and symbolic coincidence." The opening sentence of an editorial in the *New York Times* on September 11 stated: "The Pope has come and the Red Army has gone—two reasons for jubilation in Lithuania."

The Baltic countries, like so many of the other countries in the former Soviet Union, are marked by ethnic, political, and religious strife. For varying reasons, John Paul views much of the world in the post-cold-war era as spiritually threatened. He said, "Tragically, the fall of the walls which separated East and West into two camps has made more evident the scandal of walls of poverty, violence and political oppression which still divide vast sectors of humanity." Consequently, he told the Baltic peoples that "there is need for a spiritual rebirth." He warned them that, although they had overcome communism and "left the tunnel of forced atheization," their next struggles would be with "the perils of indifference and secularism."

Spirituality and Justice

With and since Vatican II the church's understanding of history and God's role in it has gone through some remarkable shifts and developments. How we respond to God's attempts to promote and expand his own presence in history is called spirituality.

The contemporary church is marked by three understandings of justice and spirituality.[12] The preconciliar understanding is predominantly pietist or privatized: the church stands over against the world in an attitude of defense and offense. In this mindset there are two histories: sacred and secular. Christ is the light of the world. God remains outside of secular history but will save us in the next world. These Christians are otherworldly. God reigns in individual hearts. Sacred history operates through the church and this is a place of special encounter with God. The Bible is not central to this spirituality. Neither does this privatized spirituality evoke a keen sense of mission for all Christians.

All of this does not mean that these Catholics do not serve others. The spiritual and corporal works of mercy are encouraged. Much good is done through schools, orphanages, and hospitals. But changes in society, it is thought, will flow from personal transformation. A good example of this mindset was manifested at the time of the worldwide depression of the 1930s. The depression was considered to be the result of moral evil. Little consideration was given to ignorance about keeping an industrial economy functioning well.

"At its worst, this spirituality was ghetto-like, individualistic and escapist. But at its best it gave people a sense of God's transcendence . . . [and] a sense of security; there was little need for agonizing, since all knew their place and how they were expected to act" (Dorr 1984, 199). It is also important to add that it is just possible that the worst dimensions of this fortress spirituality "are just the fossilized relics" of a spirituality that at first challenged Christians—in a world where many were atheistic, materialistic, anti-Christian, and anti-church—to preserve not only God's transcendence and providence, but also the significance of baptism and a personal commitment to Christ.

At Vatican II the church aimed at aggiornamento and a commitment to the world. It reversed one hundred years of teaching that began with the *Syllabus of Errors* (1864), whereby the church and world stood in opposition to one another. The Council retrieved from the Scriptures a new dominant image, namely, the pilgrim people of God. The Scriptures have an important place in this spirituality.

The great strength of this new model "is that it removes the traditional split between the sacred and the secular" (ibid., 201). There are not two histories but one, and this history has been redeemed in all its dimensions by Christ, the Lord of history. With his resurrection, Jesus made a real and powerful reentry into history. All the baptized should be involved in the church's mission to serve the world.

Instead of beginning with the church, this spirituality starts with the world redeemed by Christ, the servant of the world. At Vatican II the church applauded every human effort to build a better world. It encouraged Christians to transform their hearts. In this way the world would eventually change for the better. The truth in this approach it that a person cannot be an instrument of peace if he or she is not at peace.

In the postconciliar church the shift from service of the church to service of the world was still operative, but with a major difference. The socioeconomic developments that the council fathers optimistically anticipated never materialized. This resulted in new questions: "When you set out to serve the world, whose world are you serving? Is it the world as structured by the rich and powerful, a world built on the dominant values of competition and success at all costs? Or is it the world as God wants it to be, one in which structural poverty and powerlessness are challenged, and the poor are privileged agents of God in bringing about the kingdom?" (ibid., 202).

The postconciliar church, with its faith-justice spirituality, is, in Leonardo Boff's apt phrase, a "church in the subworld" (Boff 1989, 12–13, 191–94). It underscores that we have a history marred by structural injustices and grinding poverty. God is on the side of the poor in their efforts at liberation. Christ's disciples serve Christ the liberator and the world by overcoming injustice.

Full participation in the liturgy includes both celebrating God's saving interventions and answering his call to alleviate and eliminate injustices. The Scriptures are read and studied from the perspective of the poor. Structural transformation of society has been the message of Paul VI and John Paul II, Medellín, Puebla, Santo Domingo, and many other episcopal conferences.

This liberationist spirituality calls Christians to solidarity with the poor and to disentangle themselves from unjust structures. Such moves are not easy to make because our social, economic, and political lives are so interrelated that we are immersed in a huge interlocking system where almost all our actions play a part in maintaining structural injustice. We may be forced to make some compromises.

Compromises should not create guilt. There are several reasons it is necessary. First, although the Sermon on the Mount calls us to selfless love, it is not clear in our day-to-day living what this love requires of us. Compromise is possible because our vocation to be as holy as our heavenly Father cannot be identified with a clear and precise kind of moral perfection. Second, the proper spiritual response to our entrapment in structures of sin is mourning. The biblical word is *lamentation.* Mourning is part of the process of conversion. "Mourning unites those in the middle class with the victims of society who also mourn, even if for different reasons" (Baum 1989b, 119).

In addition to mourning, something can be done in small Christian communities, especially among the poor. Christians committed to the faith-justice spirituality will have to band together because they exist as a minority in the church. Nevertheless, they can be a countervailing current. Minorities sometimes find an appropriate strategy. Gregory Baum offered an imaginative and encouraging proposal:

> Imagine for a moment that in a city there were five just Christians in every parish, involved in local projects and joined in a lively network, what impact would such an active minority have on the church and on the city! The advantage of this minority strategy is that it does not depend on the cooperation of those in charge of the institutions, even though their cooperation is of great consequence. Thanks to such a minority strategy, moreover, there is always something we can do. We are not

caught in total impotence. We can always find others with whom to promote the countervailing current of social justice, knowing that this is not a waste of time, but a contribution that in the long run prepares significant social change (Baum 1984a, 104).

Conclusion

In chapter 4, a sacramental consciousness was described as the single most powerful force holding the devotional life of the church together. In view of what has been presented in chapters 8 and 9, this point needs to be nuanced.

The sacramental consciousness of Catholics is most tangibly expressed at the Eucharist when the presence of the risen Christ is symbolized by the assembled community, the altar, the bread and wine, the Scriptures, and the priest. The eucharistic celebration is indeed the most important thing a church community does and the Eucharist is the heart of the devotional life of the church—provided the celebration encompasses true, active participation. That is, the believing disciples not only participate in Christ's total surrender to his Father, but also bring this commitment to all facets of their lives, especially by participation in social justice.

This chapter reviewed the church's social teachings. From Leo XIII to the present, the popes have built on the teachings of their predecessors and, in view of the signs of the times, offered guidance to the church and to the world about justice and injustice. The bishops have joined in this teaching process at Vatican II, international synods, episcopal conferences, and as individuals. Theologians have illuminated, explained, and guided this teaching. However, even though the teaching has been developing, not all members of the church have received and live the social teachings in the same way. Presently, there are in the church three very distinct mindsets or spiritualities—privatized, conciliar, and faith-justice. They are present at all levels of the global and world church. They have been (and are) manifested at synods and episcopal conferences, and in theology departments, parishes, and religious communities. These mindsets represent different views of how the church should take action against the powers of injustice. These powers are presently so tenacious and demonic that only "a radical Catholicism renewed by the faith in Jesus Christ as the compassionate protector of humans on this earth" can challenge these destructive forces (ibid.). Can a radical Catholicism emerge when the church has three different mindsets? Donal Dorr, for one, does not think so. "The different mindsets do not result in a healthy pluralism but rather in suspicion and intransigence" (Dorr 1984, 204).

The church can be the compassionate protector of the world and the sacrament of the kingdom of God if it follows the injunction of Paul to his church at Philippi (2:1–2): "If there is any encouragement in Christ, any solace in love, any participation in the Spirit, any compassion and mercy, complete my joy by being of the same mind, with the same love, united in heart, thinking one thing."

10

The Church and Sexual Ethics

All human affairs have moral dimensions. We have just reviewed the church's involvement with such radically important questions of international injustice and violence as economic exploitation, political repression, and the nuclear arms race. We turn now to sexual ethics. For several reasons, it is not possible to discuss business, medical, and feminist ethics. Richard McCormick observed, for example, that the full effect of the emergence of feminism on moral theology "is probably still ahead of us" (1989, 12).

There are good reasons to single out sexual ethics, even though it was not given extensive pastoral investigation by the Council. First, in the 1960s and 1970s, the Western world went through a sexual revolution that had been spurred on by such factors as greater affluence, the contraceptive pill, the increase of women in the work force, the destabilization of traditional values during the Vietnam War (1961–75), and by a new societal emphasis on self-fulfillment. On its negative side, the revolution trivialized sexuality. There was more tolerance of prostitution, divorce, cohabitation, and of nudity and pornography in the media and theater. Sexual activity among teenagers increased—a fact verified by the number of pregnancies among the young. People were exploited and many were seriously harmed by the epidemic spread of venereal diseases and AIDS. Between June 1981 and February 1990, over 110,000 deaths from AIDS were reported in the United States—almost twice the 58,183 United States military personnel whose names are etched on the Vietnam Memorial. By the end of 1992, the number dead from AIDS had risen to over 152,000.

On its positive side, people were no longer afraid to discuss sexual matters openly. In general, Victorian prudishness and its extremely damaging patriarchal notions about sexuality (e.g., the idea that women lacked sexual feelings altogether) were debunked. Some of the constructive power of sexuality was released and gains were made in sexual justice and equality. Most importantly, there was a significant shift in appreciation of marriage. Sexual intimacy and friendship were firmly combined. Previously, people tended to keep them separated. The purpose of sexual intercourse was procreation of children; friendships were often found elsewhere.

Second, from almost the beginning, much of the church's teachings on sexuality has been at odds with the Catholic sacramental consciousness. Over the course of the church's history one can find not only popes and bishops but also outstanding theologians like Ambrose, Augustine, Albert the Great, and Aquinas fostering anti-sexual, misogynist theories. Is it any wonder that some declare that "the failure of the analogical imagination to subsume sexuality is the most grievous failure in the history of Catholic Christianity" (Greeley and Greeley Durkin 1984, 68)?

Third, since the Council, the Vatican has issued many documents on sexual matters. Nevertheless, it is common knowledge that there is a sharp difference between, on the one hand, the official hierarchical teaching on sexual morality, and, on the other hand, the practices of many faithful Catholics and the views of the majority of Catholic theologians. The Vatican teachings, no matter how vehemently repeated, have had little effect on the attitude and lifestyle of most United States Catholics (Greeley 1992). If this inconsistency continues, there can only be grave harm to the church. For example, studies have shown that, in addition to the usual reasons why people do not participate in weekly Eucharist—laziness, work, lack of desire, an inability to get to church—many do not participate because of dissatisfaction with some of the church's teachings, particularly the ban against contraceptive birth control and remarriage for the divorced (Winter 1975).

Fourth, chastity (the proper use of sex) is constitutive of the identity and mission of the church. The bishops at Vatican II reflected on this relationship when they reminded married persons that "Christ the Lord abundantly blessed [marital] love, welling up as it does from the fountain of divine love and structured as it is on the model of his union with the Church. For as God of old made himself present to his people through a covenant of love and fidelity, so now the savior of men and the spouse of the Church comes into the lives of married Christians through the sacrament of matrimony" (GS 48). Members of religious communities were reminded that their vow of chastity gives "witness to all Christ's faithful of that wondrous marriage between the Church and Christ her only spouse, a union which has been established by God and will be fully manifested in the world to come" (PC 12).

Sexual misconduct, on the other hand, tarnishes the church's identity and mission. For instance, beginning in June 1985, the institutional church in the United States was rocked by national media attention given to numerous sexual scandals involving bishops and priests. Several bishops had to resign their posts over reports of affairs with women. National estimates of the number of priests involved in the sexual abuse of children and adolescents was in the hundreds (approximately 1 percent of United States priests) and the number of children molested was in the thousands. The bishops had been quietly discussing these cases since 1985, but in 1993 reports of sexual misconduct by priests received such aggressive media attention and there was such a crisis of confidence in church leadership that the bishops formed a special national committee to deal with the problem. Pope John Paul himself spoke out publicly in a letter to the bishops, dated June 11, 1993. He stated that out of concern "for the victims so seriously hurt by these misdeeds" he would help the bishops use church law to remove child molesters from the ranks of the priesthood. He established a committee "to study how the universal canonical norms can best be applied to the particular situation in the United States."

These scandals demoralized the community, especially the many bishops and priests faithful to their commitments, and they provoked investigations into the standards governing the recruitment and training of seminarians, men who should be models of justice and order.

Society and Order

To live a full human life we must live in a society marked by order, law, justice, and freedom. But society is often marked by disorder, lawlessness, injustice, and repression. Catholicism teaches that basic principles govern societies: (1) There exists an objective moral order in which some actions are good and others are bad. (2) Humans can know this objective order. (3) The objective moral order applies universally. Actions objectively morally evil are always objectively morally evil. (4) Individuals do not always realize their fundamental ability to know the objective order (Keane 1982).

If these principles are true, then the objective moral order cannot be achieved by either of the two extremes—legalism and relativism. Legalism is strict, literal adherence to law. Under this view, morality becomes simply a matter of obedience to the law as promulgated by the authorities. One simply checks predetermined norms or commandments that establish which acts are good and which are evil. Legalism—justice without love—can subvert societies, especially religious communities. Both the Jewish prophets and Jesus condemned legalism because it changes radically the original purpose of the law, which is proper concern for and response to God's love. Legalism turns God into an exacting lawgiver and makes obedience to law the ultimate sign of faith and the principal means to holiness. In the preconciliar church, many Catholics showed legalistic leanings in their observance of Friday abstinence, the eucharistic fast, and avoidance of servile work on Sundays.

This critique of legalism does not mean societies and individuals do not need law. Since we are not completely free nor entirely conformed to the inspirations of the Spirit, laws instruct us about what is good for society and the individual, and they can correct our inconstancy in doing what is just and good. To deny the relevance of laws "would be to deny the continuity of human experience in history and all the wisdom laboriously acquired in the past" (Johann 1965).

The other extreme, relativism, is more a danger today than legalism. Alasdair MacIntyre declared in 1981 that with the

Enlightenment, Western society lost Aristotelian principles and Judeo-Christian divine law tradition so that today we have no common moral philosophy other than relativism, which bases all judgments on individual preference or feeling. Relativism is the view that whatever the individual thinks is morally right is in fact objectively right or good and for that very reason. As such, relativism rules out interference—by the state or religion or anyone—in a person's private moral and religious conduct. It maintains that there is no moral good all can agree on (ethical agnosticism), and, therefore, everyone ought to have as much freedom as possible to pursue her or his notion of the good. This perspective presumes that each person is an autonomous source of value.

Relativism is expressed in such axioms as the following: I do what seems best for me and what does not hurt anyone; judge people only by their standards; any opinion seriously entertained is as correct as any other; all lifestyles are of equal value; and every culture has its own morality.

Relativism is based on certain truths. First, it is founded on an appreciation of the importance to morality of the subjective component, including individual free choice. Second, it is also true that we are always conditioned by cultural and historical circumstances, and some practices are culturally relative. But this does not make all practices relative. While it is true that certain values can be appreciated only by one culture, there are values that are valid for all cultures. For example, "the value of persons over things or the value of life over convenience are value-hierarchies that transcend culture" (Vacek 1984, 59). Ultimately, relativism is unacceptable because it is individualistic and totally subjective. We are social beings: individualism is an inadequate account of human behavior and the means to an ordered society. Also, relativism is based on ethical agnosticism—a view incompatable with the Catholic notion that goodness and badness can be measured by objective reality.

In 1966, Joseph Fletcher (1905–1991), an Episcopal priest, professor of ethics, and founder of the field of biomedical ethics, developed a famous version of relativism that he popularized as "situation ethics." He was willing to call his theory "principled relativism" (Bennett 1966) and in 1978 he wrote, "If we were to choose the appropriate school term for it, situation ethics would be act-utilitarianism" (Fletcher 1978).

Fletcher did not coin the term *situation ethics*. The theory arose in Germany after World War II when there was serious questioning of why so many Germans had not protested the unjust Nazi rule and the morality that had permitted or at least tolerated the war with its atrocities and disregard for human dignity. In 1952, Pius XII delivered several addresses against situation ethics and those who based morality on circumstances rather than universal moral norms (Gallagher 1990, 225–35).

Fletcher rejected legalism and a morality based on abstract-universal norms. "The classic rule of moral theology has been to follow laws but do it *as much as possible* according to love and according to reason. Situation ethics, on the other hand, calls upon us to keep law in a subservient place, so that *only* love and reason really count when the chips are down!" (1966, 30).

Legalism subordinates the situation to predetermined general laws of morality and absolutizes these laws. Fletcher denied that human actions could be declared morally wrong in every circumstance. He did not totally eliminate objective laws of morality. He agreed that there are valid general moral rules that help people make moral judgments in particular cases. However, he argued that those general rules are not universal and absolute. The situationist, he wrote, "enters into every decision-making situation fully armed with the ethical maxims of his community and its heritage, and treats them with respect as illuminators of his problems. Just the same, he is prepared in any situation to compromise them or set them aside *in the situation* if love seems better served by doing so" (ibid., 26).

Fletcher forced Catholic moralists to reaffirm that "all morality, properly understood, is situational, is aware of the increasing importance placed upon circumstances, motives, historical evolution, the subjectivity of the moral agent" (Wassmer 1968, 191). In general, Fletcher's theory was roundly rejected. Karl Rahner, for example, wrote, "A situation ethic carried to its logical conclusion would become an ethical and metaphysical nominalism in which the universal could never actually bear upon the concrete with binding force" (1964a, 53). Similarly, people wondered what there was about the situation that suddenly enabled a person to choose wisely if no decision was valid outside the concrete situation. The experience of most people is that it is precisely in moments of crisis, when it is difficult to mobilize their powers of reflection to make a prudent choice, that they need guidelines; that is, values, ideals, aims, and purposes.

Vatican II

In the period before the Council, moral theology was predominantly neoscholastic. It emphasized the sins of the individual; it was act-centered and law-oriented; and it was concerned primarily with human conduct in relation to the destiny of humanity. In addition to emphasizing an objective moral order grounded in the natural law and divine revelation, it also stressed the preparation of seminarians for the proper administration of the sacrament of penance. Faith was declared the primordial Christian virtue, but Christ was not the center of morality.

Several theologians tried to renew moral theology. For example, Emile Mersch's studies (1939) on the church as the mystical body focused morality on Christ, and Gerard Gilleman (1959) put love at the center of the moral life. Bernard Häring (1961–66) integrated moral principles and the great Christian mysteries by returning to the sources of the Christian faith, especially the Scriptures. Fritz Tillman (1960) described morality as the imitation of Christ.

The council fathers picked up these themes when, in a section written by Bernard Häring (1992, 60), they declared that "special attention needs to be given to the development of moral theology. Its scientific exposition should be more throughly nourished by scriptural teaching. It should show the nobility of the Christian vocation of the faithful, and their obligation to bring forth fruit in charity for the life of the world" (OT 16).

Josef Fuchs of the Gregorian University in Rome commented on these conciliar directives. He said the Council called for a moral theology that was biblical, christocentric, social, faith-centered, and scientific.

The Scriptures, "the soul of sacred theology" (DV 24), should have a central place in moral theology because they recount God's gracious calling of individuals to a life commensurate with their salvation in Christ. Contrary to the view of the rationalists of the Enlightenment period, Jesus was not mainly a moral teacher, one who designed a code of precepts and obligations for his followers. Rather, a christocentric morality should emphasize the full and rich relationship among the Father, Christ, and those "in Christ," his community. A morality of law is not ruled out, but law is only one element in the whole context of life in Christ. A biblical and christocentric morality should be social in contrast to the neo-Thomist view, which was individualistic. Christian morality should also be faith-centered. The Christian mystery should be examined by reason enlightened by faith. Finally, moral theology should take account of psychology, anthropology, and history, as well as of ethics, dogmatic theology and other Christian traditions (Fuchs 1970, 1–55).

Traditionalists vs. Revisionists

Right after Vatican II a revolution was set in motion in moral theology. It began with a seminal essay on the principle of double effect by the Jesuit Peter Knauer (McCormick 1989, 9; see Knauer 1979, 1–39). At the heart of his article was the question of whether some of the most important rules of morality, such as those forbidding masturbation, premarital sex, and contraceptive birth control, were to be considered absolute or whether exceptions were possible. Those who follow the church's traditional teaching on these matters are called traditionalists (or deontologists). Those who advocate another methodology, a relational-responsibility model, are called revisionists (or proportionalists or teleologists).

The traditionalists maintain that morality is based on absolute moral norms and fear that the revisionists leave the door open for moral compromise and breakdown when they say there are few absolute norms and even these are not infallible. The revisionists argue that emphasis on absolute moral norms eliminates morally important elements from consideration such as circumstances, consequences, and motive. Revisionists accept formal norms, statements which inform us of values and of the kind of behavior that should be avoided. For example, the injunction not to kill recalls the value of life; and the commandment not to steal informs us about the right of private property.

Actually, revisionism and traditionalism are not two mutually exclusive models of moral theology, but are generic terms to indicate different forms of moral argumentation. Both models are committed to an objective moral order. However, the methodology of the traditionalists is deductive, comprehensive, and certain, whereas that of the revisionists is inductive, partial, and conditional (Cahill 1978, 2). Revisionism is more of a loose tendency than a school of thought, and many of its proponents believe that the kind of weighing of circumstances and motives that traditionalists say is impossible, has in fact long been characteristic of Catholic moral analysis (Steinfels 1990b).

The background of this debate is the clash between a classical and historical consciousness. Classical consciousness underscores the objective, the unchanging, the universal and abstract, and advocates a uniform approach to moral attitudes and principles. It regards the Bible as a moral code with ready-made normative laws and answers. Historical consciousness, on the other hand, looks to the subjective, changeable, particular, and practical. It accepts a certain pluralism in moral theology. The Bible is read in light of the historical-critical method, suggesting that what often seem like universal laws are actually conditional prohibitions.

Traditionalists

Traditionalists deplore both legalism and relativism. In the past, Catholic moral theology was often legalistic. It was "all too often one-sidedly confession-oriented, magisterium-dominated, canon law-related, sin-centered, and seminary-controlled" (McCormick 1989, 3). Law was stressed since morality was understood as a reflection of the eternal, divine and natural law of God. Nevertheless, there were theologians and confessors who were "very pastoral and prudent, critically respectful, realistic, compassionate, open and charitable, well-informed" (ibid., 4). Theologians knew that legalism was an enemy of true religion and encouraged *epikeia* and casuistry. The former made allowances for human weakness by informing people that at times they should look to the meaning and intention of the lawmaker rather than the law; the latter affirmed absolutes in a rigorous fashion, yet permitted a wide range of exceptions.

Traditionalists counteract relativism by teaching a normative ethic based on absolutes and principles. The way absolutes are understood has bearing on four aspects of morality: acts as intrinsically evil, the principle of double effect, the natural law, and the ability of the church to teach morality.

The church has labeled certain acts as intrinsically evil and therefore forbidden without any possible exception. Some of these acts are abortion, contraceptive birth control, rape, bestiality, and incest. Other actions are ruled immoral or sinful (e.g., killing another person or an animal) because a person acts against a basic moral good. However, since these prohibitions are conditioned applications of general moral norms or rules for specific situations, exceptions are always permitted when proportionately greater goods or evils come into play (e.g., killing a person in self-defense or an animal for food).

Traditionalists also acknowledge the principle of double effect. It often happens that an intended action can have two effects, one good and one evil. For example, it is wrong to directly take the life of an innocent person, even if doing so would save the lives of thousands. It might, however, be permissable to take innocent lives indirectly, as occurs when civilians are killed when bombs are dropped on military targets. The traditional formulation of the principle of double effect requires that an evil effect could be permitted to follow from an action if four criteria were present: the action itself must be intrinsically good or indifferent; the good effect must be the intended effect; the evil effect must not follow directly from the action, only indirectly (the good effect cannot come about by means of the evil); and the good effect must proportionately outweigh the evil effect (O'Connell 1976, 170–73; Dwyer 1987, 152–61).

Natural law also plays a part in morality, traditionalists believe. "The basic thrust of the natural law was and still is that man's being is and must be the basis for his becoming" (McCormick 1968, 771). There is a law implanted by God within every being; it is part of their very essence—this is what is meant by "natural law." The classical consciousness of the traditionalists, however, often reduces the natural law to the order of nature. They identify the demands of the moral law with biological and physical processes. Nature's norms are applicable always, everywhere, and for all. There is a blueprint in nature that needs to be uncovered and properly deciphered. The universe is a static structure reflecting the mind of God. All humans, despite variations of culture and history, are the same. There is an eternal law implanted in our rationality that is unchangeable. This law can be known by natural reason and it is often reinforced by revelation. Humans can rebel against this law, but it never changes.

Finally, traditionalists stress the teaching role of the official church. They uphold its ability to determine which actions are objectively wrong.

Revisionists

The revisionists also deplore legalism and relativism. They avoid both extremes by using a methodology that draws upon human experience and historical developments for their explanation of evil acts, the principle of double effect, natural law, and church teaching.

As for the idea of "evil actions," the revisionists dislike labeling certain human acts as in themselves intrinsically immoral. Such an approach, they maintain, neglects morally significant factors such as motive and significant circumstances. They argue that a distinction must be drawn between the kind of evil that the act as such involves in its physiological structure and the kind of evil that the person intends without proportionate reason. Evil intrinsic to the action can only have a meaning in a premoral (or ontic or nonmoral or physical) sense.

Revisionists do not say that premoral evil is morally neutral. "To the contrary," as Lisa Sowle Cahill explains, "it is regarded as something generally not fulfilling from human nature, and indeed harmful to it. It always counts as a negative factor in a total moral evaluation. But taken by itself, it is not morally decisive" (McCormick 1985, 62–63). Moral evil occurs when the person intends the premoral evil without a proportionate reason.

Our human situation is filled with "disvalues" (premoral or ontic evil) that conflict with the values already there. Each person has essential dignity and existential originality. These basic values must always be protected. Formal moral norms and principles inform us about values; for example, "You shall not lie" tells us the importance of truth in relationships, personal and social. But disvalues such as error, fatigue, ignorance, and violence are inevitable and unavoidable, due to the limitations built into our human situation. These we may cause but not intend while pursuing some course of action. These premoral qualities become moral evils against a person's essential dignity and originality when willed without proportionate reason. For example, basketball is a noncontact sport. However, when ten players scurry around the court to get position or the ball, accidents happen, sometimes even causing very serious physical harm to a player. Instinctively, the players, coaches, referees, and fans know when such a foul is accidental and when it is purposely intended to harm another. Similarly, premoral evil is present when a doctor amputates a limb, or a parent spanks a child pedagogically, or a vacationer catches fish for his dinner.

The revisionists deny that acts can be labeled intrinsically evil, but they admit the existence of moral norms that are virtually exceptionless. That is, certain acts like cruelty to children, slavery, rape, direct killing of noncombatants in war, and not assisting persons in dire distress are clearly wrong. But it cannot be proven with the sharpness of syllogistic logic that no exceptions could ever occur.

The traditionalists argue that in relativizing the notion of acts as intrinsically immoral by subsuming them under the criteria of intention and proportionate reason, the revisionists have stripped the world of any distinctively moral character. If things cannot be known as morally good in themselves, then moral knowledge has been relativized. After all, one can marshall proportionate reasons to justify whatever one wishes.

Further, the revisionists reject the principle of double effect with its third condition that the good effect must not be produced by means of an evil effect. It is positive and proportionate consequences that justify the means used. We can judge whether an evil effect follows directly or indirectly from our formally willed actions, depending on the presence or absence of a proportionate (commensurate) reason. Revisonists actually reject the distinction between directly and indirectly intending the evil effect. They maintain that the key factor is the overall purpose in mind. In many cases the exceptions of the traditionalists are the result of involuted, unconvincing logic. For example, the traditionalists' description of an abortion to save the life of the mother as indirect killing does not seem consistent. In cases like this, actions are justified, based on an estimate of all the values and disvalues involved in the total consequences.

The revisionists also question the extent of the influence of the natural law. The relational-responsibility approach to morality is more dynamic than that of the traditionalists. They do not deny human continuity amid human change. But they insist that the abiding and unchangeable structures of the human person are fewer and more general than previous ages liked to believe. The revisionists root the natural law in the order of reason and discerning love. With the use of reason, humans subordinate and adapt the biological and physical facts of life to reach humane ends. Reason reflecting on the total human experience becomes the guide for human well-being, and not the order of nature. Biological processes become subservient to the total well-being of human life. This approach is in keeping with Vatican II, which marked a distinct turn in Catholic theology "from a cosmological orientation to one decidedly more personalist. There is a difference between seeing people as contingent beings and seeing them as personal participants in dialogue with a personal God" (Modras 1979, 494).

Due to the findings of the human sciences, we have a better sense of the complexities of human nature. The structure of morality is not a static set of regulations constitutive of human nature. The natural law is "the cognitive realization of a pattern of dynamic norms generated by the human social experience of history" (Murphy 1978, 382). Humans grow more truly as they assume more consciously their responsibility for the future of humankind and the world.

The revisionists' view of church teaching is less absolute than that of the traditionalists. The revisionists are accused by the traditionalists of dismantling the authority of the magisterium in moral matters. If there is no objectively definable set of evil actions and consequences, say the traditionalists, then the official magisterium is reduced to exhorting and counseling.

While not dismantling the magisterium's authority in moral matters, many theologians today give critical attention to Vatican documents. Several have warned that these documents should not be considered the final word, a view that would stifle further theological discussion and that would label those who questioned them as disloyal. To see the documents as unquestionable "would be theologically erroneous, pastorally tragic and practically harmful to both the theology of sexuality and the moral magisterium of the church" (McCormick 1976a). The revisionists might consider an example of this to be the CDF's "Declaration on Certain Questions Concerning Sexual Ethics" (*Persona humana*, "The Human Person") issued December 29, 1975. This document maintained that it is only in marriage that the full sense of mutual self-giving and procreation is preserved. Based on this value judgment, premarital sex, homosexual relations, and masturbation fall short of this ideal.

This document had more critics than defenders, mainly because it so firmly represented the traditional arguments (McCormick 1981a, 668–82; Maguire 1976). Charles Curran criticized the document on the following five counts (1978, 30–52). First, it begins with immutable principles and a deductive approach, leaving little room for developing cultural and historical realities. This methodology stands in sharp contrast with Vatican II, which called attention to the signs of the times and to a much more inductive type of logic. Second, its conclusions are based on the finality of the physical act itself without reference to the personal dimension and the connection between love and sexuality. Third, it manifests a legalistic emphasis on principles, norms, and laws. Curran favored a relational-responsibility model that focuses on the values the laws are meant to safeguard. He argued that it is more difficult than it is assumed to discover eternal and immutable laws. Over the years, moralists always recognized there was a place for exceptions. Fourth, the document pays insufficient attention to people's actual lives. It makes unsubstantiated assertions about what people think about such topics as masturbation and homosexuality. Fifth, it takes an unhistorical approach to Scripture, treating the Bible as a moral code with ready-made answers.

The Vatican continues to monitor publications on morality and intervenes if it finds materials that deviate from the official teachings. For example, in 1977, two priest-theologians were censured for publishing books that taught sexual ethics from a revisionist viewpoint. Philip Keane's book had its imprimatur removed. Anthony Kosnik was removed from his teaching position in a Michigan seminary and told he could no longer teach sexual ethics. Kosnik edited a book that was the work of a five-member committee (two priests, two married men, and a nun) sponsored by the Catholic Theological Society of America. This book proposed that Catholic sexual ethics return to a gospel ethic of love by not centering on procreation, natural law, and the physical contours of sexual acts but by focusing instead on creative growth toward personal integration. Such growth and integration, they suggested, would be promoted by sexual expressions that manifested these seven values: it should be honest, faithful, socially responsible, other-enriching, life-serving, joyous, and self-liberating.

However, it should be pointed out that Kosnick's book was also criticized as a whole or in part by some United States bishops and some members of the Catholic Theological Society.[1] Some found the seven criteria for healthy sex unhelpful since they did not address what was specific to sex itself. The same criteria, it was said, could be applied to almost any human activity, such as athletics or a social club.

Revisionists and Relativism

Revisionists can seem like relativists, but there are several reasons they are not. First, while revisionism seems to deny the existence of concrete universal norms, it does accept the principle of universality in moral theology. Once an action is understood to be objectively immoral, it will be so whenever and wherever it occurs. Some examples that are virtually exceptionless: deliberately calculated homicide, apostasy for temporal advantages, perjury in order to ruin another, defrauding workers of their just wages, misusing funds given for the support of the helpless, such as orphans and widows.

Revisionism also seems to lead to consequentialism (i.e., the belief that actions are right or wrong depending solely on the consequences), especially since it rejects some of the language of double effect, particularly on the issue of directly and indirectly intending the evil effect. The revisionists say they are not consequentialists because they ask if there is a proportionate reason for the action and proportionate reason includes more than weighing the good and bad results of an act. It also looks to norms and principles, as well as the values and disvalues in the total consequences.

Revisionism seems individualistic. However, the revisionists insist that an action does not become moral simply because someone thinks it is moral (Keane 1982, 266). Furthermore, as a person forms his or her conscience by weighing the values and disvalues involved in an action, the priority of the community and its objective moral judgments remains in place. As we saw in the chapter on authority, these include the judgments of popes, bishops, theologians, tradition, Scripture, and the sense of the faithful. However, even here the revisionists remind the traditionalists that authoritative structures can never be final or absolute. "Not only must they continually recommend themselves by their reasonableness to the persons they are meant to serve, but, like all other human devices, they too stand in need of constant criticism and constant improvement" (Johann 1968, 66).

Revisionism seems to some to be chaotic and a cause of moral breakdown. The revisionists insist, however, that for all the vagueness of its objectives, which make it appear a threat to right order, there is an order to their method: our orientation to God and our abiding vocation to participate in God's work of promoting and expanding his kingdom. If relational-responsibility means anything, "it means determining before God the appropriate response to a situation and acting accordingly" (ibid.). The touchstone for distinguishing better from worse is intelligent recognition. Since all of us are by nature open to God (that is, we are supernatural!), then "we all share a common light by which to judge whether steps proposed are really improvements, or not" and "we all share a common calling to move beyond where we are if we are going to be true to ourselves" (ibid., 67). We may not have metaphysical certitude about moral matters, but moral certitude is possible on specific moral matters, and on such matters, moral certitude is enough.

Sexual Ethics

Before turning to six specific questions of sexual morality, it is necessary to list the three characteristics or criteria on which sexual ethics depend for its integrity:

1. Sexual activity has the potential first and foremost of being linked with love in a relationship with another person.

2. Sexual activity has the capacity of procreation.
3. Sexual activity is accompanied by an intense pleasure, which reaches its peak at orgasm.

These three—physical satisfaction, interpersonal intimacy,
and parenthood—"are not three separate 'variables,' or *possible* meanings of sex which we are morally free to combine or
omit in different ways. Sex and love as fully *embodied* realities
have an intrinsic moral connection to procreativity and to the
shared creation and nurturing of new lives and loves" (Cahill
1990). Sexuality is a relational gift.

Masturbation
Masturbation is "the pursuit of induced sexual pleasure with or
without orgasm, usually solitary but sometimes mutually, frequently involving the genitals but sometimes involving other
orifices of the body" (Dominion and Montefiore 1989, 27).

Based on some sociological studies, the conventional wisdom holds that virtually all males and most females mastur-
bate at some time during their lives and this action is not
wrong. In fact, such studies conclude that masturbation is normal, not harmful, and relieves sexual tension. The Catholic
Church and most theologians teach otherwise.

The Congregation on Catholic Education issued an instruction in 1974 in which it called masturbation a youthful dysfunction but cautioned that "fears, threats, or spiritual
intimidation are best avoided" when dealing with this conduct. The Vatican encouraged counselors to aim at helping
young people form a balanced sexual attitude. Then, in 1975
the CDF published *Persona humana*, which declared that
masturbation is objectively a grave sin because it is "a deliberate use of the sexual faculty outside normal conjugal relations
. . . that contradicts the finality of the faculty."

This 1975 document evoked considerable response from theologians and bishops (McCormick 1981a, 668–82). Many viewed
it as theologically inaccurate, psychologically harmful, and pedagogically counterproductive. Bernard Häring, for example,
granted that, on the one hand, some theologians had gone too
far in reaction to an earlier rigorism concerning masturbation
by simply dismissing it, but, on the other hand, he warned that
a too facile judgment of mortal sin in sexual matters harms the
faithful. "It must never for an instant be forgotten," he wrote,

"that conversation about mortal sin, especially the mortal sins of children, is conversation about God" (ibid., 676).

Charles Curran, who had previously written that masturbation is wrong because a person fails "to integrate sexuality in the service of love" (Curran 1970, 175–76), disagreed with the judgment that masturbation is an intrinsically and seriously disordered act. He said individual masturbatory acts, when judged in the context of the person and the meaning of sexuality, "do not constitute such an important a matter . . . providing the individual is truly growing in sexual maturity and integration" (McCormick 1981a, 676).

What constitutes the heart of morality is the individual's relationship with God. "The moral life, therefore, consists of a deepening of our fundamental orientation. It consists of a growth process whereby we stabilize, deepen and render more dominant the love poured into our hearts by the Spirit" (McCormick 1968, 770). Human or moral acts, say the revisionists, are a configuration of a person's multiple relationships with the triune God, neighbor, the world, and self (a person's fundamental option) rather than a single action. The single action must be seen against the developmental process and particular life-context. This is why it is wrong, wrote Bernard Häring, to propose that masturbation is always a mortal sin, and only then consider the difference between masturbation by adolescents, young adults, and a married person. Ethicists must "look first to the diversity of the phenomena" and "only then" ask about the moral meaning or possible sinfulness of the individual phenomenon (Häring 1979, 2:503, 560).

Jack Dominion, a British psychiatrist, noted that, according to sociologists, masturbation is very common among both males and females, especially during adolescence. He believes that although masturbation is narcissistic, it is a necessary part of growing up since it helps people discover new dimensions of their body and it prepares people for heterosexual relations. He does not believe it is a sin for adolescents. However, it lacks the three criteria for integral sexual activity listed above, since both interpersonal love and procreation are absent. When Dominion discusses other instances of masturbation (such as that practiced by someone in prison or a widow), he insists that the three criteria must be used to judge the moral criterion of this behavior also.[2]

Philip Keane wrote that masturbation involved premoral evil, which had to be weighed against a variety of factors, depending on circumstances. He was hesitant to declare it a moral evil for adolescents, but he said people should move to a higher stage of sexual maturity. For adults, the premoral evil is more serious. Masturbation can signal a moral disorder. Individual evaluation is required and the person may need counseling if the masturbation is used compulsively as a substitute for more rewarding, interpersonal relationships. When Keane and other theologians discuss self-stimulation for sperm-testing for the treatment of infertility, they are inclined to accept it as a moral act that is quite different from masturbation as generally understood.

Richard McCormick, while he respects the sociological, psychological, and theological reasons for not imputing serious sin to adolescent masturbation, cautions that the young can stagnate their sexual development if, knowing the perspective of professionals, they decide to continue the habit of masturbation. For adolescents to simply indulge the habit is to feed and strengthen "the underlying causes of such symptomatic behavior" and to compromise their growth toward maturity. McCormick says he would tell adolescents two things: first, meet the challenge to become genuinely mature and free in sexual expression; second, the habit of masturbation is a serious challenge to growth that requires a serious response, a response that is "a resolute and adult attitude. As long as you maintain this, you are on the right path and responding properly to the challenge" (McCormick 1981a, 175).

Premarital Sex
In contemporary society premarital sex has become common. For many people and certainly in much of the media and the entertainment industry, premarital sex is regarded "as a sophisticated recreational activity for which the only moral criterion is mutual consent" (Cahill 1990, 497). Most Catholics do not subscribe to this cavalier attitude, but Andrew Greeley reported in 1992 that there is a definite decline among Catholics in their acceptance of the institutional church's teaching on this topic. In his report he indicated that "only one of six American Catholics thinks that premarital sex is always wrong" (p. 345). Other Christian churches are also

divided on this issue. For example, an Episcopal bishop argued recently that "life-giving" premarital sex can be just as "holy" as marriage (Spong 1988).

The Catholic Church has maintained that sexual intercourse should be limited to publicly committed married partners. Is there any enduring and universal reason why this is so? Some argue that moral theologians have yet to produce convincing proof why sexual intercourse must be matched in *every* case by a total covenant of love that can be expressed only in marriage (Kosnik et al. 1977, 152–58; see also Cahill 1985a, 89–90; Mahoney 1990, 203).

The official church resolutely rejects premarital sex for several reasons. First, the partners have not committed themselves to one another in a stable and definitive way and, therefore, their sexual intercourse is a lie. It does not express exclusive fidelity. In the Catholic tradition, passion and commitment go together: "commitment needs passion to sustain it over the long haul, and passion needs commitment if it is to keep its flame" (Greeley and Greeley Durkin 1984, 109). Second, the procreative character of sexual intercourse demands that the couple be ready and able to secure the education of the possible child. Premarital sex does not involve an adequate context for this value.

In order to give a solid reason why premarital sex is wrong, theologians like Richard McCormick begin by discussing the values found in a Christian marriage. Sexual intercourse is commonly called "the marital act." By so speaking, we indicate that sexual intercourse "has a sense and a meaning prior to the individual purpose of those who engage in it, a significance which is part of their situation whether or not the partners turn their minds to it" (McCormick 1981a, 365–67). The *sense* that is prior is that sex should be restricted to the marriage relationship; the *meaning* that is prior is that sex is the expression of love and friendship that is permanent and exclusive. Both the sense and meaning derive from centuries of human experience. Humans have learned "that unless this type of intimacy is restricted to the marriage relationship, the integrity of sexual language is seriously threatened" (ibid., 27–31, 447–62). Marriage is a covenant relationship built on friendship and it is friendship that generates fidelity, loyalty, and constancy.

There are different patterns to premarital sex: that which occurs between a client and a prostitute; during the one-night stand; in the temporary, semi-committed relationship; between cohabitating couples; and between the engaged. All of these are different human and moral situations. All have a premoral dimension; those involved in each of these situations will have to determine before God the extent of their immorality.

The status of those engaged to be married has received special attention because there is a pledge of permanence and, in a sense, the church's sacrament is involved. The sacrament of marriage has three distinct elements that normally take place in this order: the consent of the baptized partners, the consent of the church, and consummation. These three elements are not an instantaneous action, but a process that takes time. Engaged couples sometimes put the consummation before the consent of the church for different reasons. This is sometimes called "preceremonial intercourse." Some would argue this is not always immoral because the couple is in a state of committed love. Some ask about the relationship of the formal engagement to the sacrament itself. Are not catechumens who prepare for months for baptism to some extent already Christians before the actual baptism? Does marriage begin when the couple becomes formally engaged? Can the concept of "marriage" be so extended?

Despite these theoretical questions, premarital sex for the engaged has its own special, practical difficulties. For one thing, the intention to marry can be, and frequently is, revoked. If the engagement is broken, one of the partners can feel very distressed, deceived, or exploited. Second, McCormick observes that "the intention to marry is, indeed, part of the process leading to marriage. But the process leading to marriage cannot be converted that easily to read marriage-in-process" (McCormick 1981a, 458). Third, the significance of the social and ecclesial dimensions of the marriage should not be disregarded. The "public ceremony seals a commitment in as full a human way as possible" (Dominion and Montefiore 1989, 34). The ceremony is meant to safeguard the commitment. "Treating the ceremony as if it were *merely* a ceremony . . . is an unhealthy symptom of an eventually destructive individualism" (McCormick 1981a, 458).

Finally, what Richard McCormick wrote about premarital sex in 1966 is worth citing at length today. He declared that in the Christian ethic it is always immoral to manipulate another person.

> That is why the cardinal rule of sexual conduct was and always will remain: physical expressions of intimacy express the person and therefore must correspond to the existing relationship of the persons. The unmarried are only preparing for the total relationship of marriage. They are learning, not chiefly but among other things, to fill their expressions of love with respect and protection, with more of the person; they are learning to drain off the elements that stifle personal communion. Since their love is protective, not possessive, they will give themselves to each other only to the extent that the person can be given at this point—in a limited way. Consequently, they will avoid those acts that of themselves signify total personal oblation, not out of blind servility to a negative 'thou shalt not,' but because, being in love, they will wish to speak a personal, and therefore a genuinely human language to each other.

Contraceptive Birth Control

The world is going through a population explosion. One pundit remarked that when God told Adam and Eve to increase and multiply "the population density was two persons per square world" (Wynn 1988, 107). Demographers indicate that at the time of Jesus the world population stood at some 250 million. Today the earth gains as many people in two years. In 1830, during the Industrial Revolution, the population reached one billion. By 1930 it reached two billion, and by 1975, four billion. By the year 2000 the population could be over six billion. No one with any sense is against birth control and responsible parenthood. No one wants human beings to be born into situations where they begin and end their lives as nonpersons. From the perspective of the Catholic Church, the problem is contraceptive birth control. McCormick declared that he could "think of no moral issue or event [the 1968 encyclical *Humanae vitae*] in this century that impacted so profoundly on the discipline of moral theology" (1989, 12).

Greeley judged the encyclical "the most important event of the last twenty-five years of Catholic history" (1990a, 91).

The church's first universal condemnation of contraception took place in December 1930 when Pius XI issued the encyclical *Casti connubii*. He wrote because earlier in the year, August 15, the Anglicans meeting for a Lambeth Conference approved contraceptives "in those cases where there is such a clearly felt moral obligation to limit or avoid parenthood."

From 1930 to 1960, no Catholic moral theologian openly espoused the position that contraceptives could be used in good conscience in some circumstances. But, in the late 1950s, the whole context of contraceptives changed when a Catholic doctor, John C. Rock (1890–1984), and his associates developed, popularized, and championed the anovulant pill (Nyhan 1984; McLaughlin 1982). Rock and his supporters maintained that, in arresting the ovulation process, the pill does not violate the structure of the act of sexual intercourse. Use of contraceptives is an intervention into the marital act; the pill is an intervention into the generative system. Rock and others did not see it as any different from use of the infertile periods—those times when couples can engage in sexual intercourse without achieving conception.

Shortly before his death in June 1963, John XXIII appointed a high-level, international committee of thirteen to investigate the threat of overpopulation and the morality of contraceptives. By all reports, the group, which included Bernard Häring, was afraid at first to challenge the church's teachings that were firmly in place since 1930. Then, in fall 1964, at the second session of Vatican II, Cardinals Leo Josef Suenens, Bernard Alfrink, Paul Léger, and Patriarch Maximos IV Saigh (1878–1967) spoke out for a study of the means of contraception other than total or periodic continence. Léger said, "We must affirm that the intimate union of the couple finds its legitimate end in itself, even when it is not directed toward procreation." These interventions were applauded by the majority of the bishops, but Paul VI, persuaded by Cardinal Ottaviani of the Holy Office, removed the issue from the Council's agenda and assigned it to the commission previously set up by John XXIII. During the Council, the bishops referred briefly to the church's teachings and simply reaffirmed them (GS 51).

In December 1964, Paul appointed forty more members to the commission of thirteen. Among the group was an American couple, Patrick and Patricia Crowley, cofounders of the Christian Family Movement (McClory 1988b). The committee of fifty-three met for the first time in March 1965. Although they quickly realized there were no easy answers, they did produce a large stack of documentation. In spring 1966 Paul further enlarged the committee by adding seven cardinals and nine bishops, bringing the group to sixty-nine. However, Karol Wojtyla, the future John Paul II, was invited but never attended any of the meetings. Robert Blair Kaiser said, "His absence was probably the most important no-show on record" (Kaiser 1986).

"A crucial turning-point was reached on April 23, 1966, when the four theologians on the commission who upheld the traditional opinion admitted that they could not show the intrinsic evil of contraception on the basis of the natural law alone" (Hebblethwaite 1975, 212). Another crucial point in this whole discussion was the role of the Spirit guiding the officeholders. Where was the Spirit in 1930? At Lambeth or in Rome with Pius XI? Could the church now reverse *Casti connubii?* Does the presence of the Spirit in the church guarantee lack of error or replace human analysis? Other problems surfaced: the encyclical may have indicated that the pope can choose the wrong advisers, that Rome should not be preoccupied with authority, that the church must be willing to examine its past formulations openly and critically, and that "honest theological input is called for both before *and after* official statements" (McCormick 1990, 735).

In 1967, the committee voted to change the church's teaching that all use of contraceptives is immoral. The vote was sixty-four to four. Despite the vote, Paul VI published his famous encyclical *Humanae vitae* on July 25, 1968, reaffirming the traditional teaching that contraceptive birth control was intrinsically disordered (*intrinsece inhonestum*, n. 14).

Reactions to the Encyclical
Humanae vitae "plays a role in [Paul's] pontificate comparable to the dropping of the atomic bomb in the presidency of Harry S. Truman. Taken alone, it can obscure many achievements; if one neglects it, one slights the seismic and epochal."[3]

Many bishops, priests, theologians, doctors, lawyers, organizations like Opus Dei and the Knights of Columbus accepted the encyclical in 1968 and do so now.[4] John C. Ford, a Jesuit theologian who was a member of the papal commission, and Germain Grisez, a professor of Christian ethics, have argued that the traditional Catholic teaching on birth regulation is infallibly taught (1978).[5]

Paul VI was not ready for the vociferous dissent and the ferocious debates. "The incomprehension of the world was to be expected; the incomprehension of the church was his cross" (Hebblethwaite 1975, 209). After *Humanae vitae*, Paul never wrote another encyclical and he stopped his visits to churches outside of Italy. Were these decisions the result of the negative reaction to *Humanae vitae*? Did he retreat before the moral pressure or did he remain in Rome because his arthritic hip was a source of physical pain (Wynn 1988, 61)? No one really knows. What is clear is that a storm arose in the church that has yet to abate.

Several episcopal conferences issued statements that clearly modified the papal position. The Dutch bishops directed their people to form their consciences in light of the encyclical but also to consider such factors as "mutual love, family condition, and social circumstances." The English bishops said they rejected a subjective conscience that will not accept ecclesial documents. Nevertheless, they stressed the primacy of conscience and insisted "neither the encyclical nor any other document of the church takes away from us our right and duty to follow our conscience" (Haughey 1968). The United States bishops issued the statement "Human Life in Our Day" on November 15, 1968, calling on the priests and people to form their consciences in light of the encyclical. Some people interpreted this general statement as a blank check to choose another course of action than that set down in the encyclical. But the bishops were quick to reply that whereas people form their own conscience, they must also form a correct one (ibid.; see also Sheridan 1968).

Charles Curran

Immediately after the publication of the 1968 encyclical, Curran, a priest and professor of moral theology at Catholic University since 1965, initiated a public dissent from the church's teaching that contraceptive birth control was intrinsically evil. Curran wrote that "spouses may responsibly decide according to their conscience that artificial contraception in some circumstances is permissible and indeed necessary to preserve and foster the values and sacredness of marriage." He was not alone. Over six-hundred theologians, other academics, and priests signed Curran's statement of dissent (Häring 1987; Baum 1968; McCormick 1973).

Curran's position at Catholic University and the media coverage his dissent received brought on efforts to remove him from the university. Those moves were unsuccessful at that time. However, he came under investigation by the CDF in 1979 and, after a long, drawn-out process, he was informed in August 1986 that he was "neither suitable nor eligible to exercise the function of a professor of Catholic theology" (Curran 1986, see also May 1987). His struggles to return to his teaching position at Catholic University were of no avail. After one-year appointments at Cornell University, the University of Southern California, and Auburn University, he accepted a tenured position at Southern Methodist in the fall of 1991.

Curran has documented his case and his controversy with the Vatican. The questions evoked by the removal of Curran's canonical mission, particularly the issue of public dissent, prompted McCormick to rate the Curran affair "as among the most significant developments in moral theology in the past 50 years" (1989, 17).

The Birth Control Debate

There seem to be three major points of disagreement on this topic. First, those who are against the use of contraceptives say nothing should interfere with the biological integrity of sexual intercourse. This position is in accord with the understanding of natural law as an order of nature. The morally good must be in accord with nature. Contraceptives prevent the finality of the sexual act. Every conjugal act must be open to the transmission of life. Any interference in the nature of the act is intrinsically evil.

The counterargument asks why humans cannot intervene in human affairs. They acknowledge that contraceptives involve premoral evil since they preclude procreation. However, is it not true that humans often have to sacrifice one value for another? What is marriage for? Abstinence could endanger the unitive purpose of the marriage, that is, the couple's mutual and covenant love. Also, there are often other values to consider, for example, the couple may have too many children already.

Second, those against the use of contraceptives say the unitive and procreative goals of marriage are inseparable. The unitive cannot exist independently.

The counterargument centers on the "Catholic method of birth control," namely, the rhythm method, or natural family planning. Pius XII announced in 1951 that it was permissible for a couple with "serious motives" to use natural family planning to limit births.

The rhythm method relies on the approximately six to nine days during the monthly cycle when the woman can conceive. During these times the couple practicing the rhythm method do not express love with sexual intercourse. But those who disagree argue that rhythm is not a perfect method and they accuse the church of inconsistency. The rhythm method allows sex despite the teaching that the conjugal act must be open to procreation. What is the difference, they ask, between using the "safe period" and using contraceptives? In actual practice, is the rhythm method not contraceptive? Also, the rhythm method is said to be psychologically harmful. Many couples say they cannot grow together when they have to structure their married lives around a method and a calendar.

Third, those against the use of contraceptives maintain that this is the infallible teaching of the church with a history going back to the third century. The church cannot admit error on this point without irreparably damaging its indefectibility. The counterargument holds that this teaching was never defined as infallible. The church has made errors in the past and corrected them. This, they maintain, is the case here. Also, Catholics have much to learn from other Christian communities, some of whom permit contraceptive birth control to limit or avoid parenthood.

The Effects on the Church

Humanae vitae was rejected for many reasons: the pope had not consulted all the bishops, many of whom modified the pope's position for their people; papal teachings on sex had not developed since 1930 and yet there have been many advances in the sociological, biological, and physiological understanding of human sexuality; the pope rejected the majority vote of his commission; and many found the teachings unrealistic, for some of the reasons outlined above.

Many left the church in response. Others limited their involvement, especially their participation at Eucharist. Others questioned the ability of the church to instruct people about a correct conscience. The encyclical also created a crisis of authority. If the church is wrong about this important issue, where else is it in error? The result is that today many Catholics make their own decisions on moral and religious matters and yet continue to participate as active Catholics. But most of all, *Humanae vitae* constituted the first major test for the postconciliar church. "The encyclical was a catalyst which did most to bring about the crisis of identity within the church which had been imminent since the closing of the council" (Mahoney 1990, 300).

Synod of 1980

The theme of this synod was the Christian family in the modern world. The bishops did not want a change in the teachings found in *Humanae vitae*, but some bishops requested a clearer explanation of the encyclical since it was rejected by many Catholics whose faith, learning, and dedication to the church were beyond doubt. There was also a call for worldwide dialogue between the pope and theologians on the meaning of dissent.

In *Familiaris consortio* (1981), the apostolic exhortation issued after the synod, John Paul II addressed the subject of contraception. He explained how, "in continuity with the living tradition of the ecclesial community throughout history," both Vatican II and *Humanae vitae* had "handed on to our times a truly prophetic proclamation, which reaffirms and reproposes with clarity the church's teaching and norm, always old yet always new, regarding marriage and regarding the transmission of life." It was this stance, he stated, that led the episcopal synod to reaffirm the teaching of Vatican II (GS 51) and *Humanae vitae*, "particularly that love between husband and wife must be fully human, exclusive, and open to new life" (n. 29).

John Paul then called on theologians to help the hierarchical magisterium make this teaching "truly accessible to all people of good will" by "illustrating even more clearly the biblical foundations, the ethical grounds and the personalist reasons behind this doctrine" (n. 31).

Despite these exhortations, debate and dissent continue within the church and among the Christian churches. For example, two weeks before his first meeting with John Paul II on May 12, 1992, George Carey, Archbishop of Canterbury, blasted the Catholic Church's ban on contraceptive birth control, charging that *Humanae vitae* "actually stopped theological thinking."

The context of the archbishop's comments was the worldwide preparations for the United Nations Conference on Environment and Development to be held in Rio de Janeiro in early June. Carey said the church's teachings on contraceptives would inhibit discussion of population control. He was distressed because population control was not even on the conference's agenda. The archbishop said, "The moment the pope actually says this is a dogma, it creates a very big problem for the Church of Rome. That's their problem. It's also ours, in the sense that all of us are caught up in it."

In the summer of 1993, the twenty-fifth anniversary of the encyclical, numerous church leaders, theologians, and journalists commented on how much the 1968 encyclical continues to shape church life, authority, and discipline (Untener 1993; McCormick 1993; Curran 1993; Hebblethwaite 1993b; Steinfels 1993a). The encyclical has both defenders and critics. Defenders praised the encyclical's teachings that married love should be permanent and exclusive, and offered fresh philosophical and theological defenses of the procreative teachings (Flannery and Koterski 1993). John Paul reaffirmed the encyclical at World Youth Day in Denver in August 1993. Critics, on the other hand, remained unpersuaded by the encyclical's teaching that the dual meaning of sex—marital love and procreation—must be respected in the totality of a married life and in each act of intercourse. There is evidence that United States Catholics are as likely to use contraceptives as other Americans.

These discrepancies between the official teaching and the beliefs and practices of Catholics are unhealthy for the church, its institutional, intellectual, and devotional life.

Abortion
Abortion is the removal or expulsion of a fetus from the uterus, deliberately procured or induced. There are three kinds: natural (when the fertilized egg does not get implanted

in the uterus); therapeutic (when the fetus is removed for medical reasons); elective (when a person chooses to have the fetus removed). In the United States elective abortion is a highly emotional and controversial topic that has been constantly in the headlines, especially since the Supreme Court decision that legalized it, *Roe v. Wade* of January 22, 1973. The court decreed that abortions are allowed up to the third trimester, except when it is necessary to preserve the life or health of the mother. The debate has reached a stalemate inasmuch as two values are locked in opposition: life and freedom. Prolife advocates argue for the rights of the unborn. Prochoice advocates argue for a woman's right to make her own decision about her own pregnancy. In the United States the number of abortions annually is approximately 1.5 million (or more than 4,000 a day). Daniel Callahan wrote that the permissive abortion laws in our country and around the world "bring forward a whole class of women who would otherwise not have wanted an abortion or felt the need for one" (1973).

McCormick (1981a, 474) summarized the multiple problems raised by abortion:

> Abortion is a matter that is morally problematic, pastorally delicate, legislatively thorny, constitutionally insecure, ecumenically divisive, medically normless, humanly anguishing, racially provocative, journalistically abused, personally biased, and widely performed. It demands a most extraordinary discipline of moral thought, one that is penetrating without being impenetrable, humanly compassionate without being morally compromising, legally realistic without being legally positivistic, instructed by cognate disciplines without being determined by them, informed by tradition without being enslaved by it, etc. Abortion, therefore is a severe testing ground for moral reflection . . . and probably a paradigm of the way we will face other human problems of the future.

Church Teaching

The magisterium teaches that human life begins at conception. Elective abortion, then, is alway immoral. Therapeutic abortion is allowed when killing the fetus is indirect and is done to save the life of the mother.

Abortion was not a major issue in the Catholic Church until the 1970s. Pius XII rarely discussed it. John XXIII did not include it in either *Mater et magistra* or *Pacem in terris*. Vatican II gave it a brief mention, referring to it and infanticide as "unspeakable crimes" (GS 51). Paul VI did not mention it in his great moral statement *Populorum progressio*. However, in November 1974, the CDF published a "Declaration on Procured Abortion," the most detailed and authoritative utterance on abortion in years. It asserts that human life must be given equal protection at all stages from fertilization through adulthood. Speaking of the fertilized ovum, it states that it "would never be made human if it were not human already."

In November 1983, the revised code of canon law was published. The official church declared abortion to be so serious an offense that it is one of only six offenses punishable by excommunication. Canon 1398 states that "a person who procures a completed abortion incurs an automatic excommunication." In 1988 Vatican authorities clarified the legal definition of abortion to include new drugs and surgical procedures. They said that any method used to terminate a human life from the moment of conception until birth is an abortion. For an excommunication penalty to go into effect, one must know there is a pregnancy, and there must be a free choice to abort.

Reception of the Teaching
Catholics' attitudes on abortion are not radically different from those of other citizens. In general there have been three responses to the magisterium's condemnation of abortion: acceptance, a call for further dialogue, and rejection.

Nearly all Catholics view abortion as a grave moral evil—even those who consider themselves prochoice. Many express their opposition to abortion by participating in such organizations as the National Right to Life Committee (founded in 1973) and Operation Rescue (founded by Randall Terry in 1987), joining well-organized marches on Washington each January 22, and writing letters to government officials.

The United States bishops have spoken out on a number of occasions. Individual bishops have excommunicated Catholics who direct abortion clinics and some bishops have publicly criticized Catholics in political office who refuse to support antiabortion legislation. One bishop made national headlines in January 1990 when he suggested that Catholic politicians who vote to "facilitate" abortion risk hell if they die without repenting (Dicker 1990). In May 1990, the United States bishops hired a reputable and expensive public relations firm to spread the church's message that all abortions are wrong. Building on the prochoice theme of *choice*, the bishops urged all citizens to "exercise the natural choice—choose life." Then in January 1992, the bishops canceled their contract with the public relations firm for several reasons: there was criticism of the costs, questions arose about some of the controversial clients of the firm, and the bishops said they wanted to enter a new phase of their public education program.

Some Catholics think the question needs further dialogue since there are different views on abortion in the church. For example, a full-page ad with just that message appeared in the *New York Times* on October 7, 1984. Among the ninety-seven signees were twenty nuns. All the nuns were threatened with expulsion from their communities if they did not remove their names from the statement. Two Notre Dame sisters, Barbara Ferraro and Patricia Hussey, refused. Since 1981 they had been managing a home in West Virginia for poor women. From these women they heard pathetic accounts of rape, incest, battering, and abortion. They decided they could no longer accept the Vatican teaching that every abortion is an unspeakable crime. They continued to battle for their position until 1988 when, under considerable direct pressure from Rome, they withdrew from their community, vowing to continue "loyal, authentic dissent."[6]

In the spring of 1990, the Archbishop of Milwaukee, Rembert G. Weakland, held hearings with women in his diocese to gather their views on abortion, especially so he could understand the views of those who disagreed with the church's teaching. His report on the meetings was widely publicized. The archbishop upheld the church's teachings but warned that the antiabortion movement was driving away potential supporters, including Catholics, who viewed its focus as narrow, its tactics as aggressive and some of its rhetoric as "ugly and demeaning." He also urged that politicians trying to face the abortion issue with respect for life should be given "as much latitude as reason permits." The frank discussions with the women affected Weakland so much that he declared he could never again be glib when talking about "the moment of conception" or talk glibly about bringing the baby to term and then "just give it up for adoption" (Steinfels 1990a; Martinez 1990, 7).

A Vatican follow-up to Weakland's report came in November 1990 when it barred the theology faculty of the University of Fribourg from granting the archbishop an honorary degree. The awarding of the degree was meant to open the centennial celebration of Leo XIII's pioneering social encyclical, *Rerum novarum.* The archbishop was chosen primarily because of his central role in the drafting of the United States bishops' pastoral on the economy in 1986. The Vatican's reason for barring the archbishop from receiving the degree was that his statements on abortion had caused "a great deal of confusion among the faithful" (Steinfels 1990c; Windsor 1990a; Hebblethwaite 1990d).

The church teaches that individual human life begins at the moment of conception, and that a fetus has the same rights and deserves the same legal protection as a child. These two points—when human life begins and when a human's full standing in the eyes of the law or as a member of the human moral community begins—are the kind of questions that many Catholics want discussed further since the medical, scientific, and legal communities continue to study and debate them.

Some Catholics reject the absolutism of official Catholic teaching that all abortions are immoral. A group called Catholics for a Free Choice endorses abortion rights. This organization, founded in 1970, was the force behind the *New York Times* ad of October 7, 1984 (Doerflinger 1985). Daniel Maguire, a moral theologian at Marquette University, believes some theologians and a majority of Catholics do not consider abortion immoral under a range of circumstances: rape, risk of health, genetically damaged fetus, physically disabled woman, teenage pregnancy, a mother on public aid who cannot work, and a married woman who already has a large family (1983, 1984). However, the common opinion among moral theologians, including prominent scholars such as McCormick and Häring, is that abortion is allowed only to save the mother's life. "Beyond this case," wrote Häring, "I do not see any plausible reasons that could morally justify an interruption of pregnancy" (1981, 3:33).

The Prolife-Prochoice Debate

Here are the key points made by each side in the abortion debate. First, prolife proponents say that the fertilized egg has a right to life, which begins at conception and is paramount. However, not all Catholic theologians agree that individual human life begins with conception. McCormick describes the embryo during the first two weeks as "nascent human life," but he does not consider it an "individual human life" until later (1981a, 108–9). During the first two weeks, the new life does not exhibit the stable and determining character necessary for considering it a distinct individual or a person with human dignity. Others agree with this opinion, including Albert Di Ianni (1974), Karl Rahner (1972, 236), and Charles Curran (1973). The basis of their position is the scientific view that "hominization" cannot possibly be said to occur before fourteen to twenty-two days after conception (Diamond 1975). For example, twinning is no longer possible after the first fourteen days.

Prochoice adherents maintain that women have the right to decide whether and when to become mothers. Also, many persons believe human life begins at the time it can be sustained outside the womb.

Further, prolife proponents say that abortion is murder; however, they make an exception for therapeutic abortions. Prochoice supporters maintain that stages in fetal life distinguish the fertilized egg from a human being and distinguish fetal rights from those of a human being. As we saw above, theologians agree there are different stages of human life, but they still claim that an abortion of this "nascent human life" is tragically justifiable only on very limited occasions.

Those who are prochoice accuse the prolifers of being inconsistent because they seem unconcerned about the extremely high natural abortion rate. The fact that half or more of fertilized eggs are lost after failing to implant themselves in the uterus raises many moral and theological issues. Are these fertilized eggs really images of God and our brothers and sisters?

Prolife supporters challenge the idea of choice by pointing out that a woman makes a choice to have sexual intercourse knowing that pregnancy is a possible result. Prochoice proponents argue that contraceptive failures beyond a woman's control put her at risk of an unwanted pregnancy.

The prolife view claims that women do not appreciate what an abortion is. The prochoice stand maintains that women know what abortion entails and to force on them information they do not require is punitive.

Those who support prolife maintain that abortion can be an unsafe medical procedure; those who promote prochoice maintain that it is safe.

The prolife view maintains that adoption is a "loving alternative" to abortion and that there are many couples who wish to adopt children. The prochoice view says women are not obliged to provide babies for those who cannot conceive on their own.

Prolife adherents argue that the prochoice movement has made a woman's right to choose more important than the choice itself, which is wrongly portrayed as morally neutral. Abortion, they say, inflicts such harm on the fetus and its right to life that it cannot be considered a private issue but should be a matter of legitimate government regulation. Prochoice supporters maintain that abortion is a private issue best left to individual conscience and without the interference of law.

Divorce and Remarriage: A Sacramental Marriage

The church has always defended marriage. It teaches that a sacramental marriage has three dimensions: the consent of two baptized persons to live together in love until death, the consent of the church through the witnessing priest, and consummation.

In a sacramental marriage the couple are baptized. This should not be understood in a juridical way. A sacramental marriage entails a commitment to be Christian disciples who publicly witness the covenant love of God through Jesus Christ and his Spirit. This is no easy commitment and some theologians wonder just how many couples are ready for it (Cahill 1987; Cooke 1987).

The priest witnesses the ceremony, symbolizing the ecclesial and social dimensions of a sacramental marriage.

Consummation, too, must not be understood juridically, that is, occurring at least once after the church ceremony. Consummation involves more than this. It requires a lifelong commitment and struggle to deepen intimacy and love.

The church grants an annulment when it declares that the marriage was not a sacramental union in the first place. The church does this when, after examining the evidence, it has moral certitude there was no marriage. This annulment does not mean the couple were not legally married or that the children are illegitimate.

In the United States annulments have increased considerably. Pope John Paul II complained in 1984 about the "alarming increase" (15,000 percent in fifteen years) and warned marriage tribunals about "easy and hasty" annulments (Farrell 1984).[7]

Perhaps one of the reasons for the increase in annulments is the increase in second marriages. Many couples in second marriages have a stable relationship, try to live up to all their other obligations, and seek an annulment of their first marriage. John Catoir suggested in 1967 that "even if the evidence does not convince the judges of moral certitude, if it enables them to arrive at a well-founded possibility that the [first] marriage was null, an annulment should be granted."

Vatican II

The Council did not change the traditional ideals and standards concerning the indissolubility of marriage (AA 11). It "did achieve a total turnabout in the church's appreciation of the physiological, psychological and conjugal aspects of marriage that has resulted in a basic shift in its evaluation of mankind's sexual propensities" (Murphy 1978).

This change reflects the deeper understanding of human behavior achieved by the human sciences and the change in understanding of marriage in society. We witness today the change from a male-dominated, child-centered, ethnically defined marriage to one in which the man and woman are seen as equals, interdependent, growth-oriented, and open to many expanded relationships.

The Council introduced two fundamental changes in the Catholic definition of marriage (see GS 48–50). First, it did not list two ends of marriage, primary (the procreation and education of children) and secondary (mutual love and assistance). This is how Augustine, Aquinas, and Pius XI had ranked them. Instead, love and procreation were joined equally as the purposes of marriage. The bishops spoke of marriage as a "togetherness in love and life" rendered by the spouses to each other. The couple should nourish and develop their marriage "by pure conjugal love and undivided affection." Sexual love was endowed by God with "special gifts of healing, perfecting and exalting" in grace and love. Second, it did not refer to marriage as a contract but rather as a "covenant of conjugal love."

Divorce

United States Catholics now divorce as frequently as other citizens. In the United States divorces have nearly quintupled since 1940. In 1940 there were 131 million Americans and 250,000 divorces; in 1990, there were 250 million people and 1,190,000 divorces.[8]

At the fourth session of Vatican II, Melchite Archbishop Elias Zoghbi proposed that the church consider a pastoral practice for the divorced-remarried that more closely resembled the discipline of the Eastern Catholics. Since that intervention, there has been a great deal of writing on divorce and remarriage, and Zoghbi's suggestion is often considered to be the stimulus for it (McCormick 1981a, 332–33).

One of the first questions asked concerns the indissolubility of marriage. Some, like canon lawyer Stephen J. Kelleher, say this is an ideal and a goal (1973; see also Brunsman 1985; Curran 1974a, 1974b); others, like Richard McCormick (1981a, 554–61), that it is an absolute norm (see also P. F. Palmer 1975).

Those who believe marriage is an ideal accept divorce and remarriage. When Catholics get divorced and remarried, their first marriage is one of two kinds. It was a true sacramental marriage that failed or it was not truly a Christian marriage except in a canonical sense. For example, some of these marriages died because, right from the start, there was a radical incapacity to sustain the duties and obligations of marriage.

The questions of indissolubility and remarriage received national attention in 1968 through the writings of Stephen Kelleher, a Catholic priest with twenty-five years of active experience in church courts and, at that time, presiding judge of the marriage tribunal in New York City. Kelleher wrote that many marriages had become "intolerable," that is, one "in which it cannot be realistically foreseen that the couple would be able to continue or to resume a common life" (1968; see also Kelleher 1975, 1977, 1978).

He had three main contentions. First, he said that the church's marriage tribunals had no place in the life of the church. They are not a Christian structure. They produce very few annulments. "What they do produce is delayed justice (sometimes no justice), frustration, humiliation, distrust, suspicion and fear. They are as much the enemies of law as of freedom."

Second, he recommended that each person should decide "in his own conscience whether or not he is free before God from one marriage and free to enter another." The bond no longer exists when love, commitment, and other signs that visibly manifest a marital relationship have been irretrievably lost.

Third, Kelleher suggested that the church establish a system of marriage commissions (not courts) to assist individuals and the church to reach responsible decisions on marital status. Kelleher had always maintained that the church could not grant divorces but it could acknowledge that a marriage had dissolved.

Many viewed Kelleher's proposals as impractical, too subjective, and vague. By 1978, his solution to the intolerable marriage was deemed by James Young as "neither necessary nor desirable" (1978). He offered six reasons for his judgment. He pointed out that between 1968 and 1978 people became more tolerant of divorce among their loved ones. There was less stigmatization and ostracism and more support in putting together a new life, even when this entailed a second marriage without church approval. He also mentioned that the marriage tribunals had been reformed so that they were real instruments of pastoral healing; and that the church had developed a ministry to divorced Catholics in many parishes. Further, divorce and remarriage no longer resulted in automatic excommunication and its concomitant punishments: denial of funeral Mass and Christian burial, and labeling the second marriage an "adulterous union." The United States bishops had made this a church law in 1884, but Paul VI removed all these penalties in 1977. And he added, there had emerged a new pastoral theology of the Eucharist as a meal of reconciliation. This made it possible for the authentic reunion of many divorced-remarried Catholics to full communion in parish communities. Finally, the Catholic Church had learned about Protestant and Orthodox churches' experiences. These churches had normally allowed second marriages, but they were infrequent. Now they were increasing dramatically. They feared their church discipline was contributing to this increase.

Jesus and Divorce

In the Jewish Scriptures there is only one text that authorizes divorce: Deut. 24:1–4. Actually, it presupposes divorce rather than authorizes it.

In Jesus' day a man could divorce his wife, but not vice versa. The older Jewish tradition, based on Gen. 2:24, outlawed divorce. Jesus followed this tradition and forbade divorce for any cause (Luke 16:18). The constant teaching of the church has been that marriage is indissoluble.

Divorce is mentioned in five New Testament texts: 1 Cor. 7:10–16; Mark 10:1–12; Matt. 5:32 and 19:1–12; and Luke 16:18. Jesus' divorce teachings always appear in the context of his proclamation of the kingdom and his radical call to conversion and discipleship. When modern Scripture scholars examine the context of these passages, they ask if Jesus' most firm prohibition was an absolute law applicable to all times and all cases. Did Jesus teach that divorce was impossible—or that it was wrong? The opinion of many Scripture scholars (McKenzie 1980; 1985, 40–50; Fitzmyer 1981; Donahue 1981; R. F. Collins 1993) is that divorce is wrong. Jesus did not proclaim an absolute law, but, as a man of compassion, he spoke against divorce in order to protect women from being cast out of their families. The "prohibition of divorce may be rooted in a culture in which women, from birth to death, were secure only as long as they were the property of some man—father, husband, and in their old age, a son" (McKenzie 1980, 303). Furthermore, the exegetes point out that the so-called Pauline privilege of 1 Cor. 7:10–16, as well as the exceptive clauses in both Matthew texts, are exceptions made by the Pauline and Matthean churches to the prohibition. In other words, the fact that Jesus' sayings on divorce exist in so many different versions demonstrates that first-century Christians experienced a need not only to hand on Jesus' teaching on divorce but also to adapt it to ever new circumstances.

It is a fact that marriages fail for many reasons. Scripture scholars suggest that Jesus in his wisdom and compassion would allow divorce in our context—although most reluctantly. Until now, the church has maintained an "inhumane rigidity" regarding divorce. The opposite extreme would be "amoral relaxation." Between these two extremes there should be a position that would allow each individual case, as individual, to decide how best to live the life of peace to which God calls them (1 Cor. 7:15).

The Divorced-Remarried and the Sacraments

Can the divorced-remarried ever receive the sacraments? At the end of the Synod of 1980 on marriage and in *Familiaris consortio* (1981), John Paul II reiterated not only that they may not, but that this is the church's "traditional practice" (Michaels 1980; Hebblethwaite 1980e). However, this teaching flies in the face of "a virtually unanimous theological opinion that some divorced-remarried may be admitted to the sacraments" (McCormick 1981a, 120). There is a traditionalist and revisionist understanding of this issue (ibid., 82–87, 332–47, 372–81, 544–61, 826–41).

The traditionalist position assumes the existence of a permanent bond of marriage, one that lasts until death. Since the bond is permanent, the traditionalists conclude that the remarried must either separate or live as brother-sister.

They have three reasons for this conclusion. First, the couple is living in sin or at least a proximate occasion of sin. They are not disposed for the sacraments of reconciliation or eucharist because a firm purpose of amendment or change is required. The Italian episcopal conference stated in 1979 that this will to change "does not exist if the divorced-remarried remain in a condition of life that is contrary to the will of God. How is it possible at the same moment to choose the love of God and disobedience to his commandments?"

Second, the remarried couple is in a state of imperfect unity with Christ and not eligible to receive the Eucharist. The International Theological Commission said in 1978: "From the incompatibility of the state of the divorced-remarried with the command and mystery of the risen Lord, there follows the impossibility for these Christians of receiving the Eucharist, the sign of unity with Christ."

Third, scandal would result if the remarried were admitted to the sacraments. Others would conclude that it is not wrong to remarry after divorce and that the church approves second marriages.

The revisionists conclude that the divorced-remarried may be admitted to the Eucharist under certain conditions. Charles

M. Whelan, a Jesuit specialist in church-state relations, lists four: if the first marriage is irretrievably lost; if the circumstances that allow official reconciliation are not available, for example, an annulment or the death of a spouse; if the couple has indicated by their lives that they desire to participate fully in the life of the church; and if there are solid grounds for hope of stability in the second marriage that in all other respects is a Christian marriage (Whelan 1974; see also P. F. Palmer 1975).

The revisionists reject the traditionalists' arguments. They doubt that the bond of marriage perdures if the marriage is existentially and psychologically dead (McCormick 1981b). They think the traditionalists' view that the remarried can receive the sacraments as long as they live like celibates is absurd. How, they ask, is the principle of indissolubility not threatened by a second marriage without a sexual life but with sacramental participation, while it would be threatened by a second marriage with a sexual life and sacramental participation (McCormick 1981a, 550)?

The revisionists offer three reasons why some of the divorced-remarried should be admitted to the sacraments. First, the life of the couple often does not reflect a state of sin. Also, when children are involved, the church has frequently urged the remarried couple to remain together and to deepen their Christian life. Second, to exclude the divorced-remarried from the Eucharist on the basis of incompatibility with the unity between Christ and his church that the Eucharist signifies involves a static and "perfectionist" notion of the sacraments. Everyone who approaches the Eucharist admits unworthiness. Also, the Eucharist has another function: it is a means of grace. All Christians, including the divorced-remarried, need the grace of Christ. Third, if people are properly instructed, scandal need not follow from admitting the remarried to Eucharist. People should be able to weigh the premoral evil involved, namely, that remarriage undermines the stability of marriage, but understand that in this instance the Eucharist would be good for the Christian life of those involved.

A conclusion to this discussion is a seeming paradox: the official church might better foster the ideal of permanent marriage by blessing more second marriages of divorced Catholics.

Homosexuality

Homosexuality designates the psychosexual inclinations of a person who prefers sexual activity with persons of the same sex. Alfred Kinsey (1894–1956), a biologist at the University of Indiana, reported in 1948 in *Sexual Behavior of the Human Male* that 10 percent of the population is exclusively homosexual. This figure has been challenged by studies made in the 1990s.

In the United States especially, self-avowed homosexuals have become increasingly visible and even militant in their demand to be socially accepted as homosexuals and for freedom from discrimination. There is even a church that comprises mostly gay and lesbian members, the Universal Fellowship of Metropolitan Community Churches, a denomination that in 1992 had 50,000 participants in 264 congregations around the country (Hevesi 1992).

Because there is widespread and deep-seated homophobia in our society, gays and lesbians face considerable social, legal, and religious discrimination (Nugent 1981; Boswell 1981). The advent of AIDS has only heightened this fear.

At present there is no consensus among Christian churches or theologians regarding moral questions about homosexuality and homosexual behavior. In society and the Catholic Church there seem to be four views: that it is a perversion, a disease, an irreversible orientation, or a normal alternative to heterosexuality.

Those who view homosexuality as a perversion judge all homosexual activity as immoral, intrinsically evil, unnatural, and contrary to Scripture. Scripture scholars point out, however, that the Scriptures have no doctrine on homosexuality and certainly do not address the question of an irreversible orientation. The concepts of "constitutionally homosexual" and "homosexuality" are unknown during the biblical periods. It is modern science that has proposed that some persons are not heterosexual by choice or preference. Throughout the Bible, the Genesis description of male-female relationships is taken for granted as the standard. All people are heterosexual and their genital activity would reflect this point. However, whenever people turn from God and his created order, all kinds of disorders and depravities would follow, not only homosexuality but also adultery and lying (see Jer. 23:14), and pride, gluttony, and arrogance (see Ezek. 16:49–50).

There are five biblical references to homosexual activity: Gen. 19:4–11; Lev. 18:2; 20:13; Rom. 1:24–27; 1 Cor. 6:9–10; and 1 Tim. 1:9–10. In these passages homosexuality is not condemned as such, but as a sin of idolatry or a violation of the sacred duty of hospitality (Genesis 19), or as the dehumanizing pederasty that was widespread in the Greco-Roman culture of the first century.

In St. Paul's day, homosexuality "was related to temple services and therefore adoration of false gods" (Nouwen 1967; see also Wink 1979; Groppo 1986, 9; R. F. Collins 1986, 172–74). This is the context of Leviticus 18 also. In this text God commands the Israelites not to "behave as they do in Egypt where you once lived" or "as they do in Canaan where I am taking you." This concern for cultural purity suggests that homosexuality would reflect the male and female prostitution common in middle-Eastern religious cults. This prohibition, as well as those in such passages as Deut. 23:18 and 1 Kings 14:24 and 15:12, suggests that homosexual activity was prohibited because of its intimate association with idolatry (G. D. Coleman 1987). Furthermore, passages such as Rom. 1:24–31 cannot be used to establish that homosexual acts are intrinsically disordered and can in no case be approved. It is generally agreed that "St. Paul did not know homosexuality as a condition. He saw it as a human choice, and as such, a perversion which he condemned in general terms" (McCormick 1976a).

Some view homosexual orientation as a disease resulting from a pathological constitution or as a psychological dysfunction caused by harmful behavioral patterns in the familial or immediate social environment. It can be cured by depth therapy, they believe.

Modern science rejects this view. The American Psychiatric Association moved in 1973 to drop its official diagnosis of homosexuality as a mental illness (Hansen 1986). The organization declared that homosexuality "implies no impairment in judgment, stability, reliability, or general social or vocational capabilities." Similarly, the World Health Organization did not list homosexuality in the 1993 edition of its International Classification of Diseases.

Some differentiate between homosexual activity and orientation. A person's sexual orientation is a given rather than a chosen or preferred condition. This distinction was popularized by

Alfred Kinsey in 1948. What causes the orientation remains an unanswered question. Various explanations are offered: heredity or genetic factors; erratic behavior patterns in the family or the social environment.

One of the earliest statements on homosexuality as an orientation came from the United States bishops in 1973 in their document "Principles to Guide Confessors in Questions of Homosexuality." Here the bishops acknowledged that people do not choose their sexual orientation. But they went on to say that "homosexual acts are a grave transgression of the goals of human sexuality and of human personality." Confessors were encouraged to help homosexuals work out an ascetical plan of life with a view to controlling their sexual activity.

In December 1975, the CDF declaration *Persona humana* made the distinction between behavior and orientation. The document observed that some homosexuals are "innately" constituted as such and thus their "constitution" should not be thought curable. The United States bishops reiterated this distinction in their 1976 message "To Live in Jesus Christ." They condemned homosexual behavior but decried the prejudice against the basic human rights of homosexual people, especially friendship, respect, and justice.

The 1983 statement from the Congregation for Catholic Education, "Educational Guidance in Human Love," encouraged sex education. However, it did not make the distinction between behavior and orientation in condemning homosexuality. It declared that homosexual activity "impedes the person's acquisition of sexual maturity." Without whitewashing this kind of sexual activity as a likely path to sexual integration, it did instruct educators not to disturb people who were troubled in these ways with accusations of guilt (Burtchaell 1983). Robert Nugent, a priest who founded New Ways Ministry in 1977, insisted in his commentary on the document that balance is needed in dealing with the question. "Homosexual *people* should not be reduced to their *orientation*; nor should the homosexual orientation be reduced to sexual *behavior*" (1984, 488).

Disturbed by increasing challenges to the traditional teachings on homosexuality, the CDF published another document on homosexuality on October 1, 1986: "On the Pastoral Care of Homosexual Persons." In it they said too much had been made of the distinction between orientation and behavior. The orientation of the homosexual "is not a sin, it is a more or less strong tendency toward an intrinsic moral evil, and thus the inclination itself must be seen as an objective disorder." The document seemed to misunderstand homosexuality as an orientation. Ordinarily, the term refers to a psychosexual attraction toward one of the same sex, but the CDF document described it as a tendency toward evil acts. Commenting on the strong words in this analysis, an editorial in *America* said, "The letter explicitly aims at 'pastoral care' for homosexuals, but it is doubtful they will feel especially cared for."[9]

In 1990, the United States bishops again reiterated that "homosexual activity, as distinguished from homosexual orientation, is wrong." They added that homosexual orientation "in itself, because not freely chosen, is not sinful" (Steinfels 1990d).

Gregory Baum offered this advice to homosexuals: "If it is true that some people are constitutively homosexual and that homosexual relations allow for mutuality, then, from the viewpoint of Christian theology, it is the task of homosexuals to acknowledge themselves as such before God, accept their sexual orientation as their calling, and explore the meaning of this inclination for the Christian life" (1974a). Baum does not say explicitly whether homosexual behavior between homosexual persons who were growing in friendship and covenant faithfulness was morally justifiable. Philip Keane took another perspective. He said homosexual acts always involve a significant degree of premoral evil since they are not open to procreation. Yet they are not necessarily an objective moral evil (1977, 87). For other commentators, both the homosexual orientation and overt acts are not in themselves good for people and therefore generally right, but they are not necessarily immoral in all cases, especially if the persons are in a stable, loving relationship. For example, Curran offered a "theology of compromise": "One may reluctantly accept homosexual unions as the only way in which some people can find a satisfying degree of humanity in their lives" (1972, 217).

Some view homosexuality as a variation within the human condition and not something contrary to nature. As such, it is a fully normal alternative to heterosexuality. They support sexual expression by gay persons that is humane and humanizing, that is, "loving, life-giving and life-affirming." For over twenty years "Homosexual marriages" have been reported in the media.[10] Those involved insist that their domestic partnerships are the equivalent of traditional marriages.

In a 1976 book *The Church and the Homosexual*, John McNeill argued that homosexuality is part of God's plan for the world. Homosexual orientation in itself is a precondition of the affirmation of the homosexual Christian in his or her characteristic sexual lifestyle. For McNeill, gay love is morally good, even holy, when it is mutual, faithful, and unselfish, and so he objected to Curran's theology of compromise because for him the proposition that homosexual acts are permissible as the least offensive among objectively "evil" alternatives is demeaning. McNeill asked his readers to reconsider the condition of those homosexually-oriented individuals who regard themselves as Christians. These persons, he wrote, say they can express a relationship of shared love, fidelity, and responsibility. Together they can fulfill their identities as Christians-in-community and as persons-in-the-world, summoned to relate themselves in justice and love to all reality. John Giles Milhaven reviewed the book and asked the key question: "And how does one step from 'healthy and loving' to 'morally good' (1976, 12)? When John McNeill wrote his book he was a Jesuit priest and an avowed celibate homosexual. Without due process,[11] he was given an ultimatum to keep silent on the question of the morality of homosexual activity or face dismissal from his community. In 1986, right after the publication of the CDF document "On the Pastoral Care of Homosexuals" and after thirty-eight years as a Jesuit, he withdrew from the Jesuits because he could no longer keep silent about the church's ministry to gays and lesbians (McNeill 1986).

Presently, no church has a satisfying answer to the homosexuality question. This issue, McNeill wrote in 1987, challenges the church to grow. Meanwhile, many carry "in their guts the acid of guilt and shame and rejection" (Milhaven 1976). In the early 1970s, a group of Catholic homosexual men and women formed an association in Los Angeles to give witness to the church that it is possible to be both Catholic and gay. McNeill was a charter member. They call themselves Dignity and held their first national meeting in Los Angeles on a weekend in September 1973. Their national headquarters are presently in Boston. By 1992 they had one hundred chapters throughout the United States and over four thousand members. In response to the CDF document of 1986, a number of United States bishops instructed the priests of their dioceses to withdraw support for Dignity and not to allow them to meet on church property. These actions only further alienated and hurt a community already alienated and hurt (Opstrny 1988; McClory 1988a).

The gay and lesbian community in general and Dignity in particular were again deeply hurt when the CDF issued an twenty-five hundred-word statement on June 25, 1992, "Some Considerations Concerning the Catholic Response to Legislative Proposals on the Non-discrimination of Homosexual Persons." This document, "written in the United States by consultants to the CDF" (Vidulich 1992b), was offered as guidance for bishops in states considering gay-rights legislation (Steinfels 1992a; Vidulich 1992a). It contradicted its previous teaching that homosexual people have the same human and civil rights as all citizens. Ultimately, the document was against those domestic partnership laws that would assure housing, health benefits, and other protections for homosexuals. In short, the document was clearly opposed to the view that homosexuality is a fully normal alternative to heterosexuality and the traditional marriage.

After repeating the 1986 description of homosexuality as "an objective disorder," the 1992 statement declared that gays and lesbians do not have the same rights to civil liberties that heterosexuals have and it urged the bishops to oppose civil-rights legislation for gays. Since a homosexual orientation "does not constitute a quality comparable to race" or ethnic background, there are "areas in which it is not unjust discrimination to take sexual orientation into account." Teaching, coaching, and military service are among the areas cited. The document also says that, while homosexuals have the same basic rights as anyone else, those rights "are not absolute" and they can be "legitimately limited for objectively disordered external conduct." This distinction is compared to the state's authority to restrict the exercise of rights "in the case of contagious or mentally ill persons, in order to protect the common good."

This document was judged by many to be not only pastorally insensitive but also uncatholic because there is nothing in the church's moral tradition that promotes the prevention of gay and lesbian persons from participating in the social and economic life of society (Tuohey 1992). It will be interesting to see how the bishops handle the document because even before its publication a number of bishops, apparently believing that legislation to protect gay civil rights does not undermine family values, had taken steps to see that homosexuals do not suffer unjust discrimination in law and in life.

Conclusion

The popes and bishops of the twentieth century consistently opposed dehumanizing and unchristian views of human sexuality by fostering the virtues of chastity and fidelity, the holiness of marriage, responsible parenthood, the sacredness of human life, and the profundity of conjugal friendship and love. Consistent, too, has been the hierarchical teachings on the six topics of sexual morality reviewed here.

Most preconciliar Catholics agreed with the Christian principles proclaimed by the hierarchy, and, in general, followed their specific directives. Although there were many instances of divorce, masturbation, premarital and extramarital sex, etc., Catholics were renowned for their strict moral standards. Today, and particularly since the so-called sexual revolution in the 1960s, many Catholics—priests, theologians, single, and married persons—openly disagree with the official teachings about sexual morality. There is evidence that the number of Catholics involved in divorces, abortions, premarital sex, etc., is not much different from the rest of society. This striking reversal of "strict moral standards" has forced some to question just how well grounded preconciliar Catholic sexual morality was. For example, in a 1972 essay on the sexual revolution, the historian James Hitchcock argued that "emphasis on sexual purity was always, in a sense, a confession of failure on the part of Catholic educators, since they found it difficult to imbue their students with real piety and settled instead for morality. It was a morality that secular American culture also honored in theory, and hence it did not seriously estrange the young Catholic from society. He was distinguished, and heroic, for behaving in the way that other Americans secretly thought that they should behave in, too."

One of the themes of this book is that "real piety" must be grounded in a sacramental consciousness in imitation of Christ. But most Catholics would agree that our sexual morality is not sufficiently shaped by faith in Jesus as God's *incarnate* self-gift. This failure can be illustrated by the way the sexuality of Jesus is often perceived.

In his elegant 1984 book *The Sexuality of Christ in Renaissance Art and in Modern Oblivion,* Leo Steinberg, a distinguished art historian, demonstrated that the early church focused on the divinity of Jesus and skirted the full reality of his bodiliness. The Renaissance artists, on the other hand, purposely exposed Jesus' genitals. Their art was "the first Christian art in a thousand years to confront the incarnation entire . . . not excluding even the body's sexual component." By this standard, the Renaissance also produced, said Steinberg, "the last phase of Christian art that can claim full Christian orthodoxy." Steinberg admitted he did not know precisely when or why post-Renaissance Christians decided that nudity and genital disclosure were shocking. His ultimate answer is theological: sometime after the Renaissance, the Christian West lost the "mythic roots" from which incarnational art drew its compelling power. Kenneth Woodward explained: "The living Christ disappeared, transformed into a tableau of tidy, rational propositions. Once that happened, the body of Christ no longer disclosed the meaning of his spirit because the faithful no longer had eyes to see" (Woodward and Moorman 1984).

There is some evidence that many Christians are now beginning to realize that sexuality and spirituality are part and parcel of each other, and that Christ, the Word incarnate, continues to become flesh and dwell among us. James Nelson reflected on the sexual revolution and wrote in 1987, "The sexual revolution helped convince many Christians that an incarnationalist faith embraces the redemption of alienated sexuality as well as other estranged dimensions of our lives. *Justification by grace* signifies God's unconditional, unmerited, radical acceptance of the whole person: God, the Cosmic Lover, graciously embraces not just a person's disembodied spirit but the whole fleshly self—the meanings of which theology is only beginning to explore" (Nelson 1987, 189).

The whole church—and particularly parents, the hierarchy, priests, theologians, and educators—has three interrelated areas to explore: the Christian understanding of what it means to be human and chaste, the official church's teachings, and the Catholic sacramental consciousness grounded in Jesus, God's incarnate self-gift.

11

The Church and Mary

Devotion to Mary the mother of Jesus has been a hallmark of the Catholic tradition. Over the centuries, millions of women and hundreds of churches, schools, and hospitals have been named for her. Theologians and popes have extolled her virtues, and the faithful, saints, and religious orders have often had a tenacious devotion to her. Vatican II opened and closed on one of her feast days. In the postconciliar church her importance is such that Raymond Brown has suggested that the theology of Mary (mariology) "is almost a bellwether indicating theological directions in the Roman Catholic Church" (1985, 86).

What Brown suggests is true. Moreover, his use of the symbol *bellwether* implies that this chapter should begin rather than conclude this book. However, it is easier to place it last since it contains references to all the topics covered in this book: sacramental consciousness, the identity and mission of the church, tradition, historical consciousness, Vatican II, ecumenism, liturgy, spirituality, social justice, inculturation, sexual morality, and feminist issues.

Mary of History

Mary the mother of Jesus is probably the most influential woman in the history of the world. Yet, we know so little of her history and personality. As a member of the supporting cast in the Gospels, Mary's appearances are few. It is actually more difficult to discern the Mary of history than the Jesus of history. No information is offered, for example, about her parents or where and when she was born. She married Joseph, a craftsman, and gave birth to a son, Jesus. We do not know how much she really knew about her son's uniqueness. That she had other children is a debatable issue and one that cannot be decided by trying to balance all the New Testament texts. For example, Matt. 1:18 is rather clear about the virginal conception of Jesus, but Matt. 13:56–57 refers to Jesus' sisters and four brothers, actually naming the brothers. We know little of Mary's relatives. Luke relates her to Elizabeth, the mother of John the Baptist. However, the Baptist said he did not know Jesus until he baptized him (John 1:31–33).

Mary appears only once during Jesus' public ministry in the first three Gospels. Mark never mentions Joseph. Was this because he was dead by the time Jesus began to teach in the towns and cities? John's Gospel places Mary at a wedding in Cana and at the cross when Jesus died. She is next mentioned praying with the community at Pentecost. There is not a single detail about Mary after Pentecost. We know nothing of her role in the community or of any personal contacts with such important disciples as Peter and Paul. Mary is never mentioned in Paul's epistles. Finally, there is no mention of when or where she died.

Mary in the Scriptures

The Scriptures are not concerned with the Mary of history, but with mariology, the theology about Mary, a particular historical individual who has a definite, even unique, place in salvation history.

In 1979 a group of twelve Lutheran and Catholic Scripture scholars issued a study titled *Mary in the New Testament* (Brown, Donfried, Fitzmyer, and Reumann). This book is a major accomplishment that has helped place ecumenical dialogues about mariology on a sound footing. In it, rigorous exegesis is applied to all the passages in the New Testament (and some other early Christian literature) where Mary is mentioned.

The earliest New Testament writings, the letters of Paul, mention that God sent his Son, "born of a woman, born under the law" (Gal. 4:4). The text is not a reflection on the mother of Jesus but, rather, on Jesus himself, a person truly human, truly Jewish, and truly the savior of all.

The only references to Mary by name in the New Testament are in the four Gospels, plus one reference in Acts 1:14, the Pentecost story. Since we know so little of the Mary of history, what can we expect to learn about her by studying the Gospels? Catholic and Protestant scholars agree that "Mary appears consistently as a symbolic character, and that therefore symbolism, not history, is the key to mariology" (Rausch 1982).

Turning to the Gospels, we start with Mark, the earliest. The mother of Jesus appears in only one scene (3:31–35), in which Mark presents Mary in a poor light. He contrasts the natural family of Jesus who do not understand him with the family of disciples who do. Mary seems to be an outsider. A comparison of the words and the intrinsic staging of the same scene in Matt. 12:46–50 and Luke 8:19–21 indicates, say the Lutheran and Catholic scholars, that Mark's Gospel offers a "negative portrait" of Mary. This judgment is reinforced by the one other allusion to Mary in Mark. When Jesus returns to Nazareth to preach in the synagogue (6:1–6), the local people take offense and Jesus says, "A prophet is not without honor except in his native place and among his own kin and in his own house." In the parallel scenes, Matt. 13:57–58 omits the phrase "among his own kin" and Luke 4:24 omits both phrases after the words "native place".

Compared with Mark, Matthew and Luke present Mary in a more favorable light. Why? Their theology of salvation history is more advanced. Both Matthew and Luke have infancy narratives. Although both these narratives differ quite a bit in details, each does say that Mary's child was conceived through the power of God. This fact made it impossible for them to portray Mary without an understanding of and honor for her son. Actually, Luke pictures Mary more positively than Matthew. In Matthew, Joseph is the main figure in the infancy narrative. In Luke, Mary is constantly center stage: the angel announces her child will be the Son of David and the Son of God; Mary visits Elizabeth and proclaims her famous prayer, the Magnificat; Mary presents the child in the temple where she encounters Simeon and Anna; and it is Mary who questions the twelve-year-old boy Jesus in the temple.

In Luke's Gospel, Mary is presented as the first Christian and a model Christian. She accepts God's word with her *fiat*, which means "let it be to me." She proclaims that when God regarded her, a slave woman,[1] he was showing his continued mercy to Israel, and also his dethronement of the proud and mighty. During Jesus' ministry, Mary is praised by Jesus for hearing and doing God's word. After the resurrection, she waits with the community for the Spirit at Pentecost. In Luke, says Raymond Brown, Mary "serves as the most consistent disciple in the whole gospel narrative" (1985, 94).

John's Gospel does not add much to Luke's ideal picture of Mary as a model disciple. John never refers to her by name, only by title. The "mother of Jesus" appears in two scenes: Cana and Calvary. In the former she gives priority to what Jesus wills and in the latter she not only becomes the mother of the beloved disciple but with him witnesses her son's obedience to his Father's will on the cross (Grassi 1986). In John's Gospel, Jesus leaves behind a community of disciples that includes his mother and the beloved disciple.

Mary and Feminism

Our society is presently undergoing a major change "in the self-perception and self-definition of women, and consequently in the understanding of women's nature, capabilities, role, status and relationship to men and male-created structures" (Johnson 1985, 116–17). Women have been denied their full humanity in society and church because men alone have been considered the norm of authentic humanity. The image of Mary, too, has been limited by the androcentric presuppositions of society. She has been presented as a passively obedient handmaid, a woman of unparalleled holiness and purity, a submissive and subjugated sorrowful mother, and the male projection of idealized feminity both as an asexual virgin and as a domestically all-absorbed mother in a patriarchal family.

Feminists (both women and men) reject the sexist dimensions of these perspectives, claiming that not only are they based on androcentric presuppositions but also that they have contributed to the perpetuation of patriarchal power. They seek to retrieve the Mary of history as a genuine woman. They acknowledge that Mary's actual life and culture are hidden in historical shadows and are quite removed from our own. Nevertheless, as Elizabeth Johnson explains, "The very paucity of the historical record regarding her is a point of identification with all women, whose history has been largely hidden and unremarked" (ibid., 130). Furthermore, some feminists regard Mary's life as a journey of faith marked by poverty, suffering, and authenticity. Her *fiat* was the radical autonomous decision of a young woman willing "to risk her life on a messianic venture" (ibid., 126) and her Magnificat a prayer to a God of peace and justice.

Marian Dogmas

There are four Marian doctrines: immaculate conception, virginal conception, mother of God, and assumption.

Pius IX, after consulting all the bishops of the world, issued *Ineffabilis Deus* on December 8, 1854, declaring the immaculate conception a doctrine revealed by God, and, therefore, to be firmly and constantly held by all the faithful. The decree said, "We declare, pronounce and define: the doctrine that maintains that the most Blessed Virgin Mary in the first instant of her conception, by a unique grace and privilege of the omnipotent God and in consideration of the merits of Christ Jesus the Savior of the human race, was preserved free from all stain of original sin."

This teaching has an uneven history in the church. It is not found explicitly in the scriptures. This is partly the reason it was denied by Thomas Aquinas (1225–74), who believed it was contrary to the universality of Christ's redemptive work. But many others affirmed it. For example, John Duns Scotus (1266–1308) was the first major theologian to defend the belief; in 1476 the Immaculate Conception was made a feast day by Pope Sixtus IV; and in 1846, at the sixth provincial Council of Baltimore, the United States bishops proclaimed Mary the patroness of this country under this title.

What prompted Pius IX to proclaim this dogma? It seems he had a double motive: to crown his own lifelong and sincere Marian piety and to counteract the Enlightenment. The rationalists emphasized the goodness of human nature and the ability of humans to arrive at truth, progress, and success through human effort and universal consensus. The immaculate conception reminded the world that, since original sin wounds everyone's intellect, will and affections, all people are sinners and need a divine savior (Hennesey 1989, 670–71).

This doctrine, difficult as it is, has significance for Christian spirituality. While it first seems to set Mary apart from the rest of the human race, its true meaning is quite different, as Karl Rahner explained: "God did not will the difference between [Mary and] us principally because he loved us less, and therefore did not give us the gift of grace, which is himself, from the beginning, but rather so that through this difference, the full range of the significance of grace might find clear expression. . . . We who first come into existence graceless in soul, proclaim the truth that we are not the beloved children of God by our own powers" (1963, 49–50).

The virginal conception specifies that Mary conceived Jesus without a human father. The conception of Jesus was miraculous, and is attested independently by both Matthew (1:18) and Luke (1:34). Virginal conception differs from virgin birth. The latter (a second century thought) declared that Mary gave birth to Jesus in a miraculous way that preserved the integrity of her bodily organs.

The doctrine of the virginal conception of Jesus has never been given a solemn and extraordinary definition like the other three Marian teachings. Although the virginity of Mary is stated in the early creeds, these phrases are interpreted as statements "about Jesus' human reality without intending to define the historicity of the virginal conception as part of the teaching" (Tambasco 1984, 19). Nevertheless, the virginal conception is considered infallible because it has been the constant, ordinary teaching of the Catholic Church.

This doctrine, while not an "open question" for Catholics, has, nevertheless, become very problematic in the modern church for several reasons. First, the infancy narratives seem highly symbolic. Some maintain that Matthew and Luke intended to make christological statements by proclaiming that God had intervened in history with a new creation. Furthermore, it is presumed that the evangelists took over the concept of the virginal conception from their sources and simply presumed it was true. Second, this extraordinary event is not mentioned elsewhere in the New Testament. Third, there is no evidence that it was held from the beginning as a universal teaching in all the New Testament churches. Fourth, the two infancy narratives disagree on some points and contain some inaccuracies (e.g., the Roman census during the reign of Herod the Great).

The historicity of the virginal conception came into postconciliar discussion through the publication of the New Dutch Catechism in 1966. This textbook, published in 1967 in the United States as *A New Catechism*, avoided the doctrine in its traditional meaning. It stated that Jesus is "God's gift" and "the son of promise, like none other." Some Dutch Catholics complained to Rome that "the book does not affirm [Mary's] biological virginity prior and subsequent to the birth of Jesus. Its use of ambiguous expressions seems to deny her virginity."

The Vatican wrote on October 15, 1968, that "it must be openly professed in the Catechism that the holy mother of the incarnate Word remained always adorned with the honor of virginity. It must teach equally clearly the doctrine of the virginal birth of Jesus, which is so supremely in accord with the mystery of the incarnation."

The Vatican directives to the authors of the Dutch Catechism did not faze Hans Küng, who unequivocally asserted in 1976 that "the virgin birth cannot be understood as a historical-biological event," but should be interpreted as "a meaningful symbol at least for that time." As a symbol, the virginal conception signaled a new beginning for the human race brought about by God in Christ. According to Küng, there are several other ways in which this new beginning was given expression in the New Testament. For example, the geneology in Luke's Gospel that traces Jesus all the way back through Adam to God. Küng believes this new beginning by God can still be proclaimed today, but "without the aid of the legend of a virgin birth" (1976, 456–57).

Between the evasive interpretation of the Dutch Catechism and the outright denial of its historicity by Küng stands the interpretation of Raymond Brown—one in keeping with the Catholic tradition. In his research (and that of others, for example, Fitzmyer [1973]), Brown found that the story of Jesus' conception is in a form for which there are no exact parallels or antecedents in the material available to the Christians of the first century. For example, in non-Jewish literature there are stories of women giving birth to deities, but none of them are like the nonsexual virginal conception found in Matthew and Luke. In the non-Jewish literature the deity either has normal sexual intercourse or there is some other form of penetration. In the New Testament there is no male deity or element to impregnate Mary. Similarly, in Jewish literature miraculous births such as that of Isaac are the result of God's blessing on the normal intercourse of a man and a woman. Brown's conclusion: "No search for parallels has given us a truly satisfactory explanation of how early Christians happened upon the idea of a virginal conception—unless, of course, that is what really took place" (Brown 1972; see also Brown 1986a, 1986b).

The theology of Mary as mother of God received special debate in the fifth century. Bishop Nestorius (428–431), a theologian of the Antioch school, posited a double personality in Christ, one human and one divine. Cyril of Alexandria (412–444) opposed this teaching at the ecumenical Council of Ephesus in 431. Ephesus taught that since Jesus, the God-man, was one divine person, then his mother could rightly be called the mother of God. The Greek term used was *theotokos*, which literally means "she who gives birth to God." The bishops used this term to honor Mary. More importantly, they wanted to guard the belief that the Word of God took flesh from Mary and became fully man also.

Mary's title Mother of God holds a preeminent place in all the churches of the East. In the West, Mary is honored with this title in the liturgical calendar on January 1. Pius XI commemorated the fifteen hundredth anniversary of the Council of Ephesus in 1931.

Hans Küng found this title problematic for several reasons, four of which are listed here. First, the title of Mother of God has no biblical basis. In the Scriptures, Mary is called the mother of Jesus. Second, Cyril of Alexandria manipulated the bishops at Ephesus to accept "his definition of 'God-bearer' before the arrival of the other, Antiochene party at the council." Third, as Mother of God, Mary was a replacement by the Ephesians, albeit an enthusiastic replacement, for their ancient "Great Mother," who was originally the virgin goddess Artemis or Diana. Finally, the title Mother of God "might imply a Monophysite conception of divine sonship and incarnation, hypostasizing God (as if God could be born and not a man in whom as God's *son* God himself is *evident* to faith)" (Küng 1976, 459–60). Monophysites divide the humanity of Jesus from his divinity.

On November 1, 1950, and after extensive consultation with the church, Pius XII defined the assumption of Mary into heaven a dogma of faith. This doctrine had been celebrated liturgically by the beginning of the sixth century. It has no biblical or patristic warrant, but it is the conclusion of an argument from fittingess, that is, it was "fitting" that the body-person that conceived Jesus should be "preserved from the corruption of the tomb."

Pius said, "We do pronounce, declare and define as a divinely revealed dogma: The Immaculate Mother of God, Mary ever Virgin, after her life on earth, was assumed, body and soul, to the glory of heaven." Nothing was said about the manner or time of Mary's assumption, and it is not clear whether the pope intended to teach that Mary died at all.

Robert Kress offered two reflections on the meaning of this doctrine. First, this teaching "reminds us that God's original plan to give us the gifts of life and being has not been undone by sin and the obscurity of life and death caused by sin." Second, this is a feast especially for women. The sexist society in which Mary lived designated a low status to women. "In the kingdom of God there is no sexist subordination of women" (1977, 71–74). Others welcomed the doctrine as a positive response to World War II when millions of body-persons were mutilated, gassed, or destroyed by chemicals, guns, and bombs, including nuclear bombs. The assumption of Mary affirmed the dignity of the human body and rekindled faith in the resurrection of the body.

Marian Titles

In addition to the four just discussed, Mary has hundreds of titles. Some have been linked together in litanies. Often the titles are culturally and socially conditioned. For example, Mary, a poor, Jewish, Palestinian mother and wife became "Our Lady" in feudal times, "Queen of Heaven" in the age of monarchies, and "Mother of the Liberator" in liberation theology.

Some of the titles involve complicated theological and ecumenical matters. Two that became very controversial in the twentieth-century church are coredemptrix, meaning Mary merited our salvation, and mediatrix, meaning Mary obtains grace for sinners. These titles go back to the medieval period when Mary was given divine prerogatives as a result of the parallels in grace, virtue, and dignity that were drawn between her and her son, Jesus Christ (Johnson 1989).

Apparitions of Mary

Hundreds of apparitions of Mary have been reported. Three that have had significant influence on the twentieth-century church and popes are those at Guadalupe (1531), Lourdes (1858) and Fatima (1917).

Spanish explorers and missionaries arrived in Mexico around 1500. In their ethnocentricism, they systematically enslaved the Aztec Indians and tried to root out their language, religion, and culture. On Saturday morning, December 9, 1531, an Aztec peasant named Juan Diego (an imposed Spanish name) was on his way to church. On the hill of Tepeyac, just outside of Mexico City, Mary appeared to him for the first of four times. Tepeyac was the site of an ancient temple dedicated to Tonantzin, Aztec virgin mother of the deities.

Mary appeared as a short, swarthy Aztec woman, apparently pregnant. She identified herself in the Aztec language: "Know and understand that I am the ever-virgin Holy Mary, mother of the true God, from whom one lives; the Creator, the Lord of Near and Togetherness, the Lord of Heaven and Earth." Later it was to Juan Diego's uncle that she told the name Our Lady of Guadalupe.

Juan Diego was commissioned to deliver a message to the bishop: "I ardently desire that a shrine may be built on this site, so that in it I can give all my love, compassion, help and protection; for I am your most holy mother, ready to hear all your laments and to alleviate all your miseries, pains and sufferings."

As a sign of her authenticity, her picture was imprinted on Juan Diego's tunic. This garment was woven from cactus, material which normally would disintegrate in about twenty years. This relic hangs today in the cathedral built at Guadalupe in 1533. The picture has been studied by scientists using the latest technology. They have discovered in it some intricate symbols, many not visible to the naked eye.

The apparitions at Guadalupe have bearing on inculturation and liberation theology. Mary appeared as an Aztec woman. She did not come as someone foreign, nor as one identified with the dominating, albeit Catholic, Spanish culture. "She came as one of their women, clothed as they would be clothed, adorned not only with the cross of her Son but also with the symbols sacred to their nation and culture. She came to a place sacred to their goddess, a goddess of fertility . . . inviting all the symbolism that surrounded that goddess to . . . find its place within a true, enriched understanding and experience of Mary and of her Son" (Pennington 1975, 68).

In representing the righteous poor, Mary gave millions of Indians their dignity. Mary's desire to give "love, compassion, help and protection" was not the image of God conveyed by the Spaniards. Their God, while he could inspire courage, was also a judge who punished sinners with eternal hell. He showed little compassion and understanding.

John Paul II visited Mexico in 1979 and in 1990, his first and forty-eighth overseas trips as pope. In 1990 he affirmed liberation theology by beatifying Juan Diego (Hebblethwaite 1990b) and by making such points as the following: "We cannot live and sleep tranquilly while millions of our brothers, very close to us, lack that which is most indispensable to conduct a worthy human life" (Haberman 1990a). On May 12, 1992, John Paul opened a chapel in honor of Our Lady of Guadalupe in the Vatican grottoes. He said the chapel witnesses not only the "Marian vocation" of the Mexican people, "but also [their] historical roots and the unifying strength of [their] culture which enriches the entire church."

Between February 11 and July 16, 1858, Mary appeared some eighteen times to a girl of fourteen named Bernadette Soubirous (1844–79), at Lourdes, a town in southwestern France. Bernadette was a shy girl, naturally laconic but not neurotically introverted. She joined the Sisters of Charity at Nevers at the age of twenty-two and died at the age of thirty-five, after enduring years of pain from tuberculosis of the bone. She was canonized by Pius XI in 1933.

Mary appeared to Bernadette as a beautiful French woman. She announced that she was the Immaculate Conception and asked that a chapel be built where a miraculous stream had appeared. Since that time, millions of pilgrims have gone to Lourdes annually. Countless miracles, both physical and spiritual healings, have taken place there.

During the pontificate of Benedict XV in a period from May until October 1917, Mary appeared six times on the thirteenth of each month to three Portugese children in their village, Fatima. The children's names were Lucia Santos and Francisco and Jacinta Marto.

In her conversations with the children, Mary declared that her immaculate heart would triumph. She asked that the faithful recite the rosary, wear the scapular of Mount Carmel, and make daily sacrifices in reparation for sins that offended her immaculate heart. She also showed the children a terrifying vision of hell.

On July 13, Mary revealed three secrets to the children. The first was that two of the children would die young. The Marto children, brother and sister, died during a flu epidemic in 1919 and 1920, respectively. Lucia went on to become a Carmelite nun and, in 1991, at the age of eighty-four, joined John Paul II in venerating Mary at Fatima. The second secret concerned Russia. Mary predicted that this country would spread errors throughout the world but would eventually be converted and an era of peace would follow. The Russian Revolution did occur on November 7, 1917. Many viewed this event as a confirmation of Mary's prediction of imminent catastrophe for the world. The third secret has never been revealed. By all reports it was delivered to the pope. It has been the subject of endless speculation centered around some dreadful cataclysm. Cardinal Joseph Ratzinger said the secret has not been made public in order "to avoid confusing religious prophecy and sensationalism" (Riding 1991).

On October 13, 1917, the sixth and last appearance, a miracle of great magnitude occurred, one witnessed by over 700,000 people. It is reported that the unrelenting rain that had greeted the crowd suddenly ceased. The sun came out, began to "dance in the sky" and plunged toward earth. The terrified pilgrims began crying out to God for mercy and the sun retreated to its place in the sky. All the rain-soaked pilgrims were suddenly comfortably dry.

These three apparitions, while officially approved by the church, remain within the realm of private revelation and are valid only to the extent that they repeat public revelation. Since they do not rank as sources of faith, Catholics are not obliged to believe them. Church approval does not guarantee their historical truth or authenticity. What the institutional church reports is that it has sufficient evidence, especially the miracles, to allow veneration of Mary at these sites. Also, the shrines are a sign of the nearness of the triune God who always invites everyone to a personal relationship.

Many people question the validity of the apparitions. Some indicate that there is often a curious resemblance of many details in the visions to prior experiences of those involved. For example, Bernadette was naturally laconic and her vision of Mary was not talkative either. Also, the doctrine of the immaculate conception had been infallibly defined four years before. Bernadette said she had never heard the term. Some suggest she heard it at school or in church or at home. Another objection to the validity of the apparitions is that the mariology involved is often what many Catholics reject and Protestants scorn. For example, Mary is too condemnatory and threatening in these images. The Fatima children were shown a terrifying vision of hell and Mary's account of the number of damned souls is apocalyptic.

On the other hand, it is not easy to dismiss the impressive portrait of Mary imprinted on Juan Diego's cloak, the miraculous spring at Lourdes, and the powerful development of communist Russia after Fatima. Catholics continue to flock to these Marian centers. For example, in 1992 Lourdes "had a record 5.5 million visitors—1.5 million more than in 1993" (Simons 1993).

Finally, the apparitions at Medjugorje (fifty miles south of Sarajevo in what was Yugoslavia) deserve a brief mention, especially since between 1981 and 1991 some seventeen million pilgrims had visited the site. On June 24, 1981, six children, ranging in age from ten to sixteen, claimed that Mary appeared to them to urge worldwide conversion. Mary asked for more involvement in prayer, fasting, confession, and the Eucharist. She told the children that these apparitions would be her last appearances in our time and she warned of worldwide cataclysms. Some of the visionaries claimed to have had visions for years, for some as late as 1988.

True to its policy of caution in these matters, the official church often takes a wait-and-see attitude. In March 1984, the local bishop called the apparitions fraudulent and accused the alleged visionaries and the Franciscan priests who support them of lies, manipulation, and "fabricated miracles." In January 1991, the bishops' conference of Yugoslavia approved by vote of nineteen to one a statement declaring that on the basis of research, "one cannot affirm that supernatural apparitions are involved" at Medjugorje.

Mary and Protestant Christians

Martin Luther and Ulrich Zwingli (1484–1531) regularly observed and preached on the Marian feasts. Both accepted Mary's virginal conception and perpetual virginity as well as her immaculate conception and total sinlessness. "Mary was upheld as a paramount model of faith and humility and thus a chief example of Christian piety" (Elliot 1982, 227).

If this is true, why do few Protestants have a devotion to Mary? Why is Mary an ecumenical liability? Several reasons are given. First, John H. Elliott, Lutheran biblical scholar, explains that in the seventeenth century when the two churches became more entrenched in their theologies and disciplines, Mary "became a pawn in a deadly game of ecclesiastical polemics and apologetics." Whereas for Catholics, devotion to Mary became a mark of orthodoxy and fidelity to Rome, for the Reformation churches Mary's role was deemphasized and devotion neglected. In the eighteenth and nineteenth centuries when pietism arose "in reaction to the sterile intellectualism of the Counter-Reformation and Lutheran orthodoxy," Catholics stressed the loving and motherly care of Mary, and Lutherans sought the same qualities in Jesus and invested him "with feminine qualities of compassion, tenderness and care" (ibid., 228).

Second, Protestants found that Mary had been so elevated to a semidivine status that either she was given titles that parallel those given to Christ or she functioned like the Spirit.

Third, some of the Marian doctrines have a scriptural base and others do not. Protestants who accept Jesus' divinity call Mary the mother of God. The virginal conception is generally accepted because it is scriptural. But even here there are differences. Karl Barth defended this teaching for the sake of Jesus' divinity. For him, just as the spirit of God moved over the waters at creation (Gen. 1:1–2), so the Spirit overshadowed Mary to place within her God's own Son. Human initiative, particularly that of the male, is excluded. Paul Tillich, on the other hand, denied the virginal conception in order to preserve the humanity of Jesus.

The two doctrines that most Protestants say are not sufficiently supported by scripture are the immaculate conception and the assumption. John McHugh, an English Catholic professor, wrote a book in 1975 to show that these doctrines "are either plainly expressed or necessarily implied in Holy Scripture."

Raymond Brown gave this book a negative review, pointing out that "McHugh's solution is both unnecessary and impossible." Why? "There is only one source of our knowledge of Christian revelation, namely, the divinely guided reflection of the Christian community on the mystery of Jesus, a reflection that is articulated in church tradition of all ages—and the New Testament is the tradition of only the first-century church. All dogma must be expressed or implied in the revelation that is Jesus Christ, but not necessarily in the New Testament, which is a witness to the first-century understanding of Jesus Christ" (R. E. Brown 1975b, 260–63).

By 1979 Lutheran and Catholic Scripture scholars had reached a new plateau in their appreciation of the Scriptures and how they contributed to Marian doctrines. We have already seen that in their book *Mary in the New Testament*, the scholars found a definite line of development in mariology in the New Testament. Mark's rather ambiguous portrait of Mary as one who did not understand her son was followed by Matthew's assertion of the virginal conception, by Luke's portrayal of Mary as the first Christian disciple, and by John's depiction of her symbolic role in Jesus' new community as the mother of the beloved disciple.

It is precisely Mary's discipleship that is acknowledged as the key to later developments in Marian doctrine and devotion. While it is true that the immaculate conception and assumption are not explicitly in the Scriptures, as doctrines they are fitting because they are in line with the New Testament development of mariology. Disciples are freed from sin through the grace of Christ. Mary, as the first disciple, was given this grace at conception. Furthermore, disciples are called to God's eternal life as body-persons. What awaits all disciples already happened to Mary.

If Protestants accepted the immaculate conception and assumption as teachings in line with the total scriptural witness to Mary, then Mary would cease being an ecumenical liability. She could even become an asset to Protestant spirituality because they would recognize that "veneration of Mary is deeply rooted in the Christian tradition and is a practice of piety with great spiritual potential" (Bokenkotter 1985, 140).

Marian Devotion in the Eighteenth and Nineteenth Centuries

In the first half of the eighteenth century there was intense devotion to Mary as mediatrix and coredemptrix in such writings as *True Devotion to the Blessed Virgin* by Louis-Marie

Grignion de Montfort (1673–1716) and *The Glories of Mary* by Alphonsus Maria Liguori (1696–1787), the Italian Redemptorist. De Montfort went so far as to say that the devil feared Mary more than God himself.

In the second half of the eighteenth century, under the impact of the rationalism of the Enlightenment, devotion to Mary appeared to be a medieval relic and greatly declined.

In the nineteenth century, rationalism was succeeded by romanticism. This movement was spurred on in part by the libertarian and egalitarian ideals of the French Revolution. The romantics stressed, among other things, a return to nature, the innate goodness of people, the exaltation of the senses and emotions, and a keen interest in the medieval period. In harmony with this mood, devotion to Mary took on a new life, especially as it was reenforced by a series of remarkable apparitions in France. There were apparitions in Paris to Catherine Labouré (1830), at La Salette to two young illiterate children (1846), at Lourdes to Bernadette Soubirous (1858).

The attacks on Christianity by atheists, socialists, and positivists were certainly deflected by these unusual interventions of the sacred into human history. Pius IX contributed immensely to the church's triumphalism by defining the doctrine of the immaculate conception in 1854.

The Preconciliar Popes and Marian Devotion

Leo XIII wrote sixty encyclicals during his long pontificate of twenty-five years. Eleven of these were on devotion to Mary and the rosary. Leo emphasized her roles as mediatrix and coredemptrix. The same themes are found in the encyclicals of Pius X, Benedict XV, and Pius XI.

Compared to his four predecessors, Pius XII's devotion to Mary was intense, even though he tempered the titles of mediatrix and coredemptrix. Pius "was obsessed with Fatima" (Hebblethwaite 1984b). The first appearance at Fatima, on May 13, 1917, was also the day Pius was installed as an archbishop. He subsequently consecrated the world to the Immaculate Heart of Mary in 1944 and again in 1954. Also, Mary's prediction about the rise of communist Russia associated Fatima with anti-communism, a comfort to Pius's own virulent anti-communism.

Pius XII defined the assumption in 1950. In 1954, he instituted a special year of devotion to Mary, the one hundreth anniversary of the declaration of the immaculate conception. This was the first time in the history of the church that such a year of devotion had been instituted. On October 11 of that year he also instituted the feast of the Queenship of Mary. The announcement was greeted with some ambiguity. Some regarded it as an instance of triumphalism because the church found itself "politically beleaguered, in danger of losing its power on earth" (Gordon 1982). Others were more favorable. For them it was fitting to imagine "choirs of angels and the mother of God enthroned, not above her children, but in the midst of them, their voices raised in a harmony impossible to them in their life on earth" (ibid.).

The preconciliar mariology had its negative and positive sides. On the negative side, Mary was given a semidivine status. The devil feared her more than God, as DeMontfort remarked. She was mediatrix, coredemptrix, queen of heaven and earth, "uncorrupted by childbearing, sin or death." She became a model of Christ. This theology—called christotypical—had Mary and Jesus side by side facing the church and world in the work of redemption (Tambasco 1984, 10–11). To a certain extent Mary was kept distinct from the church and other Christians. It is no wonder that some Protestant Christians believed Catholics gave Mary the very same worship given to God.

Mary also played a negative part in sexual and spiritual development. Andrew Greeley (1974) wrote:

> In my adolescence, our teachers converted the gentle lady into a stern, negative sex goddess who banned 'dirty thoughts' and presided over the depth of necklines and the length of hemlines. Like most other young men who aspired to the priesthood, I said the rosary every day and would have claimed a 'strong devotion' to Mary. But in my seminary years she became identified with the sweet, sickly, sentimental piety preached by the spiritual directors—long, flowery, elaborate prayers which said nothing. She was used to reinforce a religious viewpoint in which obedience had become more important than charity, chastity more important than dedication, and

prudence more important than commitment. The people who claimed to be her devoted followers were creeps lugging statues about, preaching secret revelations rather than the gospel, and substituting ethereal pieties for both social concern and personal involvement. I turned the whole thing off.

On the positive side, Mary was a model of purity and fidelity. She was the one who helped Catholics respect women and children. Many people "experienced the love of God and the saving mystery of divine reality in the figure of a woman" (Johnson 1989, 513). She was the one to whom people entrusted their needs through novenas and other devotions. Even Andrew Greeley admits that when his generation was starting out in the parochial schools in the 1930s, "the Mary myth was for the most part benign and tender . . . a soft, gentle, reassuring aspect of religion" (1974).

Vatican Council II

During the preconciliar period when mariology was christotypical, there was also considerable thought and writing about Mary within the mystery of the church—labeled *ecclesiotypical*—due in large measure to the developments in Scripture, patristics, liturgy, and ecumenism. A good example is found in the only systematic treatise on ecclesiology in the twentieth century, *The Church of the Word Incarnate* by Charles Journet. This three-volume work, published in 1940, 1962, and 1969, was judged by Yves Congar as "the most profound dogmatic work to have been written on the church in our century" (De Fiores 1988, 481). Journet wrote that "mariology and ecclesiology can be seen as two parallel treatises." The church "finds in the Virgin its highest success." "Mary is mother, bride and virgin *before* the church and *for* the church; *in* her above all and *through her*, the church is mother, bride and virgin."

When Vatican II began, some bishops had a christotypical mariology, others an ecclesiotypical one. In the latter, there is greater recognition of Mary's identity with the rest of humanity, her need for redemption, and her development in faith and discipleship. Mary joins the church as it faces Christ, its redeemer and the only mediator of salvation. Mary and the church are part of the history of salvation and the wonderful works of God.

When the bishops took up the document on Mary there was a major disagreement about where it should be placed. Some wanted a separate document on Mary lest some Catholics deduce that Mary had been neglected. Others insisted that her chapter be restored to "the place in the schema on the church that was intended for it at the beginning of the preparatory period" (Semmelroth 1969, 285). This group argued that Mary should not be isolated from Christ and his church, and they feared that a separate document would not sit well with many Protestant communities.

The English-speaking bishops were as divided on this question as the other bishops. On the eve of the vote to resolve the issue, about 250 bishops assembled to hear a panel of experts on mariology. Barnabas Ahern, William Coyle, Godfrey Diekmann, and Eugene Maly provided theological background so the bishops could make an informed decision. On October 29, 1963, it was decided by one of the closest votes in the whole Council—1,114 to 1,074—to include the schema on Mary in the church document. It became the last chapter, number eight, in the Constitution on the Church (*Lumen gentium*). Diekmann regarded the vote as a personal triumph. From the positive response of many of the bishops to the panel discussion, he was convinced the four experts had made a difference in the extremely close vote (K. Hughes 1991, 238–40).

During the Council the Marian chapter had several titles. At one point it was "On the Blessed Virgin Mary, Mother of the Church." Most of the bishops voted against this title—though not against the teaching that Mary is the mother of the faithful. The negative vote reflected concern for sound theological terminology. Those with an ecclesiotypical mariology believed that the connection between mariology and ecclesiology ought to appear in the very title. On the other hand, these same bishops viewed the title as christotypical, with the risk that Mary would be outside the church as mother rather than inside as member. Finally, those with an eye to the Protestant communities were cautious about using titles not found in the Scripture.

The final title given the Marian chapter was "The Role of the Blessed Virgin Mary, Mother of God in the Mystery of Christ and the Church." This title satisfied both mariologies, the ecclesiotypical and the christotypical. It also showed that they need not be in complete conflict. From one point of view, they do complement one another: Christ can no more be separated from either his mother or the church any more than Mary can be separated from her Son and his community.

The final version received almost unanimous approval by a vote of 2,080 to 10, on November 21, 1964. It was not intended to be "a complete doctrine of Mary" or "to decide those questions which have not yet been fully illumined by the work of theologians" (LG 54). Like most of the conciliar documents, it represented a compromise whereby the different theologies of the various bishops could be represented.

In the christotypical sections, Mary is glorious and triumphant, and receives special cult. Yet even here the Marian privileges are toned down and Mary's cooperation with Jesus in the redemptive process is not defined. The document says that her involvement "in the work of salvation was manifested from the time of Christ's virginal conception up to his death" (LG 57). Because of her role as mother of the Son of God, Mary is "the favorite daughter of the Father," "the temple of the Holy Spirit," and "she far surpasses all other creatures, both in heaven and on earth" (LG 53). In the ecclesiotypical sections, Mary is described as "one with all human beings in their need for salvation" (LG 53). She can be invoked under the titles of advocate, helper, benefactress, and mediatrix. "These, however, are to be so understood that they neither take away from nor add anything to the dignity and efficacy of Christ the one mediator" (LG 62). Mary is "a pre-eminent and altogether singular member of the Church, and is the church's model and excellent exemplar in faith and charity" (LG 53). Finally, she is "a model of the Church in the matter of faith, charity and perfect union with Christ" (LG 63).

The final document has several strengths. Underlying the chapter and unifying it is the perspective of salvation history. Mary does have a part in saving history. For example, as a result of an accommodated and symbolic reading of Old Testament texts, Mary is seen foreshadowed in Gen. 3:15 and Isa. 7:14. Yet there is a movement away from a mariology that would feature Mary's privileges and which would obstruct ecumenical efforts. In particular, Mary is not called Mother of the Church or coredemptrix, two titles susceptible of dangerous misunderstanding.

The document has some weaknesses. It does not relate Mary to the Spirit in a clear way. Second, "the most glaring omission is of an anthropological and cultural nature" (De Fiores 1988, 474). Mary is not connected to the pastoral thrust of the Council—there are no references to the problems of daily life, to people's legitimate aspirations, and to Mary's place within the various cultures of the church. It is this point that helps explain in part the tremendous decline in Marian devotion in many parts of the global church. Certainly in the United States many forms of Marian piety disappeared. Rosaries, medals, and scapulars have been discarded; statues of Mary, if not removed, have been shunted off to the side in many parish churches; fewer Marian hymns are sung; and hardly any attention is paid to devotions on Saturdays and in the month of May.

Paul VI

Paul VI had a traditional devotion to Mary. On December 8, 1965, at the Eucharist closing the Council, he said in his homily that was heard by 100,000 people: "We are honoring Mary most holy, the immaculate one, therefore innocent, stupendous, perfect. She is the woman, the true woman who is both ideal and real, the creature in whom the image of God is reflected with absolute clarity, without any disturbance as happens in every other human creature" (Doty 1965).

Paul is remembered for three honors he bestowed on Mary: he reactivated her title Mother of the Church in 1964, visited Fatima in 1967, and wrote *Marialis Cultus* (Devotion to Mary) in 1974.

In his discourse on November 21, 1964, the closing date of the third council session, Paul said the Marian chapter in the Constitution on the Church "is the first time . . . that an ecumenical council has presented such a broad-ranging synthesis of Catholic doctrine on the place that the Blessed Virgin Mary holds in the mystery of the Christ and of the Church." Later in the homily, Paul referred to Mary as Mother of the church. When he did so, there was applause, "principally from other than bishops in the audience. [Paul] paused and beamed broadly" (Doty 1964).

Mother of the Church is not an ancient title. The earliest known reference occurs about the beginning of the twelfth century (Semmelroth 1969, 292). The Council, as we have seen, had deliberately avoided this title because its meaning is not so clear as one might at first suppose. So why did Paul VI return to this title? It could have been a gesture of reassurance to those who wanted the title and to those who wanted more doctrinal declarations about Mary.

It is interesting to note that at Puebla in 1979, the Latin American bishops accepted Mary as "Mother and model of the Church." They were able to sponsor these prerogatives once they were placed within the sociocultural circumstances of Latin America. For the people of Latin America, the church is always a family. They recognize the church "as the family whose mother is the mother of God." It is Mary who creates the family atmosphere, including such natural qualities as "receptivity, love and respect for life" (De Fiores 1988, 511–12).

Paul VI was the first pope to make overseas visits to the global church. He made nine. His third was to Fatima on May 13, 1967, the fiftieth anniversary of the first apparition there. For the liberals, this was generally regarded as a setback and a disappointment because Paul was setting the seal of pontifical approval on a secondary devotion that some Catholics mistrusted and many Protestants scorned. Many have difficulty with reports of the sun falling from the sky and a mysterious revelation about communist Russia.

In February 1974 Paul issued an apostolic exhortation, *Marialis Cultus,* offering criteria to update Marian devotion and to solve the serious neglect of Marian devotions since the Council. Marian devotion should be biblical; imbued with the great christological themes; in harmony with the liturgy; reflect ecclesial and ecumenical concerns; attend to contemporary social conditions; and eliminate exaggerations, sentimentalism, and legendary elements.

Paul's theology of Mary was biblical and very much in line with the latest Scripture scholarship. He said Mary had always been proposed as an example for Christians to imitate. However, since her specific sociocultural situation was long past, Christians today cannot imitate precisely the type of life she lived. What should be imitated is her full and responsible acceptance of the will of God. She heard the word of God and lived it. Her life was one of charity and service. "She is worthy of imitation," he concluded, "because she was the first and most perfect of Christ's disciples."

John Paul II

John Paul, the first Polish pope, has a great devotion to the Virgin of Czestochowa at Jasna Gora. He has made it known that he believes his call to the papacy is connected to his devotion to the shrine. When he first moved into his Vatican apartment, he added only one item: a replica of the Virgin of Czestochowa (Wynn 1988, 171).

The shrine is a focal point of Polish nationalism. It dates back to 1656 when King John Kasimir proclaimed Mary the Queen of Poland after a victory over the Swedes (L. S. Cunningham 1986, 27). Mary's statue is black and called the Black Madonna. Ancient black stones are connected "with the fertility power of maternal deities, black being the beneficient color of subterranean and uterine fecundity" (Johnson 1989, 506).

Like Paul VI, John Paul accepts fully the Marian chapter of Vatican II. At a general audience in Rome in May 1972, he said the Marian chapter is "in a certain sense a *magna charta* of the mariology of our era." Like Paul VI, he went to Fatima. His first visit on May 13, 1982, was to thank Our Lady of Fatima for saving his life exactly one year before when an assassin's bullets almost killed him. One of the bullets extracted from the pope's body has been set alongside diamonds in a golden crown that is placed on a statue of Mary on special occasions. His second visit on May 13, 1991, was to express thanks to Mary for saving his life in 1981 and for interceding to free Eastern Europe from communism. On that day the pope also entrusted the entire world to Our Lady of Fatima.

John Paul asked all the world's bishops on March 25, 1984, to "renew the consecration of the world to the Immaculate Heart of Mary" made by Pius XII. Like Pius XII, he called for a Marian year on January 1, 1987. The "year" lasted for fourteen months, June 7, 1987, the feast of Pentecost, until August 15, 1988. The reason he gave for the year was that he was anticipating the year 2000. Just as Mary prepared for Jesus while he was in her womb, so now she waits with us as we look forward to the two thousandth anniversary of her son's birth. Mary not only watches with us but she also accompanies and assists us, her fellow pilgrims, towards a new start in the year 2000.

On March 25, 1987, John Paul issued *Redemptoris mater*, an encyclical to mark the Marian year. In the letter he took up the themes of the Marian year just outlined. Also, with his global consciousness, he added that the purpose of the Marian year was to celebrate the anniversary of the church's seventh ecumenical council at Nicaea II in 787. That Council, by putting an end to iconoclasm, promoted a flourishing and artistic devotion to Mary. Furthermore, the Marian year commemorated the arrival of Christianity in Russia in 988, a thousand years before.

The Marian year supported the concerns of liberation theology (Hebblethwaite 1987a). John Paul declared that Mary exemplified the truth that the God who saves us is the God who has a preferential option for the poor. Her Magnificat "truly proclaims the coming of the 'Messiah of the poor.'"

John Paul also used the encyclical to treat ecumenical matters. Marian devotion in the Orthodox churches is a source of unity between the East and Rome. Mary, "our common mother," should be a sign of unity among all Christians instead of division. The encyclical did not dwell on such devotions as the rosary. Instead it sought to find in Mary as presented in the Scriptures a common ground that Christians can (and should) accept. This mariology in which care of the poor and ecumenism were linked together was welcomed in some Protestant circles. For example, Robert McAfee Brown said that "the Mary of the Magnificat is already becoming increasingly important to us as a beacon for illuminating the difficult path of being a Christian in a world of oppression" (1987b, 520–21).

Not all were enthusiastic about all parts of the encyclical. It has one paragraph (n. 46) on feminism. In this paragraph the pope lists as Marian virtues "limitless fidelity" and "tireless devotion to work." These are desirable virtues for all people. In their context in the encyclical, feminists balked.

Finally, in September 1990, John Paul went to the Ivory Coast, a very poor country that he had already visited in 1980 and 1985. Here he dedicated the largest church in the world, the cathedral of Our Lady of Peace in Yamoussoukra. At 489 feet, it is thirty-seven feet higher than St. Peter's in Rome, which it resembles. It cost 150 million dollars and was a personal gift to the institutional church from the president of the country. It was earlier rumored that the Vatican might turn down the gift because of its cost and questions about its funding.

Mariology in the Postconciliar Church

Marian devotion has declined in the church since the Council. Several reasons are offered. First, the increased appreciation of the presence of the resurrected Christ as mediator, teacher, and liberator leaves little place for Mary as a "relay station" on the way to Jesus. Second, many Marian devotions are not related to the liturgical year. At the Council the bishops urged that popular devotions be in harmony "with the liturgical season . . . since the liturgy by its very nature far surpasses any of them" (SC 13). Third, Catholics cannot agree on the role of women in the modern church. Traditional approaches to Mary as virgin and mother emphasize fulfillment in the home and family to the exclusion of all else.

This viewpoint does not sit well with women who want more involvement and decision-making power in the church. Writing in 1976, Marina Warner said that, despite the beauty inspired by veneration of Mary—superb churches and cathedrals, poetry and paintings—such veneration has led to a denigration of women. Women have been taught to interpret Mary's humility as submissiveness and her obedience as docility. Rosemary Radford Ruether took up the same theme, but much more forcefully. She says that the image of Mary as faithfully receptive to God and morally perfect has generally been used to heighten the disparity between Mary and all other women. Other women "are simultaneously disparaged and called to an impossible ethic of sexual repression and total submission to male authority. Thus Mary does not become a model of woman as autonomous person, but rather appears as a fantasy by which celibate males sublimate their sexuality into an ideal relationship with a virgin mother, while projecting the hostility caused by this sexual repression into misogynist feelings towards real women" (1987, 282).

Lisa Sowle Cahill and others think that Mary Magdalene fills the disciple and servant role model better than Mary (1985b). All four Gospels attest that Magdalene was the first witness to the resurrection of Jesus. She became "the apostle to the apostles," one entrusted with authority to teach and preach.

Mary and Language about God

We have no completely adequate name for the incomprehensible and transcendent one we call God. The best we can do is speak of God in the terms of our experience, using as metaphors persons and things. For example, the Bible was written within a patriarchal culture, one which fostered male superiority, grounded authority in physical power, and structured society hierarchically (Cooke 1983). One consequence of this unjust situation is that in Western theology male imagery has been used almost exclusively for God. God has been called king, judge, lord, warrior, and father. Jesus called God Father (*Abba*).

At Vatican II the bishops acknowledged the existence of the feminist movement when they wrote that many women "claim for themselves an equity with men before the law and in fact" (GS 9). In the early 1970s, when Christian feminists intensified their struggle against the sinful dimensions of the prevailing patriarchy, Mary Daly (1973) and others highlighted their dissatisfaction with naming God "Father."

Over the past few decades the discussion about God-language has escalated so that it now affects all dimensions of the church. For example, at the institutional level, the proposed revision of the English sacramentary will vary "the traditional titles of God to avoid a certain monotony and to show the richness of Christian revelation" (Montague 1993). At the intellectual level, Scripture scholars have examined not only the numerous biblical texts that offer powerful female images of God but also Jesus' use of cosmic and human metaphors other than father for his Father and his kingdom. Other scholars and theologians have examined the experiences of women, insisting that God-language "in female symbol emerges gracefully, powerfully, and necessarily from women's encounter with divine presence in the depths of their blessed selves. Women's reality forms part of the treasury of created excellences that can be used to refer to God" (Johnson 1993). At the devotional level, there have been discussions, even heated debates, about God-language at worship, especially the eucharistic liturgy. Should God be addressed as Father or as Mother or by such gender-free terms as Creator, Holy One, and Source of Being?

It is beyond the scope of this chapter to develop all the ramifications of this complex and controversial topic. It is enough to indicate that some authors have suggested that Mary reveals the feminine dimension of God. For example, it has been argued that, despite the doctrinal and ecumenical difficulties raised by a christotypical view of Mary, she is "a sacrament of God's life-giving, nurturing, healing, maternal love" (Greeley and Greeley Durkin 1984, 54). Mary even helps us see God as "passionately tender, seductively attractive, irresistibly inspiring, and graciously healing" (Greeley 1977, 13; see also Greeley 1980). This perspective is taken because Mary remains the "defining image" for a Catholic sacramental consciousness: "Mary is essential to Catholicism, not perhaps on the level of doctrine but surely on the level of imagination because she more than any other image blatantly confirms the sacramental instinct: the whole of creation and all its processes, especially its life-giving and life-nurturing processes, reveal the lurking and passionate love of God" (Greeley 1990a, 253).

Those who prefer to speak of God as Mother object to the view that Mary reminds us of the female element in God. This, they maintain, is a misuse of Mary. God can be called Mother if we break out of patriarchical imagery. Once God is fully envisioned as having a female face and as a loving mother who creates, nurtures, loves and saves, then Mary will no longer have to bear the burden of keeping alive the female imagery of the divine (Johnson 1989).

Conclusion

Devotion to Mary today in the institutional church and among the people is sporadic, its vitality depending in great measure on culture and local conditions. Devotion to Mary will not return to its fitting and proper place within the Catholic tradition until the intellectual dimension is clarified. There is as yet no coherent renewed mariology in the postconciliar church— even though Mary is, as Raymond Brown observed, "almost a bellwether of theological direction in the Roman Catholic

Church," as cited earlier. In order to revive a vibrant and sound devotion to Mary, a renewed mariology will have to retrieve Mary as a woman, disciple, virgin, and mother in non-sexist terms and in view of the fact that most of the world's poor are women of color and their children. Such a mariology would contribute immensely not only to the essential dignity of all women (and men) but also to the development of the church as a community of disciples with a threefold mission to promote and expand the kingdom of God, especially through a preferential option for the poor.

Postscript: Identity and Mission for the Future

Christians are disciples of Jesus Christ who respond to his call to participate in God's own work of expanding and promoting his kingdom among all people. Fulfilling this mission has not been easy during the twentieth century for several reasons: Christians themselves are divided into hundreds of churches; Christianity exists side by side with other vibrant religions; many people profess atheism and an absence of the experience of God; many, many people struggle against structural poverty and injustice.

Within the Catholic Church, the obstacles to mission are further compounded today because the church is facing perhaps its greatest crisis since the Reformation. There is a hydra-like crisis in its institutional, intellectual, and devotional dimensions. The institution faces a crisis of authority, community, freedom, identity, and mission. The intellectual dimension of the church is struggling to learn how best to hand on the tradition, with interreligious dialogue and ecumenism, and with what it means to be a world church. The devotional dimension is hobbled by a serious decline in sacramental faith, by a priest shortage, and by serious disagreements over ministries for women, sexual ethics, participation in the liturgy, and the spirituality that is fitting and proper for today. Today, the major spiritualities are the neo-Augustinian, communitarian, and liberationist. In an age of pluralism it seems tolerant to allow these to exist side by side. On paper this is possible. But bring an ecclesial body together (an international synod, an episcopal conference, a diocesan synod, a parish council, a religious community) to discuss sensitive issues—like liturgical changes, interreligious dialogue, the disposition of funds to the homeless or the victims of AIDS, or school curricula—and see how little consensus and mutual respect exist and how quickly and violently tempers fly.

Liberationist spirituality is new in the church. Many believe it represents a paradigmatic shift in theology comparable to what occurred with Augustine in the fifth century and with Aquinas in the thirteenth. It has growing support from recent popes, many bishops, and many of the faithful, clergy, and theologians. For example, Paul VI in *Octogesima adveniens* (1971) said that social justice questions, "because of their urgency, extent and complexity, must, in the years to come, take first place among the preoccupations of Christians" (n.7).

This liberationist spirituality is history and community-centered (and not ahistorical), justice and freedom-centered (and not pietist or privatized), and grace and kingdom-centered (and not self-centered). It takes these perspectives because modernity was not only too optimistic about human advancement but also self-centered. Its goal was individual autonomy through rational self-fulfillment. According to David Tracy, the postmodern and postconciliar ideal is self-transcendence, that is, "a radical commitment to the struggle to transcend our present individual and societal states in favor of a continuous examination of those illusions which cloud our real and more limited possibilities for knowledge and action" (Tracy 1975, 11). Only "a religion that promotes self-transcendence to the point, not merely of justice, but of self-sacrificing love, will have a redemptive role in human society inasmuch as such love can undo the mischief of decline and restore the cumulative process of progress" (Lonergan 1972, 55). In short, the church needs a spirituality that fosters a sacramental consciousness and focuses on the massive social evil in which we live our history and from which God promises to redeem us.

It seems that some moments in history call for a particular theology and spirituality in preference to others, and even to the exclusion of others. Many believe a liberationist spirituality is what will best enable the church to meet the challenges it faces as its moves toward the twenty-first century.

Notes

Chapter 1

1. For a summary of Von Hügel, see Dulles 1988a, 63–64. See also Imbelli 1986; Tracy 1987b, 268–72; 1989b; and M. J. Buckley 1989, 464. For an extensive examination of Von Hügel's triad, see Lash 1988, 141–77. Lash indicates that, since for Von Hügel each of the elements takes an active and/or passive form, his final name for them was historical-institutional, critical-speculative, and mystical-operative. Lash also explains that, with reference to the mystical-operative, Von Hügel stressed the pervasive sense of God experienced by all and that, while he was aware that religion has social dimensions, unfortunately he never developed the relation of religion to the social and political problems of his day. In this book the mystical or devotional will denote not only religious experience, prayer, and a sacramental life, but also involvement in works of justice and mercy.

2. Associated Press report, "9-day Funeral Rites for Pope," *New York Times*, 10 February 1939.

3. A brief news notice: "Housekeeper Breaks Long Silence on Pius XII's View of the Nazis," *National Catholic Reporter* 19 (4 March 1983): 2. For more details on Sister Pascalina, see Murphy and Arlington 1983. This book, tainted with sensationalism and inaccuracy about the close relationship between Pius XII and this sister, was given a long, decisive rebuttal by Andrew Greeley (1983).

4. A front page editorial in the *New York Journal American*, 29 October 1958.

5. An editorial in the *National Catholic Reporter* 14 (18 August 1978): 8.

6. When Marcinkus was director of the Vatican Bank, it lost more than $1.2 billion in doubtful transactions with Italy's failed Banco Ambrosiano.

7. "The September Pope," *Time*, 9 October 1978.

8. Editorial, "After Two Conclaves, A Polish Pope," *New York Times*, 6 November 1978.

9. It is estimated that thirty-three popes died by violence since Peter was crucified near the Vatican in 67: "12 martyrs; 8 sure, or relatively sure,

assassinations; and 13 quite possible assassinations" (McGinn 1985, 13–18).

Chapter 2

1. For a brief but insightful commentary on the Pope's remarks, see Spaeth 1993.

2. Historicism is the theory that all history is an account of what actually happened so that there is no room for the subjective or reflective view(s) of the historian. In other words, it is "the view that all thought is essentially related to and cannot transcend its own time" (Bloom 1987, 40).

3. Rhodes (1983, 193) says that from 1870 to 1900 the principal enemies of the Catholic Church—"the various atheist groups in a number of guises: anarchists, nihilists, positivists, freethinkers, socialists"—had different means but the same goal: the elimination of the church.

4. See also Gilhooley 1984. This is an interesting account of the effect of the condemnation of Modernism on the career of Father Francis Patrick Duffy (1871–1932), professor of philosophy at the New York diocesan seminary for fourteen years and the most celebrated chaplain of World War I.

5. This passage is from a 1916 work, *Escrits du temps de la guerre*, and found in Mooney 1967, 485.

6. See also Nichols 1989; Komonchak's appreciation of Henri de Lubac (1990c, 1992a); and Dulles 1991.

Chapter 3

1. See Greeley 1971, 1973, and 1977. *The Cardinal Sins* was his first novel (1981). His novels are usually about priests and their involvement with sex, power, and corruption in the church. Asked why he writes these novels, Greeley has one consistent answer: "Religion has been passed along through stories since it began, and *Cardinal Sins*, which is really about the power of God's love, carries on the tradition. It's as appropriate for a priest to be a novelist today as it was for priests in medieval times to make stained-glass windows" (*Wall Street Journal*, 20 April 1982).

2. Editorial, "Vatican II: 25 Years," *Commonweal* 117 (7 December 1990): 707–8.

3. Associated Press report, "Catholic Theologians Accuse Vatican of Resisting Change," *New York Times*, 14 December 1990. See also Windsor 1990b.

Chapter 4

1. Quoted in footnote 192 in Abbott 1966, 264.

2. For an excellent survey of the explanation of Catholicism by both Protestant and Catholic theologians and philosophers, see Dulles 1988a, 51–74.

3. Dulles (1988b) later replaces the servant model with "a secular-dialogic theology."

4. See Steinfels 1985; Imbelli 1986; Lamb 1986; Hebblethwaite 1986a; Dulles 1988a, 184–206; Murphy 1986.

Chapter 5

1. The older tradition was revived during the Council and placed in the Constitution on the Church (LG 22). A special postscript, dated November 16, 1964, and signed by Cardinal Pericle Felici, Secretary General of the Council, was added to the document to explain the nature of the bishopric and its relationship to the papacy.

2. "Vatican Document on Collegiality Draws Both Rejection, Support," *National Catholic Reporter* 25 (9 December 1988): 25. See *America* 158 (19 March 1988): 65–72 for four articles on the theological and juridicial status of episcopal conferences.

3. Editorial, "Refusing the Draft," *Commonweal* 115 (2 December 1988): 644–45.

4. "Ratzinger Criticizes Postconciliar Changes," *National Catholic Reporter* 21 (21 June 1985): 26.

5. Editorial, "Vatican Limits Dissent," *Christian Century* 107 (11 July 1990): 665.

6. Dulles is quoted in an editorial, "Dangerous Opinions," *Commonweal* 117 (10 August 1990): 435–36.

7. Gregory Baum is quoted in an editorial, "Gorbachev and John Paul Must Face Contradictions," *National Catholic Reporter* 26 (19 January 1990): 32.

8. Quoted by John Tracy Ellis in a letter to the editor, *Commonweal* 117 (9 February 1990): 66, 94.

Chapter 6

1. *National Catholic Reporter* 23 (25 September 1987): 31. See also De Nevi and Moholy 1985.

2. *New York Times*, 25 September 1988.

3. This whole section is based on such works as the following: Bishops of the Philippines 1974; Baum 1969, 1972a, 1973; Dulles 1972; MacEoin 1973; Schineller 1976. See also Richard 1981; Hick and Knitter 1987.

4. Schineller presents four views. There are actually more. The three outlined here are those most Catholics would accept.

5. See Hebblethwaite 1987b, 4; 1989f, 8; see also an editorial, "Mr. Waldheim Visits the Vatican," *America* 157 (25 July 1987): 27. At the time of the fiftieth anniversary of the Warsaw uprising, Pope John Paul told fourteen Carmelite nuns to move from their convent at the site of the Auschwitz death camp. Some Jews viewed the presence of a Catholic convent at the place where 1.5 million Jews perished an affront to Jewish sensibilities. See Perlez 1993.

6. See a brief notice, "A Papal First," *Christian Century* 103 (30 April 1986): 432.

Chapter 7

1. "No Forgiveness for Luther," *Christian Century* 97 (27 February 1980): 223.
2. For a more thorough description of Luther see Bokenkotter 1977, 204–19; Woodward 1983; McDonnell 1983; Marty 1983; Sheets 1983.
3. "Paisley vs. the Pope," *Christian Century* 105 (2 November 1988): 978.
4. "Protesters Denounce Anglican Archbishop over Ecumenism," *National Catholic Reporter* 26 (2 February 1990): 9.
5. "Cardinal Questions Church's Ecumenical Stance," *National Catholic Reporter* 23 (29 May 1987): 24.
6. "COCU Consensus," *Christian Century* 106 (4 January 1989): 8; Moede 1984; Horgan 1990.

Chapter 8

1. There are too many to list here. Some of the more prominent scholars were Karl Adam, Louis Bouyer, Odo Casel, Pierre-Marie Guy, Johannes Hofinger, Clifford Howell, Josef Jungmann, A. G. Martimort, Pius Parsch, A. M. Roguet, and Gerald Vann.
2. This is part of H. A. Reinhold's tribute to Virgil Michel after his death as reported in Hughes 1991, 18.
3. "Pope Urges End to Abuse of Liturgy Changes," *National Catholic Reporter* 25 (26 May 1989): 15.
4. Editorial, "Lefébvre Knows How to Hurt Rome," *National Catholic Reporter* 13 (26 August 1977): 10.

Chapter 9

1. An editorial, "After Ten Years Romero's Death An Invitation," *National Catholic Reporter* 26 (23 March 1990): 32.
2. This quote on nuclear war and the headline that follows were taken from an unsigned article in the *New York Times*, 9 October 1958.
3. Murray also wrote the sixty-two footnotes to the text. For a detailed history, see Linnan 1986 and Pavan 1969. For an appreciative review of Murray's career, his education in Europe in the mid-1930s, his conflicts with the Vatican in the 1950s, and his contribution to the Council, see Komonchak 1992b.
4. *Wall Street Journal*, 30 March 1967.
5. Boff adds on page 65: "Liberation theology's starting point is ethical indignation in the face of the 'humiliating scourge' of poverty, together with an encounter with the Lord in the effort to search out, in company of the poor, the pathway of liberation."
6. For a first-person account of this experience, see Sobrino 1991.
7. *New York Times*, 30 January 1979.
8. For a lengthy and disturbing analysis of the problems of the welfare state in response to the encyclical, see Moynihan 1991. Moynihan, a United States senator from New York, warns that "there is no equivalent

in our history to such a number or such a proportion" as the one-quarter of children on welfare. These children come of age "unemployable" and with no "vision of a secure future." These dependent people could very well become the central issue of social justice for the next century and more state interventions will be required.

9. A special report, "Pope, in India, Prays for the Bhopal Victims," *New York Times*, 6 February 1986.

10. For a clear and full explanation of "communion ecclesiology" and the Vatican's own interpretation of it used to condemn Boff, see Doyle 1992.

11. Editorial, "Santo Domingo Foreruns Church of Next Millenium," *National Catholic Reporter* 29 (6 November 1992): 1.

12. Dorr (1984) speaks of four spiritualities or mindsets: fortress, pilgrim, people of God, and power pyramid. The fourth is complicated and is explained on pages 55–56 and 202–4. While I do not accept his four divisions nor do I use all of his "models," I do find some of his explanations of the spiritualities presently operative in the church helpful and insightful.

Chapter 10

1. See Kosnik et al. 1977; News service, "Sex Book Provokes Critical Statements from Bishops," *National Catholic Reporter* 15 (29 July 1977): 8; Winiarski 1977, 1979a.

2. Dominion and Montefiore 1989, 27–29. They add a fourth criterion: sexual activity relieves sexual tension.

3. An editorial at the time of Paul VI's death, "The Pilgrimage of Pope Paul," *Christian Century* 95 (30 August 1978): 779–80.

4. There were two meetings in Rome in November 1988, the first attended by sixty bishops and the second by three hundred moral theologians. See Hebblethwaite 1988b, 4; 1989b. See the report on a symposium held at Princeton University, August 7–12, 1988, by Lefevere (1988). See also an editorial, "Anniversary Waltz," *Commonweal* 115 (15 July 1988): 387–88.

5. A response was made by Hallett (1982); Grisez followed (1986). See also Hebblethwaite 1990a.

6. "Former Nuns Vow to Keep Dissenting," *National Catholic Reporter* 26 (12 October 1990): 15. See their book: *No Turning Back* (Ferraro and Hussey 1990).

7. See also an editorial: "John Paul II on Annulments," *America* 144 (14 February 1981): 112.

8. *New York Times*, 1 April 1990.

9. Editorial: "Consulting Stephen's Experience: Pastoral Care of Homosexuals," *America* 155 (23 November 1986): 313–14. See also Williams 1987; McManus 1986; Quinn 1987.

10. See editorial, "Homosexual Marriages," *America* 123 (30 December 1970): 621; "For Same-sex Marriage," *San Francisco Chronicle*, 16 December, 1990; Dean 1991; Hartinger 1991.

11. Baum and several other major North American theologians protested the silencing of McNeil (Baum et al. 1977; see also Berrigan 1977).

Chapter 11

1. Raymond Brown (1985, 99) indicates that the translation of Luke 1:48 as "handmaiden" does not do justice to the fact that Mary is speaking from within the stratified society of the Roman Empire where slave women were among the lowest of peoples.

Bibliography

Abbott, Walter M., ed. 1966. *The Documents of Vatican II*. New York: America Press.

Allen, Diogenes. 1989. "Christian Values in a Post-Christian Context." In *Postmodern Theology: Christian Faith in a Pluralistic World*, edited by Frederic B. Burnham, 20–36. New York: Harper and Row.

———. 1990. "The End of the Modern World: A New Openness to Faith." *The Princeton Seminary Bulletin* 11.1 (Supplement): 11–31.

Anton, Angel. 1988. "Postconciliar Ecclesiology." In vol. 1 of *Vatican II*, 407–38. *See* Latourelle 1988a.

Aubert, Roger. 1978. *The Church in a Secularized Society*. New York: Paulist Press.

Balasuriya, Tessa. 1991. "Mission Encyclical's Dubious Claim of Church Monopoly." *National Catholic Reporter* 28 (25 October): 22.

Baum, Gregory. 1968. "The Encyclical: The Right to Dissent." *Commonweal* 95 (23 August): 553–54.

———. 1969. "The New Ecclesiology." *Commonweal* 91 (31 October): 123–28.

———. 1970a. *Man Becoming*. New York: Herder and Herder.

———. 1970b. "Vatican II and the Reinterpretation of Doctrine." *The Ecumenist* 9 (November): 1–4.

———. 1972a. "The Jews, Faith and Ideology." *The Ecumenist* 10 (July): 71–76.

———. 1972b. "Eucharistic Hospitality." *The Ecumenist* 11 (November): 11–16.

———. 1973. "Mission and Power." *The Ecumenist* 11 (March): 44–46.

———. 1974a. "Catholic Homosexuals." *Commonweal* 99 (15 February): 479–82.

———. 1974b. "Faith after Auschwitz—and Belfast." *Commonweal* 101 (8 November): 153–59.

———. 1975. *Religion and Alienation: A Theological Reading of Sociology*. New York: Paulist Press.

———. 1976. "Liberation Theology: First the Theory." *National Catholic Reporter* 12 (8 October): 8–9.

———. 1979a. "The First Papal Encyclical." *The Ecumenist* 17 (May): 55–59.

———. 1979b. "Catholic Foundations of Human Rights." *The Ecumenist* 18 (November): 6–12.

———. 1982. *The Priority of Labor: A Commentary on* Laborem Exercens. New York: Paulist Press.

———. 1983a. "After Twenty Years." *The Ecumenist* 21 (January): 17–19.

———. 1983b. "Gutierrez and the Catholic Tradition." *The Ecumenist* 22 (September): 81–84.

———. 1984a. "Faith and Liberation: Development Since Vatican II." In *Vatican II: Open Questions and New Horizons*, edited by Gerald M. Fagin, 75–104. Wilmington, Del.: Michael Glazier.

———. 1984b. "Class Struggle and the Magisterium: A New Note." *Theological Studies* 45 (December): 690–701.

———. 1985. "After Liberal Optimism, What?" *Commonweal* 112 (21 June): 368–70.

———. 1986a. "The Theology of the American Pastoral." *The Ecumenist* 24 (January): 17–22.

———. 1986b. "Catholic Inconsistencies." *The Ecumenist* 24 (January): 23–30.

———. 1987. *Theology and Society.* New York: Paulist Press.

———. 1988. "The Churches, Israel and the Palestinians." *The Ecumenist* 27 (November): 1–6.

———. 1989a. "Liberal Capitalism." In *The Logic of Solidarity*, 75–89. *See* Baum and Ellsberg 1989.

———. 1989b. "Structures of Sin." In *The Logic of Solidarity*, 110–126. *See* Baum and Ellsberg 1989.

———. 1989c. "Sociology and Salvation: Do We Need a Catholic Sociology?" *Theological Studies* 50 (December): 718–43.

Baum, Gregory et al. 1977. "Documentation." *The Ecumenist* 16 (November): 9.

Baum, Gregory, and Robert Ellsberg, eds. 1989. *The Logic of Solidarity.* New York: Orbis Books.

Bellah, Robert, Richard Madsen, William M. Sullivan, Ann Swidler, and Stephen M. Tipton. 1985. *Habits of the Heart: Individualism and Commitment in American Life.* Berkeley, Calif.: University of California Press.

Benjamin, Don C. 1984. "Roman Catholics and the Lima Document." *The Ecumenist* 22 (March): 36–37.

Bennett, John C. 1966. Review of *Situation Ethics*, by Joseph Fletcher. *Religious Education Review* 61 (November): 482–83.

Berrigan, Daniel. 1977. "The Leveling of John McNeill." *Commonweal* 104 (9 December): 778–83.

Bishops of the Philippines. 1974. "On Evangelization and Development." *Catholic Mind* 72 (January): 46–64.

Bloom, Allan. 1987. *The Closing of the American Mind.* New York: Simon and Schuster.

Boff, Leonardo. 1989. *Faith on the Edge: Religion and Marginalized Existence.* New York: Harper and Row.

Bokenkotter, Thomas. 1977. *A Concise History of the Catholic Church.* New York: Doubleday.

———. 1985. *Essential Catholicism.* New York: Doubleday.

Boswell, John. 1981. *Christianity, Social Tolerance and Homosexuality.* Chicago: University of Chicago Press.

Briggs, David. 1993. "Spiritual Leaders Gather to Counter Religious Violence." *Los Angeles Times,* 28 August.

Brockman, James R. 1979. "Seventeen Days in Puebla." *America* 140 (10 March): 180–83.

Brouwer, Arie R. 1986. "The Steps of Ecumenical Formation." *Christian Century* 103 (24 September): 803–5.

Brown, Grayson Warren. 1990. "Bringing All Nations As a Gift to the Lord." *America* 163 (22 September): 149–50.

Brown, Raymond E. 1970. *Priest and Bishop: Biblical Reflections.* New York: Paulist Press.

———. 1972. "The Problem of the Virginal Conception of Jesus." *Theological Studies* 33 (March): 3–34.

———. 1975a. *Biblical Reflections on Crises Facing the Church.* New York: Paulist Press.

———. 1975b. Review of *The Mother of Jesus in the New Testament,* by John McHugh. *America* 133 (25 October): 260–63.

———. 1984. *The Churches the Apostles Left Behind.* New York: Paulist Press.

———. 1985. *Biblical Exegesis and Church Doctrine.* New York: Paulist Press.

———. 1986a. "Gospel Infancy Narrative Research from 1976 to 1986: Part I (Matthew)." *Catholic Biblical Quarterly* 48 (July): 468–83.

———. 1986b. "Gospel Infancy Narrative Research from 1976 to 1986: Part II (Luke)." *Catholic Biblical Quarterly* 48 (October): 660–80.

Brown, Raymond, Karl P. Donfried, and John Reumann. 1973. *Peter in the New Testament.* New York: Paulist Press.

Brown, Raymond, Karl P. Donfried, Joseph A. Fitzmyer, and John Reumann. 1979. *Mary in the New Testament.* New York: Paulist Press.

Brown, Robert McAfee et al. 1972. "A Round Table: Where Are We in Ecumenism?" *America* 126 (22 January): 50–66.

———. 1978. *Theology in a New Key.* Philadelphia: Westminster.

———. 1980. "Starting Over: New Beginning Points for Theology." *Christian Century* 97 (14 May): 545–49.

———. 1986. "Leonardo Boff: Theologian for All Christians." *Christian Century* 10 (2 July): 615–18.

———. 1987a. "A Protestant Looks at an Aggressive Papacy." In *The Church in Anguish*, 177–85. *See* Küng and Swidler 1987.

———. 1987b. "Protestants and the Marian Year." *Christian Century* 104 (3 June): 520–21.

Brunsman, Barry. 1985. *New Hope for Divorced Catholics.* New York: Harper and Row.

Buckley, Michael J. 1989. "Experience and Culture: A Point of Departure for American Atheism." *Theological Studies* 50 (September): 443–65.

Buckley, William F. 1961. "This Week." *National Review* 11 (12 August): 88.

Buhlmann, Walbert. 1977. *The Coming of the Third Church.* New York: Orbis Books.

Burtchaell, James T. 1983. "Vatican Sex Document 'On the Whole a Postive Step.'" *National Catholic Reporter* 20 (16 December): 1, 24.

Butterfield, Herbert. 1966. *The Origins of Modern Science, 1300–1800.* New York: Macmillan.

Cahill, Lisa Sowle. 1978. "Sexual Ethics in Christian Theological Ethics: A Review of Recent Studies." *Religious Studies Review* 4 (January): 1–14.

———. 1985a. "Humanity as Female and Male: The Ethics of Sexuality." In *Called to Love: Towards a Contemporary Christian Ethic*, edited by Francis A. Eigo, 79–95. Pennsylvania: Villanova University Press.

———. 1985b. "Morality: The Deepening Crisis." *Commonweal* 112 (20 September): 496–99.

———. 1987. "Divorced from Experience: Rethinking the Theology of Marriage." *Commonweal* 114 (27 March): 171–76.

———. 1990. "Can We Get Real about Sex?" *America* 163 (14 September): 497–99, 502–3.

Callahan, Daniel. 1973. "Abortion: Thinking and Experience." *Christianity and Crisis* 32 (8 January): 295–98.

Callahan, Sidney. 1986. "Conscience Reconsidered." *America* 155 (1 November): 251–53.

Carmody, Denise Lardner, and John Tully Carmody. 1983. *Christianity: An Introduction.* Philadelphia: Westminster Press.

Castillo, Dennis. 1992. "The Origin of the Priest Shortage: 1942–1962." *America* 167 (24 October): 302–4.

Catoir, John T. 1967. "The Church and Second Marriage." *Commonweal* 94 (14 April): 13–14.

Chadwick, Owen. 1987. *Britain and the Vatican During the Second World War.* New York: Cambridge University Press.

Champlin, Joseph M. 1989a. *The Marginal Catholic.* Notre Dame, Ind.: Ave Maria Press.

———. 1989b. "Barriers to the Sacraments." *Commonweal* 116 (20 October): 559–61.

Cheetham, Nicholas. 1983. *Keepers of the Keys.* New York: Charles Scribner's Sons.

Clebsch, William A. 1979. *Christianity in European History.* New York: Oxford University Press.

Coleman, Gerald D. 1987. "The Vatican Statement on Homosexuality." *Theological Studies* 48 (December): 727–34.

Coleman, John A. 1981. "The Future of Ministry." *America* 144 (28 March): 243–49.

———. 1989. "Who Are the Catholic 'Fundamentalists'?" *Commonweal* 116 (27 January): 42–47.

Collinge, William, Daniel Sheridan, Denise Lardner Carmody, William P. Lowe, and William Cenkner. 1986. A review symposium of *No Other Name?: A Critical Survey of Christian Attitudes toward the World Religions,* by Paul Knitter. *Horizons* 13 (Spring): 116–30.

Collins, Patrick W. 1984. "Liturgical Renewal, Twenty Years Later." *Commonweal* 111 (1 June): 330–34.

Collins, Raymond F. 1986. *Christian Morality: Biblical Foundations.* Notre Dame, Ind.: University of Notre Dame Press.

———. 1993. *Divorce in the New Testament.* Collegeville, Minn.: Liturgical Press.

Congar, Yves. 1968. *A History of Theology.* New York: Doubleday.

Cooke, Bernard. 1977. *Ministry to Word and Sacrament.* Philadelphia: Fortress Press.

———. 1983. "Non-patriarchal Salvation." *Horizons* 10 (Spring): 22–31.

———. 1985. "U.S. Lay Ministry Bouncing Over Old Boundaries." *National Catholic Reporter* 21 (15 March): 17.

———. 1987. "What God Has Joined Together." *Commonweal* 114 (27 March): 178–82.

———, ed. 1989. *The Papacy and the Church in the United States.* New York: Paulist Press.

———. 1990. "Entire Faith Community Performs Eucharist." *National Catholic Reporter* 26 (14 May): 14.

Cornwell, John. 1989. *A Thief in the Night: The Death of John Paul I.* New York: Simon and Schuster.

Cortesi, Arnaldo. 1962. "Pomp and Prayer Reign on Sunny Day at Vatican." *New York Times,* 11 October.

Cowell, Alan. 1991. "Europe's Bishops Unable to Heal Rifts." *New York Times,* 15 December.

———. 1992. "After 350 Years, Vatican Says Galileo Was Right: It Moves." *New York Times,* 31 October.

Cox, Harvey. 1980. "Theology: What Is It? Who Does It? How Is It Done?" *Christian Century* 97 (24 September): 874–79.

———. 1988a. *The Silencing of Leonardo Boff: The Vatican and the Future of World Christianity.* Oak Park, Ill.: Meyer Stone.

————. 1988b. "Many Mansions or One Way? The Crisis in Interfaith Dialogue." *Christian Century* 105 (17 August): 731–35.

Crow, Paul A. 1986. "Assisi's Day of Prayer for Peace." *Christian Century* 103 (3 December): 1084–85.

Cuddy, Edward. 1979. "The Rebel Function in Catholicism." *Commonweal* 106 (14 September): 495–97.

Cullmann, Oscar. 1988. *Unity through Diversity*. Philadelphia: Fortress Press.

Cunningham, Agnes. 1986. "Decree on Ecumenism." In *Vatican II and Its Documents*, 62–77. *See* O'Connell 1986.

Cunningham, Lawrence S. 1986. *The Catholic Experience*. New York: Crossroad.

Curran, Charles E. 1970. *Contemporary Problems in Moral Theology*. Notre Dame, Ind.: Fides Publishers.

————. 1972. *Catholic Moral Theology in Dialogue*. Notre Dame, Ind.: University of Notre Dame Press.

————. 1973. "Abortion: Law and Morality in Contemporary Catholic Theology." *Jurist* 33 (Spring): 180.

————. 1974a. "Divorce: Catholic Theory and Practice in the United States." *American Ecclesiastical Review* 168 (January): 3–34; 168 (February): 75–79.

————. 1974b. "Two Signs of the Times." *National Catholic Reporter* 10 (18 October): 7–8.

————. 1978. *Issues in Sexual and Medical Ethics*. Notre Dame, Ind.: University of Notre Dame Press.

————. 1986. *Faithful Dissent*. New York: Sheed and Ward.

————. 1993. "Encyclical Left Church Credibility Stillborn." *National Catholic Reporter* 29 (16 July): 14–15.

Daly, Gabriel. 1980. *Transcendence and Immanence*. Oxford: Clarendon Press.

————. 1985. "Catholicism and Modernity." *Journal of the American Academy of Religion* 53 (December): 773–96.

Daly, Mary. 1973. *Beyond God the Father*. Boston: Beacon Press.

D'Costa, Gavin. 1984. "John Hick's Copernican Revolution Ten Years After." *New Blackfriars* 65 (July): 323–30.

————. 1990. *Christian Uniqueness Reconsidered*. New York: Orbis Books.

Dean, Craig R. 1991. "Legalize Gay Marriage." *New York Times*, 28 September.

De Fiores, Stephano. 1988. "Mary in Postconciliar Theology." In vol. 1 of *Vatican II*, 469–539. *See* Latourelle 1988a.

De Nevi, Don, and Noel Francis Moholy. 1985. *Junipero Serra*. San Francisco: Harper and Row.

Deschner, John. 1986. "What To Do with 'Convergence.'" *Commonweal* 113 (31 January): 50–52.

Desseux, Jacques. 1983. *Twenty Centuries of Ecumenism*. New York: Paulist Press.

Diamond, James J. 1975. "Abortion, Animation and Biological Hominization." *Theological Studies* 36 (June): 305–24.

Dicker, Fred. 1990. "Judgment by a Higher Authority." *New York Post*, 23 January.

Di Ianni, Albert. 1974. "Is the Fetus a Person?" *American Ecclesiastical Review* 168 (May): 323–24.

———. 1989. "Faith and Justice: A Delicate Balance." *America* 161 (22 July): 32–36, 45.

Dinges, William D. 1988. "Quo Vadis, Lefébvre?" *America* 158 (18 June): 602–6.

Dinter, Paul E. 1989. "Standing in the Way of Worship." *Commonweal* 116 (16 June): 367–70.

Dionne, E. J. 1985. "Pope and Jews: Strain Amid Celebration." *New York Times*, 29 October.

Doerflinger, Richard. 1985. "Who are Catholics for a Free Choice?" *America* 153 (16 November): 312–17.

Dolan, Jay P. 1975. *The Immigrant Church*. Baltimore: Johns Hopkins University Press.

———. 1978a. *Catholic Revivalism: The American Experience: 1830–1900*. Notre Dame, Ind.: University of Notre Dame Press.

———. 1978b. Review of *A Concise History of the Catholic Church*, by Thomas Bokenkotter. *Critic* 36 (Spring): 75–77.

———. 1985. *The American Catholic Experience: A History from Colonial Times to the Present*. New York: Doubleday.

Dominion, Jack, and Hugh Montefiore. 1989. *God, Sex and Love*. Philadelphia: Trinity Press International.

Donahue, John R. 1981. "Divorce: New Testament Perspectives." *The Month* 242 (April): 113–20.

Donohue, John W. 1981. "The Centennial of John XXIII." *America* 145 (22 November): 314.

Dorr, Donal. 1983. *Option for the Poor: A Hundred Years of Vatican Social Teaching*. New York: Paulist Press.

———. 1984. *Spirituality and Justice*. New York: Orbis Books.

———. 1989. "Solidarity and Integral Human Development." In *The Logic of Solidarity*, 143–54. *See* Baum and Ellsberg 1989.

Doty, Robert C. 1964. "Pontiff Adjourns Council and Honors Mary." *New York Times*, 22 November.

———. 1965. "Pope Paul Closes Vatican Council Amid Pagentry." *New York Times*, 9 December.

Doyle, Dennis M. 1992. "Communion Ecclesiology and the Silencing of Boff." *America* 167 (12 September): 139–43.

Duffy, Regis. 1987. "The RCIA Misunderstood." *America* 156 (9 May): 385–86.

Dugan, George. 1962a. "Study of Liturgy Begun at Council." *New York Times*, 23 October.

————. 1962b. "2nd Rome Session Will Open May 12." *New York Times*, 13 November.

————. 1962c. "Vatican Council to Reopen September 8." *New York Times*, 28 November.

Dulles, Avery. 1972. "Current Trends in Mission Theology." *Theology Digest* 20 (Spring): 26–34.

————. 1974. *Models of the Church*. New York: Doubleday.

————. 1980. "The Symbolic Structure of Revelation." *Theological Studies* 41 (March): 51–73.

————. 1981. "Imaging the Church in the 1980's." *Thought* 56 (Spring): 121–38.

————. 1982. "Toward a Christian Concensus: The Lima Meeting." *America* 146 (20 February): 126–29.

————. 1983. "The Teaching Authority of Bishops' Conferences." *America* 148 (11 June): 453–55.

————. 1985. "Authority: The Divided Legacy." *Commonweal* 112 (12 July): 400–3.

————. 1986. "Sensus Fidelium." *America* 155 (1 November): 240–42.

————. 1988a. *The Reshaping of Catholicism: Current Challenges in the Theology of the Church*. New York: Harper and Row.

————. 1988b. "Vatican II and Communications." In vol. 3 of *Vatican II*, 528–47. *See* Latourelle 1988a.

————. 1989. "A Half Century of Ecclesiology." *Theological Studies* 50 (September): 419–42.

————. 1990. "Episcopal Conferences: Their Teaching Authority." *America* 162 (13 January): 7–9.

————. 1991. "Henri de Lubac: In Appreciation." *America* 165 (28 September): 180–82.

————. 1992. *The Craft of Theology: From Symbol to System*. New York: Crossroad.

Dwyer, John C. 1985. *Church History: Twenty Centuries of Catholic Christianity*. New York: Paulist Press.

————. 1987. *Foundations of Christian Ethics*. New York: Paulist Press.

Eagleson, John, and Philip Scharper, eds. 1979. *Puebla and Beyond*. New York: Orbis Books.

Egan, John J. 1983. "Getting Liturgy and Justice to Merge." *National Catholic Reporter* 19 (30 September): 9, 16–17.

Elliott, John H. 1982. "The Image of Mary: A Lutheran View." *America* 146 (27 March): 226–29.

Empereur, James L. 1992. "Liturgy Reform Flounders in Sea of Ambiguity." *National Catholic Reporter* 29 (11 December): 11–12.

Falconi, Carlo. 1967. *The Popes of the Twentieth Century*. London: Weidenfelf and Nicolson.

Farrell, Michael J. 1984. "Annulments: 15,000% Increase in 15 Years." *National Catholic Reporter* 21 (16 November): 1, 9.

Fauss, Jose I. Gonzalez. 1989. *Where the Spirit Breathes: Prophetic Dissent in the Church*. New York: Orbis Books.

Ferm, Dean William. 1986. *Third World Liberation Theologies: An Introductory Survey*. New York: Orbis Books.

———. 1988. *Profiles in Liberation: 39 Portraits of Third World Theologians*. Mystic, Conn.: Twenty-Third Publications.

Ferraro, Barbara, and Patricia Hussey. 1990. *No Turning Back*. New York: Poseidon Press.

Feuerherd, Joseph. 1990. "Theologians Tossing Vatican's Latest Hot Potato." *National Catholic Reporter* 26 (13 July): 10.

Fichter, Joseph H. 1988a. "Married Priests and Ecumenism." *The Ecumenist* 26 (January): 26–30.

———. 1988b. "The Ordination of Anglican Priests." *America* 159 (24 September): 157–61.

Fiorenza, Francis Schüssler. 1975. "Political Theology and Liberation Theology: An Inquiry into Their Fundamental Meaning." In *Liberation, Revolution and Freedom: Theological Perspectives*, edited by Thomas M. McFadden, 3–26. New York: Seabury.

———. 1982. "The Church's Religious Identity and Its Social and Political Mission." *Theological Studies* 43 (June): 197–225.

———. 1984. *Foundational Theology: Jesus and the Church*. New York: Crossroad.

Fitzmyer, Joseph A. 1973. "Virginal Conception in the New Testament." *Theological Studies* 34 (December): 541–75.

———. 1981. *To Advance the Gospel: New Testament Studies*. New York: Crossroad.

Fitzpatrick, Joseph P. 1978. "Justice as a Problem of Culture." *Catholic Mind* 76 (January): 10–26.

Flannery, Kevin, and Joseph Koterski. 1993. "Paul VI Was Right." *America* 169 (25 September): 7–11.

Fletcher, Joseph. 1966. *Situation Ethics*. Philadelphia: Westminster Press.

———. 1978. "Love and Utility." *Christian Century* 95 (31 May): 592–94.

Ford, John C., and Germain Grisez. 1978. "Contraception and Infallibility." *Theological Studies* 39 (June): 258–312.

Fox, Matthew. 1979. *A Spirituality Named Compassion*. New York: Winston Press.

Fox, Tom. 1988. "Inside NCR." *National Catholic Reporter* 24 (29 July): 2.

French, Howard W. 1992a. "Pope Arrives in Dominican Republic." *New York Times*, 10 October.

———. 1992b. "Protests Follow the Pope on Santo Domingo Visit." *New York Times*, 14 October.

Fries, Heinrich, and Karl Rahner. 1985. *Unity of the Churches: An Actual Possibility*. Philadelphia: Fortress Press.

Fuchs, Josef. 1970. *Human Values and Christian Morality*. Dublin: McGill and Macmillan.

Gaffney, James. 1986. "From Models of the Church to Models of the Model." *America* 155 (13 December): 377–80.

Gaine, Michael. 1991. "The State of the Priesthood." In *Modern Catholicism*, 246–55. *See* Hastings 1991.

Gallagher, John. 1990. *Times Past, Time Future: An Historical Study of Catholic Moral Theology*. New York: Paulist Press.

Geffre, Claude. 1989. "The Political Dimensions of a New Theological Paradigm." In *Paradigm Change in Theology*, 390–96. *See* Küng and Tracy 1989.

Geyer, Alan. 1983. "The Pains of Peace at Vancouver." *Christian Century* 100 (31 August): 765–67.

Gibeau, Dawn. 1976a. "WCC Finale Mood: Sense of Struggle, Spirit of Unity." *National Catholic Reporter* 12 (9 January): 4.

———. 1976b. "God Puts His Foot in History." *National Catholic Reporter* 12 (15 September): 7–9.

———. 1989. "Advances, Retreats Since Medellin." *National Catholic Reporter* 25 (31 March): 3–4.

Gilhooley, James. 1984. "Father Duffy: Priest with a Tin Hat." *America* 150 (24 March): 204–7.

Gilkey, Langdon. 1989. "The Paradigm Shift in Theology." In *Paradigm Change in Theology*, 367–83. *See* Küng and Tracy 1989.

Gilleman, Gerard. 1959. *The Primacy of Charity in the Moral Life*. Westminster, Md.: Newman Press.

Goldman, Ari L. 1992. "Support Fading for Document about Women." *New York Times*, 19 June.

Gonzalez, Justo L. 1984. *The Story of Christianity*. Vol. 2. New York: Harper and Row.

Gorday, Peter. 1989. "Raimundo Panikkar: Pluralism without Relativism." *Christian Century* 106 (6 December): 1147–50.

Gordon, Mary. 1982. "Coming to Terms with Mary." *Commonweal* 109 (15 January): 11–13.

Goslin, Tom. 1988. "New Struggles for Spanish Catholics." *Christian Century* 105 (31 August): 759–60.

Graham, Robert A. 1966. "Non-Christians." In *The Documents of Vatican II*, 656–59. *See* Abbott 1966.

Granfield, Patrick. 1987. *The Limits of the Papacy*. New York: Crossroad.

Grassi, Joseph A. 1986. "The Role of Jesus' Mother in John's Gospel: A Reappraisal." *Catholic Biblical Quarterly* 48 (January): 67–80.

Greeley, Andrew M. 1970. "Myths, Meaning and Vatican III." *America* 123 (19 December): 538–42.

———. 1971. *The Jesus Myth*. New York: Doubleday.

———. 1973. *The New Agenda*. New York: Doubleday.

———. 1974. "Hail Mary." *New York Times*, 15 December.

———. 1977. *The Mary Myth: On the Feminity of God*. New York: Seabury.

————. 1980. "Mary Survives." *America* 142 (23 February): 135–37.

————. 1981. "*Quadragesimo Anno* after Fifty Years." *America* 145 (8 August): 46–49.

————. 1982a. "The Failures of Vatican II After Twenty Years." *America* 146 (6 February): 86–89.

————. 1982b. "Going Their Own Way." *New York Times*, 10 October.

————. 1983. Review of *La Popessa*, by Paul I. Murphy and René Arlington. *National Catholic Reporter* 19 (6 May): 22–23.

————. 1990a. *The Catholic Myth*. New York: Charles Scribner's Sons.

————. 1990b. "Good Liturgy Is Little More Than a Good Weave." *National Catholic Reporter* 26 (16 March): 12–13.

————. 1992. "Sex and the Single Catholic: The Decline of an Ethic." *America* 167 (7 November): 342–47, 358–59.

Greeley, Andrew M., and Mary Greeley Durkin. 1984. *How To Save the Catholic Church*. New York: Viking Press.

Greene, Jack P. 1975. "The 'New History': From Top to Bottom." *New York Times*, 8 January.

Greenhouse, Steven. 1991. "Archbishop Lefébvre Dies; Traditionalist Defied the Vatican." *New York Times*, 26 March.

Grisez, Germain. 1986. "Infallibility and Contraception: A Reply to Garth Hallett." *Theological Studies* 47 (March): 134–45.

Groppo, Dan. 1986. "The Vatican Can Slight Scripture for Its Purposes." *National Catholic Reporter* 23 (26 December): 9,12.

Gros, Jeffrey. 1990. "Discerning the Gospel: Dialogue in the Catholic Church." *Christian Century* 107 (2 May): 460–63.

Gustafson, James M. 1978. *Protestant and Catholic Ethics*. Chicago: University of Chicago Press.

Haberman, Clyde. 1989. "Gorbachev Lauds Religion on Eve of Meeting Pope." *New York Times*, 1 December.

————. 1990a. "Pope, Amid Mexico's Poor, Laments." *New York Times*, 8 May.

————. 1990b. "Vatican Synod Studies 'Burnout' and 'Identity Crisis' among Priests." *New York Times*, 1 October.

————. 1990c. "Synod in Vatican Bars Change in Celibacy Rule." *New York Times*, 28 October.

Haight, Roger. 1990. "Modernism: Vatican Had to Create It to Condemn It." *National Catholic Reporter* 26 (27 July): 14–15.

Hallett, Garth L. 1982. "Contraception and Prescriptive Infallibility." *Theological Studies* 43 (December): 629–50.

————. 1988. "Infallibility and Contraception: The Debate Continues." *Theological Studies* 49 (September): 517–28.

Hansen, Susan. 1986. "Vatican's Homosexual Letter Disputed." *National Catholic Reporter* 23 (26 December): 5.

Hanson, Eric O. 1987. *The Catholic Church in World Politics*. Princeton: Princeton University Press.

Happel, Stephen, and David Tracy. 1984. *A Catholic Vision*. Minneapolis, Minn.: Fortress Press.

Häring, Bernard. 1961–66. *The Law of Christ*. 3 vols. Westminster, Md.: Newman Press.

————. 1978–81. *Free and Faithful in Christ*. 3 vols. New York: Crossroad.

————. 1987. "The Curran Case." In *The Church in Anguish*, 235–50. *See* Küng and Swidler 1987.

————. 1992. *My Witness for the Church*. New York: Paulist Press.

Hartinger, Brent. 1991. "A Case for Gay Marriage." *Commonweal* 118 (22 November): 681–83.

Hastings, Adrian, ed. 1991. *Modern Catholicism: Vatican II and After*. New York: Oxford University Press.

Haughey, John C. 1968. "Conscience and the Bishops." *America* 119 (12 October): 322, 324.

————, ed. 1977. *The Faith That Does Justice*. New York: Paulist Press.

Hebblethwaite, Peter. 1975. *The Runaway Church: Postconciliar Growth or Decline*. New York: Seabury.

————. 1976. "Not about But for Liberation." *National Catholic Reporter* 13 (12 November): 11, 13.

————. 1978a. *The Year of the Three Popes*. Cleveland, Ohio: Collins.

————. 1978b. "Pope John Paul, the Smiling Pope, Dead at 65." *National Catholic Reporter* 14 (6 October): 1–5.

————. 1979a. "Was Archbishop Lured into Candid Comments?" *National Catholic Reporter* 15 (2 March): 19.

————. 1979b. "John Paul's Renewal Engulfs Aggiornamento." *National Catholic Reporter* 16 (16 November): 1, 4.

————. 1979c. "John Paul Welcomes Galileo Back." *National Catholic Reporter* 16 (23 November): 3,20.

————. 1980a. "Orthodox Dialogue Continues." *National Catholic Reporter* 16 (28 March): 7.

————. 1980b. "Rome Ignored Lefébvre Mass." *National Catholic Reporter* 16 (18 April): 1.

————. 1980c. "Orthodox-Roman Meeting 'Troubled.'" *National Catholic Reporter* 16 (6 June): 16.

————. 1980d. "Is the Pope Committed to Ecumenism?" *National Catholic Reporter* 16 (4 July): 14–15.

————. 1980e. "Synod Ending 'Anticlimactic'; Some Bishops 'Disappointed.'" *National Catholic Reporter* 17 (7 December): 1, 18.

————. 1981a. "Bishops Will Aid Converts." *National Catholic Reporter* 17 (12 April): 18.

————. 1981b. "What John Thought of the Popes He Knew." *National Catholic Reporter* 18 (27 November): 13–14.

————. 1982. "The Council Opens." *National Catholic Reporter* 18 (8 October): 34.

————. 1983. "Why John XXIII Wrote *Pacem in Terris.*" *National Catholic Reporter* 19 (8 April): 9, 20–21.

————. 1984a. "New Concordat." *National Catholic Reporter* 20 (2 March): 5.

————. 1984b. "Consecration to Mary a Loyalty Test." *National Catholic Reporter* 20 (3 April): 10.

————. 1984c. "Tridentine Decision a Slap at Collegiality." *National Catholic Reporter* 21 (21 December): 5.

————. 1986a. *Synod Extraordinary.* New York: Doubleday.

————. 1986b. "Letter to Brazilian Bishops Termed Papal Turning Point." *National Catholic Reporter* 22 (2 May): 4.

————. 1986c. "Encyclical on Holy Spirit Judged Pessimistic." *National Catholic Reporter* 22 (20 June): 8.

————. 1987a. "Marian Year Shores Up Liberation Theology." *National Catholic Reporter* 23 (5 June): 4.

————. 1987b. "Vatican Seems to Lack 'Prudence' over Waldheim." *National Catholic Reporter* 23 (23 July): 4.

————. 1987c. "Lefébvre 'Dialogue' His Vindication?" *National Catholic Reporter* 24 (13 November): 1, 16.

————. 1988a. "A Private Note and What It Wrought." *America* 158 (18 June): 598–601, 614.

————. 1988b. "Meetings Celebrate Twenty Years of *Humanae Vitae.*" *National Catholic Reporter* 25 (16 December): 4.

————. 1989a. "Pope Lists Two 'Shadows' in State of Church Speech." *National Catholic Reporter* 25 (27 January): 4.

————. 1989b. "Häring on *Humanae Vitae.*" *National Catholic Reporter* 25 (10 February): 7.

————. 1989c. "Hope, Anguish of the People of Our Time." *National Catholic Reporter* 25 (17 March): 15–17.

————. 1989d. "Apostolic Letter Throws 'Dynamite' into Lefébvre Camp." *National Catholic Reporter* 25 (26 May): 15.

————. 1989e. "Papal Style at Issue Between Rome, Canterbury." *National Catholic Reporter* 25 (2 June): 15.

————. 1989f. "Auschwitz Legacy an 'Unholy Mess.'" *National Catholic Reporter* 25 (25 August): 8

————. 1989g. "Runcie Leaves Hardly a Ripple in Rome." *National Catholic Reporter* 25 (13 October): 8–9.

————. 1989h. "Australian to Head Vatican Unity Council." *National Catholic Reporter* 26 (29 December): 4.

————. 1990a. "Excavating for Foundation of Infallible *Humanae Vitae.*" *National Catholic Reporter* 26 (4 May): 16.

————. 1990b. "Beatification of Juan Diego Affirms Liberation Theology." *National Catholic Reporter* 26 (11 May): 8.

————. 1990c. "Alternative of Cowed Silence Strange Way to Defend Faith." *National Catholic Reporter* 26 (13 July): 28.

————. 1990d. "Weakland and the Theology of Fribourg Doctorate." *National Catholic Reporter* 27 (23 November): 8.

————. 1991a. "John Paul I." In *Modern Catholicism*, 444–46. *See* Hastings 1991.

————. 1991b. "Lefébvre Was a Traditionalist to the End." *National Catholic Reporter* 27 (5 April): 2.

————. 1992a. "Boff Leaves Priesthood and Order for 'Periphery.'" *National Catholic Reporter* 28 (17 July): 12–13.

————. 1992b. "From John Paul II Superstar to a Super Surprise?" *National Catholic Reporter* 28 (11 September): 5–7.

————. 1993a. "Ratzinger Comments on Changing Papacy." *National Catholic Reporter* 29 (26 February): 10.

————. 1993b. "Encyclical Insists Intercourse Is Language of Love." *National Catholic Reporter* 29 (16 July): 15–16.

Hehir, J. Bryan. 1981. "A New Era of Social Teaching." *Commonweal* 108 (23 October): 585, 607.

————. 1991. "From Leo XIII to John Paul II: The Evolution of Catholic Social Teaching." *Commonweal* 118 (3 May): 281–82.

Heim, Mark S. 1986. "BEM Finds Favor with American Churches." *Christian Century* 103 (14 May): 476–77.

Hennelly, Alfred T. 1986. "The Red Hot Issue: Liberation Theology." *America* 154 (24 May): 425–28.

Hennesey, James. 1971. "The Two Vatican Councils: The Church Becomes Universal." *The Catholic Mind* 69 (June): 22–31.

————. 1989. "Catholicism in an American Environment: The Early Years." *Theological Studies* 50 (December): 657–75.

Henriot, Peter J., ed. 1988. *Catholic Social Teaching*. New York: Orbis Books.

Hevesi, Dennis. 1992. "Gay Church Again Rejected by National Council Group." *New York Times*, 15 November.

Hewitt, W. E. 1986. "Basic Christian Communities in Brazil." *The Ecumenist* 24 (September): 81–86.

Hick, John. 1973. *God and the Universe of Faiths*. New York: St. Martin's Press.

Hick, John, and Paul Knitter, eds. 1987. *The Myth of Christian Uniqueness: Toward a Pluralistic Theology of Religion*. New York: Orbis Books.

Hillman, Eugene. 1980. "From Tribal Religion to a Catholic Church." *America* 143 (15 November): 303–5.

————. 1989. *Many Paths: A Catholic Approach to Religious Pluralism*. New York: Orbis Books.

Hitchcock, James. 1972. "The Church and the Sexual Revolution." *America* 127 (23 September): 197–201.

Hobgood, Mary E. 1989. "Conflicting Paradigms in Social Analysis." In *The Logic of Solidarity*, 167–85. *See* Baum and Ellsberg 1989.

Hollenbach, David. 1977. "Modern Catholic Teaching Concerning Justice." In *The Faith That Does Justice*, 207–32. *See* Haughey 1977.

———. 1979. *Claims in Conflict: Retrieving and Renewing the Catholic Human Rights Tradition*. New York: Paulist Press.

———. 1991. "The Pope and Capitalism." *America* 164 (1 June): 590–91.

Holmes, J. Derek. 1981. *The Papacy in the Modern World 1914–1978*. New York: Crossroad.

Horgan, Thaddeus D. 1990. "The Second Vatican Council's Decree on Ecumenism." *America* 162 (2 June): 548–52.

Howell, Leon. 1984. "Emilio Castro's Election as WCC Secretary." *Christian Century* 101 (1 August): 732–34.

Huck, Gabe. 1989. "Why Settle for Communion?" *Commonweal* 116 (27 January): 37–39.

Hughes, John Jay. 1971. "Infallible? An Inquiry Considered." *Theological Studies* 31 (June): 183–207.

———. 1980a. "Hans Küng and the Magisterium." *Theological Studies* 41 (June): 368–89.

———. 1980b. "Episcopalians and Rome." *America* 143 (13 September): 111–12.

Hughes, Kathleen. 1991. *The Monk's Tale: A Biography of Godfrey Diekmann, OSB*. Collegeville, Minn.: The Liturgical Press.

Imbelli, Robert P. 1982. "Vatican II: Twenty Years Later." *Commonweal* 109 (8 October): 522–26.

———. 1986. "Theology after the Synod: Boundaries." *Commonweal* 113 (31 January): 41–44.

Irwin, Kevin W. 1986. "The Constitution on the Sacred Liturgy." In *Vatican II and Its Documents*, 9–38. *See* O'Connell 1986.

Jay, Eric G. 1978. *The Church: Its Changing Image Through Twenty Centuries*. Atlanta: John Knox Press.

Johann, Robert O. 1965. "Responsible Parenthood: A Philosophical View." *Catholic Theological Society of America* 20:115–28.

———. 1967. "Love and Justice." In *Ethics and Society*, edited by Robert T. De George, 25–47. New York: Doubleday.

———. 1968. *Building the Human*. New York: Herder and Herder.

John, Eric., ed. 1964. *The Popes*. New York: Hawthorne Books.

Johnson, Elizabeth A. 1985. "The Marian Tradition and the Reality of Women." *Horizons* 12 (Spring): 116–35.

———. 1989. "Mary and the Female Face of God." *Theological Studies* 50 (September): 500–26.

———. 1993. "A Theological Case for God-She: Expanding the Treasury of Metaphor." *Commonweal* 120 (29 January): 9–14.

Jones, Alfred H. 1985. "Edinburgh 1985." *Christian Century* 102 (17 July): 671–72.

Jones, Arthur. 1987. "Pope's South Carolina Stop Is a Major Move to Ecumenism for Evangelicals." *National Catholic Reporter* 23 (11 September): 1, 25.

———. 1992. "Apostolic Delegate Left Seal on U.S. Church." *National Catholic Reporter* 28 (25 September): 5–8.

Jossua, Jean-Pierre. 1987. "Jacques Pohier: A Theologian Destroyed." In *The Church in Anguish*, 205–11. *See* Küng and Swidler 1987.

Jungmann, Joseph Andreas. 1969. "Constitution on the Sacred Liturgy." In vol. 1 of *Commentary on the Documents of Vatican II*, 1–87. *See* Vorgrimler 1969.

Kaiser, Robert Blair. 1986. *The Politics of Sex and Religion*. Kansas City, Mo.: Leaven Press.

Kaspar, Walter. 1989. *Theology of the Church*. New York: Crossroad.

Keane, Philip S. 1977. *Sexual Morality: A Catholic Perspective*. New York: Paulist Press.

———. 1982. "The Objective Moral Order: Reflections on Recent Research." *Theological Studies* 43 (June): 260–78.

Keifer, Ralph A. 1975. "Rite or Wrong: Ten Years after the Constitution on the Liturgy." *Commonweal* 102 (15 August): 328–30.

Kelleher, Stephen J. 1968. "The Problem of the Intolerable Marriage." *America* 119 (14 September): 178–82.

———. 1973. *Divorce and Remarriage for Catholics?* New York: Doubleday.

———. 1975. "The Laity, Divorce and Remarriage." *Commonweal* 102 (7 November): 521–24.

———. 1977. "Catholic Annulments: A Dehumanizing Process." *Commonweal* 104 (10 June): 363–68.

———. 1978. "Looking Back, Looking Ahead." *America* 139 (18 November): 355–57.

Kelly, George A. 1982. *The Crisis of Authority*. New York: Regnery Gateway.

Kelly, J.N.D. 1986. *The Oxford Dictionary of the Popes*. New York: Oxford University Press.

Kennedy, Eugene. 1976a. "Insufficient Guilt in the Room." *America* 134 (27 March): 244–51.

———. 1976b. "A Myth for Ministers." *America* 134 (12 June): 509–12.

———. 1988a. *Tomorrow's Catholics, Yesterday's Church*. San Francisco: Harper and Row.

———. 1988b. "The Problem with No Name." *America* 158 (23 April): 423–25.

Kerlin, Michael. 1973. "A New Modernist Crisis? Hardly." *America* 129 (6 October): 239–42.

Kilmartin, Edward. 1979. *Toward Reunion: The Orthodox and Roman Catholic Churches*. New York: Paulist Press.

King, Thomas M. 1985. "The Milieu Teilhard Left Behind." *America* 152 (30 March): 249–53.

Kirk, Robin. 1986. "Gustavo Gutierrez's New Way to Be a Christian." *National Catholic Reporter* 23 (31 October): 7–8.

Knauer, Peter. 1979. "The Hermeneutical Function of the Principle of Double Effect." In *Moral Norms and the Catholic Tradition*, 1–39. No. 1 of *Readings in Moral Theology*, edited by Charles Curran and Richard McCormick. New York: Paulist Press.

Knitter, Paul F. 1985. *No Other Name?: A Critical Survey of Christian Attitudes toward the World Religions*. New York: Orbis Books.

———. 1986. Knitter's response to a review symposium of his *No Other Name? Horizons* 13 (Spring): 130–35.

———. 1990. "Key Questions for a Theology of Religions." *Horizons* 17 (Spring): 92–102.

Kolden, Mark. 1984. "Marxism and Latin American Liberation Theology." In *Christians and the Many Faces of Marxism*, edited by Wayne Stumme, 123–31. Minneapolis, Minn.: Augsburg Press.

Komonchak, Joseph A. 1983. "The Return of Yves Congar." *Commonweal* 110 (15 July): 402–5.

———. 1985. "What's Happening to Doctrine?" *Commonweal* 112 (6 September): 456–59.

———. 1987. "Issues Behind the Curran Case" *Commonweal* 114 (23 January): 43–47.

———. 1990a. "Marie-Dominique Chenu." *Commonweal* 117 (20 April): 252–54.

———. 1990b. "What They Said Before the Council." *Commonweal* 117 (7 December): 714–17.

———. 1990c. "Theology and Culture at Mid-Century: The Example of Henri de Lubac." *Theological Studies* 51 (December): 579–602.

———. 1992a. "Recapturing the Great Tradition." *Commonweal* 119 (31 January): 14–17.

———. 1992b. "The Coldness of Clarity, the Warmth of Love: The Measure of John Courtney Murray." *Commonweal* 119 (14 August): 16–17.

Kosnik, Anthony, William Carroll, Agnes Cunningham, Ronald Modras, and James Schulte. 1977. *Human Sexuality: New Directions in American Catholic Thought*. New York: Paulist Press.

Kress, Robert. 1977. "Mary's Assumption, God's Promise Fulfilled." *America* 137 (30 August): 71–74.

Küng, Hans. 1976. *On Being a Christian*. New York: Doubleday.

Küng, Hans, and Leonard Swidler, eds. 1987. *The Church in Anguish*. New York: Harper and Row.

Küng, Hans, and David Tracy, eds. 1989. *Paradigm Change in Theology*. New York: Crossroad.

Lamb, Matthew L. 1986. "Theology after the Synod: Beyond Culture." *Commonweal* 113 (31 January): 46–49.

Lamboley, Kathryn. 1979. "Leo XIII, 'The Workers' Pope,' Favored Unions." *National Catholic Reporter* 15 (7 September): 37.

Lapomarda, Vincent A. 1986. "Some Reflections on Catholics and the Holocaust." *America* 155 (27 December): 424–27.

Lash, Nicholas. 1988. *Easter Is Ordinary.* Charlottesvile, Va.: University Press of Virginia.

———. 1992a. "Theology on the Way to Stuttgart." *America* 166 (4 April): 266–68.

———. 1992b. "The Broken Mirror." *America* 166 (16 May): 432–34.

Latourelle, Rene, ed. 1988a. *Vatican II: Assessment and Perspectives.* 3 vols. New York: Paulist Press.

———. 1988b. "Absence and Presence of Fundamental Theology at Vatican II." In vol. 3 of *Vatican II,* 378–415. *See* Latourelle 1988a.

Lauret, Bernard, ed. 1988. *Fifty Years of Catholic Theology: Conversations with Yves Congar.* Minneapolis, Minn.: Fortress Press.

Lavin, Henry St. C. 1984. "A View from Rome: The Concordat." *America* 150 (5 May): 340–41.

Lefevere, Patricia. 1988. "*Humanae Vitae* Celebrated 20 Years Later." *National Catholic Reporter* 24 (26 August): 10.

Lernoux, Penny. 1985. "Act 'Shocks' Brazilians United With Theologians." *National Catholic Reporter* 21 (24 May): 1, 23.

———. 1989. *People of God: The Struggle for World Catholicism.* New York: Viking.

Lindbeck, George A., Monika Hellwig, and George Higgins. 1985. "The Ratzinger File." *Commonweal* 112 (15 November): 635–42.

Linnan, John E. 1986. "Declaration on Religious Liberty." In *Vatican II and Its Documents,* 167–79. *See* O'Connell 1986.

Lonergan, Bernard. 1972. *Method in Theology.* New York: Seabury.

———. 1974. *A Second Collection.* Edited by William Ryan and Bernard Tyrrell. Philadelphia: Westminster Press.

———. 1985. *A Third Collection.* Edited by Frederick E. Crowe. New York: Paulist Press.

Lyles, Jean Caffey. 1983. "Unity and Diversity at Vancouver." *Christian Century* 100 (28 September): 836–37.

MacEoin, Gary. 1973. "Maryknoll Adopts New Mission Concept." *National Catholic Reporter* 10 (6 April): 1, 20.

———. 1984. "Liberation Theology under Fire." *The Witness* 67 (December): 12–14.

———. 1991a. "Struggle for Latin American Soul Quickens." *National Catholic Reporter* 27 (22 January): 15–19.

———. 1991b. "Lay Movements in the United States before Vatican II." *America* 165 (10 April): 61–65.

———. 1992a. "View of Rome Neocolonialism Issue Clearer." *National Catholic Reporter* 28 (28 August): 10.

———. 1992b. "Curia Faction Goes for Total Control over CELAM IV." *National Catholic Reporter* 29 (6 November): 14–15.

MacEoin, Gary, and Nivita Riley. 1980. *Puebla: A Church Being Born.* New York: Paulist Press.

MacIntyre, Alasdair. 1981. *After Virtue*. Notre Dame, Ind.: University of Notre Dame Press.

Maguire, Daniel C. 1976. "The Vatican on Sex." *Commonweal* 103 (27 February): 137–40.

———. 1983. "Abortion: A Question of Catholic Honesty." *Christian Century* 100 (14 September): 803–7.

———. 1984. "Visit to an Abortion Clinic." *National Catholic Reporter* 20 (5 October): 9, 14.

———. 1986. *The Moral Revolution*. New York: Harper and Row.

Mahoney, John. 1990. *The Making of Moral Theology*. New York: Clarendon Press.

Mainelli, Vincent P. 1986. "RCIA: Option or Panacea?" *America* 154 (5 April): 279–80.

Maloney, Donald. 1970. "Rahner and the 'Anonymous Christian.'" *America* 123 (31 October): 348–50.

Martinez, Demetria. 1990. "Weakland on Abortion: Who's Confusing Whom?" *National Catholic Reporter* 27 (23 November): 7.

Marty, Martin E. 1983. "Martin Luther's Reckless Grasp of Grace." *Commonweal* 110 (26 October): 962–65.

———. 1988. "The State of the Disunion." *Commonweal* 115 (29 January): 43–46.

———. 1989. "Rites of Passage I." *Christian Century* 106 (5 July): 671.

May, William W., ed. 1987. *Vatican Authority and American Catholic Dissent: The Curran Case and Its Consequences*. New York: Crossroad.

McBrien, Richard P. 1973. *The Remaking of the Church*. San Francisco: Harper and Row.

———. 1978a. "Who Is a Catholic?" *National Catholic Reporter* 14 (10 February): 7, 9.

———. 1978b. "Catholic Social Action." *National Catholic Reporter* 14 (3 March): 7–8.

———. 1979. "The Roman Catholic Church: Can It Transcend the Crisis?" *Christian Century* 96 (17 January): 42–45.

———. 1981. *Catholicism*. Minneapolis, Minn.: Winston Press.

———. 1992. "Capitalists Should Worry about Pope." *National Catholic Reporter* 28 (18 December): 2.

———. 1993. "Social Justice the Conservative's Achilles' Heel." *National Catholic Reporter* 29 (5 February): 2.

McClory, Robert J. 1988a. "Archdiocesan Mass for Gays Ruptures Catholic Dignity." *National Catholic Reporter* 24 (1 August): 4.

———. 1988b. "Patty Crowley, at 75, Bruised But Unbowed." *National Catholic Reporter* 24 (12 August): 5–6.

McCormick, Richard A. 1966. "Modern Morals in a Muddle." *America* 115 (30 July): 116.

———. 1968. "The New Morality." *America* 119 (15 June): 769–72.

———. 1973. "The Silence Since *Humanae Vitae.*" *America* 129 (21 July): 30–33.

———. 1976a. "Sexual Ethics: An Opinion." *National Catholic Reporter* 12 (30 January): 9.

———. 1976b. "Human Rights and the Mission of the Church." *Theological Studies* 37 (March): 107–19.

———. 1981a. *Notes on Moral Theology 1965 through 1980.* Lanham, Md.: University Press of America.

———. 1981b. "Notes on Moral Theology." *Theological Studies* 42 (March): 119–24.

———. 1984. "The Chill Factor: Recent Roman Interventions." *America* 150 (30 June): 475–81.

———. 1985. "Notes on Moral Theology." *Theological Studies* 46 (March): 50–64.

———. 1986. "The Search for Truth in the Catholic Context." *America* 155 (8 November): 276–81.

———. 1989. "Moral Theology 1940–1989: An Overview." *Theological Studies* 50 (March): 3–24.

———. 1990. "Changing My Mind about the Changeable Church." *Christian Century* 107 (8 August): 732–36.

———. 1993. "*Humanae Vitae* 25 Years Later." *America* 169 (17 July): 6–12.

McCormick, Richard A., and Richard P. McBrien. 1991. "Theology as a Public Responsibility." *America* 165 (28 September): 184–89, 203–6.

McDade, John. 1991. "Catholic Theology in the Postconciliar Period." In *Modern Catholicism*, 422–43. *See* Hastings 1991.

McDonagh, Enda. 1991. "The Church in the Modern World." In *Modern Catholicism*, 96–112. *See* Hastings 1991.

McDonagh, Francis. 1990. "With Eyes to CELAM IV." *National Catholic Reporter* 27 (16 November): 10.

McDonnell, Kilian. 1982. "Anglicans and Catholics: Where We Stand." *America* 147 (27 November): 326–30.

———. 1983. "Luther and Catholics on Justification." *America* 149 (3 December): 345–48.

McGinn, Bernard. 1985. "Papal Assassinations: An Historical View." *Criterion* 24 (Winter): 13–18.

McGovern, Arthur F. 1989. "Liberation Theology Adapts and Endures." *America* 161 (3 November): 587–90.

McGovern, Arthur F., and Thomas L. Schubeck. 1988. "Updating Liberation Theology." *America* 159 (16 July): 32–35.

McHugh, John. 1975. *The Mother of Jesus in the New Testament.* New York: Doubleday.

McKenzie, John L. 1980. "A Bill of Divorce." *Commonweal* 107 (30 May): 301–5.

———. 1985. *Source.* Chicago: Thomas More.

McLaughlin, Loretta. 1982. *The Pill, John Rock and the Church: A Biography of a Revolution.* New York: Little, Brown.

McManus, Jim. 1986. "New Homosexuality Guidelines Seen as a Step Back." *National Catholic Reporter* 23 (7 November): 7.

McNeill, John J. 1976. *The Church and the Homosexual.* Kansas City, Mo.: Sheed Andrews and McMeel.

————. 1986. "No Time for Silence." *Commonweal* 113 (5 December): 647.

————. 1987. "Homosexuality: Challenging the Church to Grow." *Christian Century* 104 (11 March): 242–46.

Mecklenburger, Ralph D. 1979. "Are Christians 'Honorary Jews'?" *Christian Century* 96 (21 March): 302–3.

Mersch, Emile. 1939. *Morality and the Mystical Body.* New York: P. J. Kenedy and Sons.

Metz, Johann Baptist. 1969. *Theology of the World.* New York: Herder and Herder.

————. 1970. "Political Theology." In vol. 5 of *Sacramentum Mundi: An Encyclopedial of Theology,* 34–38. New York: Herder and Herder.

————. 1980. *Faith in History and Society.* New York: Crossroad.

————. 1981. *The Emergent Church: The Future of Christianity in a Postbourgeois World.* New York: Crossworld.

————. 1989. "Theology in a New Paradigm: Political Theology." In *Paradigm Change in Theology,* 355–66. *See* Küng and Tracy 1989.

Michaels, James W. 1980. "U.S. Theologians' Hopes 'Dashed' by Synod Results." *National Catholic Reporter* 17 (7 December): 1, 19.

Milhaven, John Giles. 1970. "The Abortion Debate: An Epistemological Interpretation." *Theological Studies* 31 (March): 106–24.

————. 1976. Review of *The Church and the Homosexual,* by John J. McNeill. *National Catholic Reporter* 14 (8 October): 12.

Miller, J. Michael. 1983. *What Are They Saying about Papal Primacy?* New York: Paulist Press.

Misner, Paul. 1983. "Vancouver 1983: A Catholic View." *The Ecumenist* 22 (November): 1–4.

Modras, Ronald. 1979. "Solidarity and Opposition in a Pluralitic Church." *Commonweal* 106 (14 September): 493–95.

Moede, Gerald R. 1984. "Covenanting: New Directions for Ecumenism." *Christian Century* 101 (31 October): 1014–15.

Molineaux, D. J. 1987. "Gustavo Gutierrez: Historical Origins." *The Ecumenist* 25 (July): 65–69.

Moltmann, Jurgen. 1967. *Theology of Hope.* New York: Harper and Row.

————. 1975. *The Church in the Power of the Spirit.* San Francisco: Harper and Row.

Montague, George T. 1993. "Freezing the Fire: The Death of Relational Language." *America* 168 (31 March): 5–7.

Mooney, Christopher F. 1967. "Teilhard de Chardin and Christian Spirituality." *Thought* 42 (September): 483–502.

Moore, Arthur J. 1983. "More Than Politics." *Commonweal* 110 (9 September): 452, 454–55.

Moran, Gabriel. 1966a. *Catechesis of Revelation*. New York: Herder and Herder.

———. 1966b. *Theology of Revelation*. New York: Herder and Herder.

———. 1972. *The Present Revelation*. New York: Herder and Herder.

Moynihan, Daniel Patrick. 1991. "Social Justice in the Next Century." *America* 165 (14 September): 132–37.

Murphy, Francis X. 1978. "Christianity, Marriage and Sex." *Commonweal* 105 (16 June): 380–86.

———. 1981. *The Papacy Today*. New York: Macmillan.

———. 1986. "The Politique of the Synod." *America* 154 (25 January): 49–51.

———. 1990. "Aggiornamento to Perestroika: Vatican Ostpolitik." *America* 162 (19 May): 494–98.

———. 1991. "Oswald von Nell-Breuning: Papal Surrogate." *America* 165 (26 October): 293–95.

———. 1992. "John's Council as Catholic Camelot." *National Catholic Reporter* 28 (2 October): 2.

Murphy, Paul I., and René R. Arlington. 1983. *La Popessa*. New York: Warner Books.

Murray, John Courtney. 1966a. "Religious Freedom." In *The Documents of Vatican II*, 672–74. *See* Abbott 1966.

———. 1966b. "Freedom, Authority and Community." *America* 115 (14 September): 734–37, 740–41.

Nelson, James B. 1987. "Reuniting Sexuality and Spirituality." *Christian Century* 104 (25 February): 187–90.

Nelson, J. Robert. 1976. "The World Council's Second Generation Takes Over." *Christian Century* 93 (18 February): 144–47.

Neuhaus, Richard John. 1992. *Doing Well and Doing Good: The Challenge of the Christian Capitalist*. New York: Doubleday.

Nichols, Aidan. 1989. *Yves Congar*. Wilton, Conn.: Morehouse-Barlow.

———. 1990. *From Newman to Congar*. Edinburgh: T. and T. Clark.

Norman, Edward. 1991. "An Outsider's Evaluation." In *Modern Catholicism*, 457–62. *See* Hastings 1991.

Nouwen, Henri J. M. 1967. "Homosexuality: Prejudice or Mental Illness?" *National Catholic Reporter* 4 (29 November): 8.

Novak, Michael. 1975. "Theology of Liberation." *National Catholic Reporter* 11 (21 November): 12.

———. 1987. *Will It Liberate?* New York: Paulist Press.

Nugent, Robert. 1981. "Homosexuality and the Hurting Family." *America* 144 (28 February): 154–57.

———. 1984. "Homosexuality and the Vatican." *Christian Century* 101 (9 May): 487–89.

Nyhan, David. 1984. "The (Catholic) Father of the Pill." *National Catholic Reporter* 21 (28 December): 7.

O'Collins, Gerald. 1990. "Catholic Theology (1965–1990)." *America* 162 (3 February): 86–87, 104–5.

O'Connell, Timothy, 1976. *Principles for a Catholic Morality.* New York: Seabury.

———, ed. 1986. *Vatican II and Its Documents: An American Reappraisal.* Wilmington, Del.: Michael Glazier.

Oesterreicher, John M. 1969. "Declaration on the Non-Christian Religions." In vol. 3 of *Commentary on the Documents of Vatican II,* 1–136. *See* Vorgrimler 1969.

Ogden, Schubert M. 1980. "Faith and Freedom." *Christian Century* 98 (17 December): 1241–44.

O'Grady, Desmond. 1977. "Reassessing the Missioner's Role." *National Catholic Reporter* 13 (15 April): 3.

O'Malley, John. 1989. *Tradition and Transition: Historical Perspectives on Vatican II.* Wilmington, Del.: Michael Glazier.

Opstrny, David J. 1988. "Gay Catholics Evicted from San Francisco Church." *San Francisco Examiner,* 20 November.

Orsy, Ladislas. 1990. "Magisterium and Theologians: A Vatican Document." *America* 163 (21 July): 30–32.

Osborne, Kenan B. 1993. *Ministry: Lay Ministry in the Roman Catholic Church.* New York: Paulist Press.

Ostling, Richard. 1992. "The Second Reformation." *Time,* 14 November.

Outler, Albert C. 1982. "Protestants Found Three Councils." *National Catholic Reporter* 18 (8 October): 4, 37–38.

Palmer, Parker J. 1986. *The Company of Strangers.* New York: Crossroad.

Palmer, Paul F. 1975. "When a Marriage Dies." *America* 133 (22 February): 126–28.

Parker, James. 1992. "The Mother of Christian Initiation." *Commonweal* 119 (31 January): 19–21.

Pavan, Pietro. 1969. "Declaration on Religious Freedom." In vol. 3 of *Commentary on the Documents of Vatican II,* 49–63. *See* Vorgrimler 1969.

Peerman, Dean. 1979. "Did the Pope Apply the Brakes at Puebla?" *Christian Century* 96 (28 February): 203–4.

———. 1993. "CELAM IV: Maneuvering and Marking Time in Santo Domingo." *Christian Century* 110 (17 February): 180–85.

Penfield, Janet Harbison. 1980. "COCU at 20: An Anniversary Waltz." *Christian Century* 97 (3 December): 1186–91.

Pennington, M. Basil. 1975. *Mary Today.* New York: Doubleday.

Perlez, Jane. 1993. "Pope Orders Nuns Out of Auschwitz." *New York Times,* 15 April.

Piccolino, Alberta. 1991. "Pope Confronts a Different 'Less Catholic' Brazil." *National Catholic Reporter* 28 (1 November): 12.

Portier, William L. 1983. "Catholic Theology in the U.S., 1840–1907: Recovering a Forgotten Tradition." *Horizons* 10 (Fall): 317–33.

Pottmeyer, Hermann J. 1992. "The Traditionalist Temptation of the Contemporary Church." *America* 167 (5 September): 100–104.

Provost, James H. 1989. "The Papacy: Power, Authority and Leadership." In *The Papacy and the Church in the United States,* 189–215. *See* Cooke 1989.

Putney, Michael E. 1992. "Come, Holy Spirit, Renew the Whole Creation: Seventh Assembly of the World Council of Churches." *Theological Studies* 52 (December): 607–35.

Quinn, John R. 1987. "Towards an Understanding of the Letter on the Pastoral Care of Homosexual Persons." *America* 156 (7 February): 92–95.

Radano, John A. 1985. "Consultation on Church Union: Recent Developments, New Directions." *Religious Studies Review* 11 (April): 151–59.

Rahner, Karl. 1963. *Mary, Mother of the Lord.* New York: Herder and Herder.

———. 1964a. *Nature and Grace.* New York: Sheed and Ward.

———. 1964b. "On the Question of a Formal Existential Ethics." In vol. 2 of *Theological Investigations,* translated by Karl-H. Kruger, 217–34. Baltimore: Helicon Press.

———. 1966. "Christianity and the non-Christian Religions." In vol. 5 of *Theological Investigations,* translated by Karl-H. Kruger, 115–34. New York: Herder and Herder.

———. 1969. *Grace in Freedom.* New York: Herder and Herder.

———. 1972. "The Problem of Genetic Manipulation." In vol. 9 of *Theological Investigations,* translated by Graham Harison, 225–52. New York: Herder and Herder.

———. 1979. "Towards a Fundamental Theological Interpretation of Vatican II." *Theological Studies* 40 (December): 716–27.

Ranly, Ernest W. 1977. "Constructing Local Theologies." *Commonweal* 104 (11 November): 716–19.

Ratzinger, Joseph Cardinal, with Vittorio Messori. 1985. *Ratzinger Report.* San Francisco: Ignatius Press.

Rausch, Thomas P. 1982. "The Image of Mary: A Catholic Response." *America* 146 (27 March): 231–34.

———. 1984. "An Ecumenical Eucharist for a World Assembly." *America* 150 (21 January): 25–29.

———. 1985. "Rome and Geneva: The Experience of Ecumenism." *America* 152 (19 January): 41–45.

———. 1986. *The Roots of the Catholic Tradition.* Wilmington, Del.: Michael Glazier.

———. 1989a. *Authority and Leadership in the Church.* Wilmington, Del.: Michael Glazier.

———. 1989b. "Ethical Issues and Ecumenism." *America* 160 (21 January): 30–33.

———. 1990. "The Ecumenical Movement in the 1990's: Is It Still Moving?" *America* 163 (3 November): 218–22.

Rawls, John. 1971. *A Theory of Justice*. Cambridge, Mass.: Harvard University Press.

Redington, James D. 1983. "The Hindu-Christian Dialogue and the Interior Dialogue." *Theological Studies* 44 (December): 587–603.

Reese, Thomas J. 1984. "The Selection of Bishops." *America* 151 (24 August): 65–72.

———. 1988. "Archbishop Lefébvre: Moving Toward Schism." *America* 158 (4 June): 573–74.

Rhodes, Anthony. 1983. *The Power of Rome*. New York: Franklin Watts.

Richard, Lucien. 1981. *What Are They Saying about Christ and World Religions?* New York: Paulist Press.

Riding, Alan. 1991. "Pope Visits Fatima to Tender Thanks." *New York Times*, 14 May.

Riley, Maria. 1989. "Feminist Analysis: A Missing Perspective." In *The Logic of Solidarity*, 186–201. *See* Baum and Ellsberg 1989.

Riley, Michael C. 1978. "Teaching All Nations . . . and Learning." *America* 138 (18 March): 202–6.

———. 1979. "Cross–cultural Evangelization." *America* 141 (22 December): 409–11.

Rohter, Larry. 1990. "Pope, in Mexico, Faces Rising Protestant Tide." *New York Times*, 12 May.

Rosato, Philip J. 1992. "The Church of United Europe: Reflections on the Recent Special Synod." *America* 166 (11 January): 4–7.

Ruether, Rosemary Radford. 1985. *Women-Church*. San Francisco: Harper and Row.

———. 1987. "John Paul II and the Growing Alienation of Women from the Church." In *The Church in Anguish*, 279–83. *See* Küng and Swidler 1987.

Rusch, William G. 1985. *Ecumenism*. Philadelphia: Fortress Press.

Ryan, Thomas. 1991. "Report on the World Council of Churches General Assembly." *America* 164 (25 May): 566–71.

Scharper, Philip. 1978. "Toward a Politicized Christianity." *Commonweal* 105 (16 June): 392–99.

Schillebeeckx, Edward. 1981a. *Interim Report on the Books Jesus and Christ*. New York: Crossroad.

———. 1981b. *Ministry*. New York: Crossroad.

Schineller, Peter J. 1976. "Christ and Church: A Spectrum of Views." *Theological Studies* 37 (December): 545–66.

Schlette, Heinz Robert. 1976. "Anonymous Christianity: A Disputed Question." *Theology Digest* 24 (Summer): 125–31.

Schoof, Mark T. 1970. *A Survey of Catholic Theology: 1800–1970*. New York: Paulist, Newman Press.

Schüssler-Fiorenza, Elizabeth. 1986. "Theology after the Synod: Acknowledging Women." *Commonweal* 113 (31 January): 44–46.

Searle, Mark. 1988. "Renewing the Liturgy—Again." *Commonweal* 115 (18 November): 617–22.

Semmelroth, Otto. 1969. "The Role of the Blessed Virgin Mother." In vol. 1 of *Commentary on the Documents of Vatican II*, 285–96. *See* Vorgrimler 1969.

Sheets, John. 1983. "The Luther Year: 1983." *America* 148 (30 April): 337–40.

Sheppard, L. C. 1967. "Catholic Liturgical Movements." In vol. 8 of *New Catholic Encyclopedia*, 900–904. New York: McGraw-Hill.

Sheridan, Edward F. 1968. "Canadian Bishops on Human Life." *America* 119 (31 October): 349, 352.

Sigmund, Paul E. 1990. *Liberation Theology at the Crossroads: Democracy or Revolution?* New York: Oxford University Press.

Simons, Marlise. 1993. "Pilgrims Crowding Europe's Catholic Shrines." *New York Times*, 12 October.

Smith, Huston. 1991. *The World's Religions*. San Francisco: Harper San Francisco.

Smith, Karen Sue. 1988. "Michel Blows His Horn: Social Justice and Liturgy." *Commonweal* 115 (9 September): 456–57.

Sobrino, Jon. 1991. "Awakening from the Sleep of Inhumanity." *Christian Century* 108 (30 April): 364–70.

Sölle, Dorothee. 1967. *Christ the Representative: An Essay in Theology after the 'Death of God.'* London: SCM.

Spaeth, Robert L. 1993. "The Galileo File: Still Open." *Commonweal* 120 (26 March): 6–7.

Spong, John Selby. 1988. *Living in Sin? A Bishop Rethinks Human Sexuality*. San Francisco: Harper and Row.

Stahel, Thomas H. 1992. "The Cry from Santo Domingo." *America* 167 (31 October): 315–17.

Stammer, Larry B. 1993. "Meeting of World Religions Leads to Ethics Rules." *Los Angeles Times*, 5 September.

Steinberg, Leo. 1984. *The Sexuality of Christ in Renaissance Art and in Modern Oblivion*. New York: Pantheon.

Steinfels, Peter. 1985. "Conflicts and Code Words: A Sober Look at the Synod." *Commonweal* 112 (20 December): 698–700.

———. 1989. "A Champion of Tradition." *New York Times*, 30 June.

———. 1990a. "Flexibility Urged on Abortion Issue." *New York Times*, 21 May.

———. 1990b. "Theology Awaits the Vatican's Word on Evils Lesser and Greater." *New York Times*, 2 September.

———. 1990c. "Vatican Bars Swiss University from Honoring Archbishop of Milwaukee." *New York Times*, 11 November.

———. 1990d. "Bishops Issue Warning on Birth Control." *New York Times*, 15 November.

———. 1990e. "Pope Endorses Prague Statement on Anti-Semitism." *New York Times*, 7 December.

———. 1991. "Papal Letter Spreads the Faith and the Debate." *New York Times*, 29 January.

————. 1992a. "Vatican Urges Restrictions on Homosexual Rights." *New York Times*, 18 July.

————. 1992b. "Struggling for Unity." *New York Times*, 6 September.

————. 1992c. "A Pivotal Conference Is Begun by Latin Bishops." *New York Times*, 13 October.

————. 1992d. "Pastoral Letter on Women's Role Fails in Vote of Catholic Bishops." *New York Times*, 19 November.

————. 1992e. "Why Did God Make These Debates So Hard?" *New York Times*, 22 November.

————. 1993a. "Papal Birth-Control Letter Retains Its Grip." *New York Times*, 1 August.

————. 1993b. "More Diversity Than Harmony." *New York Times*, 7 September.

Stransky, Thomas F. 1986a. "Surprises and Fears of Ecumenism: Twenty Years after Vatican II." *America* 154 (25 January): 44–48.

————. 1986b. "The Catholic-Jewish Dialogue: Twenty Years after *Nostra Aetate*." *America* 154 (8 February): 92–97.

Swidler, Leonard. 1987. "A Continuing Controversy: Küng in Conflict." In *The Church in Anguish*, 193–204. *See* Küng and Swidler 1987.

Tambasco, Anthony J. 1984. *What Are They Saying about Mary?* New York: Paulist Press.

Tavard, George H. 1960. *Two Centuries of Ecumenism*. Notre Dame, Ind.: Fides Publications.

————. 1980. "The Anglican-Roman Catholic Agreed Statements and Their Reception." *Theological Studies* 41 (March): 74–97.

Thompson, Betty. 1985a. "W. A. Visser't Hooft: Mover and Shaker." *Christian Century* 102 (17 July): 668–70.

————. 1985b. "Eugene Carson Blake: A Noble Prophet." *Christian Century* 102 (28 August): 756–57.

Tierney, Brian. 1988. "Pope and Bishop: A Historical Survey." *America* 158 (5 March): 230–37.

Tillard, J. M. R. 1983. *The Bishop of Rome*. Wilmington, Del.: Michael Glazier.

Tillman, Fritz. 1960. *The Master Calls*. Baltimore: Helicon Press.

Timmerman, Don, Gordan Zahn, and John F. Baldovin. 1988. "The Eucharist: Who May Preside?" *Commonweal* 115 (9 September): 460–63, 466.

Toolan, David. 1982. "Is There Life after Ecumenism?" *Commonweal* 109 (29 January): 43–46.

Tracy, David. 1975. *Blessed Rage for Order*. New York: Seabury.

————. 1981. *The Analogical Imagination*. New York: Crossroad.

————. 1987a. "On Hope as a Theological Virtue." In *The Church in Anguish*, 268–72. *See* Küng and Swidler 1987.

————. 1987b. *Plurality and Ambiguity*. New York: Harper and Row.

————. 1989a. "Hermeneutical Reflections in the New Paradigm." In *Paradigm Change in Theology*, 34–62. *See* Küng and Tracy 1989.

————. 1989b. "The Uneasy Alliance Reconceived: Catholic Theological Method, Modernity and Postmodernity. *Theological Studies* 50 (September): 548–70.

————. 1990. "God, Dialogue and Solidarity: A Theological Refrain." *Christian Century* 107 (10 October): 900–904.

————. 1991. *Dialogue with the Other: The Interreligious Dialogue.* Grand Rapids, Mich.: William Eerdmans Publishing.

Tuohey, John F. 1992. "The CDF and Homosexuals: Rewriting Moral Tradition." *America* 167 (12 September): 136–38.

Tyrrell, George. 1910. *Christianity at the Crossroads.* London: Longmans, Green.

Untener, Kenneth E. 1984. "Local Churches and Universal Church." *America* 151 (13 October): 201–5.

————. 1993. "*Humanae Vitae:* What Has It Done to Us?" *Commonweal* 120 (18 June):12–14.

Vacek, Edward. 1983. "Authority and the Peace Pastoral." *America* 149 (22 October): 227.

————. 1984. "Popular Ethical Subjectivism: Four Preludes to Objectivity." *Horizons* 11 (Spring): 42–60.

Van Beeck, Franz Josef. 1985. *Catholic Identity after Vatican II.* Chicago: Loyola University Press.

Vidulich, Dorothy. 1990. "Weakland: Vatican II Spirit Has 'Spun Itself Out.'" *National Catholic Reporter* 26 (12 October): 7.

————. 1992a. "Vatican Strikes at Legal Protection for Gays."*National Catholic Reporter* 28 (31 July): 9.

————. 1992b. "Gay Groups Say 'Outing' Bishops Is Out of Bounds." *National Catholic Reporter* 28 (14 August): 3.

Vidulich, Dorothy, and Thomas Fox. 1992. "Women's Letter Draft Moves Sharply Right."*National Catholic Reporter* 28 (11 September): 3.

Visser't Hooft, Willem A. 1982. *The Genesis and Formation of the World Council of Churches.* Geneva: World Council of Churches.

Voegelin, Eric. 1956–87. *Order and History.* 5 vols. Baton Rouge: Louisiana State University Press.

Von Hügel, Friedrich. 1932. *The Mystical Element in Religion as Studied in St. Catherine of Genoa and Her Friends.* 2nd edition. London: J. M. Dent and Sons.

Vorgrimler, Herbert, ed. 1969. *Commentary on the Documents of Vatican II.* 3 vols. New York: Herder and Herder.

Walsh, Michael. 1980. *An Illustrated History of the Popes.* New York: St. Martin's Press.

Warner, Marina. 1976. *Alone of All Her Sex.* New York: Alfred A. Knopf.

Wassmer, Thomas A. 1968. "The New Morality." *America* 118 (10 February): 190–92.

Watson, Russell. 1978. "A Death in Rome." *Newsweek,* 9 October.

Watts, A.M. 1989. "Christian Claims in a Pluralistic Society." *Christian Century* 106 (1 March): 222–23.

Weakland, Rembert G. 1992. "Crisis in Orthodox-Catholic Relations: Challenge to Hopes." *America* 166 (25 January): 30–35.

Welsh, John R. 1986. "Comunidades Eclesiais de Base: A New Way to Be Church." *America* 154 (8 February): 85–88.

Whelan, Charles M. 1974. "Divorced Catholics: A Proposal." *America* 131 (7 December): 363–65.

White, Nancy. 1979. "Collision Course." *Newsweek*, 16 July.

Willems, Ad. 1987. "The Endless Case of Edward Schillebeeckx." In *The Church in Anguish*, 212–22. *See* Küng and Swidler 1987.

Williams, Bruce. 1987. "Homosexuality: The New Vatican Statement." *Theological Studies* 48 (June): 259–77.

Windsor, Pat. 1989. "Häring Fears 'Psychological Exodus' from Church." *National Catholic Reporter* 25 (28 April): 5.

———. 1990a. "Vatican Vetoes Doctorate for Weakland." *National Catholic Reporter* 27 (16 November): 1, 8.

———. 1990b. "Theologians' Statement Benign Yet Critical of Vatican." *National Catholic Reporter* 27 (21 December): 9.

———. 1991. "Neoconservatives Capitalize on Papal Encyclical." *National Catholic Reporter* 27 (17 May): 3.

Winiarski, Mark. 1977. "Theologians Debate Resolutions on Sex Report." *National Catholic Reporter* 13 (1 July): 1, 6.

———. 1979a. "Vatican Chides 'Human Sexuality' Authors." *National Catholic Reporter* 15 (29 July): 4, 20.

———. 1979b. "Pope Didn't Boost, Harm Ecumenism." *National Catholic Reporter* 15 (19 October): 15.

Wink, Walter. 1979. "Biblical Perspectives on Homosexuality." *Christian Century* 96 (7 November): 1082–86.

Winter, Art. 1975. "Doctrinal Stands Lurk Below 'Usual Reasons' for Mass-going Dropoff." *National Catholic Reporter* 12 (31 October): 4.

Wirpsa, Leslie. 1992a. "Rome Sails into Carribbean against the Wind." *National Catholic Reporter* 29 (23 October): 11–14.

———. 1992b. "Curia Ignites Angry Protest at CELAM IV." *National Catholic Reporter* 29 (6 November): 12–13.

Woodward, Kenneth. 1983. "Luther in Excelsis." *Notre Dame Magazine* 12 (October): 11–15.

Woodward, Kenneth, and Margaret Moorman. 1984. "The Sexuality of Christ." *Newsweek*, 23 April.

Woodward, Kenneth, Rod Nordland, and Fred Coleman. 1989. "The Highest Summit." *Newsweek*, 11 December.

World Council of Churches. 1982. *Baptism, Eucharist and Ministry*. Geneva: WCC.

Wynn, Wilton. 1988. *Keepers of the Keys*. New York: Random House.

Yallop, David A. 1984. *In God's Name.* New York: Bantam.

Young, James J. 1978. "Six Factors in a Climate of Change." *America* 139 (18 November): 347–51.

Index